Sentence Comprehension

Sentence Comprehension

The Integration of Habits and Rules

David J. Townsend and
Thomas G. Bever

A Bradford Book
The MIT Press
Cambridge, Massachusetts
London, England

This book was set in Times New Roman in '3B2' by Asco Typesetters, Hong Kong and was printed and bound in the United States of America.

Library of Congress Cataloging-in-Publication Data

Townsend, David J.
  Sentence comprehension / David J. Townsend and Thomas G. Bever.
    p. cm.—(Language, speech, and communication)
  "A Bradford book."
  Includes bibliographical references and index.
  ISBN 0-262-20132-1 (alk. paper)—ISBN 0-262-70080-8 (pbk. : alk. paper)
  1. Grammar, Comparative and general—Sentences. 2. Psycholinguistics.
3. Comprehension. I. Bever, Thomas G. II. Title. III. Series.
P295.T68 2001
415—dc21   00-067882

To all colleagues and students
who take the time to figure out
where we are wrong

Contents

Acknowledgments

Many people helped to develop this book. The National Science Foundation supported our research. David Townsend was supported by a Distinguished Scholar Award from Montclair State University, with the help of George Miller. Montclair State University also provided support through a sabbatical leave and grants from the Student-Faculty Research program, the Faculty Scholarship Incentive Program, and a Princeton Faculty Fellowship.

Merrill Garrett, Director of Cognitive Science at the University of Arizona, provided financial support. Several individuals contributed detailed reviews of early drafts: Brian McElree, Colin Phillips, Zohar Eviatar, Andrew Carnie, Steve Seegmiller, and an unnamed reviewer provided by MIT Press. Montse Sanz assisted in writing chapter 3. Students in the Honors Seminar at Montclair State University and in the graduate Psycholinguistics Seminar at the University of Arizona performed test readings of early drafts. Donna Amato and Linda Kuentje provided valuable assistance with the bibliography. Jason Haugen, Chris Nicholas, and Erin O'Bryan read a late draft. Jennie Bradley assisted in innumerable ways.

Most critical to completion of this book was the support and encouragement that Janis Townsend and Cindy Bever provided.

Chapter 1
The Sentence as a Case Study in
Cognitive Science

Much of the work of modern cognitive science has assumed that cognition is at least in part computational. That is, "to think" means "to manipulate symbols in a particular manner." In cognition, the symbols are mental representations that possess meaning or "stand for" mental objects. Regardless of the domain, the formal manner of manipulating symbols constitutes the syntax of the domain. Syntax is not a unique formal property of linguistic computation, but it is part of vision, motor behavior, and every other activity with a computational basis.

This canon of modern cognitive science recently has been under attack. One of the major problems of the syntactic conception of cognition has centered around how the formal operations take on appropriate meanings. That is, how does it come about that the formal manipulations of symbols produce computational effects that have meaning in our world? What we will try to show is that, in the case of language, the sentence provides the minimal domain into which elementary meanings can be placed and combined. Thus, when more elaborate structures are derived from sentences, the more elaborate structures will also have meaning.

A second line of attack on the assumption that cognition involves symbol processing comes from impressive demonstrations that models of intelligent behavior need not encode symbols at all. The nonsymbolic connectionist approach has attained remarkable success in predicting language behavior with networks of simple processing units that are associated with one another in various ways. Importantly, none of these simple processing units needs to represent anything. Nevertheless, connectionist models are able to behave in ways that mimic the behavior of human beings as they carry out such complex tasks as understanding language.

In this book we present a model that addresses both of these attacks on the symbol-processing metaphor for cognitive science. This chapter makes the point that mental processes in general and linguistic processes in particular come in two flavors —habits and computations. We argue that the sentence level is a natural level of linguistic representation, and that, despite many valid arguments for an associative aspect of sentence comprehension, sentence comprehension also is fundamentally computational. Our integration of computational and associative approaches, furthermore, can resolve difficult problems that each approach faces when independently considered as a complete model of comprehension.

1.1   The Sentence Is a Natural Level of Linguistic Representation

One argument for the sentence level flows from consideration of a widespread phenomenon in cognitive science, inductive learning. Inductive learning is the acquisition of general knowledge based on experience with specific examples. Since it is based on experience, this type of learning should be influenced by how frequently specific patterns occur. We will see in this section that inductive learning of language requires considering the sentence as a natural level of representation, defined by a grammar.

Cognitive science has been founded on two alternate truths:

· Most of the time what we do is what we do most of the time.
· Sometimes we do something new.

Both statements are intuitively correct. Yet each alone has dominated the cognitive sciences for sustained periods of scientific history. For example, during the first half of the twentieth century, the first statement was enshrined within associationistic behaviorism as the only relevant fact. In this view, complex behavior was concocted out of associations between individual mental entities. The behaviorist constraint further restricted the associated entities themselves to being observable in actual stimuli and behaviors.

The basic paradigm was *stimulus-response* (S-R) theory, in which patterns of behavior are built up out of the environmental reinforcement of connections between particular stimulus configurations and response sets. Language was recognized as an extremely complex behavior because it involves stringing words together into long sequences. S-R theory was elaborated to explain this in terms of long S-R chains in which each successive word served as both the reinforcement of the previous word and the stimulus for the next one.

The S-R paradigm for language never got very far for several reasons. First, it was never implemented in a way complex enough to begin to approach the intricacies of actual speech. Second, by the late 1950s it was clear that associative behaviorism was not adequate to explain many different kinds of facts, ranging from animal behavior in nature and the lab to human language. For example, Karl Lashley (1951) noted that spoken language comprehension cannot be explained in terms of simple direct associations, because of the frequent presence of relations at a distance. When the following sentence is spoken

(1) Rapid righting with his uninjured hand saved from loss the contents of the capsized canoe.

the interpretation of the spoken form of *righting* depends on material presented much later in the sentence. Examples like these provided evidence against a simple chaining associative model of language behavior, in which the interpretation of a word is a conditioned response to the previous word.

The final reason was a logical failure of the S-R paradigm as a scientific theory. The problem here is that there is no independent way to define what counts as the relevant "stimulus," the relevant "response," or the relevant "reinforcement" all at the same time (Chomsky 1959). Even simple examples of conditioning, such as training a rat to press a lever to a particular tone, face this logical problem. When the rat appears to learn to press the bar correctly, there is still no evidence that it has conceived of the situation in the same way as the experimenter. Is the stimulus the tone? Is it the tone in a particular cage? Is it the tone a particular amount of time after some other event? Is it something else that the tone affects, such as vibrating the sawdust in a particular way? Of course, each of these possibilities can be studied, and the field of learning was becoming littered with evidence that any or all of the alternatives could be true (see Saltz 1971 for a review).

The problem is even more manifest when considering a complex behavior such as language. When children who have not yet mastered English hear the sentence

(2) The sky is blue today.

how do they know what to relate it to? What conceptual probabilities are reinforced? Which parts of the utterance are reinforced? Even if one restricts the domain of inquiry to sentence-internal pattern learning, the problem remains. *The* can be viewed as a stimulus for *sky*, but what is the stimulus for *is* or *blue*, and most specifically, *today*? Chomsky (1959) argued that a theory requires an independent definition of the natural objects under study, before one can investigate the effects of frequency and reinforcement on learning those objects. In the case of language, he suggested that the natural object is the sentence, and its definition is provided by a grammar. His arguments were generally taken as persuasive, and the S-R attempts to deal with language faded. From our standpoint, the important idea is that even inductive learning models of complex behaviors require structures that can define relevant patterns over which learning can be reinforced. The sentence is a level of organization at which such patterns can be defined.

Associationism is an ever-renewable resource. Connectionist models recently have resuscitated the power of habit-based theories and have rehabilitated the reputation of inductive learning. These models recapture the intuition that most behavior is made up of accumulated habits, themselves based on frequency. While they are descendents of associationist behaviorism, many connectionist models have broken with the behaviorist stipulation that only observable entities can be associated.

Connectionist models consist of simple processing units analogous to neurons. These processing units are interconnected in various ways, and the activity of any particular unit depends on the input it receives from other units. Applied to language, units can be triggered by more than one word, by "memory" of prior words, or by internal units that have no direct correspondence to overt stimuli. As the system gains experience with language, the weight, or value, that is assigned to any particular input and internal connections may change depending on feedback about whether it has responded correctly. That is, a connectionist system can encode environmentally appropriate modifications to its behavior, meeting at least a rough definition of *learning*.

Connectionist models explicate comprehension as a matter of satisfying various constraints formed through experience with language. For example, the spoken form of *righting* has been used a certain number of times as "righting" and a certain number of times as "writing." The immediate interpretation of *righting* in Lashley's example above will depend on the frequency of use of the alternative meanings of the word. Contextual constraints that depend on the frequency of use of a word in particular contexts, such as how frequently the sequence *rapid writing* has been experienced, apply as well to influence the immediate interpretation of a word. Syntactic constraints, such as how frequently an adjective like *rapid* precedes a nominalized verb (like *righting*—a verb based on the noun *right*), also influence the immediate interpretation of a word. Thus, comprehension involves the application of many kinds of habits simultaneously to determine the most likely interpretation. This procedure is often called *constraint satisfaction* (e.g., Rumelhart 1989).

Most connectionist theorists maintain that "rules" are mimicked by the network of processing units as a by-product of the constraint satisfaction process. This is expressed in terms of *pattern completion*. Incomplete or ambiguous information is "filled in" by triggering the closest available pattern that has been learned by the system. Since patterns can involve abstract units that connect to many actual parts of an utterance, the patterns can be quite complex and can approach representations of sentence-level dependencies.

A brief consideration of a connectionist treatment of object recognition illustrates pattern completion. If you see this book at a distance and obliquely, its retinal projection might be a crooked rhomboid with some correspondingly crooked markings. You will immediately see it as a rectangular "book" with normal writing on it. In connectionist terms what happens is that isolatable features of the oblique book activate selected features that are strongly connected to an actual book, four corners, a certain thickness, recognizable letters (e.g., *o* or *l*). All those features are best integrated from experience as part of a book, which is why that is what you perceive. This homely example sets us up for the formal requirement: *In order for pattern completion to work, the environment has to have real objects that can be experienced with variable frequencies*. The visual system cannot build up frequency-based activation patterns to objects that do not exist independently. Since physical objects do exist independently, the models can work swimmingly well, and may indeed capture important features that are neurologically relevant.

But what about language? Where are the "objects" of language over which learning can occur? Utterances do not have a constant independent existence, and they certainly do not wear their internal structure on their surface. Thus, Chomsky's suggestion that simple S-R theory required a prior theory of the sentence is exactly relevant to connectionist models, for exactly the same reasons. The sentence level defines the fundamental object of language perception and provides the mechanism for modifying weights in the processing system.

We noted at the beginning of this section that it may be surprising to find that inductive models, including current sophisticated ones, require an independent theory of linguistic structures. It is surprising (and disappointing) only to those who wish to eradicate symbolic structures as relevant to mental models of ongoing behavior. We find it heartening that both systems of symbolic creativity and of habits converge on the same double-edged truth: we mostly behave out of habit, except when we do something novel.

1.2   The Integration of Habits and Symbols

This book is devoted to meeting the challenge of how to integrate the symbolic computational basis for language with acquired habits. The more specific focus is on how sentence-level syntax might be organized together with frequency-based perceptual templates to be efficient and to predict a wide range of empirical phenomena. One can view this as an example of the current goal of creating "hybrid" systems, which have elements of symbolic and spreading activation models. We explore a version of *analysis by synthesis* as a theoretically attractive model with a surprising array of both trite and unexpected empirical support.

Our first task is to consider the classic history of psycholinguistics and current models of comprehension. Chapter 2 reviews the trials and tribulations of the concept of the sentence over the past century. We give special attention to the experimentally grounded revival of the sentence level as an independent representation during comprehension, mostly due to George Miller and his students. We recount the rise and fall of attempts to treat linguistic syntax as a direct model of behavior, and the emergence of the notion of a frequency-sensitive component of comprehension. Through all this, an essential psychophysical feature of sentences remains true —*words are especially behaviorally compelling when they are arranged in sentences.*

Chapter 3 presents some essential facts that psychologists need to know about syntax. We present a sketch of modern syntactic theory, with as little jargon and technical apparatus as possible. The essential features are that syntactic operations apply to abstract categories, they include movement, and they occur cyclically over sentences. That is, sentences have computational *derivations* underlying them. This property motivates some form of sentence-level application of syntactic structure, rather than a simple left-right one (for reasons related to Lashley's observations). It is also difficult to attach statistical information to entire sentence derivations, since they involve a series of abstract computational steps, they are not susceptible to direct reinforcement, and the derivations are not susceptible to direct modeling in constraint-based systems.

Chapter 4 reviews many recent and contemporary approaches to comprehension, focusing on the influential structural model of Marcus and its many witting inheritors, and on the equally influential associative model of Osgood and its modern unwitting inheritors. The reader may find that we miss some of the virtues of particular models because our focus is specifically on the ways structural and habit-based knowledge of language are handled. For some theorists, this is either an oblique or an obnoxious question. Despite many differences, there are some consistent grains of agreement across sets of models. In particular, both statistical and structural constraints are evident in language comprehension.

Chapters 5 and 6 present an analysis-by-synthesis theory of sentence comprehension and some basic evidence for it. The analysis-by-synthesis model offers a way to accommodate the facts that comprehension is both inductively statistical and computationally derivational. In this model, statistically valid perceptual templates assign an initial hypothesized meaning, which is then checked by regeneration of a full syntactic structure. Accordingly, the model proposes that we "understand" every sentence twice, once when we project an initial meaning-form pair and then again when we assign a complete syntax to it. Hence, we refer to our specific analysis-by-synthesis model as *Late Assignment of Syntax Theory* (LAST). The model is completely consistent with current syntactic theories that include inflected lexical items and semantic functional projections in early stages of a derivation. It is also consistent with recently developed evidence that statistical properties of sentences play an immediate role in comprehension, captured in the frequency-based perceptual templates that assign the initial meaning.

LAST offers interesting twists on a number of classic and recently developed psycholinguistic phenomena. We contrast LAST with the nearly ubiquitous "syntax-first" models, which assume that syntax must be assigned before meaning can be analyzed. Perhaps the most salient fact in favor of LAST is that people understand sentences immediately, yet a number of syntactic features appear to have a behavioral role very late in processing, in some cases after a sentence is over. This fact is puzzling from the standpoint of any "syntax-first" theory. It is important to note that the initial comprehension is not purely semantic and syntax-free. Rather, it is based on "pseudosyntactic" structures that can be reliably assigned based on superficial cues. This has the consequence that in some cases, sentences are initially understood with an incorrect syntax that felicitously converges on the correct semantics. For example, we argue that passives are initially understood as complex adjectives. That is, the following sentence

(3) *Passive*
   Clinton was impeached by Congress.

is initially assigned a structure like that of either of the following:

(4) *Adjectival sentences*
   a. Clinton was impeachable by Congress.
   b. Clinton was insensitive to Congress.

This incorrect assignment leads to a correct semantic interpretation, which in turn is part of the basis for later regenerating the correct syntax that reflects the passive construction, as in:

(5) *Passive with trace*
   Clinton was impeached [t] by Congress.

In chapter 6 we report a variety of experimental evidence suggesting that indeed the correct syntax in passive sentences is assigned very late in comprehension.

Chapter 7 explicates how the model treats garden-path constructions—perhaps the single most pervasive object of study in today's psycholinguistics. A garden-path sentence is one in which the initially assigned structure turns out to be wrong. A frequent example from the last three decades of study in psycholinguistics is the *reduced relative* construction,

(6) *Ambiguous reduced relative*
   The horse raced past the barn fell

which is much more complex perceptually than its corresponding unreduced relative:

(7) *Unreduced relative*
   The horse that was raced past the barn fell.

or a corresponding unambiguous reduced relative:

(8) *Unambiguous reduced relative*
   The horse ridden past the barn fell.

LAST explains the strength of the illusory complexity of the ambiguous reduced relative as a function of the application of a pervasive perceptual template that assigns simple declarative "agent-action-patient" patterns to sequences. In this case, the first salient organization of the sentence is like that in

(9) The horse raced past the barn. Fell.

which is hard to avoid even though the result is an ungrammatical sentence.

Indeed any property of the initial sequence that increases its salience as a simple sentence also increases the garden-path effect. This includes information about the animacy of the first noun, the conceptual fit of the first noun as an agent of the verb, and the kind of roles required by the verb, as well as other types of information. The role structure of verbs turns out to be a critical controller of how the garden-path effects appear and how they interact with context. We review much of the current experimental literature along with some new studies showing that most of the processing difficulties with reduced relatives occur only with verbs that are potentially intransitive, such as *raced*, and less so with verbs that must have an object, such as *frightened*.

(10) *Reduced relative with potentially intransitive verb*
      The horse raced in the barn fell.

(11) *Reduced relative with transitive verb*
      The horse frightened in the barn fell.

Chapter 8 focuses on applications of LAST. We return to the question of why the sentence level is a basic unit of analysis in comprehension. The NVN pattern and its variations, such as NV for intransitive verbs and NVNN for "double-object" verbs, is a powerful template just because the sentence is the fundamental unit in our analysis-by-synthesis model. The sentence is the object of pattern-recognition processes in comprehension, and therefore serves as the conduit for modifying associative connections. Thus, the existence of canonical sentence patterns solves the problem of isolating a relevant analytic level for inductive learning. This chapter reviews recent experimental evidence for sentence-level templates.

The next two chapters broaden the application of the model and integrate it with other systems of language behavior. Chapter 9 extends the model to multiclause and discourse-level structures. It is useful to think of comprehension as simultaneously building up meanings and structural representations at different levels of representation at the same time. This gives a special status to the ends of clauses, which is the point at which word-, sentence-, and discourse-level structures can be integrated together. A variety of behavioral studies show that clause boundaries indeed involve rapid swings in attention from being internally to externally oriented—that is, oriented toward mental activities or the world. It is in this context that we discuss the issue of the "modularity" of sentence-comprehension processes and corresponding experimental evidence. We will suggest that LAST renders the issue of modularity a nonissue, since the comprehension system can be seen as both modular and non-modular at different points during comprehension.

Chapter 10 sketches theories of acquisition and the neurology of language. In each case, the goal is to explore the implications of and for LAST. We do not propose to present complete or even correct models of acquisition or the representation and processing of language   he brain. Rather, our goal is to see if these behaviors give evidence for the kinds   distinct processes that we postulate in the analysis-by-synthesis model. We th   k they do.

A natural model of acquisition has an analysis-by-synthesis form, in which children continually create structural representations for the sentences they can understand, which in turn are extended by statistically valid generalizations to understand more kinds of sentences. A model of this kind emphasizes the dual role of innate (or easily available) structural descriptions and statistically validated generalizations. It also offers a potential explanation of how the analysis-by-synthesis model of comprehension is naturally acquired.

The most stable neurological property of language representation is that it has a unique relation to the left hemisphere. Examination of some data from aphasics and some developmental data suggest that what may actually be lateralized is the *pseudosyntax*, the set of initial operations in the formation of an immediate initial structure and meaning. Knowledge of actual syntax might be represented more diffusely. This could explain why certain aphasics can make syntactic grammaticality judgments about sentences that they cannot understand.

The neurological experimental data we focus on primarily are evoked brain potentials, which can be collected during comprehension and language behaviors of other kinds. A common contemporary method is to introduce an anomaly of some kind into a sentence and study how long it takes to have a measurable effect, and what kind of effect it has. This allows contrast between quite local features, such as inflections, and global syntactic properties. Intriguingly, the evidence suggests that anomalies in features involved in pseudosyntax have immediate effects, while derivational syntactic properties are detected much later. The distinction between the kinds of syntactic features and the timing of their computation is exactly predicted by the analysis-by-synthesis model.

We hope that this book serves several purposes. First, we review a large segment of classic and current psycholinguistic research and theory. We also outline how current syntactic theory can fit well with behavioral theories in general. Most generally, we offer and adduce evidence for a model that integrates structural and habit-based knowledge. We hope that this inspires others to develop corresponding models in other domains of cognitive science.

Chapter 2
Classical Evidence for the Sentence

This chapter and the next present the historical background for contemporary models of sentence comprehension. The long history of scientific approaches to the sentence also serves as a cautionary historical tale about the scientific study of what we know, what we do, and how we acquire what we know and do. As we discussed in the first chapter, two opposing paradigms in psychological science deal with these interrelated topics. The behaviorist *prescribes* possible adult structures in terms of a theory of what can be learned from explicit data. The rationalist *explores* adult structures, including those that are implicit, to find out what a developmental theory must explain. In this chapter, we outline a century of alternations between approaching the sentence as defined by linguistic knowledge, and treating it as an associatively processed behavioral concept. This history leaves a residue of consistently reappearing associative and structural facts about language that any comprehension theory must account for. In addition, it lays out some options on how to integrate structural theories of linguistics knowledge with associative and statistical properties of language behavior.

2.1 Early Ideas about the Sentence

Experimental cognitive psychology was born the first time at the end of the nineteenth century. The pervasive paradigmatic work in psychology by Wundt (1874) and the thoughtful organization by James (1890) demonstrated that experiments on mental life both can be done and are interesting. Language was an obviously appropriate object of this kind of psychological study. Wundt (1911), in particular, summarized a century of research on the natural units and structure of language (see especially Humboldt 1835/1903; Chomsky 1966). Wundt came to a striking conclusion: The natural unit of linguistic knowledge is the *intuition* that a sequence is a sentence. He reasoned as follows:

· We cannot define sentences as sequences of words because there are single-word sentences (e.g., "Stay").

• We cannot define sentences as word uses that have meaningful relations because there are meaningful relations within certain word sequences that, nevertheless, are not sentences (e.g., "Monday, Tuesday, Wednesday, Thursday, Friday, Saturday, Sunday").

• Hence, the sentence must be defined as a sequence that native speakers of a language intuitively believe to convey a complete proposition in a linguistically acceptable form.

At the outset, this framed the problem of linguistic description as the description of linguistic knowledge: The goal of linguistic description is to describe what speakers of a language know when they know a language. Wundt's formal analyses of this knowledge summarized a tradition of continental research on local and exotic languages. Most important was the assignment of purely abstract syntactic structures to sentences, independent of their meaning. The structural features included levels of representation, which expressed grammatical relations between words and phrases. At a surface level, a set of hierarchically embedded frames symbolized the relative unity of word sequences grouped into phrases. For example, in sentence (1), *the* is clearly more related within a unit to *Rubicon* than to *crossing*, despite being adjacent to both. Similarly, in sentence (2), *was* is intuitively closer to *crossed* than to *Rubicon*.

(1) Caesar was crossing the Rubicon.

(2) The Rubicon was crossed by Caesar.

(3) Cross the Rubicon was what Caesar did.

The surface level also defines a set of surface grammatical relations between the phrases. In sentence (1), *Caesar* is the grammatical subject—that is, the phrase that determines the morphological agreement with the verb. In sentence (2), the corresponding grammatical subject is *the Rubicon*. In sentence (3), it is the entire act, *crossing the Rubicon*.

It was obvious that surface grammatical relations could not capture the propositional relations between the phrases. Wundt noted that *Caesar* is the acting one in each of sentences (1) to (3) despite its different positions. The propositional relations between phrases are represented by a separate level that Wundt called the *inner form* of the sentence. At this level, sentences (1) to (3) share the same relations between *Caesar* (agent), *cross* (action), and *Rubicon* (patient). The different actual sequences at the surface grammatical level are related to the propositional level by mapping processes called *Umwandlungen* (literally, "transformations"). These processes reorder surface phrases into the surface patterns allowed by the particular language. The relations between elements of a proposition are not purely semantic, but are the formal expression of relations between semantic units of meaning (Blumenthal 1970, 1975). That is, even the propositional form is arranged according to a system.

2.2 Banishment of the Sentence

The continental model of language was rich and made many claims about the capacity of humans to manipulate abstract entities. But the theory never became an object of experimental importance. The reasons are, no doubt, scientifically, even politically complex. One sufficient fact is that Wundt classified the study of language as a branch of social psychology, and hence, for him, not a subject fit for laboratory experimental investigation. His vast structural catalog of language is more an anthropological survey than a scientific scrutiny of mental processes. The continental linguistic model and its richness became lost to scientific psychology.

But Wundt's model was not lost to everybody interested in language. It was popularized in the infant field of linguistics by a young professor of German, Leonard Bloomfield. Bloomfield's (1914) enthusiastic exegesis of Wundt's multileveled model might have installed it as the basis for the newly emerging science of language. However, in all social sciences at the time, there was a growing preoccupation with behaviorist injunctions against unobservable entities and relations. The notions "intuition" and "inner grammatical level" were not acceptable in a framework that required operational definitions.

Even Bloomfield capitulated to such restrictions as enthusiastically as he had earlier espoused the Wundtian model. His foundational book, *Language* (1933), presents a behaviorist framework for linguistic theory. In that book, the sentence is hardly mentioned, while meaning is given cursory treatment in terms of the reinforced association of stimuli and responses.

2.2.1 Behaviorism, Stimulus-Response Theory, and the Sentence

Behaviorism is a seductive doctrine that dominated psychological theories of learning for most of the twentieth century. It is seductive because it *simultaneously* purports to answer three questions:

- What do we learn?
- How do we learn?
- Why do we learn?

According to behaviorism, the reason we learn is that the environment provides pleasure when we do. That is, the environment reinforces only certain activities in certain circumstances, and those activities become habits. This selective reinforcement accounts for the way we learn; it associates environmentally successful pairs of behaviors and situations as permanently learned units. Accordingly, what we learn must be expressed in terms of definable pairs of behaviors and situations. These principles provide an appealing chain of inference from the motive to learn back to the structure of what is learned.

The classic behaviorist model in behavioral science is the S-R schema, laid out by Watson (1919) and given more formal definitions and philosophical justification by Skinner (1957). This model of behavior describes every behavior as a response to a particular stimulus, ranging from relatively automatic behaviors such as ducking at a loud noise to obviously learned behaviors, such as stopping at a red light. In each case, a period of training inculcates the habit of producing a particular response to a particular stimulus. The training consists of presentation of the stimulus S and then some form of positive reinforcement if the correct response R is produced: every time a S-R sequence is followed by a positive reinforcement, the S-R bond is strengthened, (4a), just as it is weakened when followed by punishment, (4b). That is, behaviors are "associated" with stimulus configurations, by virtue of independent "reinforcement." This simple architecture has tremendous power implicit in it, and the principles dominated behavioral science for roughly four decades.

(4) a. Red light → stop, Positive Reinforcement (driving instructor says "good")
     b. Red light → go, Punishment ("crash!")

Part of the philosophical surround of associationism is behaviorism, the principle that only observable stimuli, responses, reinforcements, and punishments can count as part of a theory. This restriction seemed viable so long as fairly simple behaviors were at issue, but a complex behavior such as language seemed to resist such treatment —where are the stimuli, the responses, the reinforcements? Ultimately, various S-R theorists proposed that language behavior could be accounted for with a model in which each word served as a stimulus for the next, building up an overall structure out of local associative relations (e.g., Staats 1961; Kendler and Kendler 1962). For example, in producing the sentence in (5a), *the* can be taken as the stimulus that elicits *horse*, which in turn elicits *races*, as in (5b).

(5) a. The horse races.
     b. The → horse → races.

The S-R treatments of language also formulated a distinction between function words (e.g., *the*) and content words, based on the different kinds of references they have (content words ostensibly have externally definable reference; function words do not). This allowed differential reinforcement of two kinds of sequence information, function-to-function and content-to-content. For example, sentence (5a) is composed of two overlapping sequences:

(5) c. The → X_ → Y es
     d. horse → races

From a structural standpoint, (5c) captures part of the structural regularities relating to noun-verb agreement, and contrasts with a different sequence (5f) when the noun is plural, as in (5e). The sequential probability in (5d) captures the meaning relation, in which it is frequently true of *horses* that they are the agent of *race*.

(5) e. The horses race.
   f. The → X es → Y_

While initially couched as a model of how language behavior could be learned and maintained, this scheme can also be interpreted as a model of language comprehension. In that model, the learned sequences of adjacent elements are internally represented as automatically characterizing a sentence as it is encountered.

Chomsky and others noted fifty years ago that such a classic S-R sequencing of elements is not adequate to describe linguistic facts and that similar limitations apply to unadorned S-R theory for the interpretation of sentences. The most salient reason is that sentences manifestly have elaborate hierarchical structure and long distance dependencies in which the two parts of associated components are separated by an arbitrary distance. Any model limited to expressing the associative relation between elements no more than a limited distance apart will not be able necessarily to represent hierarchical relations, and will surely be inadequate to represent long distance dependencies.

(6) a. The hors*es* that were raced past the barn *are* falling.
   b. The horse_ that was raced past the barn *is* falling.

Chomsky generalized his critique of Skinner's proposals on language to the entire S-R program. At a general level, he noted that it is impossible to define independently what *counts* as a stimulus, a response, or a reinforcement in any normal complex situation. There is no independent definition of stimulus, or of response or reinforcement for that matter—it is all determined after the fact. If a motorist stops at an intersection, if we did not know already about stoplights, how would we know what had actually controlled the behavior, how would we know what the effective behavior is, and how would we know where the reinforcement is? Rather, we think we know each of the three components because after the fact we can analyze them. Similarly, without already knowing about the relation between noun-number and verb inflection, how would we (or the listener) know what aspect of the speaker's behavior controlled the relation; indeed, how would we know there is a relation? Furthermore, in language, how do we know exactly which pieces of the preceding string should be taken as the stimulus for the current word—that is, what exactly should be reinforced? We will see that this problem corresponds in modeling language comprehension with associative models to the "grain" question, namely, how does a system select the "relevant" amount and level of information to form complex associations subject to reinforcement?

2.2.2 Mediation Theory and Linguistic Knowledge

The first proposals within the S-R framework that attempted to meet Chomksy's challenge also antedate the classic psycholinguistic period and are primarily due to Charles Osgood (1963; Osgood, Suci, and Tannenbaum 1957). Osgood was a S-R psychologist trained by Clark Hull, who elaborated the role of internal entities that "mediate" external stimuli with external responses. Hull and his students had addressed the problem of how to adapt simple S-R theory to the learning of complex chains—for example, when a rat learns a maze with two turns before reaching the reinforcing goal (as in (7a)). The last correct turn (R_2) is reinforced by the presence of the reward in the goal location, but how does the final reinforcement affect the first correct turn (R_1)? Hull's proposal (1943) was that both "responses" and "reinforcement" could be analyzed as "fractionating" into parts that can be related to each other at points prior to the final response and reinforcement. For instance, the first turn has two components, the actual immediate response (e.g., R_1, "turn right") and a fraction of the goal response (e.g., "Go toward the goal")—that is, the initial correct turn is both a local behavior and part of the final goal-directed behavior. Hull represented this by postulating a fractional response (r_{g_1}) and fractional reinforcement (s_g) at early points in a chain, as in (7b):

(7) a. $S_1 \rightarrow R_1$, $S_2 \rightarrow R_2$, reinforcement by Goal
     b. $S_1 \rightarrow R_1$
         r_{g_1}, reinforced by s_g
         $S_2 \rightarrow R_2$, reinforced by Goal

Of course, this leads to the postulation of a kind of variable that can intervene between the stimulus and response, a hypothesis anathema to behaviorists. There were many proposals and much worry about how such intervening variables could come to exist, based on the principle that only observable stimuli, responses, and reinforcements can play a causal role in behavior.

Even if it is not possible for behaviorist principles to account for the theoretical notions of fractionated responses and reinforcements, those concepts can be applied to the description of a complex behavior like language, and at least potentially maintain the usefulness of associationism. Osgood first explored the application of this kind of schema to the representation of word meaning. According to his proposal, a word stimulates a set of particular intervening response components with varying strength (r_{g_1}, r_{g_2},...), which in turn are connected to a set of intervening stimulus components (s_{g_1}, s_{g_2},...), which connect to overt responses.

For subsequent developments it is instructive to analyze some critical features of this model. First, the input is an explicit word. Each word is connected to an intervening set of meaning "r-s" *components* or *features* in which the *r* is a fractional, or internal, part of the goal response and serves as an internal stimulus for other behaviors, which may also be internal. Each word has an activation strength level associated with each feature, ranging from 0 to a ceiling level. The features themselves are characteristically learned by way of massed exposure to a wide range of word-word pairs. The claim was that out of many such pairs, similarities in meanings would coalesce around activations of particular intervening r-s components, thereby isolating them as relevant to differentiating meanings from each other. Random intervening components would tend to fall out of general use because they would not be relevant to extracting unique responses from any input words. (At times, Osgood also entertained the view that at least some of the intervening components could be innately constrained, while the connection strength to them would be based on experience.) One might label the separate intervening r-s to the word *elephant* as in (8).

(8) a. r_g-s_1 = "animate"
    b. r_g-s_2 = "large"

Finally, any given word could be the critical factor in a variety of actual output responses, because the intervening components could be stimulated by other mental factors, adjacent words, background level, local context, and so on. Thus, while *elephant* as an input always resulted in raising the activation level of each intervening component by a fixed amount, the resulting output could vary because of other factors that govern which response receives the overall highest activation: sometimes *elephant* can elicit *cat* or *house*, but rarely *force*.

Thus, unlike Skinner, Osgood recognized explicitly that in a S-R explanation of a complex phenomenon like language, a fundamental problem was how to reinforce and therefore represent "abstract" intervening r-s connections that mediate between explicit stimuli and responses. Osgood built on the Hullian concept of fractional responses and reinforcement to explain language behavior. In Osgood's scheme for representing and learning word meaning, an overt stimulus (e.g., an appearance of a word) automatically stimulates the universal set of intervening "semantic" r-s modules (what we might think of as intervening "features"). The overt response results from a particular set of those r-s modules. Reinforcement of that response spreads "backward" to reinforce the particular intervening r-s modules that played a positive role in eliciting the overt response. Osgood (1963) extended these principles to explain the role of syntactic structure in language behaviors.

In this sense, Osgood was an enlightened associationist who postulated intervening entities that seem quite abstract. But he was also a "behaviorist," hewing to the position that all causally relevant intervening variables in behavior must ultimately be resolvable to components of actual stimuli or responses. He shared with most psychologists of his day the view that mental life is made up of the componentially reinforced shards of overt stimuli and overt responses. In this way, he wedded himself to the fundamental weakness of the Skinnerian program, despite his enlightened views on linguistic representations. Osgood's behaviorism made him continually vulnerable to the same kind of attacks as did Skinner's.

For example, J. A. Fodor (1965) articulated a number of difficulties with this model of meaning. Many of these were technical matters involving the mechanics of how any associative model could work. Most general was the observation, like Chomsky's on Skinner, that the model does not offer independent behaviorist definitions of its independent terms. In particular, there is no principled way to determine which aspects of an input word are just the ones that should be reinforced with a strengthening of connections to intervening components. The same question arises with respect to the connections from those components to the output responses.

Despite its shortcomings, Osgood's attempt to deal with meaning in an associative framework offers a background and general description of features of such models, including some that are contemporary (see chapter 4). A specific input (a word) can activate a set of internal components, which along with activations contributed by other sources, can result in a range of outputs in which the specific input is a critical, but not the sole, factor. In light of current connectionist models that we discuss below and in chapter 4, Osgood was a pioneer—he saw how a distributed representation model could be integrated with fundamental principles of associationism to explain complex abstract behavior.

Reinforcement was an important concept because it justified the scientific investigation of isolated sources of pleasure and displeasure. The focus on behavior-situation pairs licensed investigation of the learning of meaningless associations between situations and behaviors. The requirement that learned associations occur between definable entities transferred to the operationalist requirement that we reduce theoretical terms to observable entities.

By the late 1950s, sophisticated elaborations of these principles had crystallized, most notably in the proposal by Hull (1943) that these principles could account for chains of behavior. Even when transferred to descriptions of language behavior, these principles retained the basic behaviorist doctrine about the structure of what was learned (Osgood, Suci, and Tannenbaum 1957): There must be recognizable links between isolatable situations and behaviors (Fodor 1966; Bever 1968a). The implications of this doctrine for theories of language were severe. Consider how these procedures affected theories of the relationship between words and phrases. Following Bloomfield's conversion, linguists had adopted the behaviorist restrictions on how to pursue the analysis of language structure. They imposed on themselves a set of *discovery* procedures that would guarantee the scientific acceptability of linguistics and the learnability of the resultant linguistic descriptions. Language was to be described in a hierarchy of levels of learned units such that the units at each level can be expressed as a grouping of units at an intuitively lower level. The lowest level in any such hierarchy was necessarily composed of physically definable units. For example, sentences (9a) to (9d) could all be resolved to a basic sequence of the same kinds of phrases—a noun phrase, a verb, and an adjective phrase.

(9) a. Harry was eager.
    b. The boy was eager.
    c. The tall boy was eager to leave.
    d. He was something.

The behaviorist principles demanded that phrases not be free-floating, abstract objects. Each must be reducible back to a single word that could serve as a lexical substitute for the entire phrase, as in sentence (9d). In this way, they rendered "phrases" theoretically as units that could be resolved as "words." At the same time, the description gave an account of the fact that words within phrases seem to be more closely related to each other than across phrases. Finally, it was possible to hope for a description of all possible types of phrases, since longer ones seemed to resolve into combinations of shorter ones, which in turn could resolve into single words.

In the 1930s and 1940s, psychological research on language proceeded largely without explicit benefit of linguistic analysis. Psychologists studied the processing of unrelated word sequences with the goal of discovering how universal laws of learning apply to human beings. This deceptively simple paradigm, called *verbal learning*, became the focus of an enormous amount of research. There were many hundreds of such studies, with several journals devoted to little else (for representative reviews see Underwood and Schulz 1960; Cofer 1961; Cofer and Musgrave 1963). Great effort was devoted to exploring the formation of associations between adjacent and remote words in strings and the influence of different kinds of practice, of different kinds of reinforcement, of subjects' age, mental capacity, and so on.

These studies might appear to be about language as well as learning because they used words as stimuli. But they were about words only coincidentally. Words were merely handy units that humans could learn to string together in unrelated ways. The focus was on learning, motivation, and memory, not language. Of course, one could have viewed this as leading to an understanding of how words are processed when they are organized in whole sentences. Unfortunately, this promise was never realized. As we will see shortly, words in whole sentences are processed differently from words in random sequences.

Just as wholes are the natural enemies of parts, Gestalt psychology was the natural enemy of associationist behaviorism. Crucial demonstrations had long been available that percepts have higher-order structures that cannot be accounted for by merely associating the parts. It would appear that linguistic structures are prime candidates for gestalt investigations. After all, sentences are wholes that bind together and transcend words and phrases as their parts (Lashley 1951; Mandler and Mandler

1964). Such an obviously true observation, however, rarely stops associationists from going about their business, and, in this case, it had absolutely no impact on the prediction that the study of verbal learning would lead to an understanding of language (Skinner 1957). The failure of the Gestalt demonstrations that "good figures" undercut associationistic accounts of language was due in part to the inability of Gestalt psychology to develop a general theory of possible good figures. In any domain, most "principles" of how gestalten are formed seemed true but inexplicable. Furthermore, Gestalt psychologists themselves had little interest in language, since to them it seemed obvious that language was both abstract and learned, and therefore not the proper object of their investigation (Koffka 1935). Once again, a methodological preconception barred a potentially fruitful approach to language.

Until the 1950s, linguists and psychologists worked apart even though they shared the fundamental theoretical restrictions of behaviorism and some beliefs about the basic role of S-R associationism. An early burst of psycholinguistics occurred when the two groups discovered that they could mate their theories. Learning theory with mediating responses of the sort developed by Osgood was allegedly capable of describing the acquisition of "behavioral hierarchies" of just the type that linguists had found to be the ultimate grammatical aspect of language, namely, words-in-phrases (Osgood and Sebeok 1954). Although the first mating between psychology and linguistics was briefly intense, it was sterile. The reason was that the two disciplines were mutually compatible just because they shared the same behaviorist preconceptions. Psychologists were willing to postulate of the language learner only the inductive capacity to learn what linguists had already restricted themselves to describing. Yet the shared descriptive restrictions robbed linguistic theory and psychology of the sentence. The project of the first psycholinguistics, to show how linguistic structures followed from psychological laws of learning, was successful— brilliantly and pyrrhically.

2.3   Revival of the Sentence

We now turn to the beginning of modern times, starting about fifty years ago. Syntactic investigations increasingly focused on sentence-level analyses. Correspondingly, experimental investigations of real-language behavior lead psychologists to the empirically demonstrated explanatory power of the sentence level.

2.3.1   The Sentence in Behaviorist Linguistics
The behaviorist implementation of linguistics may seem harmless enough, but it had a particular result: linguistic theory could not describe the sentence. This is true for three empirical reasons. First, the number of sentences in unfathomably large. Second, in a single sentence, there are often relations between words in different phrases.

Third, there are grammatical relations between phrases that cannot be described as superficial facts about the phrases themselves. In addition, as Wundt had noted, it is impossible to define sentences without appealing to speakers' intuitions. To deal with such phenomena as these, linguistic theory would have required levels of representation and theoretical entities that could not be resolved by reduction to independently observable units. Most behaviorist linguists were sufficiently aware of these problems to leave the description of the sentence alone. The reducible phrase was the pinnacle of behaviorist linguistics.

One unconventional linguist attempted to apply the operationalist descriptive principles to sentences. Harris (1957, 1958) invoked the operationalist view that the sentence is a component of a complete discourse in the same sense that a phrase is a component of a sentence. He developed a descriptive scheme in which sentences (and clauses) that can occur in the same discourse frame are reduced to canonical sentence forms. This scheme depends on the fact that sentences occur in structural families. For example, sentences (1) to (3) are part of a larger set of constructions, as follows:

(10) a. Caesar crossed the Rubicon.
     b. It is the Rubicon that Caesar crossed.
     c. What Caesar did was cross the Rubicon.
     d. The Rubicon is what Caesar crossed.
     e. that Caesar crossed the Rubicon ...
     f. Caesar's crossing the Rubicon ...
     g. the Rubicon's being crossed by Caesar ...
     h. the crossing of the Rubicon by Caesar ...

Harris noted that each of these variants can occur in the same discourse environment. That is, we can substitute each of them for the blank in the following discourse frame (ignoring changes needed to accommodate the clausal variants):

(11) a. Caesar marched north.
     b. Then _____.
     c. This surprised the local inhabitants.

Harris intended the notion of co-occurrence to be the same as that describing the substitutability of phrases in discourse-based sentence frames. The difference is that we cannot reduce sentences—unlike phrases—to canonical words (*it*, *did*). Rather, Harris suggested that we can reduce the sentences of a structural-sentence family to a standard canonical sentence form that he called the *kernel*. A kernel sentence is the simple declarative construction. Co-occurrence "transformations" express the relation between the kernel sentence and its variants. For example, the kernel and the passive sentence (2) are related by the following co-occurrence transformation:

(12) "NP_1 V + ed NP_2 ↔ NP_2 was V + ed by NP_1"

There are several important points to retain about this theory. First, the co-occurrence transformations can only relate specific observable sentences. Second, the relative priority of the kernel-sentence form had an intuitive appeal but still did not unambiguously meet the requirement that it be both observable and operationally definable. Finally, it was inordinately difficult to make the program work in detail. In retrospect, one can view co-occurrence transformational grammar as an insightful attempt to describe sentence structure within a taxonomic paradigm. The failures of the attempt were illuminating and set the scene for the later developments in linguistic theory, to which we return after reviewing progress in the psychology of the day.

2.3.2 The Unit of Perception

During the same period (the 1950s) there was a separate stream of research on how adults organize language behavior independent of any theoretical preconceptions about learning (Miller 1951a, 1951b). It was unarguable that at some point in the understanding of the sounds of spoken language, listeners arrive at an abstract conceptual analysis of its meaning and structure, but it was still arguable that the meaning conveys the structure and not the reverse. In particular, Miller and Selfridge (1950) demonstrated the behavioral relevance of sentence structure by showing that memory for word sequences improves as they approach the statistical regularities of English. This result suggested that language behavior involves a transfer of the physical signal into a linguistic model that can access regularities of structure and meaning. The perceptual question was formulated in terms of a search for the units of speech perception in which the acoustic-to-linguistic transfer takes place.

A standard experimental method to investigate the nature of the unit of perception was based on the ordinary fact that spoken language is extremely resistant to acoustic interference. Imagine yourself next to a large waterfall. Even though the noise is tremendous, you are able to understand somebody talking to you so long as the conversation is in your language. The question is, why? Clearly, you are using your knowledge of your language to aid your perception. But which aspect of your linguistic knowledge do you access first and how does it help you hear better? A straightforward hypothesis is that you have memorized the *words* of your language. In this view, the unit of transfer from acoustic to linguistic information in speech perception is the word: a listener first maps the acoustic signal onto separate words and then computes the meaning from their sequence.

The proposal that the unit of speech perception is the word may seem daunting, since there are so many of them. But one thing we know: people do learn thousands of words in their language. Since the number of effectively necessary words is finite (though large), it is possible to imagine that they are the learned basis for speech perception.

A laboratory-controlled variant of the speech-by-waterfall experience offered a technique to test the word hypothesis (Miller, Heise, and Lichten 1951; Miller and Isard 1963). Suppose we adjust the loudness of a noise source relative to recordings of the words in a two-word sentence (13) so that each word is recognized correctly 50 percent of the time when it is heard alone.

(13) a. Horses eat.
     b. Horses cry.

If it is the word level at which the acoustic information is mapped onto linguistic representations, a sentence composed by stringing together the same words should be perceived 25 percent of the time. This follows from the hypothesis that the acoustic shape of each word is mapped independently onto a linguistic representation. The actual facts, however, are striking. When strung together into a sentence, the word sequence is often recognized much more than 50 percent of the time (Miller, Heise, and Lichten 1951). Most important is the intuitive fact that when the words are in a sentence they seem acoustically clearer *as you hear them*. The outcome of a series of such studies was the conclusion that it is at least the sentence that is the unit of speech perception. Even well-formed sentences that do not make semantic sense (e.g., 13b) enhance perception of the words in them.

Miller's conclusion on the role of sentences in speech perception created two questions that still dominate investigations of language:

· How do we use our knowledge of sentences in behavior?
· What do we know when we know the sentences of our language?

The first question is a direct example of the problem of integrating abstract knowledge with concrete behavior. For decades, psychologists had assumed that beliefs cannot affect perception except in very limited cases. This ideal was consistent with the behaviorist strictures on what we can learn: if beliefs can influence perception, what the child learns cannot be limited to what is in the world to be perceived. The apparent influence of abstract sentence structure on acoustic decisions (and other kinds of sensory judgments; see Miller, Bruner, and Postman 1954) suggested that perceptual activity involves the *simultaneous* integration of abstract and concrete levels of representation.

There are two views about how this integration occurs. Abstract levels of knowledge can directly influence concrete levels ("top-down processing") or can interact only after lower-level representations are formed ("bottom-up processing"). Research on language perception has vigorously pursued the nature of the integration of different levels of knowledge because there are well-defined, distinct levels of structure in language. The pendulum of scientific fashion has swung back and forth, with some investigators in favor of a bottom-up theory of perception (Forster 1979; Fodor

1983; Pylyshyn 1984, to name a few) and others in favor of a top-down theory (e.g., Marslen-Wilson and Welsh 1978). While the issue may never be entirely resolved, Miller's clear experimental demonstration of the behavioral importance of the sentence level discredited behaviorist restrictions on theories of language comprehension. More enduringly, the issue has been the engine for decades of empirical and theoretical research.

The acoustic clarity of sentences raised another question. How can something as varied as the sentence be the unit of transfer from acoustic to linguistic representations? Unlike the number of words, there is no meaningful upper bound to the number of sentences. Hence, when we listen, we cannot transfer information from acoustic to linguistic structure using prememorized sentences. Clearly, we must know a system of rules for describing the sentences in our language, and we must apply that categorical knowledge actively during speech behaviors such as comprehension.

The experiments on adult behavior presented an unanticipated challenge to the behaviorist doctrine about learning. The sentence level of knowledge plays an active role in perception, yet that level cannot be described or acquired according to behaviorist principles. By ignoring the problem of learning altogether and focusing on adult behavior, it was discovered that adults use representations that cannot be learned by induction. Once some thought was given to the question, it seemed clear that people actively use categorical rules in many sorts of behavior (Miller, Galanter, and Pribram 1960). Behaviorism was surely doomed as a theory of language, but the final fall awaited a viable theory of what kind of knowledge generates the sentences of a language. Such a theory emerged at the time that Miller's research on speech perception raised the question of the nature of knowledge about language.

2.3.3 Transformational Grammar

What *is* a sentence? Harris had attempted to include the sentence level within an operationalist framework, but discovery procedures limited his success. In the late 1950s Chomsky (1957) offered a new kind of grammar as a formal answer to this question: A sentence is what the grammar describes as a sentence. The motivations and details of this new theory were similar in many respects to those of Wundt (Chomsky 1957).

The configuration of the syntactic model that described sentence structure was also similar to that of much earlier times and included a reformulated notion of transformation. But the new transformational grammar had novel formal devices as well as a completely new goal for grammatical description. The grammar was generative: it described the sentence structures of a language as a natural and creative part of human knowledge.

The new approach flatly rejected operationalist discovery procedures and allowed abstract terms and rules that were not reducible to observable entities. This approach represented in linguistics the same kind of shift away from behaviorist principles of learning that was occurring within psychology. Chomsky was also diligent in pointing out the general failures of behaviorist accounts of language (Chomsky 1959). For Chomsky the goal of linguistic anlaysis was to describe an adult's linguistic knowledge, not language behaivor. The staple facts that reflect that knowledge are intuitions about the acceptability of sentences in one's language. Hence, masses of data relevant to linguistic analysis are easy to collect. One merely consults a native speaker on how he or she feels about a language sequence. By assigning sentence status to only those sequences that are intuitively acceptable, the grammar constitutes a theory of the speaker's underlying linguistic knowledge.

The most important feature of the new syntactic model was that several levels of representation are included in the description of every sentence. Obviously, only one of these levels is relatively observable. This level, the surface structure, corresponds roughly to the kind of phrase structure Wundt described for surface grammatical relations, as well as that arrived at by behaviorist linguists. Every sentence at this level is paired with an underlying kernel or "deep" structure, which presents the propositional relations for each verb in a canonical form. A set of transformations specifies the possible pairs of deep and surface phrase structures. Unlike Harris's co-occurrence transformations, these transforamtions operate in one direction only. Each transformation applies a successive deformation of the input tree, for example, changing a structure that would end up as an active into one that will end up as a passive:

(14) tree 1 ⸻⟶ tree 2

Certain transformations combined kernel trees into complex sentences. The way different kernel sentences are combined reveals interesting differences in the deep structure organization of sentences that are superficially similar. For example, sentences with *desire* and *defy* have superficially identical structures:

(15) a. John desired Bill to go.
       b. John defied Bill to go.

But (15a) and (15b) represent the combination of very different kernel sentences. This is reflected in the fact that the entire phrase *Bill to go* is the intuitive object of *desired*, but only *Bill* is the intuitive object of *defied*. We can illustrate these kernel sentences with the following, where $\Diamond$ represents a position into which a complement sentence is to be inserted:

(16) a. John past desire $\Diamond$ Bill to go
           → John desired Bill to go
       b. John past defy Bill $\Diamond$ Bill to go
           → John defied Bill to go

Also attesting to the underlying distinctness of (15a) and (15b) are their different structural variations. For example, with *desire* but not with *defy*, we can use the whole complement sentence as a unit in a passive sentence. Contrast your intuitions about the acceptability of the following two sequences:

(17) a. For Bill to go was desired by John.
     b. *For Bill to go was defied by John.

(We follow standard practice of indicating unacceptable sentences with an asterisk.) The fact that the complement sentence can act as a whole unit in passive constructions demonstrated that at the deep structure level the entire complement sentence is a direct object of verbs like *desire*, whereas only the following noun phrase is the direct object of verbs like *defy*.

Similar kinds of reasons demonstrated the difference at the underlying structure level of other superficially identical sentence structures:

(18) a. John was eager to please.
     b. John was easy to please.

(19) a. John past BE eager $\diamondsuit$ John please someone
         $\rightarrow$ John was eager to please
     b. It past BE easy $\diamondsuit$ Someone please John
         $\rightarrow$ John was easy to please

In (18a) *John* is the underlying subject of both *eager* and *please*, but in (18b) *John* has only the underlying object position of *please*.

In Chomsky's (1957) syntactic theory, knowing the syntax of a language consisted of knowing a set of phrase structure rules that generate the underlying kernel structures and the transformations that deform and combine those underlying structures into sentences. The kernel structures were not representations of the meaning of sentences but of their underlying syntactic configuration. The meaning of a sentence was a function of semantic operations on underlying structure representation (Katz and Postal 1964; Chomsky 1965). The sound was produced by operations on the surface representation.

2.3.4 A Direct Link Between Knowledge and Behavior

Linguists made a firm point of insisting that, at most, a grammar was a model of "competence"—that is, what the speaker knows. This was contrasted with effects of *performance*, actual systems of language behaviors such as speaking and understanding. Part of the motive for this distinction was the observation that sentences can be intuitively "grammatical" while being difficult to understand, and conversely. For example, Chomsky and Miller (1963) noted that center-embedded sentences become very difficult once there is an embedding within an embedding. This is not a conceptual problem, as shown by the transparent comprehensibility of the same propositions with no embedded structures; see (20c).

(20) a. The house the boy built fell.
  b. The house the boy the cat scratched built fell.
  c. The cat scratched the boy who built the house that fell.

Furthermore, some center-embedded sentence are sometimes comprehensible (Bever 1970a).

(21) The reporter everyone I met trusts had predicted the coup.

Thus, it seemed clear that there is a distinction between what we "know" about sentences and what we can "do" with them. The grammar offered a precise answer to the question of what we know when we know the sentences in our language. We know the different coherent levels of representation and the linguistic *rules* that interrelate those levels. Linguistics distinguished competence from "performance"— how the speaker implements this knowledge. Despite this distinction the syntactic model had great appeal as a model of the processes we carry out when we talk and listen. It was tempting to postulate that the theory of what we know is a theory of what we do, thus answering two questions simultaneously:

· What do we know when we know a language?
· What do we do when we use what we know?

Chomsky's (1957) syntactic model provided an answer to the first question. We know two systems of syntactic rules and the levels of representation that they describe; phrase structure rules define underlying kernel structures, and transformations derive surface phrase structures from the kernels. When the model first appeared, the initial answer to the second question was couched in terms of the linguistic model and a direct assumption about how to link the model to behavioral systems. It was assumed that this knowledge is linked to behavior in such a way that every syntactic operation corresponds to a psychological process. The hypothesis linking language behavior and knowledge was that they are identical. This hypothesis was explicit in the so-called derivational theory of complexity, that the behavioral complexity of processing a sentence corresponds to the number of transformations in its found description. Of course, that hypothesis was only one of many that might be postulated about the relation between grammar and processing mechanisms, as Chomsky and Miller noted.

The distinction between competence and performance created an aura in which it could appear that "competence' was some kind of abstraction that had no particular implication for mental structures: it was performance that carried out that mapping and created behavioral expressions of the grammar. Technically (and importantly), this common view was a mistake: "competence" itself was a theory of actual knowledge, and therefore it pertained directly to mental structures. Furthermore, the most essential behavior in determining competence was the linguistic intuition of native speakers about well-formed sentences (just as it was for Wundt). Grammaticality intuitions are real behaviors in their own right, and a grammar that accurately distinguishes between grammatical and ungrammatical sentences already explains a vast range of behavior. Nonetheless, many believed that it was important to demonstrate a direct link between knowledge and behavior and thereby to demonstrate the so-called psychological reality of linguistic structures in ongoing behavior.

It was not controversial to claim that surface phrase structures were "psychologically real" because they were allegedly definable within the behaviorist framework. (In fact, they probably are not. See Bever 1968a; Bever, Fodor, and Garrett 1968.) But the claim that *deep* structures were psychologically real was a direct challenge to behaviorism. Deep structures were abstract in the sense that they are not actual sentences, but rather the "inner form" of sentences like that to which Wundt referred. Note that even the simplest kernel structure, "he (past leave)," is not an actual sentence. A set of morphological transformations always applies to even the simplest sentences, as in changing "he past leave" to "he left." The further claim that transformations are real mental processes was an additional challenge, both because the rules are themselves abstract and because they define intermediate levels of phrase structure representations as they do their transformational work.

The first step in testing the hypothesis of a direct link between linguistic knowledge and behavior was to define a structural paradigm that would generate a family of studies of the "psychological validity" of the grammar as a mental model. Three optional transformations defined eight sentence types in a three-dimensional cube (Miller 1962b; see figure 2.1). Sentences can be either active (i.e., kernel, K) or passive (P), declarative or interrogative (Q), positive or negative (N). In the linguistic theory of the day, each of these dimensions corresponded to transformation:

(22) a. Mary hit Mark.   K
     b. Mary did not hit Mark.   N
     c. Mark was hit by Mary.   P
     d. Did Mary hit Mark?   Q
     e. Mark was not hit by Mary.   NP
     f. Didn't Mary hit Mark?   NQ
     g. Was Mark hit by Mary?   PQ
     h. Wasn't Mark hit by Mary?   PNQ

Accordingly, in testing the behavioral implications of the formal relations between these sentences as arrayed on the sentence cube, as shown in figure 2.1, one could test the psychological relevance of the grammatical model.

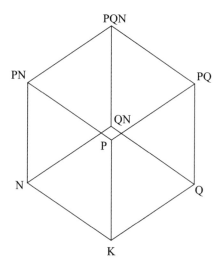

Figure 2.1
The sentence transformation cube (Miller, 1962b, adapted from fig. 12).

The initial results were breathtaking. The amount of time it takes to produce a sentence, given another variant of it, is a function of the distance between them on the sentence cube (Miller and McKean 1964). For example, given "Mary hit Mark" it is easier to produce the negative variant than to produce the negative passive version. Transformational distance between sentences also predicts confusability between them in memory (Mehler 1963; Clifton, Kurcz, and Jenkins 1965; Clifton and Odom 1966). For example, a passive-question sentence is more often recalled as a passive than as an active. Furthermore, the ease of memorizing the sentences was predicted by the number of transformations that have applied to them: simple declaratives are easier than passives, which are easier than passive questions, and so on (Mehler 1963). Finally, such transformationally complex sentence forms as passives were more resistant to acoustic distortion (Compton 1967), took longer to comprehend than corresponding actives (McMahon 1963; Gough 1965, 1966), and put a greater load on immediate memory (Savin and Perchonock 1965).

It is hard to convey how exciting these developments were. It appeared that there was to be a continuing direct connection between linguistic and psychological research. Linguistic analysis would support structural analyses, which would directly become hypotheses for investigation in language behavior. Abstract models of linguistic structure and performance could give clear direction and critical importance to empirical research (Chomsky and Miller 1963; Miller and Chomsky 1963). The linking hypothesis of a direct mapping from the structure of linguistic knowledge and the processes of language behavior was wildly successful. The golden age had arrived.

2.4   Unlinking Knowledge and Behavior

Alas, it soon became clear that either the linking hypothesis was wrong or the grammar was wrong, or both. The support for the psychological relevance of transformations had been based only on those three that defined the sentence cube. But the overall program implied a broad empirical hypothesis about the relation between all rules in a grammar and sentence processing.

It had long been known that the derivational hypothesis was wrong for many constructions. As a predictive principle, it was both too strong and too weak (Fodor and Garrett 1967). It was too weak because it failed to predict the obvious complexity of numerous kinds of sentences.

(23) *Center embedding*
     a. The oyster the oyster the oyster split split split.
     b. The reporter everyone I met trusts predicted the coup.

(24) *Reduced-object relative clauses*
     a. The horse raced past the barn fell.
     b. The horse ridden past the barn fell.

In both (23) and (24) the two versions are structurally identical, but in each case the (b) version is easier to understand. (We return to reduced relative structures in chapter 7.)

The derivational hypothesis was too strong because it incorrectly predicted that various sentence constructions with more transformations are harder to understand than corresponding sentences with fewer transformations:

(25) *Heavy noun phrase (NP) shift*
     a. We showed the long-awaited and astoundingly beautiful pictures of the Himalayan trip to Mary.
     b. We showed Mary the long-awaited and astoundingly beautiful pictures of the Himalayan trip.

(26) *Extraposition*
     a. That Bill left early with Mary surprised Hank.
     b. It surprised Hank that Bill left early with Mary.

In both (25) and (26) the (a) version is transformationally less complex than the (b) version but is harder to understand.

Further research backed up these direct demonstrations of the inadequacy of the derivational theory of complexity. These experiments examined the implications for perceptual difficulty of transformations other than those that defined the sentence cube. Several studies of specific transformations failed to show that perceptual difficulty corresponds to the number of transformations (Bever et al. 1966; Bever and Mehler 1967; Fodor and Garrett 1967; Jenkins, Fodor, and Saporta 1965).

Consider, for example, the transformation that optionally moves a particle/preposition to the position following the verb. This transformation was well motivated as starting with the *(Verb + particle) + NP* deep structure, in which *(Verb + particle)* is a complex lexical item, and then being transformed to the *Verb + NP + particle* sequence:

(27) John called up Mary → John called Mary up
   verb prt NP → verb NP prt

The fact that verbs are lexically associated with some particles/prepositions and not others supports this order of structures. For example, we have "call over NP" and "call NP over":

(28) a. John called over the waiter.
   b. John called the waiter over.

And, although we have "call under NP," we do not have "call NP under":

(29) a. John called under the bridge.
   b. *John called the bridge under.

If *Verb + particle* sequences are entered as complex lexical items and *then* transformed, we can capture these lexical facts. Despite this clear motivation for treating the *Verb + particle + NP* variant as less complex transformationally, such sentences turned out to be processed more slowly than the corresponding transformed versions (Bever and Mehler 1967).

Such failures were baffling in light of the initial success of the structure arranged on the sentence cube. The failures motivated reconsideration of the theoretical interpretation of the three-dimensional model. This further consideration revealed that if we take the grammatical theory literally, it would not have motivated many of the original predictions. That is, the linguistically provided route from one construction to another is not along the surface of the three-dimensional cube. Rather, it must involve returning to the underlying kernel structure and then reemerging to the target structure. For example, the grammatically defined pathway from the negative-passive to the active construction does not involve undoing the negative and then the passive. Rather, it involves undoing the morphologically necessary transformations, the passive transformation, and then the negative transformation, to recover the kernel structure. Then that structure must have the morphological transformations reapplied to it to produce the declarative sentence. Each time two sentences are related, it must be by way of a return to the inner kernel structure and a new path out to the target sentence structure. This strict interpretation of the grammar had the consequence that confusions between two sentences adjacent on the sentence cube (figure 2.1)—for example, between the negative passive and the passive question—would be far less likely than between two simpler structures, such as the negative and the question. Yet this was not confirmed. Sentences were confusible as a function of their adjacency on the *surface* of the sentence cube.

In light of the lack of motivation due to a strict implementation of the grammar, the question remained of why the experimental results on the sentence cube were obtained. One possibility was that the sentence cube was a real but temporary representation that subjects themselves constructed to deal with the temporarily repetitive experimental problem set for them. The repeated presentation of a small number of sentence types with constant superficial relations between them stimulated their arrangement on a cube (Bever 1970a). This offered an explanation of why small variations in response technique could change the evidence for the sentence cube. For example, the frequency of decisions that a sentence is appearing for the first time is low if a transformational variant of it appeared recently (Clifton and Odom 1966). The amount of interference, however, appears to be a function of the similarity of the two sentences at the underlying structure level. For example, active and passive constructions mutually interact more than active and negative constructions. This is explained by the fact that the "negative" is marked in the deep structure, as well as occasioning a transformational rule (Katz and Postal 1964; Chomsky 1965).

Another explanation for why the transformational distance from the kernel structure on the sentence cube predicted the relative difficulties of comprehension and perception appealed to meaning. For example, the question and negative transformations actually changed the meaning of the sentence. It is therefore not surprising that such sentences might be relatively hard to process precisely because of their semantic complexity. That is, the negative has the same propositional structure as the declarative, with an additional semantic operator. The finding that passive constructions are relatively complex *only* when they are semantically reversible supported the importance of semantic analysis (Slobin 1966; Walker, Gough, and Wall 1968). For instance,

(30) The chief of the Gauls was overcome by Caesar.

is more difficult than its corresponding active construction, but

(31) The river Rubicon was overcome by Caesar.

is not. The conclusion of such demonstrations and further theoretical analysis was that there is no direct evidence for the step-by-step application of grammatical transformations in speech behaviors.

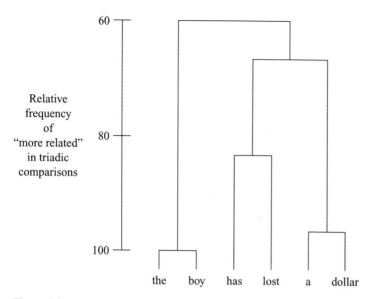

Figure 2.2
A hierarchical clustering analysis of a sentence (adapted from Levelt 1970).

The behavioral relevance of grammatical levels of representation fared better. We can construe surface phrase structure as making the behavioral claim that the members of a phrase have a stronger bond to each other than to the members of other phrases. Levelt (1970) directly tested this idea. He demonstrated that a hierarchical clustering analysis can produce a surface phrase structure. Levelt asked subjects to judge the relatedness among the word triads of a sentence, and then used a hierarchical clustering procedure to analyze the judgments. A sample of Levelt's results, shown in figure 2.2, corresponds closely to linguists' analysis of phrase structure. Accordingly, words are better prompts for other words in the same surface phrase than in different phrases (Johnson 1965; Stewart and Gough 1967; Suci, Ammon, and Gamlin 1967; Townsend and Saltz 1972). For example, once subjects have read

(32) The tall boy saved the dying woman.

tall is more successful in producing recall for *boy* than for *saved*.

Surface structure is behaviorally relevant for perception as well as for memory. Several studies demonstrated that we impose surface phrase structure on sentences as we perceive them (Mehler, Bever, and Carey 1970; Mehler and Carey 1967). Studies on the perceived location of brief nonspeech sounds that interrupt a sentence dramatically revealed the importance of the surface structure pattern. Subjects characteristically report such sounds as having occurred in a phrase break, especially between clauses, rather than in their actual location (Fodor and Bever 1965; Garrett 1965). For example, listeners judge such nonspeech sounds objectively located at the O in (33a) and (33b) to have occurred at the position of the R:

(33) a. In her *hope of marrying Anna was impractical.*

                          O   R

   b. Harry's *hope of marrying Anna was impractical.*

                             RO

That is, the syntactically driven clause boundary determines judgments of the location of the nonspeech sound. Carefully designed materials showed that this effect is not dependent on variations in intonation. For example, the italicized sequence in sentences (33a) and (33b) is common to both syntactic organizations (Garrett, Bever, and Fodor 1966). Nor is the effect due to guessing biases (Garrett 1965; Holmes and Forster 1970; Bever and Hurtig 1975) or to variation in word sequence probability (Bever, Lackner, and Stolz 1969). As Garrett, Bever, and Fodor (1966) put it, the use of surface phrase structure to organize speech during perception is "active." This was a convincing demonstration of what was foreshadowed by Miller's studies of the comprehension of speech-in-noise: listeners actively deploy grammatical knowledge in a way that clarifies the speech signal. In the next section, we review evidence on the role of deep structure in language behavior.

2.4.1 The Coding Hypothesis and Deep Structure

The most tendentious hypothesis in generative grammar was that every sentence has a deep structure representation, which is abstract. This hypothesis was the subject of greatest debate in linguistic circles because it was the most striking challenge to behaviorist principles. On the one hand, we cannot directly observe deep structure in the surface sequence. On the other hand, we cannot define deep structure in semantic terms. Rather, deep structure is a formal structure that mediates between surface form and meaning. Several psychologists proposed that deep structure was, in fact, the basic schema in which we organize and retain sentences, with transformations specifying modifications of the basic schema (Mehler 1963; Miller 1962b). The *coding hypothesis* was formulated in terms of a "schema plus correction" model for memory, proposed as a general principle by Bartlett (1932). According to the coding hypothesis, we retain sentences in the simple declarative form, plus transformationally motivated "tags" such as passive, negative, and so on that express the actual construction of the sentence (Mehler 1963; Miller 1962a). The coding hypothesis also is a literal interpretation of the sentence cube in which the simple declarative sentence is a kernel structure.

There was further support for the interpretation that the coding hypothesis applied to Chomsky's (1957) abstract underlying structures. All other things being equal, the perceived relatedness between words is greater when they are in the same deep structure phrase (Levelt 1970). For example, in (18a) and (18b), repeated here as (34)

(34) a. John was eager to please.
      b. John was easy to please.

John and *eager* are perceived to be more closely related than *John* and *easy*, since, as we noted earlier, in (34a) *John* appears in the same deep structure clause as *eager*, but in (34b) *John* does not appear in the same deep structure clause as *easy*. Words also are better prompts for other words in the same deep structure phrase than in other phrases (Walker, Gough, and Wall 1968; Davidson 1969). In fact, a word is a better prompt for recall of the entire sentence if it appears several times in the deep structure representation. For example, *John* is a better prompt in sentence (34a) than in sentence (34b), since only in sentence (34a) is it the subject of two deep structure predicates (Blumenthal 1967; Blumenthal and Boakes 1967; Wanner 1968).

The studies on locating nonspeech sounds in sentences offered evidence that listeners actively compute deep structure during speech perception. The perceived location of a brief nonspeech sounds is influenced by the "clause" structure at the *deep* structure level of representation, as shown in sentences (35a) and (35b) (Bever, Lackner, and Kirk 1969). The O indicates the objective location on the nonspeech sound, and the R indicates the relatively dominant perceived location of the sound.

(35) a. The general defied the troops to fight.
                        O   R
      b. The general desired the troops to fight.
                        R O

The fact that the nonspeech sound is heard after *troops* in (35a) makes sense if we recall that the noun phrase after *defy* appears in the same deep structure clause as *defy*. The tendency to hear the nonspeech sound before *troops* in (35b) follows from the fact that *troops* is not in the same deep structure clause as *desire*.

These studies vindicated the levels of representation proposed by transformational grammar as active participants in sentence perception. Listeners actively compute the deep structure level of representation as an active part of comprehension. But it seemed clear that the grammatical rules that defined these levels of representation did not systematically correspond to psychological operations. In that case, the question emerged: How does speech processing elicit grammatical levels of representation?

2.4.2 Perceptual Strategies

One possibility is that the processes that form perceptual representations are entirely distinct from grammatical operations (Fodor and Garrett 1967; Fodor, Bever, and Garrett 1974). In a version of this view, listeners acquire an extragrammatical set of *perceptual strategies* that map surface structures onto deep structures (Bever 1968b, 1970a). These strategies are not grammatical rules but state relations between levels of representations based on salient features at the surface level. The most powerful of these strategies (in English) is that the surface sequence NP-verb-NP corresponds to "agent action patient." That strategy gives a nontransformational explanation for the one fact that unambiguously had supported the hypothesis that transformations correspond to psychological operations: passives are harder than actives. The fact that passives violate the NP-verb-NP strategy explains the difficulty of the passive. Similarly, the strategy explains the salience of NP-verb-NP structures in sentences with reduced relative clauses, as in *The horse raced past the barn fell*. It also explains the preference for the transformed version of sentences with particle/prepositions, since the transformed version places the patient directly after the action.

Research on sentence comprehension in children confirmed the behavioral independence of such perceptual strategies. During their third year, children rely heavily on this strategy for comprehension even though there is no concomitant change in their linguistic knowledge. During this period, for example, older children actually perform more poorly than younger children on acting out passive sentences (Bever et al. 1969; Bever 1970a; Maratsos 1974; DeVilliers and DeVilliers 1972; Slobin and Bever 1982).

Distinguishing grammatical rules from psychological strategies stimulated investigation of how the latter interact with other psychological processes, such as attention, perception, and memory. There are capacity limits that require immediate memory to be cleared periodically for new input (Miller 1957; Miller, Galanter, and Pribram 1960). The perceptual strategies can clear immediate memory by recoding surface sequences on deep structure propositions. This reasoning motivated the hypothesis that the proposition is the unit of recoding during speech perception (Bever 1970a; Bever, Kirk, and Lackner 1969; Fodor, Bever, and Garrett 1974). The recoding hypothesis gives special status to the end of each proposition since it is there that definitive recoding can take place. In fact, just at the end of clauses, reaction times to clicks are slow (Abrams and Bever 1969), detection of clicks is poor (Bever, Hurtig, and Handel 1975), tones are hard to discriminate (Holmes and Forster 1972), and evoked potentials are suppressed (Seitz 1972), whereas the relative magnitude of orienting responses to shock suggest greatest preoccupation at that point (Bever et al. 1969). The loss of attention capacity was ostensibly due to the mental load associated with the final stage of recoding the sentence into a deep representation (Abrams and Bever 1969; Bever, Garrett, and Hurtig 1973). At first, it appeared that the surface clause was the unit that defined the scope of the perceptual strategies (Fodor and Bever 1965). Then it appeared that the deep structure "sentence" was the relevant unit (Bever, Lackner, and Kirk 1969). Finally, it became clear that the relevant unit as a psychological object was as a "functionally complete" proposition consisting of fully specified grammatical roles (Carroll 1978; Carroll and Tanenhaus 1975).

The decade of research on speech processing between 1965 and 1975 offered an account of the relation between certain linguistically defined representations and behavioral systems. Grammar defines the levels of representation, but ordinary behavior depends on statistically valid strategies. Grammatical rules may find behavioral instantiation, but only as a backup system slowly brought into play in the rare cases when the behavioral strategies fail (Bever 1972).

The moral of this experience is clear. Cognitive science made progress by separating the question of what people understand and say from how they understand and say it. The straightforward attempt to use the grammatical model directly as a processing model failed. The question of what humans know about language is not only distinct from how children learn it, it is distinct from how adults use it. In retrospect, this should not have been a surprising result. It is a philosophical truism that there is a difference between knowing *that* X and knowing *how to* X. For example, knowing that a sound sequence is an arpeggio on a French horn is quite different from playing one. Musical knowledge may inform both performers and listeners about the structure inherent in their shared experience, but the knowledge does not describe the actual experiential processes. The same distinction is available for linguistic knowledge.

Further consideration also suggests a straightforward functional reason why grammars are not models of specific kinds of language behaviors. There are too many classes of language behavior. Each of these language behaviors has its own neurological and physical constraints. In particular, humans ordinarily both talk and comprehend. Yet the constraints on the ear are obviously different from those on the mouth. A grammar represents exactly those aspects of language that are true, no matter how the language is used. The representation of such knowledge must be abstracted away from any particular system of use.

The most positive result of this phase of research was the demonstration of the importance of abstract levels of linguistic representation during language behavior. It definitively rejected a behaviorist model of language learning, which cannot account for the incorporation of such abstract structures. It also offered the hope of a new kind of Gestalt psychology in which the relevant "good figures" would be given a theoretical foundation. The grammar could be called on to define the "good figures" of language (Neisser 1967). The golden age was tarnished, but there was a solid prospect for a period of normal science in which abstract mental structures could be taken as the object of serious inquiry.

2.5   The Search for a Behaviorally Relevant Grammar

Behaviorism springs eternal. New theories in both linguistics and experimental psychology proposed arguments against the notion of a syntactic deep structure.

Generative semanticists in linguistics grappled with the problem of the relationship between deep structure and semantic representations. Their argument was that if a common deep structure represents the relation between an active and a passive construction, a common deep structure can underlie both an active and a causative structure, expressing the structural relation between the following two sentences:

(36) a. John killed Bill.
     b. John caused Bill to die.

A common deep structure can also underlie an active and a superficially remote construction, as in:

(37) I'm telling you that what happened was that the thing that John caused Bill to do was changed from being alive to being not alive.

Generative semanticists also noted technical problems with the transformational syntactic model that focused on its relation to semantic structure. They eventually proposed that the semantic representation of a sentence *is* its deep structure (Lakoff 1971; Lakoff and Ross 1976; McCawley 1968a, 1968b; Postal 1967). In this view, there was no intermediate, purely syntactic configuration that represented the inner grammatical structures. Rather, they were viewed as an arbitrary subset of the semantic representation (Lakoff 1972). The entire semantic representation itself served as the input to the transformations, which derived surface phrase structures from it.

This theory had great appeal and caused considerable controversy among syntacticians. It appeared to simplify linguistic description and to do so without recourse to a purely formal level of syntactic representation. However, this position was not tenable. Semantic representations themselves either must be stated in a normal form, or they must comprise all conceptual knowledge. Either way, the generative semantics program collapsed. If the semantic representation is in a canonical, propositional, or some other normal form, the model still included an intermediate formal level of representation that mediates structurally between thoughts and the outer form of language (as in McCawley 1976). If semantic representations are purely conceptual, they must include all possible human knowledge (Lakoff 1971, 1972). This conclusion was a reductio ad totam, since it is impossible to define grammatical rules for all possible knowledge (Katz and Bever 1975). For this and other reasons, generative semantics was largely abandoned as a grammatical project (see Katz and Bever 1975; Newmeyer 1980, for general discussions).

The wars in linguistics highlighted the problem that linguistic theory changes like quicksilver. Just when psychologists think they have their hands on it, it slips through. The rapid development of linguistic theory is one of the reasons it is such an influential discipline in behavioral science. It is also one of the reasons that merging linguistics and experimental psychology is difficult. It takes a month to develop a new syntactic analysis of a phenomenon, but it takes a year to develop an experimental investigation of it. All too often, the psychologist is in the position of completing an arduous series of empirical studies only to discover that the linguistic theory underlying them is no longer "operative." During the 1970s, syntactic theory received particularly great attention in linguistics. The transformational model evolved and alternative models emerged. The rejection of the early transformational grammar as a literal model of processing had discouraged psychologists from attending to linguistic theory. The sudden multiplicity of syntactic theories confirmed the psychologists' suspicion that linguists were hopelessly fickle.

For all that, psychologists were not to be left out of attempts to develop a behaviorist revival of language. The salient target was the deep structure coding hypothesis, which gives priority to deep syntactic structure as the code for remembered sentences. The obvious alternative hypothesis is that people actually remember sentences in terms of semantic schemata. Many experimental demonstrations of the syntactic coding hypothesis seemed interpretable as degenerate cases of semantic rather than syntactic coding. For example, *John* in *John is eager to please* is not only the subject of two deep structure clauses, it is also the agent of two propositional "ideas." There were also positive demonstrations of the importance of nonsyntactic representations. Sentences in a story are misrecalled or gratuitously imputed to the story in a way consistent with the story line (Bransford and Franks 1971, 1972). For example, a story originally with sentences about a robbery, shots, and dying may be incorrectly recalled as having included a sentence about killing. Such results, and the apparent disarray in linguistic theory, encouraged many to assume that linguistics-based psychology of language was an adventure of the past. In fact, some took this discouraging thought to its behaviorist conclusion, namely, that syntax is not real, and that only probabilistic language behavior exists. What appears to be evidence of syntax is the gratuitous by-product of perceptual processes (Clark and Haviland 1974), speech behavior learning strategies (Bates 1976; Bates and MacWhinney 1982), or an overimaginative and flawed linguistic methodology (Schank 1973, 1976).

Nonetheless, the same crucial empirical problem remained for both linguistics and psychology. That is, sentences have behaviorally relevant inner forms, and phrase grouped representations that are neither conceptual nor superficial. Independently of how they are behaviorally integrated with conceptual world knowledge, these structures play a role in the formal description of linguistic knowledge, aspects of sentence comprehension, and language learning.

During the 1980s there were some clear trends in the evolution of syntactic theory that led to a renewed collaboration between psychology and linguistics. The overwhelming shift was away from restrictions expressed in transformations to verb-based structural restrictions. Three syntactic models emerged in this direction (see Sells 1985 and Tanenhaus 1988 for a review of linguistic and psycholinguistic issues, respectively, and chapter 3).

Government and Binding   This theory was the original transformational model with the following changes:

- Increase in the importance of lexical information in determining sentence structure
- Reduction in the variety of transformations to one movement rule
- Introduction of explicit "filters" that constrain the distinct levels of representation and relations between the levels of representation

In the original transformational model, the transformations themselves specify the relation between the deep and the surface level. A derivation is possible only if there are particular transformations that construct it. In the government-and-binding variant, there is only one transformational rule, essentially a universal movement rule that randomly changes the deep tree. Constraints on possible trees then filter out potentially ungrammatical structures (Chomsky 1981, 1985).

Lexical-Functional Grammar   A separate model that may be a notational variant of the government-and-binding model treated most transformational variations as specified within the lexicon itself (Bresnan and Kaplan 1983). (Note that this kind of model still treated recursion and unbounded dependencies in the same manner as standard transformational models.)

Generalized Phrase Structure Grammar   A variant of phrase structure proposed to describe sentence structure. Unlike earlier models of phrase structure, this model included an enriched repertoire of the kinds of abstract constituent nodes that are intended to overcome the empirical inadequacy of earlier phrase structure systems (Gazdar et al. 1985).

Each of these syntactic models had its champions as a model of speech behavior. For example, Frazier (1985) and Freedman and Forster (1985) worked within government-and-binding theory, Bresnan and Kaplan (1983) in Lexical-Functional Grammar, and Crain and Fodor (1985) in generalized phase structure grammar. The common argument was that the only thing wrong with the previous attempts to take the syntactic theory as a psychological model was that the syntactic theory itself was wrong. Yet the old difficulties persisted: it is hard to state consistent linking assumptions between the formal model and the behaving person. A consistent theory of direct implementation of grammatical knowledge in behavior continued to be elusive. (See Bever 1987 for a discussion of attempts to formulate direct linguistic linking assumptions.)

2.6   The Reemergence of Associationism

In the 1980s several developments in cognitive psychology and the study of language exhibited a certain recycling of previous approaches. Concomitant with the increasing emphasis on lexically driven grammatical analyses, a large body of research was devoted to "lexical access." This research focused on the recognition, immediate processing, and recall of single words in various contexts including sentences (for reviews, see Simpson 1981; Seidenberg and Tanenhaus 1986; Tanenhaus, Carlson, and Seidenberg 1985).

At the same time, sentence-level syntax offered only a few structures for a psychologist to study after establishing the behavioral relevance of abstract levels of representation. A language has a small number of constructions that can act as crucial cases such as paired constructions like sentences (38a) and (38b) or (39a) and (39c), which are identical in their surface representation but different at the underlying level, repeated here:

(38) a. John was eager to please.

   b. John was easy to please.

(39) a. The general defied the troops to fight.

   b. The general desired the troops to fight.

or paired constructions like sentences (40a) and (40b):

(40) a. In her *hope of marrying Anna was impractical.*

   b. Harry's *hope of marrying Anna was impractical.*

which can share a substantial acoustic segment with distinct surface phrase structures.

But a language has a large number of words. It will take a long time to run out of things to study about them. And it appears that such work will always be relevant. Surely, it is reasonable to expect that whatever we find out today about processing words will be relevant to an integrated theory of language behavior in the future. Unfortunately, our scientific history tells us that this is not necessarily so. The only people who we can be absolutely sure will profit from our scientific work, brilliant or parochial, are the future historians of science. Otherwise, we would today be profiting from the decades of research on verbal learning.

Today's studies seem to offer more hope. They typically (but not always) involve the relation among words in sentences. They sometimes focus on the relation between lexical levels and other levels of processing. Such studies offer an unequivocal answer to the question of how much of sentence processing is controlled by categorical information in words. But many lexically focused studies are done entirely without the benefit of a more general theory of language behavior.

Associationism returned reinvigorated at the end of the 1980s, in the form of "connectionist" models of complex behavior (Feldman 1986; McClelland and Rumelhart 1986), which are now in high fashion in cognitive science. *Connectionism* is a descriptive term for a class of theories based on associative connections between elements: in this sense, it is a framework for associative models, which makes no particular claims until utilized in a particular way. There are few constraints on how abstract the units themselves can be or how many clusters they are arranged in. In this sense, connectionism is associationism without a necessary link to behaviorism.

Practitioners of the art take the laudable stance that the theories should be precise enough to be testable. But "testability" is easily conflated with "modeled," and much energy is given to instantiating specific proposals in computer programs. This is intriguing and guarantees a theory's local consistency, but by no means guarantees its correctness. Superficially, successful computational models can be the undoing of the science they purport to aid. The ability of a model to deal with a large but manageable number of isolated facts has little to do with having a correct theory. In fact, factual success can unnaturally prolong the life of an incorrect theory. As the unknown wag says, if Ptolemy had had a computer, we would still believe that we are the center of the universe.

One of the things we know about words is that a language has a manageably large number of them. Hence, studies of lexical processes and connectionist models go well together. Such associative models can even simulate the effect of morphological combination rules (Rumelhart, Hinton, and Williams 1986). This success tempts one to speculate that the consequences of such linguistic rules are represented in an associative network without any actual representation of the rules themselves. That is, the system as a whole allegedly recapitulates behavior only approximated by the rule (see Rumelhard and McClelland 1968, chap. 18; Feldman 1986).

The connectionist approach to language is often an intentional merging of competence and performance in a manner opposite the conflation of transformational grammar and a performance model, discussed above (see, e.g., Elman 1990). Thirty-five years ago, some psycholinguists claimed that the grammar is the performance system; the corresponding connectionist claim would be that the performance system is the reality that the grammar captures only approximately and vaguely.

The grammarian's claim was wrong because categorical grammatical knowledge cannot explain the continua of actual behavior. The connectionist claim may turn out to be wrong for the complementary reason, namely, that contingent probabilities cannot explain categorical knowledge. Of course, given enough associative connections between explicit and internal elements, any rule-governed behavior can be approximated. Such models are the equivalent of the sculptor's plaster of paris: give them an articulate structure and enough internal associative connectivity and they will shape themselves to it.

Associative simulations do not explain morphological structure in lexical morpheme combinations. They only conform to it as an automatic consequence of simulating a description of the combinations. If there is anything we know about sentences, it is that a language has an unmanageably large number of them. This contrast was one of the strong motivations for embarking on the study of the acquisition and deployment of rules in behavior rather than memorized connections and automatic elicitations (Miller, Galanter, and Pribram 1960). No doubt connections and elicitations exist and dominate much measurable behavior in an adult. The perennial puzzle is how to prestructure associations so that they systematically *impose* rulelike organization on what they learn. The specific challenges for an associative theory of language learning remain:

• What is the nature of the categorical information encoded in words, sentences, and rules?
• How is such categorical information learned and represented?
• Last (but not least), how does it come to be used and translated into relevant contingent connections?

2.7   Conclusion: The Mystery of Structure

The listing of classical approaches to the sentence is a tale about the merits of being methodologically flexible and answering only one question at a time. Progress was made in understanding how language behavior works by divorcing it from the question of how it is learned. Further progress depended on making a distinction between the models of linguistic knowledge and language behavior. Elaboration of structural models of linguistic knowledge has actually laid out a number of consistent features about the nature of language for the psychologist to ponder. The reemergence of a powerful framework for associative modeling offers new ways to embrace frequency-based information within processing models, without embracing behaviorist learning principles as well.

Despite all of this progress, however, we are left with an essential empirical puzzle, the answer to which will involve solutions to most of the issues raised in this chapter: How does the knowledge of syntactic structure improve the acuity of the ear?

Note

This chapter is based on a chapter by Bever that appeared in Hirst 1988. We have received comments from many linguists and psychologists on an earlier version of the chapter. Generally, psychologists find it an accurate picture of the intellectual period; linguists tend to think that it overlooks much of what was happening within linguistics at the time. The typical comment is: "But linguists were not confused about that matter (e.g., the derivational theory of complexity), so why report the psychologists' confusion over it?" We are not convinced that most linguists were—and are—not just as confused as most psychologists on most matters. However, such responses prompt us to add an explanatory caveat: this chapter is intended to give an account of how the world looked to psychologists and psycholinguists at the fore-front of the field during the years from 1955 to 1980, and a bit beyond. A parallel history of developments within linguistics would be of parallel interest—especially with respect to how linguists viewed language behavior. For example, during the period covered in this chapter, almost all linguists disdained research on the role of syntactic and semantic structures in language processing. This situation has changed somewhat in the last decade, though not always with a clarifying effect.

Chapter 3
What Every Psychologist Should Know about Grammar

The preceding chapter presents the classical evidence that when a word sequence is organized into a sentence, it takes on a special psychological status. Some of the evidence suggested that this status was not only dependent on the fact that sentences have independent meanings, but that they also have a rigorous and characteristic syntactic structure. Psycholinguistic research between 1960 and 1975 focused on the role of a transformational grammar in language behavior. The ultimate conclusion was that while grammatically defined representations appear to be computed during language behavior, the grammatical rules that define them may not be used.

This conclusion reminds us that the process of understanding sentences may be very different from the representation of linguistic knowledge. It cleaves grammatical knowledge from comprehension and sets the problem we address in this book: How should the grammar be embedded in a comprehension theory? This question requires that we have a more specific notion of grammar than the past one we have assumed up to this point. However, it is difficult and risky to rest a comprehension model on any particular syntactic architecture. Linguistics is the producer of detailed grammatical theories, and the production of generative syntactic theories has evolved rapidly over the last half century. Psychology is a consumer of generalizations about grammars, but especially in the last two decades, the rapid changes in syntactic theories have left psychologists in large part baffled as to how to integrate grammatical knowledge and behavior in rigorous models.

We think that syntactic theory in the last few years has returned to a model that is more tractable as a component of behavioral models (Chomsky 1995). However, in this chapter we first review certain features of syntactic theory that have remained a critical part of most generative models of grammar. This will help the reader focus on durable features of syntax and will help ensure the longevity of our specific proposals about the architecture of a comprehension model that includes grammatical knowledge. In the second section of the chapter we review the history of different architectures of grammar that relate to meaning, and we end with a more discursive presentation of the current syntactic theory, "minimalism."

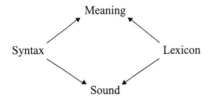

Figure 3.1
The components of grammar and their interfaces.

3.1 The Architecture of Syntax

Language relates meanings to sounds. Meanings themselves are closely linked to general cognitive and perceptual structures; sounds are closely liked to motoric properties of the mouth and acoustic properties of the ear. Thus, the domains of meanings and sounds are constrained by their output interface to other psychological structures, as shown in figure 3.1. The structures and processes that relate meanings and sounds in orderly ways comprise the grammar. The lexicon maps meanings onto sounds by memorized connections; the syntax operates on words to compose meaning-sound relations that are not already memorized in the lexicon. Arguments in linguistic theory often revolve around how much of the mapping is carried out by structures memorized in the lexicon, how much by syntactic operations. But it is commonly accepted that sentence-level meanings are compositional, modifying the impact of the isolated meaning of the individual words. Consider the meaning of the verb *call* in different sentential contexts.

(1) a. Mary called Bill.
    b. Mary called Bill over.
    c. Mary called Bill, "Bill."
    d. Mary called Bill a fool.
    e. Mary called "Bill."
    f. Mary called Bill up.
    g. Mary called Bill on his phone.
    h. Mary called Bill on his mistake.
    i. Mary called Bill on the carpet.

Native speakers of English have a vague feeling that there is a central core of the meaning of *call* that is elaborated in different ways, depending on the sentential context. This core meaning of *call* has something to do with verbal expression to get another's attention, but that is about as precise as one can be. Because of that difficulty, one might argue that these examples only show that *call* is lexically ambiguous between a variety of meanings, and the sentential context serves only to select one or another of the predefined meanings. But careful analysis of apparently unambiguous words shows that the sentence level can play a role in refining and focusing the compositional meaning in a particular direction. Consider the following words in isolation:

(2) a. hate
   b. Sparta
   c. Athens

Hate at root is a state in which some entity has a negative attitude toward another; Sparta is an ancient Greek city, known for its warlike behavior; Athens is an ancient and current Greek city, known for its philosophers. If we now put those words into a sentence, the whole entity has a particular meaning that picks out certain aspects of the root meanings of the words and composes them into a new whole.

(3) Sparta hated Athens.

The likely interpretation is now limited to ancient times, by virtue of the fact that Sparta is best known as an ancient city. The notion of *hate* is now enriched by general contextual knowledge of how hatred might be effected by one city-state against another (for example, this hatred could not result in a suit in the world court, but rather a disposition to send an army to its the city walls). The sentence level arrangement not only isolates certain meanings of the words; it provides a structure that can access conceptual knowledge to yield a new and specific sense.

3.2 Constant Features of Syntactic Structures

We now review essential features of syntax that set constraints on how to integrate a grammar within a comprehension theory. Our syntactic theory of reference is the Minimalist Program (Chomsky 1995). However, we emphasize the features of syntactic description that are shared among a number of theories that compete within the framework of purely linguistic research. It is inevitable that the details of our comprehension theory will be influenced by the syntactic theory we choose. But the architecture of how syntax is embedded in a comprehension model transcends those details and holds for a wide range of syntactic approaches.

3.2.1 Lexical Categories

The most basic syntactic information is the category information on each lexical item. Every word in the lexicon must have a categorization that describes how it can fit into syntactic frames, regardless of its meaning. This kind of information not only includes traditional categories, such as Noun and Verb, but also information about subcategories, defined by particular patterns of categories that define its allowed contexts. For example, *hate* is not merely a verb; it is a verb that ordinarily requires exactly one noun phrase object within the verb phrase, which we indicate with the following "subcategorization frame" inside angle brackets:

(4) hate = verb
$\langle$NP hate NP$\rangle$

This subcategorization frame is justified with an example ungrammatical sentence, indicated by *:

(5) *Sparta hated.

Even when the object appears to be missing, it is implied. For example, the fact that *the* is required with *victim* below shows that it is presupposed somewhere prior in the sentence.

(6) a. ?Sparta hated frequently, but that never impressed the victim.
b. *Sparta hated frequently, but that never impressed a victim.

The postulation of basic lexical categories is one of the driving theoretical concepts of syntactic theory, whether described as units or as collections of syntactic features. The most essential distinctions are between words that characteristically select arguments (for example, verbs and prepositions), words that characteristically serve as arguments (such as nouns), and words that characteristically are predicated of other words (i.e., modify them, such as adjectives and adverbs). Argument-taking words are incomplete and uninterpretable without their argument—for example, *hate* requires both a subject and an object.

(7) a. *hated
b. *Sparta hated
c. *hated Athens
d. *Xenophon went into

Nouns serve as arguments while adjectives and adverbs, which appear in parentheses below, modify other words.

(8) a. The city (violently) hated the other (rich) city.
b. Xenophon (quickly) went (almost) into the city.

It is important to be clear about the fact that the syntactic aspects of lexical categories are not derived from their conceptual attributes. The distinction between words that have argument positions and words that fill argument positions is strictly formal and resides within the framework of syntax alone. As we will see, the substantive generalization and corresponding formal requirement that verbs and prepositions must fill their argument positions has unexpected and interesting consequences for more abstract levels of syntactic description.

3.2.2   Morphology

Words also have cases and inflections assigned by their position in the syntactic configuration. In English, the presence of case is revealed by pronouns that carry different forms. For example, in (3), which we repeat here

(3) Sparta hated Athens.

Sparta has subject case and *Athens* object case, as revealed by the different forms of the pronoun in (9). Note that *they* is the normal subject or nominative form, while *them* is the normal object or accusative form.

(9) a.   they hated them
    b. *them hated they
    c. *them hated them
    d. *they hated they

It is important to note that we cannot make complete decisions about the lexical or syntactic structure assigned to single sentences. As in the case of *Sparta hated Athens*, even to determine the morphological-case assignment status of a sentence, we may have to refer to other similar sentences to extract a complete picture. This reflects the fact that even a relatively obvious property of sentences, such as lexical category and morphology, is actually an abstract layer of representation that cannot always be directly observed on the surface of a particular sentence.

Morphological units assist in the representation of functional categories, categories that are purely syntactic and provide the structural skeleton of sentences. Thus, case, auxiliaries, and other morphological structures serve in part as the glue that binds different components of a sentence. In languages with relatively free word order, morphological agreement cues can be critical.

3.2.3   Phrase Structure

It is intuitively clear that lexical sequences are segregated into larger units.

(10) The city hated Athens.

It is obvious that *the city* is a unit in some sense different from *city hated*. This is represented by a higher bracketing that defines a phrase. At first, it might seem obvious that such a level is discovered directly because it is often so clearly marked in such overt features as pronunciation, with explicit pauses allowed between phrases more readily than within them. But, technically, the evidence that a sequence is a phrase also depends in part on examination of related sequences that are and are not allowed. Evidence for a phrase typically rests on the integrity of the sequence when the unit is placed in other syntactic contexts.

(11) a.   Sparta hated Athens.
     b.   It was Athens that Sparta hated.
     c.   Sparta hated the city.
     d.   *It was the that Sparta hated city.
     e.   *It was city that Sparta hated the.
     f.   It was the city that Sparta hated.

The cases in (11) show that *the* cannot be stripped from the rest of its phrase, as in (11d) and (11e), but can be moved together with *city*, as in (11f). Similar sorts of data show that *hated Athens* is a phrase, more closely knit than *Sparta hated*:

(12) a.   It was hate Athens that Sparta did.
     b.   *It was hate that Sparta did to Athens.

The phrasal unity of a verb with its object does not depend on the fact that *hate* must have an object somewhere in the sentence. For example, *attack* may or may not have an explicit object, as shown by

(13) a. Sparta attacked.
     b. Sparta attacked Athens.

Nevertheless, any explicit object it does have is still carried with the verb, while the subject is not.

(14) a.   It was attack Athens that Sparta did.
     b. ?It was attack that Sparta did to Athens.
     c. *It was Sparta attack that happened to Athens.

Thus, the fact that phrases exist is crucially confirmed by the fact that phrases tend to move together in alternate structures.

Another more traditional kind of evidence for phrase structure is that phrase sequences of varying lengths can be shown to serve the same function in a given sentence context.

(15) a. *Sparta* attacked Athens.
     b. *The city* attacked Athens.
     c. *The ancient city* attacked Athens.
     d. *The ancient city known to be warlike* attacked Athens.
     e. *The ancient city said to be known to be warlike* attacked Athens.

Each of the italicized initial noun phrase sequences intuitively serves as the subject of the verb. Thus, phrases come in different "kinds," defined by their function in the sentence. While the italicized phrases above are all called *noun phrases*, from a functional standpoint they are *determiner phrases*, defined by the functional category determiner, which includes words like *the* and *a*. The other salient kind of phrase is traditionally the *verb phrase*. The verb phrase too can actually be defined in terms of its functional role in the sentence, namely, as predicate that carries tense/aspect and modal information.

3.2.4   Sentence-Internal Reference between Nouns, Pronouns, and Positions

Sentences have syntactic devices to cross-refer from one part of the sentence to a phrase in another part. In the examples below, elements with common subscripts indicate reference relations:

(16) *Reflexive*
  When Sparta$_i$ attacked itself$_i$, Athens$_j$ did not survive long.

(17) *Pronoun*
  When Sparta$_i$ attacked it$_j$, Athens$_j$ did not survive long.

The difference between a reflexive such as *itself* and a normal pronoun such as *it* plays a large role in syntactic investigations. This is because a pronoun must have "exogenous" reference—that is, it must refer to some antecedent not immediately in the domain of its own sentence. The reflexive has "endogenous" references—that is, its antecedent is strictly limited to the domain of its own clause. The difference between exogenous and endogenous reference allows syntactic theorists to identify the domain of the scope of various kinds of syntactic rules. These domains do not always depend on relative proximity, but to "locality" that is defined in terms of a hierarchical phrase structure.

(18) a.   Bill$_i$ was believed by Mary$_j$ to be speaking to her$_j$.
  b.   *Bill$_i$ was believed by Mary$_j$ to be speaking to herself$_j$.
  c.   Bill$_i$ was believed by Mary$_j$ to be speaking to himself$_i$.
  d.   *Bill$_i$ was believed by Mary$_j$ to be speaking to him$_i$ (= Bill).

The sentences in (18) show that *Bill*, but not *Mary*, falls within the structural domain of the verb *speaking*. For our purposes, the important feature of sentence-internal reference is that it is an example of a purely syntactic device. Thus, phrases can be related to other phrases at an arbitrary surface distance, so long as certain functional relations are maintained.

The syntactic structures we have discussed so far are technically "abstract," but they often have overt local reflexes. Thus, case, functional categories, phrase structure, and pronouns can have specific indicators in certain cases. But sometimes case, functional categories, and phrase structure information can be inaudible in the pronunciation of sentences. The same is true of anaphoric devices. Consider first the problem of verbs without subjects.

(19) a.   Sparta$_i$ attacked Athens, and it$_i$ also hated Athens.
  b.   Sparta$_i$ attacked Athens, and also hated Athens.

Where is the subject of *hated* in the second sentence? Intuitively, it is understood to be present, but its absence appears to violate the grammatical generalization that all verbs have subjects. One kind of solution to this is to postulate an empty pronoun, which can stand in for the generic subject under certain syntactically defined circumstances. This is an instance of a so-called empty category.

(20) Sparta$_1$ attacked Athens, and also e$_1$ hated Athens.

In these sentences, the subject of *hated* can be an overt pronoun, or the covert pronoun, PRO, coindexed with its antecedent in the same way as an overt pronoun. This can get complicated:

(21) a. Sparta$_1$ not only attacked it$_2$, but it$_1$ also hated Athens$_2$.
    b. Sparta$_1$ not only attacked e$_2$, but e$_1$ also hated Athens$_2$.

Once the notion of an empty unit that coindexes to an explicit unit is established, it becomes available for the treatment of certain kinds of sentential complements.

(22) a. It was easy for one to hate Athens.
    b. It was easy to hate Athens.
    c. It was easy PRO to hate Athens.

In this case, the empty unit labeled PRO accounts for free variation between verbs with and without explicit subjects with a potential referent external to the sentence. That is, in these cases PRO is "exogenous." But, once postulated, PRO can also account for the existence of constructions in which PRO is "endogenous." In these cases, its referent is restricted to a phrase elsewhere in the sentence, in which a verb may not ever be allowed to have an overt subject, as in:

(23) a. Sparta$_i$ wanted (itself) [PRO$_i$] to attack Athens.
    b. Sparta$_i$ was eager (for itself) [PRO$_i$] to attack Athens.

Complement constructions such as those above pose a threat to the generalization that verb arguments are always filled with something. PRO and analyses like those given preserve this fundamental property that differentiates the lexical category of verbs from nouns.

3.3   Arguments, Movement, and Derivations

Up to now, we have assumed that each verb has a canonical set of arguments. The theoretical situation is a bit murky with respect to how large the stock of arguments actually is. In English, every verb requires an overt subject, as in (24a). Most also require an object within the verb phrase as in (24b), and some also require an indirect object within the verb phrase (see (24c)).

(24) a. He ran.
        Ran: ⟨intransitive⟩ (i.e., requires a subject only)
     b. He attacked them.
        Attack: ⟨NP⟩ (requires an object)
     c. He donated them to her.
        Donate: ⟨NP PP⟩ (requires both direct and indirect object)

Semantically, it is intuitive that every verb must have an agent or experiencer of some kind:

(25) a. John left.
     b. *left
     c. John is sad.
     d. *is sad

Transitive verbs by definition have patients, and certain verbs can have goals as well.

(26) a. John hates carrots.
     b. *John hates.
     c. John gave the carrots to his sister.
     d. John gave his sister the carrots.

It is tempting to enumerate the argument roles in terms of their semantic/thematic properties. The difficulty with this is that there is no semantic criterion for deciding whether a particular thematic argument is also a syntactic one. One standard method of distinguishing syntactic arguments is to limit them to instances that require case marking. In English, however, case marking is not overt except for pronouns. In the preceding examples, every position is directly case-marked by the verb alone, which justifies positing those arguments as syntactic. This is explicit only when pronouns are used:

(27) a. He hates them.
     b. He gave them to her.
     c. He gave her them.
     d. *He gave them (except elliptically).
     e. *He gave her (where *her* means *to her*).

In general every obligatory syntactic argument position must always be filled with something. We saw above that in some cases an inaudible pronoun, PRO, can serve that purpose. PRO is like an overt pronoun, in that it is coindexed with an antecedent, possibly one outside the current sentence.

(28) Sparta attacked at twilight, but Athens was ready.

The object of *attack* most likely is Athens, as shown by the use of the antecedent-dependent article *the* in the subject of the second clause:

(29) a.   Sparta attacked at twilight, but the city was ready for it.
      b.   ?Sparta attacked at twilight, but a city was ready for it.
      c.   Sparta attacked Carthage at twilight, but Athens was ready.

However, the object of the attack could be some other city, as paraphrased in (29c).

Pronouns also serve a crucial role in linking phrases to modifying propositions. It is a vital part of language that it be possible to infinitely modify noun phrases. This property of language plays a role in the ability of language to provide a sentence for every sense. For example, (30a) to (30c) form a short discourse that can be more directly and unambiguously expressed in (30d):

(30) a.   A city attacked a city.
      b.   The first city was from the North.
      c.   The second city was from the South.
      d.   A city (that was) from the North attacked a city (that was) from the South.

Each relative pronoun *that* appears to serve as subject of an embedded modifying clause. At the same time, each *that* is coindexed with the appropriate head noun in the main clause. It appears on the surface that *that* is actually in the subject position of the embedded clause. Analysis of other constructions, however, suggests that this may not be quite right. In general, relative pronoun connectors can be drawn from many locations in an embedded clause. The generalization is that they must always appear at the front of the embedded clause.

The cases below raise a puzzle:

(31) a.   The church which the rich parishioner gave [X] the found money, is poor.
      b.   The money which the rich parishioner gave the church [X], was found.

If obligatory argument positions must be filled, the relative clauses should be ungrammatical, since one argument position in each is unfilled [marked by X]. *Give* ordinarily requires both a direct and an indirect object. Intuitively, we know that the relative pronoun itself stands for the missing argument. But how do we account for the fact that it is in the wrong position? One possibility might be to assume that the argument position is filled with a PRO, which is coindexed with the relative pronoun and the head noun:

(32) The church which the rich parishioner gave PRO the found money, is poor.

There is a problem with this solution. PRO characteristically occurs as an optional filler for a missing coreferring argument, which could be explicit, but an explicit pronoun is ungrammatical in the case of relative clauses:

(33) a.   *The church that the rich parishioner gave it the found money, is poor.
      b.   *The church that the rich parishioner gave the hospital the found money is poor.

One crucial point is that PRO is characteristically an optional filler for an explicit noun phrase (see section 3.2.3). Another crucial point is that the referent of PRO can have more than one thematic role. In *Sparta wanted to attack Athens*, *Sparta* is agent/experiencer of both *wanted* and *attack*. Finally, PRO remains in the location that assigns its thematic role. In relative clauses the argument position is obligatory but must *not* be filled with an explicit pronoun. Furthermore, the referent of this category has only one thematic role. In this representation the referent pronoun appears in two positions but receives its thematic role from the position it does not occupy on the surface. We need to find some device other than PRO to account for the superficially missing arguments in relative clauses.

A natural solution is to link the relative pronoun to the argument position syntactically, rather than by coindexing. Graphically, we want something like the following:

(34) The church that the member gave [NP] the money is poor.

It is not possible to establish this link between the pronoun and the argument position within the framework of simple phrase structures. To do so, we would have to have some kind of tree structure with crossing trees, but such a structure would violate the strict hierarchical nature of phrase structure organization. Thus, we need a mechanism that transcends the power of phrase structure.

Several current syntactic theories offer mechanisms that establish a syntactic link between the overt relative pronoun and its related argument position. The exact details may not matter for psychological theory. Syntactic theories appear superficially to be very different, but they share a property that is crucial for behavioral models of language: they involve "movement" and a logical "derivation" during which movement occurs. Consider first Head-driven Phrase Structure Grammar (HPSG) and Generalized Phrase Structure Grammar (GPSG), which are elaborated versions of phrase structure theory (Bennett 1995; Gazdar et al. 1985; Sells 1985 section 2.5). The structure of a simple declarative sentence in GPSG appears in figure 3.2. In this diagram V0 indicates that the lexical category of *hates* is verb, N2 indicates that the syntactic category of *Sparta* and *Athens* is noun phrase, and V2 indicates that the syntactic category of *hates Athens* is verb phrase. The critical elaboration in GPSG is the introduction of features and elements that can pass up (and down) the phrase structure tree as part of the computation of a grammatical sentence. For example, the feature that the head noun *Sparta* is singular must match or "percolate" up to the noun phrase.

Another example of a feature that passes up the phrase structure tree is "missing an argument NP," or MNP. A feature like this is "satisfied" when it finds a noun phrase that is not an argument of a verb. This device offers a neat solution to the syntactic description of relative clauses. The initial tree description of a relative

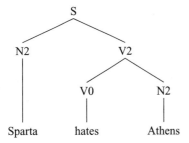

Figure 3.2
The structure of *Sparta hates Athens* according to Generalized Phrase Structure Grammar.

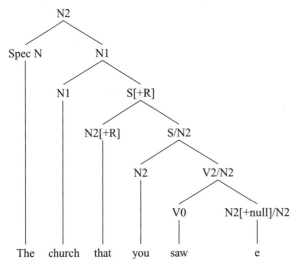

Figure 3.3
The structure of a relative clause in Generalized Phrase Structure Grammar (adapted from Bennett 1995:153).

clause includes markers of argument positions that require a noun phrase, as shown in figure 3.3. In the canonical case of declarative sentences, the argument positions are filled directly by noun phrases (see figure 3.2). But with relative clauses, the special feature MNP is part of the description of the verb. In figure 3.3, the feature [+null] allows insertion of the empty lexical item e. V2/N2 reads a verb phrase with a missing noun phrase, and it indicated that the phrase that contains the transitive verb *saw* is missing an object noun phrase. One way to compute this is to "pass" the feature up the tree. If it finds a noun phrase that is not already taken by some other verb or preposition as an argument, that noun phrase can fill the MNP feature so the

(a) D-Structure:

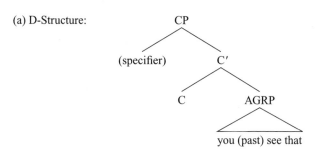

(b) S-Structure:

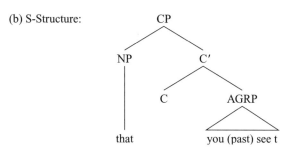

Figure 3.4
The movement in a relative clause according to government-and-binding theory (adapted from
Cook and Newson 1996:200).

NP is no longer missing. In the case of relative clauses, the relative pronoun, N2[+R]
in figure 3.3, itself can serve as such an argument, thus completing the structure
syntactically.

A somewhat different but critically similar solution uses "transformations" to
move the crucial noun phrase. It assumes that initially there is a noun phrase in the
canonical argument position. That is, the position is filled at the beginning of the
syntactic computation, as shown in figure 3.4. In this framework, some NP from
elsewhere in the sentence must be attached to the relative pronoun: movement of the
NP and attachment of it to the relative pronoun position affect this attraction. The
moved NP leaves behind a 'trace" *t* of its original position, coindexed with it.

These solutions to the problem of verb arguments-at-a-distance appear superficially quite different, and indeed, the theories from which they spring are often pitted
against each other in linguistics debates. Yet, when considering the potential behavioral implications, they are identical for our purposes. Each assumes that there is a
special marker for the missing canonical argument position. Each assumes that an
element is computed from the unfilled argument position in relation to the relative
pronoun position. And, most important for us, each assumes a computational
hierarchy or ordering—that is, terminological differences aside, each assumes a

derivation. The computation calculates well-formedness by starting with a structure, recursively moving or relating elements and checking the well-formedness of the resulting structure.

3.3.1   Clausal Locality of Movement

Once we allow movement of syntactic elements as part of syntactic computation, it is important for behavioral modeling to know what the constraints on movement are, if any. If we are to take syntactic theory as the framework for hypotheses about processing, constraints on distance or structural barriers to movement may be a part of a behavioral model. In fact, a principle potentially of great interest restricts possible movements: roughly, *movement is as local as it can be.*

Consider the following sentence, which has several layers of embedded clauses:

(35) a. Sparta was the city which the Athenians that we attacked hated.

On either syntactic theory, the source structure for this looks like:

(35) b. Sparta was the city which the Athenians that we attacked NP hated NP.

In the example above, we have not indexed the noun phrases and the relative pronouns with their correct interpretation. But we need a principle to guarantee the correct outcome as in (35c).

(35) c. Sparta was the city$_1$ which$_1$ the Athenians$_2$ that$_2$ we attacked NP$_2$ hated NP$_1$.

In the case of a theory with overt movement, it is required that the most embedded sentence be treated first. This ensures that the noun phrase that is moved to a given relative pronoun is in the same sentence domain. Thus, the notion of "local" movement is not defined serially, but in terms of domains delineated by phrase structure. A similar treatment follows within the HPSG framework. The first MNP feature that is filled by a *wh*–noun phrase must be the innermost empty noun (36a). Since relative clauses modify nouns, they are the more embedded structure and must be treated first.

(36) a. Sparta was the city$_1$ which$_1$ [the Athenians$_2$ that$_2$ + NP$_2$ we attacked] t$_2$ hated NP$_1$.

Then the remaining noun phrase in the matrix sentence can be correctly related to the remaining, higher, empty relative pronoun (36b).

(36) b. Sparta was the city$_1$ which$_1$ + NP$_1$ the Athenians$_2$ that$_2$ + NP$_2$ we attacked t$_1$ hated t$_2$.

We see that fairly simple facts motivate the notion of a syntactic derivation. The treatment of relative pronouns requires a notion of some kind of displacement from the canonical position of an argument. This recovers the generalization that verb arguments must always be filled in their canonical position. In HPSG, generative syntactic theory, and other theories the relative pronoun is attached to the canonical position by an element that (logically) moves from one position in the syntactic tree to another. In HPSG, the linking element (MNP) is related leftward and up the syntactic tree, until it merges with the *Wh*–noun phrase. In a generative treatment, the linking element moves leftward and attaches to the *Wh*–noun phrase, which is automatically higher in the tree at that point. Thus, the underlying notion of movement is a notion of a derivation in which the syntactic structure starts in one form and changes to another, or is computationally related to another, by the application of computational processes. We will see that the notion of an element that links one location in a sentence to another has implications for processing models.

The proposal that there is a special behavioral status for noun phrases linked to relative pronouns is not radical. First, the local form of the sentence often appears completely to lack the canonically required arguments. For example, *hate* requires an object, and one is obviously missing below:

(37) The city *Athens hated* attacked it.

Second, relative pronouns are characteristically overt lexical items; they are deleted only in certain clearly recognizable cases. Thus, while they are often not in the canonical argument position that they are linked to, it is relatively easy to construct comprehension models that look for a gap when a relative pronoun is encountered and to fill a likely gap position. This processing strategy is enhanced by the third fact: relative pronouns are pure syntactic elements. Relative pronouns have only sentence-internal status and always acquire their semantic interpretation from other phrases within the sentence (hence, the term *relative* pronoun). Other pronouns sometimes can derive their interpretation from the sentence, but that is a coincidence since they may also acquire it from information external to the sentence. For example, in (38a)

(38) a. Harry said he wanted to win.
      b. Harry said she wanted to win.

the *he* may refer to Harry, but the interpretation of *she* in (38a) must come from outside the sentence.

There is another kind of displaced argument construction in which the canonical position is not overtly filled and can never be filled. Consider the passive construction (39a).

(39) a. Athens was attacked by Sparta.

In this case, there is no overt object of *attacked*, nor is one optionally allowed (see (39b)).

(39) b. *Athens was attacked it by Sparta.

Rather, the distributed passive morphology, ... *was V + ed by* ..., indicates the correct arrangement, in which the apparent subject is the object of the verb and the prepositional noun phrase is the agent of the action. It is also characteristic that these kinds of constructions are always superficially similar to canonically well-formed ones that occur elsewhere in the language. For example, true passives are superficially similar to complex predicate constructions with lexical adjectives. Consider the sentences below. In each of these sentences except the first, *was* can be replaced with *remained*. Thus, the predicate modifier is an adjective-like state rather than a particular action with an agent.

(40) a. Athens was attacked by Sparta.
      b. Athens was unattacked by Sparta.
      c. Athens was ruined by Sparta.
      d. Athens was located near Sparta.
      e. Athens was insecure near Sparta.

In brief, the object in the passive does not have an optional overt pronoun of any kind that can be linked to the empty argument position. Nor does it reveal its special status by having a unique and superficially defective argument structure. It is primarily for these reasons that certain syntactic theories treat the unusual location of the verb object in passives as essentially a lexical rather than a syntactic phenomenon. Such solutions essentially argue that certain lexical items, such as the passive forms of verbs, raising verbs such as *happen ... to*, and adjectives such as *likely ... to*, can lack standard argument positions and fill them with unusually located arguments. For this exposition we will adopt the alternative treatment from generative grammars, in which such constructions involve movement, with a resulting empty trace.

The true passive construction expresses an event that apparently is missing an object. The apparent patient is in subject position, while the apparent agent is in an auxiliary phrase. That is, the passive has no obvious object, its "subject" is not the agent, and the actual agent is outside the verb domain. This is all very puzzling from a structural standpoint and appears to violate the core lexical the requirement that verb arguments be filled. But it can be neatly described with the kind of mechanisms we have seen that allow movement of a noun phrase from one position to another. Suppose we start with a structure like (41b):

(41) a. Athens was attacked by Sparta.
      b. NP was attacked Athens by Sparta.

Athens is initially generated as the object of *attack*, and then can move to fill the empty noun phrase in apparent subject position (41c):

(41) c. Athens₁ was attacked [t₁] by Sparta.

Similar kinds of descriptions apply to conventional raising constructions. For example, (42a) follows from raising *John* in the source structure in (42b) to produce the trace in (42c):

(42) a. John was likely to leave.
     b. NP was likely John to leave.
     c. Johnᵢ was likely [tᵢ] to leave.

3.3.2 Upward Movement and the Syntactic Cycle

We now can see how delicately sequenced the syntactic operations must be. Consider the interaction of raising and passive, as in (43a):

(43) a. This horse is likely to be raced tomorrow.

This sentence derives from something like (43b):

(43) b. NP₁ is likely NP₂ to be raced this horseᵢ tomorrow.

It is clear that before NP₂ can raise to NP₁, *this horseᵢ* must first raise to NP₂ as in (43c):

(43) c. NP₁ likely NP₁ + this horseᵢ to be raced tᵢ tomorrow.

Then NP₂ can raise to NP₁ as (43d):

(43) d. NP₁ + NP₂ + this horseᵢ is likely [tᵢ] to be raced [tᵢ] tomorrow.

This example is another illustration of the principle that syntactic processes occur cyclically. They first start with the most embedded verb domain and then work up to the less embedded ones. In the case of relative clauses and *wh*-attachment, we have considered object relatives because it is easy to see that the object phrase must be moved to the *wh*-position. Technically, there is movement as well in subject relatives. However, movement of the subject phrase in a subject relative sentence is more obscure because the *wh*-phrase appears to be in the subject position. Certain cases, though, show that the *wh*-phrase in a subject relative is not actually in the subject position. For example, adverbs can regularly appear between the subject phrase and verb, and also before the subject phrase.

(44) a. This horse frequently raced.
     b. Frequently this horse raced.

But in a relative clause, adverbs cannot appear before the relative pronoun:

(45) a.   This is the horse that frequently raced.
     b. *This is the horse frequently that raced.

Such examples show that the relative pronoun is outside the regular domain of the subject position. The derivation begins with a structure like the structure in (46a).

(46) a. This is the horse WH NP frequently raced.
      b. This is the horse WH + NP_i t_i frequently raced.

Then the noun phrase is moved and attached to the *wh*, leaving a trace behind in subject position, as in (46b).

3.4   The Architectures Relating Meaning and Syntax

We have sketched the overlapping components of the syntactic description of sentences. These impose constraints on what structure is assigned to sentences as they are understood. Every sentence must have some form of phrase structure, a verb with arguments, an agreement/case system, and so on. But a complete account of the assignment of such structures is not an account of how meaning is related to them. Our concern is sentence comprehension, not just sentence recognition, so we must include a sketch of how sentence meaning is connected to sentence form. Since generative grammar is our chosen grammar of reference, the question is, how is meaning derived from the structures that generative grammar assigns?

   The first problem is, what are the important aspects of meaning as we focus on sentence comprehension? Intuitively, a sentence can "mean" many things, depending on our purposes. Consider the following sentence:

(47) I'm happy to meet you.

This can be taken in its "basic meaning" as predicating pleasure on the part of the speaker at meeting the listener. But it also can have other interpretations. On the one hand, it is potentially a formulaic idiomatic greeting, meaning "hello." More broadly, it might be a signal inviting further contact. Thus, there are three general kinds of interpretation of a sentence, which can be thought of as its "meaning" (see (48a) to (48c)). An operational demonstration is that each of the three kinds of meaning could be the only one retained a week after it was uttered and heard: one could legitimately recall that the speaker was happy, or said hello, or indicated further interest, even though the speaker might have meant only one of those.

(48) *Basic meaning*
      a. The speaker is pleased to meet the listener.

      Idiomatic meaning
      b. Hello.

      Intention
      c. I hope we see each other again.

For our purpose, and for much of psycholinguistics and linguistics, the focus has been on the "basic meaning." We recognize that this addresses only a subset of the complete panoply of communicative functions of sentences. And we also note, as will come up in later chapters, that some current psycholinguists believe that it is not possible to separate idiomatic and intentional uses of sentences from the processing of their basic meaning. We agree that this is an important question. Our approach follows the convention in linguistics, as in many fields, that separates components for analysis, in the expectation that understanding them will lead to a larger integration with other components.

What, then, is the "basic meaning" of a sentence? There are three main components, which we will briefly sketch:

(49) a. The interpretation of verb arguments, in "thematic roles"
    b. "Binding" relations between anaphoric elements and their antecedents
    c. "Scope" relations among quantifiers and similar units

Thematic roles have a formal and an intuitive aspect. Intuitively, they correspond to basic conceptual participants related by a predicate. The canonical predicate has an "agent" and a "patient," as in (50a); this reflects the idea that the basic concept conveyed by a sentence is that "somebody does something to somebody," and that understanding a sentence generally involves grasping "who did what to whom." Much psycholinguistic research on sentence comprehension has concentrated on this specific kind of sentence. But some verbs have only agents, as in (50b); some have more than one kind of patient (see (50c)); some have an "experiencer" instead of agent, as in (50d), or patient (see (50e)).

(50) a. Sparta(agent) attacked Athens(patient).
    b. Athens(agent) left.
    c. Sparta(agent) sent Athens (beneficiary) a message (patient).
    d. Sparta(experiencer) disappeared.
       Sparta(experiencer) was rich.
    e. Sparta surprised Athens(experiencer).

Formally, the number and kind of roles a predicate can have can be used to define classes of predicates: it is an object of ongoing research to determine the relationship between what a verb means, the kind of thematic roles it can have, and the influence of that on syntactically specified argument positions. For example, the verb *attack* implies both intent on the part of the subject and some kind of patient that is the recipient. Thus, *attack* must have an agent and (at least an implied) patient, and is syntactically a transitive verb, requiring both a subject and object. *Leave*, on the other hand, assumes intent but does not require a patient, and hence is syntactically "intransitive." In general, it is appealing to think that once we know the meaning of a verb, we (and children) can derive its thematic and argument structure from that and vice versa. We certainly agree that there is a great deal of statistically valid predictive power, and in chapter 5, we will outline how this might be an important factor in comprehension. But there are several issues that indicate that thematic roles may not be the fundamental source of all the other types of relations verbs enter into. First, there seem to be a large number of thematic-role types, and it is not clear that there is any interesting limit on them. Consider the different kinds of experiencer relations in (51) alone.

(51) a. Sparta was rich.
     b. Sparta was aggressive.
     c. Sparta was a winner.
     d. Sparta was old.

Second, verbs with quite similar thematic roles can nonetheless have quite different syntactic argument structures.

(52) a. Sparta sent Athens a message.
     b. Athens got a message from Sparta.

Third, verbs with quite distinct thematic roles can share syntactic argument structures. Consider the different kinds of roles that *Athens* has in (53).

(53) a. Sparta supported Athens.
     b. Sparta pleased Athens.
     c. Sparta destroyed Athens.
     d. Sparta preceded Athens.

It is an object of ongoing research how specific and how independent the set of thematic roles really are. But, whether independent or not, the notion of thematic role captures an intuitively important aspect of meaning, which is a significant factor in sentence comprehension.

   Binding and scope have played a relatively minor role in psycholinguistic studies of sentence comprehension. But we include them here for completeness and because certain facts about them have played a critical role in the evolution of the architecture of syntax. *Binding* basically refers to the determination of coreference between antecedents and anaphors. In (54a), the subject and object must be coreferenced, in (54b) each member of a group in the subject is coreferenced with everyone but that member in the object, and in (54c) there is an ambiguity between those two kinds of relations between subject and object. (Did all the men like all the men, or did each man like himself?)

(54) a. Harry liked himself.
     b. The men liked each other.
     c. The men liked themselves.

Scope refers to relations to between quantifiers and between quantifiers and verbs. In (55a), the subject has a relation to every person, in (55b) to some.

(55) a. Harry disliked every man.
      b. Harry liked some men.
      c. Harry liked many men, but he did not like every man.
      d. Harry liked many men, but he liked not-every man.

In (55c), the scope of the negative *not* is not the verb *like* that it seems to modify, but is the object noun phrase, as shown by (55d). This fact turns out to be important to certain theoretical developments that we discuss below.

3.4.1 The Evolution of Generative Architecture and the Source of Meaning

The classic findings reviewed in chapter 2 document our assumption that comprehension involves both syntactic and semantic representations. In general, most researchers who think syntax is relevant at all, think it is logically and often behaviorally prior to semantics. That is, syntax is assigned to a sentence first, and then semantic analysis is a function of some operations on the syntactic representation. To understand the history of psycholinguistics and at least its near future, it is useful to review the last fifty years of evolution of architectures that describe how semantic and syntactic representations interact.

In chapter 5 and later chapters, we are going to argue that the process of comprehension is more iterative than this traditional "syntax-first" view: comprehension involves an early stage of crude syntax, then an initial semantic assignment, with a final syntactic derivation filling in missing components. But for the moment, we start with architectures that have the more traditional view that semantic analysis is a direct function of syntactic representations. In doing this, we choose particular stages in the evolution of grammatical theory that enjoyed stability and influence for a number of years. This inevitably means that we will gloss over most specifics and ignore most of the intermediate steps between models. Our goal is partly to inform the psychological reader about the history of generative grammar. But most important, we hope it gives a rounded picture of the nature of syntactic architecture and the kind of relations it can have with semantic representations.

***Syntactic Structures* (Chomsky 1957)** The first modern model involving explicit derivations was laid out by Chomsky in *Syntactic Structures*. Schematically this model started with basic phrase structure rules, then filled in lexical items to create the "deep structure" forms, clause by clause: generalized transformations merged one clause into another, and singular transformations rearranged word orders and assigned case. Semantic interpretation was assumed, but not specified within the model itself. The general idea was that semantic analysis would be based on the

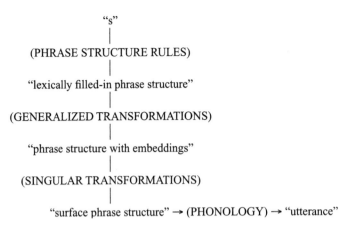

Figure 3.5
The architecture of grammar in *Syntactic Structures*.

"kernel structures"—individual clauses—but it was less clear how to analyze the meaning of complex sentences with more than one clause; the model did not present, in any single place, all the information needed to analyze the meaning of such sentences. The technical problem was that as sentences are embedded within higher sentences, movement transformations must apply to the embedded sentence, thereby distorting the canonical form of underlying structures. That is, singular transformations applied to each embedded clause, immediately after the generalized transformation merged it into a higher clause. This reflects, at an early stage, the kind of upward-moving cycle of operations discussed in the first section of this chapter. It is not surprising that the initial burst of classic psycholinguistic research focused almost entirely on single-clause sentences, and on the effects of a small number of singular transformations. In the sketch of the architecture in figure 3.5, we use (CAPITAL LETTERS INSIDE PARENTHESES) to indicate rule types, and "lowercase letters inside quotation marks" to represent intermediate and final representations produced by the rules. We do not articulate a particular representation that provides meaning information in this scheme, because it was never really resolved. It was taken for granted that the kernel structures somehow provide basic meaning information, but the integration of multiple clauses was less clear.

***Aspects of the Theory of Syntax* (Chomsky 1965)**   About a decade after *Syntactic Structures*, Chomsky presented a reformulation of the *grammatical* architecture, which solved many technical problems and also afforded a natural level for semantic analysis. In this model (see figure 3.6), phrase structure rules generate a hierarchical scheme that includes all the embedded clauses: a so-called super phrase marker. The

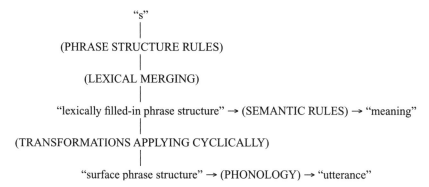

Figure 3.6
The architecture of grammar in *Aspects of the Theory of Syntax*.

terminal nodes of this tree are not lexical items but lexical categories: Noun, Verb, Determiner, and so on. Immediately subsequent lexical transformations merge lexical items with the categories—for example, when a terminal node is a noun, any lexical item (or other phrase structure tree) headed by "noun" can merge with the category label. This results in a lexically filled-in deep structure tree that has all the words and phrases in canonical positions. Further transformations and indexing processes then apply to each level, cyclically from the most to least embedded: the cycle is motivated by the kind of considerations we outlined earlier in this chapter. For example, an object noun in a relative clause has to be moved to the front of the clause first, to provide a structural basis for coindexing it with the relative clause marker in the higher clause.

This model was integrated with a proposal by Katz and Postal (1964) that the deep structure provides all the information required for a semantic analysis of basic meaning—that is, meaning is a function of lexically filled-in deep structure. Katz and Postal then spelled out a set of functions that operate on deep structures to create a semantic representation. This model offered a clear, unequivocal answer to the question about the syntactic level that provides all information needed for the semantic interpretation of sentences.

Generative Semantics (McCawley 1976; Lakoff and Ross 1976) We have already touched on the historical fact that "abstract," "autonomous" mental structures have always posed a problem for behavioral scientists. The transformational model, in particular, postulates many "hypothetical variables" and processes not directly observable. This was an immediate challenge within academic linguistics to the older taxonomic program we outlined in the preceding chapter. But for about a decade, all was quiet within the generative camp. There was general acceptance that syntax is

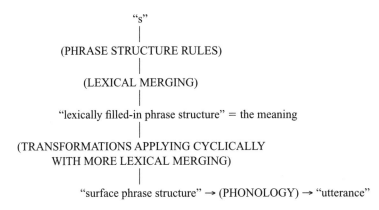

Figure 3.7
The architecture of grammar in generative semantics.

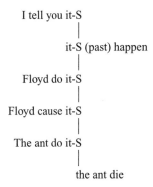

Figure 3.8
The deep structure of *Floyd killed the ant*.

"autonomous" from both meaning and sound—that is, that syntactic principles are sui generis and not reducible to other systems of linguistic knowledge.

As we have seen and will see, behavioral scientists feel a constant pressure to return to some form of behaviorism when an apparent opportunity arises. In the late 1960s a group of young syntacticians working within the Aspects framework developed the idea that the underlying structure actually is the semantic representation: in that view, transformations gradually coalesce features and predicate structures into a linear string of words and surface structure (see figure 3.7). A famous example (Ross 1974) exemplifies how rich the deep structure was according to this view. The sentence in (56) has a deep structure like that schematized in figure 3.8.

(56) Floyd killed the ant.

This view had great appeal for a variety of reasons. First, it offered a possibility that semantic representations could be generatively defined. Second, it avoided the view that syntax includes a deep structure representation that intervenes abstractly between meaning and sound: rather, the process fluidly connects meaning to sound. Since meaning is obvious (if hard to define or operationalize) and sound is physical, this schema seemed to meet the behaviorist stricture against intervening, "abstract" structures. The abstract verbs like *happen, do, cause* were drawn from a small set of basic semantic primitives. They are merged with lexical primitives, via upward transformations. For example, at a later stage in the derivation of (56) it would appear as something like (57). At that point, the abstract verbs are deleted or replaced by surface correspondents: in this case, *cause-die* is represented in the lexicon as *kill*, which has actually not appeared before in the derivation.

(57) Floyd ((past (cause-die)) the ant)

These proposals generated a great deal of controversy among generative grammarians. This is a bit puzzling in light of the deep similarity between the architectures, once one strips away the behaviorist and rationalist rhetoric. Figures 3.6 and 3.7 differ only in that lexical items can be selected after some transformations have merged components, as in merging *cause* and *die* into *cause-die*. Otherwise, the main substantive difference lies in the richness of the recursively defined initial phrase structures, and the use of abstract verbs. Generative grammarians made much of the claim that their proposal did away with "autonomous" syntax. But really it was primarily concerned with the question of when lexical items are introduced. They replaced "super-p-markers as deep structure" with such notions as "abstract verbs" and with license for extremely rich (and intuitively, extremely abstract) initial hierarchies.

Unfortunately, the potential for lasting and substantive contribution was lost in the noisy rhetoric, which presented generative semantics as a radical alternative to current theory, as opposed to an interesting variant. As we see below, the latest versions of transformational grammar have certain similarities that are intriguing.

Interpretive Semantics   Up to this point, meaning was viewed as based on an initial hierarchical structure. But certain facts emerged, suggesting that some aspects of meaning depend also on surface structure. Classic examples showed, for example, that reordering major phrases with stylistic variants, like the passive, can change scope relations (Jackendoff 1969).

(58) a. One arrow hit every target during the match.
     b. Every target was hit by one arrow during the match.

For many native speakers, (58a) indicates that there was a particular arrow that hit every target at least once during the match; (58b) indicates that every target was

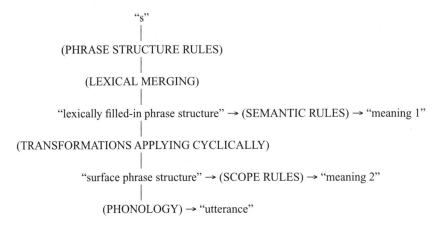

meaning 1 = basic thematic relations, NP binding relations

meaning 2 = scope relations of quantifiers

Figure 3.9
The architecture of grammar in interpretive semantics.

hit by at least one arrow (but not the same one): a formal account of this is that the first-appearing quantifier dominates a later-appearing quantifier. This was deeply puzzling within the context that meaning is derived entirely from a deep structure. How can surface order determine something as fundamental as scope? This and other facts suggested that the input to meaning was both deep and surface structure: deep structure provides information about basic thematic relations, and surface structure provides scope information (see figure 3.9).

Government and Binding Theory (Chomsky 1981)   The elevation of surface phrase structure as a contributor to meaning became part of a more general exploration of formal properties of surface phrase structure. One long-standing puzzle was how it can be that a verb can be missing its arguments at any given level of representation. For example, in (59), there is no actual object of the verb *hate* that is lexically coded as requiring an object.

(59) a. Athens was hated [ ] by Sparta.
     b. Athens was rich enough for Sparta to hate.

And correspondingly, there is no subject for *hate* in (60).

(60) a. Sparta seemed [ ] to hate Athens.
     b. Sparta was likely [ ] to hate Athens.

Our informal discussion of grammatical mechanisms from the first section of this chapter already introduced the notion that "traces" left behind from movement can fill such positions. An important feature of traces is that they fill required argument positions in surface structure. This allows one to maintain the principle that every argument is filled at every level of representation.

The presence of traces has another implication. By hypothesis, traces are automatically coindexed with their original head phrase. Since they are coindexed, binding relations can also be read off of surface structure rather than deep structure. The net result of such considerations was a radical increase in constraints on surface structures rather than constraints on particular transformations. The ultimate conclusion was that the main transformation was basically unconstrained movement. Structural constraints on possible movement took over the force of limits on what can occur. Movement transformations such as the passive were formerly described in specific terms, requiring the presence of the passive morphology ($be + en$) and a specific marker. In the reformulation, the only movement transformation was "move [constituent]", with all the descriptive and formal work done by constraints on when such movement is required. For example, the passive transformation was now expressed in terms of the requirement that a subject position be filled with an actual noun of some kind during the derivation. Thus, the underlying structure of the passive would become (as discussed above).

(61) NP be hated Athens by Sparta

The requirement that the subject position be filled requires movement, or the derivation is not successful and is blocked.

(62) Athens$_1$ be hated t$_1$ by Sparta.

The opportunity grew to derive more aspects of meaning from the surface structure, but certain kinds of facts motivated the invention of a new level of representation, *logical form*, which reconstitutes a semantic analysis that contains the information about both scope and binding. The need for a distinct level of representation that feeds off of both deep and surface structure was motivated by structures that required "reconstitution" of some aspects of deep structure after rearrangement for surface structure organization. For example, in (63), it is not possible to correctly assign the coreference relations based on the surface structure, because the subject position is higher in the hierarchy yet it contains a pronoun coreferenced with the object. This violates the otherwise universality of the principle that pronouns are always lower in their tree than their antecedents.

(63) His$_1$ mother praised John$_1$.

Examples like this (and many others, much more sophisticated) motivated the idea that the actual semantic representation that derives from surface structure can result from rearrangement transformations, which reconstitute certain relations originally stated in the deep structure. In the case of (63) the structure might look something

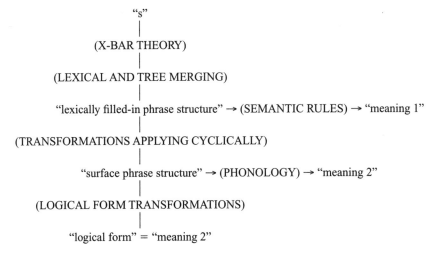

"s"
|
(X-BAR THEORY)
|
(LEXICAL AND TREE MERGING)
|
"lexically filled-in phrase structure" → (SEMANTIC RULES) → "meaning 1"
|
(TRANSFORMATIONS APPLYING CYCLICALLY)
|
"surface phrase structure" → (PHONOLOGY) → "meaning 2"
|
(LOGICAL FORM TRANSFORMATIONS)
|
"logical form" = "meaning 2"

meaning 1 = basic thematic relations

meaning 2 = scope relations and binding relations

Figure 3.10
The architecture of grammar in government-and-binding theory.

like (64). In this case, there are also traces that result from the "inverse" movement that reconstructs the proper government relations.

(64) John's₁ mother praised t₁.

The result is a schema that looks like figure 3.10.

The simplicity of the transformational operation of movement in this model is balanced against a family of constraints that restrict what movements and other processes can actually occur. First, phrase structures can now be defined as the same, regardless of whether they are in the deep or surface structure: so-called *X-bar theory* formulates the notion that a phrase structure subtree can be projected upward from the lexical category of its head noun. For example, *dog* is a noun, which can automatically be projected onto a tree, (Spec(N))np, in which "specifier" is interpreted as some kind of determiner. This means that phrase structure "rules" are no longer required to generate the deep structure. Rather, subtrees are projected from lexical heads and then joined by merging with other trees. Possible trees are constrained by the limits on X-bar theory and merging operations.

A second constraint on derivations involves the *projection principle*, the principle discussed above that requires every argument position of a verb to be filled at every defined level of representation. This motivates the postulation of traces, and other features of derivations as well. Other systems of constraints include *case theory*, which requires every noun to be marked for case, and *theta-role theory*, which requires every argument of a verb to be assigned a thematic role. These and other constraints were intended to capture natural generalizations about language, each within its own subset of constraints. Derivations wended their way through the maze of constraints, with only the correct derivations becoming complete.

The Minimalist Program **(Chomsky 1995)**   The architecture was becoming quite ornate. A derivation started with phrase structure, then transformations to create surface structure, then other transformations to undo some of what the first set of transformations had done, as part of logical form. Nature has exhibited stranger architectures than this, but a paramount goal of linguistic theory is to capture generalization with the greatest clarity and simplicity possible. In addition, the collection of sets of constraints was becoming increasingly unwieldy, sometimes contradictory, and less and less revealing of generalizations. Recently, Chomsky proposed a paradigm that captures elements of the preceding architectures, while giving a rather different model of the relation between semantic representations and syntactic structures. (A good introduction to the minimalist model appears in Radford 1997.)

The theory states the following: a linguistic derivation consists of lexical items (i.e., content words like *boy*, *run*, and so on) and functional categories that glue those words together. Functional categories are reflected in elements like *the*, *-ed* for past tense, and *-ing* for progressive tense, and also in unpronounced elements. The meaning of a sentence is a result of the way content words combine with each other through functional elements. In figure 3.11, the domain of the verb, the VP (verbal phrase), contains all the content words that are arguments of the verb. The functional component, also called inflection, is located above the VP. The inflectional component of a sentence carries information specific to that particular sentence (whether the sentence is third person, past, and so on).

Functional categories head their own projections, similarly to nouns and verbs. These projections have some features that may be pronounced (*-ed*, *-s*) and structural features such as Case that are unpronounced in English. These are called *formal features*. In figure 3.11, for instance, Tense, a functional category, projects onto Tense Phrase and has the formal features [+present], [+3rd person sg] and [+nominative]. Formal features of functional projections must be checked for agreement by a content word in the sentence. For instance, in a derivation like *the boy runs*, as we said, the Tense Phrase contains the features [+present], [+3rd person], among others. For the sentence to be grammatical, there must be a verb in the third-person present form (i.e., with a third-person present morpheme) among the lexical items of the sentence. The content word and the functional category must agree in features or the derivation will crash. If the verb were inflected for past tense or for first person, the derivation would have to stop for lack of agreement between

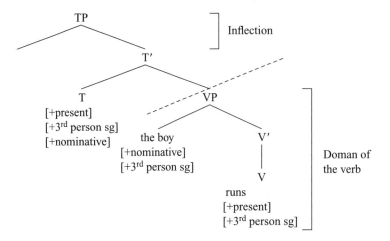

Figure 3.11
The underlying structure of *The boy runs* (adapted from Sanz and Bever 2000).

the features of the functional component and those of the content word. This is
called *checking of features*. To check the features of a functional category, the verb
must move to the functional projection (Tense Phrase in this case) that needs to be
satisfied. In this way, formal features of functional categories are the cause of syntactic operations like movement of lexical categories. In figure 3.12 both *the boy* (a
projection from a lexical item) and *runs* (a verb) move to the functional component
of the sentence.

Formal features are, therefore, those that must be pronounced in the form of morphemes or that cause visible syntactic operations, like movement of lexical items.
Figure 3.12 exemplifies the checking of Tense in the sentence *the boy runs*. The
verb checks third-person present, and the noun checks Nominative. In the end,
both noun and verb are contained in the same functional projection (Tense Phrase).
Within formal features, a distinction is established between purely formal (like structural Case) and interpretable features (e.g., number). The model establishes that a
derivation must be interpreted at two interface levels. One is the interface with the
sensorimotor systems (Phonological Form or PF as shown in figure 3.13). The other
is the interface with the cognitive-intentional system (Logical Form or LF). A derivation is computed from a set of elements or numeration by merging those elements
with each other. At some point, it must be sent to both interface levels and be
interpretable at both. The point at which the derivation is sent to the interface levels
is called *spellout*. The purely formal features must be checked and erased from the
derivation before spellout, because they are not interpretable at either PF or LF.
This is overt checking of features, which leads to overt movement of elements within

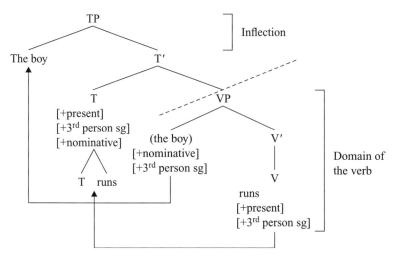

Figure 3.12
The movement of lexical categories in *The boy run* (adapted from Sanz and Bever 2000).

a sentence, as we exemplified in figure 3.12. Interpretable features, on the other hand, must survive until LF, since they bear on the meaning of the derivation. They are checked covertly and do not cause visible operations of movement.

Some of the interpretable features are also formal features (e.g., number in figure 3.12). They must be checked in the computation prior to spellout, but they are not erased. Purely formal features and features that are interpretable but formal at the same time (i.e., that must be checked prior to spellout) are called *strong*. The features that are interpretable and do not cause overt syntactic operations are called *weak*. The connection with semantics is established because only functional projections with some semantic import are allowed in the structure (Chomsky 1995). That is, projections like AgrO, which were postulated in the previous government-and-binding framework and contain purely formal features only (features whose only purpose is to be accessed by the syntactic computation before spellout) are not justified under minimalist premises. This is so because language design is assumed to be motivated by the conditions imposed by the systems with which language interacts (the sensorimotor or the cognitive system). Language mechanisms should have the shape they have in response to the conditions imposed from external systems. If there is no motivation from those systems for a certain construct or operation, minimalist considerations force us to discard it from the model.

This means that understanding the syntax/semantics interface under minimalism involves determining what functional projections there are in the inflectional component and what formal features (including interpretable features) are embedded in

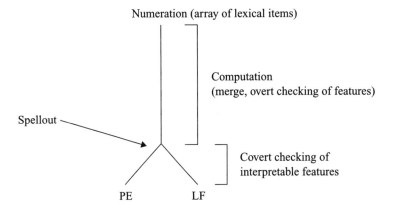

Figure 3.13
Computations and representations in the Minimalist Program (adapted from Sanz and Bever 2000).

them. Variation between languages is attributed to the difference in strength of features between languages. As stated above, a feature of a functional projection is strong when it requires that a lexical category in the sentence with the same feature moves overtly to the functional projection to check it. A feature is weak when it does not hold such a requirement. The next section presents the case of a parameter between English and Spanish that hinges on features related to events. The parameter will be illustrated through the different syntactic (visible) consequences that these features have in both of those languages.

So far we have been using the term *interpretable* to refer to features that must be interpreted at LF. It is crucial to understand the difference between conceptual and interpretable features in this sense (which we will call *semantic* from now on, for clarity's sake). *Conceptual features* or just concepts are assumed to be common to all human beings. For instance, the difference between a young individual and an old one is a universal that applies to all languages: *youth* is a concept that humans share. Likewise, normal adults understand the concept of time as being past, present, or future. *Semantic features*, on the other hand, are linguistic features: they represent the concepts that must be encoded in the grammar of many languages for sentences to be grammatical. For example, the concept of sexual identify gets encoded into the grammar of languages as gender. Sex is a concept. Gender features are semantic features. If we found a language in which the sentence *the boy runs* were grammatical but the sentence *the man runs* were not, we would have to posit that the concept of youth becomes grammaticalized as a semantic feature in the syntax of languages. In the absence of any such evidence, we assume that youth is a concept with no grammatical relevance: it is not a semantic feature. Words are stored with their

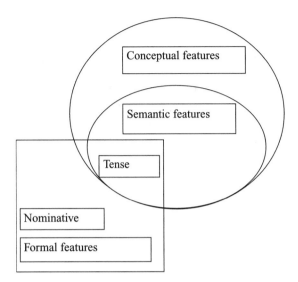

Figure 3.14
Types of features (adapted from Sanz and Bever 2000).

conceptual features. The word *boy* in English refers to a young (male) individual. This word (or its equivalent in other languages) has the conceptual feature *youth*, which does not get grammaticalized as a semantic feature. Figure 3.14 illustrates the types of features under the model we are presenting. Semantic features are a subset of conceptual features. Some of these semantic features are formal features of syntax causing syntactic operations. This is the case of Tense, which is semantic but must be pronounced through morphemes. This theory of the mapping of semantic onto syntactic structures poses the following question: Which conceptual features need to be encoded as semantic features in the grammar of languages?

In this section we provide partial answers to this question, which we think will become increasingly important in psycholinguistic research. We outline a minimalist analysis of the semantic literature on events (Davidson 1967; Dowty 1979, 1991; Tenny 1987, 1994; Kratzer 1995; Harley 1998; Higginbotham 1996, among others), which involves semantic features that vary in strength in English. We develop this as an example of a concept that we claim must be encoded in the syntax of languages through semantic features: the difference between *states* and *events* and the various action types that sentences can express. This difference explains certain syntactic phenomena involving unaccusative verbs and passive constructions in English.

This model gives a new character to the relation between semantics and syntax. In particular, there is no longer a specific deep structure tree that can be identified. Lexical items and phrase structure subtrees are successively merged in an upward direction, and elements of a lower tree are successively checked against elements in a higher tree. This kind of process iterates until a complete tree dominated by *S* is formed. The "meaning" of the sentence is built up out of various kinds of lexical items and features that are checked or passed through the derivation to logical form. The end result is that the final linguistic meaning is represented in logical form, which serves as the interface between linguistic meaning and other cognitive structures.

This model is also striking in that the initial input numeration includes a listing of the actual words, with inflections, as they appear morphologically. This results in an interesting three-faced model, which interrelates the three aspects of sentences that are most salient: words, meaning, sound. Behaviorists may find this model more acceptable because it does not present seriously "abstract" entities at its interfaces. But, like every preceding architecture (including that of generative semantics), the internal mechanisms are extremely abstract, not just the operations of merge and of movement, but also the postulation of abstract nodes and verbs. The model is missing a single coherent "deep structure" level of representation, but this is replaced with a fluid set of processes and a model driven by abstract features.

The Classification of Verbs by Action Type   This model involves some changes in the role of verb-argument structure. The explicit role of conceptual features opens up the possibility that the semantic structure of verbs can have direct implications for their potential derivations. Verbs themselves come in types, not just expressed in the specific roles their arguments can have but in the kind of action they describe, the so-called action type. This is a relatively new area of large-scale research in semantic theory and as yet has had little impact on psycholinguistic investigations of language learning and sentence behavior. We present an initial description of some aspects of it here, because we think it is in fact a very important factor in early stages of sentence comprehension; it plays a potential role in the comprehension model we present in chapter 5.

In the last three decades, there has been an increasing interest in the semantics literature about the nature of the differences between the predicates in figure 3.15 (Vendler 1967; Dowty 1979, 1991; Tenny 1987, 1994; Davidson 1967; Carlson 1977; Parson 1990; Kratzer 1995; Higginbotham 1996, among others). The sentences in the upper part of figure 3.15 contrast with those in the lower part in that they are events. It is a property of events that they can be telic (i.e., they can have a specific end point in time) or atelic. The progressive aspect distinguishes events from nonevents: whereas one can say *He is writing a letter* or *He is running*, *He is knowing math* is ungrammatical. Thus, the progressive morpheme in English (*-ing*), a grammatical operation, is sensitive to the semantic distinction between events and nonevents.

The distinction between telic and atelic events is reflected in the possible modifiers allowed in the VP. The sentence *He wrote a letter in two hours* is grammatical, in

EVENTS [+eventive]	[+telic]	[+measure]	write a letter drink a lemonade	accomplishment
		[−measure]	cross the finish line recognize John	achievement
	[−telic]		run drink lemonade	activity
NONEVENTS [−eventive]	[+permanent state]		know math be tall	individual-level property
	[−permanent state]		be tired be here	stage-level property

Figure 3.15
The classification of sentences according to their action type (adapted from Sanz and Bever 2000).

contrast with the ill-formed *He ran in two hours*. The former is an accomplishment, a telic event, because the letter is completed at the end. Observe what happens when the adverbial phrase is changed to *for two hours*. In this case, *He ran for two hours* and *He wrote a letter for two hours* pattern together in their grammaticality. But the sentence *He wrote a letter for two hours* has a different meaning from *He wrote a letter in two hours*: it does not express an accomplishment. It simply indicates that the subject engaged in the activity of letter writing for a period of time, without specifying whether he finished the letter or not. Applying this kind of durative adverbial phrase to the other telic type of event (achievement) yields ungrammaticality: *He finally crossed the finish line for two hours*. Crossing the finish line is an instantaneous event and thus cannot last any amount of time.

Three conclusions can be drawn from the previous facts. First, events have different properties from nonevents, and telic events are different from nontelic events. Second, accomplishments have two components (an activity and an end in which a new state of affairs is reached), whereas achievements do not have any internal structure of this sort. Third, the telicity of accomplishments is different from the telicity of achievements. In particular, the role of the object or delimiting goal phrase is crucial in determining whether the final end is reached in accomplishments. If the letter is completed, we have an accomplishment and the adverbial *in two hours* is allowed to appear in the VP. If the letter is not completed, the sentence expresses an atelic activity. In that case, modification with *in two hours* is out, but phrases of the type *for two hours* are grammatical, as is the case with *run*. Tenny (1987, 1994) refers to this as measuring out of the event by an object. In contrast, achievements do not transpire over time and the object cannot measure out the event. The sentence *I crossed the finish line in two hours* means that it took two hours to arrive at the moment of crossing the finish line, not that the actual crossing lasted so long. But the object is obligatory in this sentence. We will call this *delimitation (without measure) by an object*. In the next section the concepts of measuring out and delimitation by objects are developed further.

Measuring out (Tenny 1987, 1994) works as follows: a verb that is underspecified for telicity takes an object that, by its nature, measures out the event and makes it telic. The event travels through the object until it finishes. As we pointed out above, activity verbs are atelic. However, observe the following pair of sentences:

(65) a. *I ran in two hours.
     b. I ran the race in two hours.

The object *the race* provides what the verb *run* lacks: a beginning and an end to the action. In sentence (65b), *run* has been measured out and hence delimited by its object. The verb in this particular construction is not underspecified anymore for telicity: it has acquired the semantic feature [+telic] by having been measured out by the right kind of object in a syntactic configuration.

Not all objects are capable of measuring out an event. For instance, the verb *drink* (unspecified for telicity) is measured out in (66a) but not in (66b) in the following pair of examples:

(66) a. John drank a lemonade.   (accomplishment)
     b. John drank lemonade.   (activity)

The subevents of drinking a lemonade cannot be described with sentence (66a), whereas the subevents drinking lemonade (a mass noun) are all describable with sentence (66b) (Dowty 1991). Mass nouns are not measurers because they are unlimited.

The object in transitive achievements does not measure out the event in the same way. However, observe the obligatoriness of the object in (67a).

(67) a. John crossed the finish line.
     b. *John crossed.

The object in this case delimits the event by providing an entity on which the event can take place, but the event does not progress through the object and there is not change in the object at the end. The event of crossing simply cannot take place unless the agent crosses something. But since there are no intermediate steps to this event, we cannot interpret the object as a measurer.

There are syntactic consequences of the distinction between action types. The difference between accomplishments and achievements exemplified through the use of adverbs above has syntactic consequences for the grammar of English (Sanz 1996). The next pairs of sentence illustrate them:

(68) a.   The blacksmith pounded the metal flat. (accomplishment)
     a′. *The blacksmith crossed the finish line dirty. (meaning that he made the finish line dirty by crossing it)
     b.   This bread cuts easily. (accomplishment)
     b′. *This wall hits easily. (achievement)
     c.   John ran (*in two hours). (activity)
     c′. John ran to the store in two hours. (accomplishment)

The sentences in (68a) contain a resultative (an adjectival phrase that expresses the new state of the object after the action has been completed). The adjectival is ungrammatical unless we consider the object of the sentence a measurer of the action. Resultatives disambiguate an expression that could be atelic or telic and make it definitely telic: when the resultative is present, we must interpret the object as a measurer.

3.5   Conclusion and Implications

Classic research on comprehension has suggested that grammatical information is computed as part of the process. This makes us turn to linguistic theories to gain information about what grammatical information is made of. The role of syntax in linguistic theory is to mediate between sound and meaning. Most theories of syntax include notions of lexical category, morphology, phrase structure, and some kind of sentence-level organization. All theories must deal with some degree of iterative processes, since sentences can be embedded within other sentences. Generative grammars have consistently included a notion of derivation, in which a source structure is built up and modified until it fills out a complete utterance. For fifty years, the primary structure-building mechanisms have been "merging" of constituents where there is a formal category overlap, and "movement" of words or features, almost always upward in a phase structure hierarchy.

The conclusion regarding the derivational theory of complexity was that the processes (transformations) might not be "real," but the levels of representation are, most critically, the deep structure. What are we to make of that claim in light of minimalist syntax? First, we may want to argue that the point in a derivation just before spellout has some special behavioral role, it may turn out that the prior data are best explained as a reflection of logical form. In the worst case, it may turn out that the prior data are not a natural kind and have a compound explanation, drawing on different features of the grammar.

So, comprehension models aside, what do we test today, if we want to explore the behavioral implications of syntax? Our review of what has consistently played a role in generative theories suggests that we should consider examining the psychological basis for the two primary and ever-present operations, merge and move. They may be unique to linguistic computations, or a reflex of more general computations involving symbols.

Perhaps we can move toward some answers by considering the narrower question of comprehension and how a grammar can be embedded in a model of understanding sentences. The next chapter reviews a range of recent and current theories of how that works, and chapter 5 presents our model. We conclude that because derivations are not built left to right, nor necessarily top-down, nor from meaning to form, the logically best architecture for a comprehension model is analysis by synthesis. In that model, the grammar is allowed to generate syntactic representations, using its own processes, operating independently from the input stream.

Note

Portions of section 3.4, including figures 3.11 through 3.15, are based on Sanz and Bever (forthcoming).

Chapter 4

Contemporary Models of Sentence Comprehension

The previous two chapters outline the logical arguments and "classic" evidence that knowledge and use of language involves sentence-level syntactic structures. In this chapter, we take up current theories of whether and how syntactic structures are deployed during comprehension.

4.1 The Problem of Comprehension

When we understand a sentence we are hardly conscious of its structure: rather, we usually grasp its "meaning" and move on to the next sentence, leaving behind the words, the phrasing, the entire syntactic architecture. For example, it is true of (1a) that it has the word order in (1b), the structures in (1c), and the meaning depicted in (1d). But we are ordinarily aware only of the literal word sequence and the meaning.

(1) a. The horse raced.
    b. the, horse, raced
    c. "the (= determiner) + horse (= noun)" = *subject*
       "raced" (= verb, past participle) = *predicate*
    d. [conceptual representation of horse racing]

This focuses us on the main theme of this book: How do syntactic structures support language comprehension? There are two lines of thought about this:

1. Meaning is assigned by reference to contextual and internal semantic constraints. Syntax, at most, is a perceptual or cognitive afterthought.
2. Syntax is assigned logically and, in fact, prior to meaning. Syntax is an unavoidably automatic perceptual prerequisite.

Similar conflicts have occurred in other perceptual domains, where critical experiments are possible. For example, there are two opposing views on the relationship between visually recognizing an object and perceiving all the details of its contours:

1. We first recognize the object and then "fill in" its shape.
2. We first perceive a shape and then recognize the object.

In the case of vision, one can come close to distinguishing these alternatives experimentally. At one extreme, it is possible to study the perception of "objects" (e.g., a face) with blurry or no contours. At the other extreme, one can study the perception of lines, spatial frequency gradients, or "contours" that do not correspond to real objects.

In the case of language, it is far more difficult to distinguish meaning- versus syntax-based comprehension theories. *Every* sentence has some meaning, even (2a), and meaningful sequences, such as (2b), can be interpreted, though they are relatively syntax-free.

(2) a. Twas brillig and the slithey toves did gyre and gymbal.
    b. Politician speak with forked tongue.

Thus, as a practical matter, we cannot contrast the perception of meaningless but well-formed sentences with meaningful ungrammatical sequences. We are consigned to indirect demonstrations and logical arguments. The most powerful logical argument would be a working comprehension model that either rests only on meaning, or only on syntax. Such a model would be an existence proof of the possibility of the corresponding claim about actual comprehension.

The problem is that we have a surfeit of alleged comprehension models, based on contradictory principles, and none of them actually works. Consider two extremes, a pure semantic model and a pure syntactic model as they would apply to (1a), which we repeat here:

(1) a. The horse raced.

In the semantic model, each lexical item has a unique meaning that it carries independently, as in (3). On purely semantic grounds, there is only one way they can be put together into a meaningful thought. Neither syntax nor sensitivity to surface order is required to arrive at the appropriate meaning.

(3) a. *The* = an aforementioned entity
    b. *horse* = domestic four-footed animal ...
    c. *raced* = run very fast, past tense

In the syntactic model, each word initially is categorized and placed within a phrase, and phrases are assigned functional labels. In most models, this process occurs from left to right, as each new word comes in (see figure 4.1).

With sentences of normal complexity, it immediately becomes clear that at least surface order must be attended to, even in a semantics-based model. In (4a), the individual words can be put together in only one sensible manner, but in (4b), the word order makes all the difference.

| *the* | *horse* | *raced* |

the = determiner

        the = determiner
        horse = noun
        the horse = NP

                the = determiner
                horse = noun
                the horse = NP
                raced = verb
                the horse = subject
                raced = predicate

Figure 4.1
A parse of a simple sentence based on lexical information.

(4) a. The horse raced past the barn.
    b. The horse raced past the greyhound.

Furthermore, certain words have meaning only in regard to the structural functions they convey, which a semantics-based model must also respect. In (5a), *was* must be recognized as a "past passive marker" that inverts the normal effect of word order, in this case making the initial noun the patient rather than the agent of the action. In (5b) and (5c), *that* must be recognized as a modifying clause marker, marking the following verb as a modifying predicate rather than a main predicate. Such examples show that at best, a pure lexical semantics-based model cannot succeed without a significant syntactic armamentarium.

(5) a. The horse was raced past the greyhound.
    b. The horse that raced past the barn fell.
    c. The horse that was raced past the barn fell.

Conversely, it often appears that syntactic assignment relies crucially on conceptual knowledge of the world. In (6a), the adjunct prepositional phrase is attached to the sentence node and modifies the initial noun phrase; in (6b), the corresponding phrase is attached to the second noun phrase, which it modifies. Yet the difference in level of modification is entirely conveyed by our world knowledge.

(6) a. The jockey raced the horse *with a big smile*.
    b. The jockey raced the horse *with a big mane*.

A similar point is made by the contrast between (7a) and (7b), both parallel in structure to (7c), in which *the horse* is unambiguously the patient of the first verb.

While (7b) may be a bit confusing, it is nowhere near as difficult to comprehend as (7a). The only difference is that it is very unlikely that a horse can lasso anything, and simultaneously very likely that it is the patient of that patient-requiring verb; thus, the comprehension process is lead into the correct interpretation by virtue of this conceptual knowledge. In (7a) the corresponding knowledge does not help, because, in fact, horses do race at least as often as they get raced—in fact more often, by definition.

(7) a. The horse raced near the barn fell.
    b. The horse lassoed near the barn fell.
    c. The horse ridden near the barn fell.

Finally, even very basic segmentation aspects of syntactic structure may be controlled by local semantic knowledge. In both (8a) and (8b), *the socks* must be interpreted as the agent of *fell*. But in (8a) it is more likely to be miscoded as the patient of *darn*, and thereby attached as the object of the preceding verb. This is much less strong following *wiggle*, with correspondingly less miscoding.

(8) a. When Mary was darning *the socks* fell off her lap.
    b. When Mary was wiggling *the socks* fell off her lap.

The inescapable conclusion from these examples is that comprehension involves a combination of knowledge about the likelihood of conceptual combinations with knowledge of possible syntactic structures. It is not reasonable to argue that comprehension is based entirely on either conceptual or syntactic knowledge alone, but it is possible to specify an architecture in which one or the other kind of knowledge has logical and temporal priority of application. Thus, contemporary theories still fall into two classes: those that emphasize the priority and independence of rule-governed syntax, and those that emphasize the priority and independence of frequency-based associations.

4.2 Structural Models

The usual architecture in a structural theory first assigns the syntactic structures, and then semantic analyses. Semantic facts about the analyzed meanings may ultimately lead to choice of syntactically ambiguous structures or rejection of conceptually anomalous ones. But, in general, "syntax proposes, semantics disposes" (Crain and Steedman 1985).

By definition, the only information available to a structural parser is the syntactic category and related syntactic frame information conveyed by each word. The sparse nature of lexically carried syntactic information underlies the central problem of a left-to-right online syntax assignment scheme:

• At almost every point, there are multiple possible syntactic assignments.

Consider first (1a), which we repeat here:

(1) a. The horse raced.

In figure 4.1 we assumed that it had only one assignment that was unambiguous, as the parser moves through it. But consider the actual state of affairs as the process proceeds from left to right. Even at the word *horse*, the continuation could be quite different, one in which *the horse* is not a separate noun phrase, as in sentences (9a) and (9b).

(9) a. The horse races ended.
    b. The horse and buggy raced.

That means that at the word *horse*, more than one structural option must be available. In a case like (9a), the next word—*races*—would seem to determine which option is correct: *horse* is part of a compound phrase, with *the horse races* being the actual noun phrase. But this, too, can be wrong, as in (10a) and (10b). In these cases, the original decision that *the horse* is a phrase, rescinded at the following word *races*, is ultimately correct.

(10) a. The horse races frighten whinnied.
     b. The horse races usually frighten whinnied.

Accordingly, in almost all sentences there are multiple options at many points. This provides a dimension on which specific parsing architectures can differ. On the one hand, the parser can assign the "best" structure and be configured to allow multiple backtracking, or the parser can assign multiple structures in parallel and wait for the ultimately irrelevant ones to be excluded. We return to modern studies of this question later in the chapter. We start with a specific proposal by Mitchell Marcus (1980) that laid out most of the issues and many of the proposals that have dominated the structure-based approach for more than two decades. It is not our purpose to explicate the Marcus model with its original detail or nomenclature. Rather, we now review some salient properties of it, which are relevant to subsequent structural models.

Marcus argued that models that make incorrect assignments and then backtrack, or that hold alternate parses in parallel, simulate a "nondeterministic" model. He noted that these approaches set no limits on what a parsable structure could be, which means that they cannot aspire to be explanatory models, nor can they reveal how parsing constraints themselves might shape the form of language. He suggested that the parser should be "deterministic," that it should make only structural commitments that it never recants. Part of the motivation for this is to explore what such a parser must have in order to work. That is, the deterministic constraint actually weakens the power of the parser, and makes more revealing the particular properties it requires. A related motivation is to explore the extent to which a limited

The Active Node Stack

S16 (S DECL MAJOR S)/(SS-FINAL CPOOL)
[Rule for Declarative Sentence]
      NP: (John)
      AUX: (has)
      VP: ↓

C: VP14 (VP)/(SS-VP INF-COMP CPOOL)
        VERB: (scheduled)

The Buffer

1.   NP41 (MODIBLE NS INDEF DET NP): (a meeting)
2.   PP11 (PP):(for Wednesday)
3.   WORD133(*.FINALPUNC PUNC):(.)

Yet unseen words: (none)

Figure 4.2
A snapshot of Marcus's parser (adapted from Marcus 1980).

parser can explain certain linguistic phenomena as a function of the parsing limits themselves.

Marcus outlined a model, *Parsifal*, with two major data structure components: an active-node stack of incompletely analyzed constituents, and a buffer of stored completed constituents. As he put it, the active-node stack is a set of high nodes in a phrase structure tree, awaiting nodes to dominate. The buffer is a set of low nodes, with analyzed material they dominate, awaiting dominating nodes to complete a connected tree. At each word, one or more nodes are placed in the active-node stack, and as they are filled, the completed nodes are moved to the buffer. For example, the beginning of sentence (1a) would access an S and a subordinate NP in the active-node stack at the initial word *the*. The word *horse* could then complete the NP, which could be sent to the buffer, allowing for new incomplete high nodes to be activated.

Figure 4.2 illustrates a snapshot of the model during a parse. There are two data structures. The *active node stack* has two memory cells, while the *buffer* has three memory cells.

One cell of the active-node stack contains structures that are attached to higher-level nodes but that need to have additional lower-level nodes (daughters) attached. The second cell in the active-node stack is a workspace for assembling constituents. This is called the *current active node*. The active-node stack operates as a pushdown stack in which the last item entered is the first retrieved. Thus, when a constituent is assembled but has not been attached to a higher node, it is dropped into the second data structure.

The second data structure is the buffer. The buffer consists of three cells that contain words or phrases that need to be attached to a higher node. The buffer corresponds to the look-ahead component of the parser. Each buffer cell can hold either a word or a complete multiword constituent.

So far, this model seems vulnerable to the difficulties enumerated above, basically that there are too many options at each point. The model is able to parse deterministically because it can examine cells in the active-node stack and the buffer. By examining the active node stack, the model is able to look down the tree to see where it is going; by examining the buffer it is able to look past already-completed nodes. This gives the model the power to consider more than one level in the hierarchy the grammar is building, and to skip over completed constituents. If the model could consider any number of active nodes and of completed constituents it would surely be deterministic, and would never make a mistake. In the limit, it could consider an entire sentence before definitively assigning any grammatical rule-based structures. However, to reduce Parsifal's undifferentiated power, Marcus limits the number of nodes that can be examined in the active stack to two, and in the buffer to three.

This framework has a number of features relevant for current models.

I. The grammar provides a rich annotated surface structure.

Every structural parser must presuppose some kind of grammatical framework that defines the possible and particular grammatical structures that the parser must assign to each well-formed sentence. That is, there is a "covering grammar," which describes sentences and their full descriptions independently of the mechanisms of the parser. For this, Marcus chose an "annotated" phrase structure, roughly the surface structure of the then-emergent government-and-binding theory (Chomsky 1981; see sections 2.5, 3.4.1). The model includes the usual phrase hierarchies and grammatical relations such as "subject" and "object." For example, in sentence (11a), *the horse* and *raced past the barn* are phrases, with further internal structure for the latter.

(11) a. (The horse) = subject (raced (past (the barn))).

In addition, there are two notions of "trace," inaudible noun phrase elements that connect overt noun phrases with distant locations. For example, (11b) would be given an additional kind of structure, an NP-trace that marks the fact that there is an object relation assigned to *the horse* in its underlying structure, as well as the subject relation in the surface structure.

(11) b. (The horse)$_1$ = subject (was (raced (NP$_1$) = object (past (the greyhound)))).

"*Wh*-trace," another kind of trace, links questioned phrases to their grammatical relation in a clause:

(12) a. Who$_1$ did *wh*$_1$ race the horse?
      b. Who$_1$ did the horse race *wh*$_1$?

II. Rules for constructing constituents occur in hierarchical packets, which result in giving simple declarative main clauses default status.

Another critical part of the parser is a set of pattern-action rules (sometimes called *productions*). One of these rules applies when the contents of the active node stack and the buffer match the conditions (or "structural description") of the rule. When a match occurs, the parser either attaches the contents of a buffer cell to the contents of the active node stack, or creates a new node in the active node stack.

To take a simplified example that ignores details, the presence of *the* triggers an application of a left–noun phrase bracket before it. The presence of a noun phrase bracket at the beginning of a sentence triggers an application of a sentence clause node and also the assignment of "subject" to that noun phrase. The presence of a verb following a noun phrase triggers the formation of a verb phrase, which then triggers an attachment to the S-node, and the default assignment of "simple declarative" sentence.

The fact that the conditions that trigger rules can trigger parallel rules in cascades, motivates grouping rules into "packets," in part defined by the triggering conditions they share. Packets themselves can be assigned rankings of priority or can be given default status. For example, the packet that assigns simple declarative sentence status at the potential main verb is the default—in other words, what happens if no other condition has triggered a more exceptional rule application.

Marcus notes that packets and rule priorities are not strictly necessary, nor are they a crucial component of the fundamental motivation or architecture of the model. Rather, he argues that they make the model work much more efficiently by capitalizing on statistical facts about the likelihood of particular constructions. The moral we draw from this is that even structural models may include statistical information to their advantage. In addition, we note that the prime statistically predominant construction from which others depart is the simple declarative transitive sentence.

III. Noun phrases are easy to isolate, based on surface cues.

This is important to the model, because many of the rules that assign structure at the clause level must presuppose that noun phrases have been isolated and already stored in the buffer. In effect, the parser can shift the buffer within a sentence, find noun phrase left edges, segregate and store the noun phrases, and then return to its original preshift serial location for higher-level structure assignments.

As a result, Marcus has two stages of syntactic processing: assembling constituents and attaching them. Phrases are first assembled, then attached to higher nodes. In a sentence like (13),

(13) Is the block sitting in the box red?

the word *is* initiates the creation of an S-node and is attached to the S-node in the active node stack as auxiliary in a yes-no question. When the noun phrase node is completed NP, it is attached as well to the S-node. The phrase *sitting in the box* is assembled as a verb phrase in the second cell of the active node stack but is not attached initially, because it may be the main verb phrase or a reduced relative clause. Hence, the verb phrase is dropped back into the first cell of the buffer. Once the word *red* is read, the parser recognizes that *red* can serve as the main predicate with *is*. At this point the verb phrase is attached to the noun phrase *the block* as a reduced relative clause.

Of course, being able to shift like this changes the intuitive clarity of the limit of considering three nodes in the buffer. It is still technically the case that the limit holds for any given constructive operation. The general importance of this feature is that it emphasizes the role of various closed-class morphemes and syntactic category patterns that define the left edges of noun phrases.

IV. NP-traces are treated as normal noun phrases stored in the buffer; wh-traces are treated in a special wh-*comp position.*

It is characteristic of language that noun phrases can have a role in more than one clause. In (14a), *horse* is the subject/object of *proposed* and the subject of *race*. In (14b), it is the subject of both *raced* and *fell*.

(14) a. The horse was proposed to race.
       b. The horse that raced fell.
       c. *The horse$_1$ was proposed Bill to have raced NP$_1$
       d. (The horse)$_1$ = subject ((that)$_1$ (wh_1) = subject (raced (past the barn))) (fell)
       e. (The horse)$_1$ = subject ((that)$_1$ (Bill) = subject (raced (WH_1) = object (past (the barn))) (fell)

NP-traces across clauses are limited to the overt subject position in the lower clause. Thus, we can have (14a) but not (14c).

This restriction does not hold for *wh*-trace, which can be either subject or object in its own clause. The grammar marks the difference between the traces as a function of how they are generated. *Wh*-trace is assumed to be in a special *wh*-node, known as *wh*-complement, of its own at the beginning of sentences and clauses. Whenever a clause-initial *wh* is encountered, it is attached to *wh*-complement and placed in the buffer. It then can join with the first available empty position in its own clause, or be passed down to the next clause and placed in the *wh*-node for that clause. In this sense, the parsing of *wh*-words is cyclic, moving from clause to clause, until a clause-internal position is available for it to fill.

In Parsifal, NP-trace is also placed in the buffer when the morphology indicates— for example, passive morphology ("was + pp") is a trigger to link a trace to the surface subject of the sentence and place the trace in the buffer. It is then available to be assigned to a constituent anywhere in the sentence, including its rightmost boundary. But it cannot literally move to a node of its own in a lower sentence. The result is that it can be assigned to fill the initial position of a lower sentence, since it is adjacent to it. But it can never be moved elsewhere in the lower sentence. This explains why NP-trace is always linked to the surface subject of a lower sentence, never any other surface position. The implication of this differentiation of kinds of traces in the parser is that *wh*-trace and NP-trace may be parsed by quite different mechanisms.

V. In certain cases, semantics determines constituency.

We come back to the problem of how semantic information might be embedded in the parser. To quote from Marcus (1980:52, including his numbering system):

[Consider] the problem of prepositional phrase attachment. In sentence (.1) for example, the parser can be sure that "with" starts a prepositional phrase when this word enters the buffer, but it cannot possibly decide at that time whether the resulting PP should be attached to "the man" ... or to the clause itself, as in the most plausible reading of .2

.1 I saw the man with the red hair
.2 I saw the man with the telescope

To solve this attachment problem deterministically requires access to some sort of semantic reasoning capability, but a necessary precursor to the application of this knowledge is the ability to first parse the prepositional phrase independent of its higher level role. This part of the problem can be solved simply by creating an unattached PP node when the preposition comes into the first buffer position, attaching its preposition and object, and dropping the resulting PP into the buffer where whatever [processes that] bring non-syntactic knowledge into play can examine the PP at their leisure.

The implication of this move is that adjunct phrases can be computed and held in abeyance until semantic information guides the particular attachment most consistent with their meaning.

VI. Cases in which the model fails correspond to human failures.

Even with its rich structure, the model makes systematic errors. For example, the priority of building verb phrases in simple declarative sentences can create misparsings that span such a distance that the model cannot recover from them. In (15a) the model gives priority to treating *has* as an auxiliary when it precedes a past participle, as opposed to treating it as the main verb and the past participle as an adjective. This priority leads to a garden-path misparse in sentences like (15b) that unambiguously require that *has* be a main verb.

(15) a. The store has assembled models.
     b. The store has assembled models, as well as kits, in stock.

Marcus argued that such cases in fact correspond to cases in which humans also misparse the sentence, and have to access higher-level problem-solving strategies to recover from it. Thus, if the model is garden pathed just in those cases that humans are as well, this actually increases its plausibility as a psychologically correct model.

VII. There must be a means of recovery when the parser fails.

When the parser fails, it does not simply restart. Instead, repairs are carried out by "some higher level 'conscious' grammatical problem solving component" (Marcus 1980:204). In a garden-path sentence, the parser actually continues to the end of the sentence to produce two grammatical sentence fragments. The grammatical problem solver uses heuristics to operate on the grammatical fragments. For example, the parser initially produces for the garden-path sentence (16a)

(16) a. The cotton clothing is made of grows in Mississippi.

two grammatical sentence fragments, (16b) and (16c):

(16) b. [[The cotton clothing]$_{NP}$ [is made [of [???]$_{NP}$]$_{PP}$]$_{VP}$]$_S$
     c. [[???]$_{NP}$ [grows in Mississippi]$_{VP}$]$_S$

The following heuristic applies:

Given two consecutive sentence fragments, if the first fragment is a sentence that is complete through some part of the verb phrase and the second fragment is a clause that lacks a subject, then see if the bulk of the first fragment can be turned into a relative clause of some type (using another set of heuristics), thereby converting the entire fragment into a single NP which will become the subject of the second fragment. (Marcus 1980:205)

The use of this heuristic leads to the realization that *clothing is made of* is a relative clause; see (16d):

(16) d. [The cotton [clothing is made of t]$_S$]$_{NP}$

The heuristic therefore converts the two grammatical fragments, and the actual structure becomes available immediately; see (16e):

(16) e. [[The cotton [clothing is made of t]$_S$]$_{NP}$ [grows in Mississippi]$_{VP}$]$_S$

To summarize, in order to make parse assignment deterministic by application of grammatical rules, it is necessary to postulate that the parser can operate on several vertical nodes and can examine at least three horizontal constituents. These vertical and horizontal windows provide enough information in combination with a repertoire of syntactic possibilities to arrive at the uniquely correct syntactic assignment. In the course of making this model clear, Marcus defined a variety of dimensions along which all subsequent structural models can be examined. We now turn to a review of several models that have driven more recent and current research.

4.2.1   Minimal Attachment: Garden Paths and Construal

Frazier's Garden Path Theory (GPT) makes two basic assumptions about the process of combining words into phrases. First, processing resources are limited. This limitation means that the parser attempts to minimize complexity in order to preserve resources. Second, to generate candidate structures for a sentence, the parser uses only syntactic category information, such as whether a word is a noun, verb, or adjective. Thus, the GPT proposes that, as each word is received, the parser selects the structure that integrates the word into the previous structure with minimal structure change. Because of limitations on processing resources, only the first analysis that becomes available is maintained. The first available analysis is the "minimal attachment." Other analyses that are possible but not preferred are called "non-minimal attachment." In cases in which the first available analysis ultimately does not prove to be correct, there is a garden path, and the parser must perform relatively costly reanalysis. (See Frazier 1987a, 1987b for reviews.)

Basic evidence for initial computation of only the simpler, minimal attachment structure comes from the existence of garden-path sentences, such as (17):

(17) *Sentential complement*
     John knew the answer was wrong.

In this sentence, readers frequently believe that the sentence is complete on reading *answer*. Reading *was*, however, makes this initial decision incorrect, forcing reanalysis. The GPT explains this phenomenon by noting that *knew* may have a noun phrase object (e.g., *the answer*), or it may have a sentential complement (e.g., *the answer was wrong*). Since the latter structure will require rules for expanding the verb phrase in the complement clause whereas the former does not, the parser adopts the simpler structure in which *the answer* is a noun phrase object.

Similar considerations apply in the more complex garden path in (18).

(18) *Reduced relative clause*
     The horse raced past the barn fell.

This sentence is difficult because the active structure for *the horse raced past the barn* is initially adopted as soon as *raced* is received. At the point of receiving *raced*, the only rule needed is (19).

(19) VP → V (NP) (PP) (Adv)

When *fell* is processed, it becomes apparent that *raced past the barn* is actually a relative clause reduced from

(20) *Full relative clause*
     The horse that was raced past the barn fell.

The reduced relative structure requires more elaborate phrase structure compared to the active structure, and so is not initially followed.

Much of the work on the GPT concerns its second assumption: *only* syntactic category information is used to develop the initial hypothesis about structure regardless of conceptual information. Rayner, Carlson, and Frazier (1983), for example, found evidence for a garden-path effect in sentences with reduced relative clauses similar to those in (21a) and (21b)

(21) *Reduced relative clause, plausible garden path*
  a. The florist sent the bouquet of flowers was very flattered.

  Reduced relative clause, implausible garden path
  b. The performer sent the bouquet of flowers was very flattered.

compared to the control sentences:

  Full relative clause
  c. The performer who was sent the bouquet of flowers was very flattered.

  Coordinate clause
  d. The performer sent the bouquet of flowers and was very flattered as well.

Reading times were longer in the reduced relative sentences for the words *was very*, where it first becomes clear that the active structure is not viable. The fact that this increased reading time occurred equally for the reduced relatives with *florist* versus *performer* suggests that plausibility is not relevant for the initial syntactic decision. If plausibility were relevant, we might expect a smaller garden-path effect for the reduced relative with *performer*, since performers are more likely than florists to receive a bouquet of flowers.

Even though the GPT does not use plausibility information in the initial decision about structure, it may use this information to reject a structure that has been proposed on purely syntactic grounds. The effects of plausibility may appear rapidly, according to the GPT, but they do not appear initially.

The parser uses the *most recent filler strategy* to determine the structure of sentences with *wh*-movement. According to this strategy, a gap is coindexed with the most recent potential filler (Frazier, Clifton, and Randall 1983). The most recent filler strategy correctly predicts that (22a) is easier than (22b).

(22) *Late filler*
  a. This is the girl$_1$ the teacher$_2$ wanted t$_2$ to talk to t$_1$

  Early filler
  b. This is the girl$_1$ the teacher wanted t$_1$ to talk.

Whenever the parser detects a gap, it searches backward from a gap to the first noun phrase, and assumes that this noun phrase fills the gap. The late filler sentence above is easier because the most recent filler strategy provides the correct structure. In making decisions about which noun phrases fill gaps, the parser uses only syntactic category information. Not only does it ignore plausibility constraints, it does not even use verb subcategorization constraints, even though they are arguably "syntactic." Frazier, Clifton, and Randall (1983) found that the late filler sentence (22c) is easier to understand than the corresponding early filler sentence (22d):

(22) *Late filler*

c. This is the girl$_1$ the teacher$_2$ decided t$_2$ to talk to t$_1$

Early filler

d. This is the girl$_1$ the teacher forced t$_1$ to talk.

They argue that decision times are longer for the second sentence because the parser initially posited the incorrect noun phrase (*teacher*) as the filler. If the parser used verb subcategorization information to assist in filling gaps, this mistake would not occur: one can "decide" to take action oneself, but one ordinarily "forces" someone else.

Frazier and Clifton (1996) have suggested that the parser makes initial decisions solely on the basis of syntactic information only for "primary phrases." Primary phrases include subject, predicate, sentential complements, and syntactic positions that occupy argument positions such as agent, goal, instrument, and theme. Initial syntactic attachment explains the processing differences in the following pairs of sentences, in which the minimal attachment sentence appears in (a) and the non-minimal attachment appears in (b):

(23) 1. *Main clause/relative clause*
   a. The horse raced past the barn and fell.
   b. The horse raced past the barn fell.

2. *Noun phrase as object/verb complement*
   a. John knew the answer very well.
   b. John knew the answer was wrong.

3. *Direct object of initial clause/subject of second clause*
   a. While Mary was mending the sock it fell off her lap.
   b. While Mary was mending the sock fell off her lap.

4. *Coordinate object/coordinate sentence*
   a. Jacob kissed Miriam and her sister.
   b. Jacob kissed Miriam and her sister laughed.

5. *Verb, direct object, indirect object/verb, object, modifier*
   a. Sandra [wrote [a letter] [to Mary]].
   b. Sandra wrote [[a letter] [to Mary]].

6. *Complement object/relative clause*
   a. John [told [the girl] [that Bill liked the story]].
   b. John [told [[the girl [that Bill liked]] [the story]]].

7. *Direct object/relative clause*
   a. Fred gave the man the dog.
   b. Fred gave the man the dog bit the package.
8. *Purpose/rationale*[1]
   a. Nixon bought [Trivial Pursuit] [to amuse us].
   b. Nixon bought [[Trivial Pursuit] [to amuse us]].

Nonprimary phrases are attached using the *construal principle*. These phrases are first "associated" with a thematic processing domain, then interpreted within that domain using both structural and nonstructural information. Nonprimary phrases are phrases that are elaborations of arguments, such as relative clauses, prepositional phrases, and adjunct phrases. Examples of sentences that use the construal principle are[2]

(24) 1. *Main clause/subordinate clause—prepositional phrase*
        I put the book that you were reading in the library (into my briefcase).
     2. *High vs. low adverb attachment*
        We remembered that the assignment will be due yesterday/tomorrow.
     3. *Relative clauses with a complex head*
        The reporter interviewed the daughter of the colonel that had had the accident.
     4. *Secondary predication*
        John ate the broccoli yellow/raw/naked.
     5. *High vs. low adjunct clause attachment*
        The doctor didn't leave because he was angry.

Figure 4.3 shows a flowchart of the GPT. Using words and syntactic rules, a constituent structure module determines the constituent structure. A thematic processing module operates in parallel to determine whether the constituent structure is consistent with the argument structure. The thematic processing module also indicates the most plausible host for associating adjunct phrases. The flowchart shows that plausibility enters into the processing system in two ways. One way is through the thematic processing module. This module uses all available information to check whether the constituent structure module has attached phrases in plausible argument positions. The second way plausibility information has an effect is through construal. The construal process establishes which of two or more ways of attaching an adjunct is most plausible.

To recapitulate, the recent versions of the GPT establishes some general concepts:

1. Following the simplest possible structure yields the correct interpretation in many cases, and in the long run may be cost-effective.
2. Purely structural theories cannot live without semantics. Semantics can have a role in initial hypotheses about sentence structure.

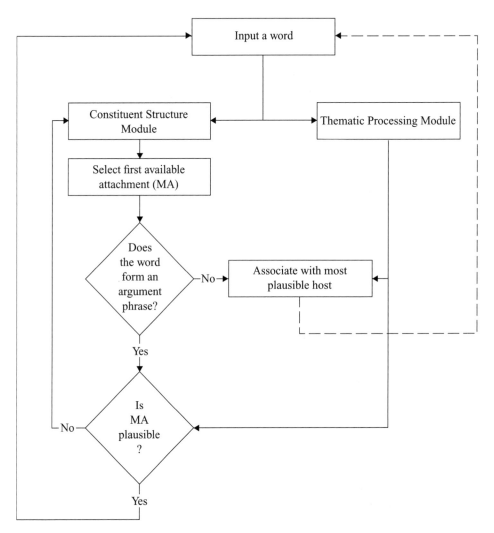

Figure 4.3
An information processing model of the Garden Path Theory.

4.2.2 Simplicity in Structure Building

Gorrell (1995) starts with two assumptions. First, the parser may work most efficiently by adopting the simplest allowable structure. The simplest structure generally provides the correct interpretation. It also costs less in terms of processing resources. Second, if the need arises, making a simpler structure more complex is easier than making a more complex structure simpler, if the simple structure is preserved as part of the complex one.

Gorrell expanded on these assumptions by proposing that the structural component of the parser can only build structure. It cannot destroy structure that has already been built. As each word is received, the parser builds the simplest possible dominance and precedence relations, a skeletal tree that indicates which syntactic category precedes another and which dominates another. The rationale for this is that the parser cannot change dominance and precedence relations.

Like Frazier's parser, Gorrell's builds a simple structure. Unlike Frazier's parser, however, Gorrell's uses plausibility information to guide initial decisions about dominance and precedence. This is allowed on the grounds that changing these relations is to be avoided. Since plausibility information can help the parser arrive at the correct structure, its use can reduce the need for subsequent reanalysis.

Figure 4.4 shows the architecture of Gorrell's parser. The structure builder utilizes words, including subcategorization information, semantic context, and principles of X-bar theory, to build a phrase structure tree. The structure interpreter uses this information together with principles such as those of government, binding, and case theory to interpret the tree for government, case, and so on. An example will clarify how these components work. Consider sentence (25):

(25) Bill knows Ian buys books.

When processing *knows*, the structure builder has access to the subcategorization information that *know* can have a NP-object or a sentential object. Since the NP-object is simpler, the parser builds a tree in which there is a VP dominating V and NP, with the V preceding the NP. This information is presented to the structure interpreter, which assigns a theta role and case to the NP that is forthcoming. When the structure builder receives *buys*, it builds a node for the complement phrase (CP) that is dominated by VP and preceded by V. Nodes are added to the tree structure so that the CP now dominates the NP for *Ian*. With the additional structure that arises from changing the NP *Ian* from an object of *knows* to subject of the embedded *buys*, there is no change in dominance or precedence relations. There has been a change in direct dominance, but the VP-node still dominates the NP for *Ian*. Consequently, there is no conscious garden path.

The situation is different when the parser must change precedence relations. When processing *raced* in a sentence like (26),

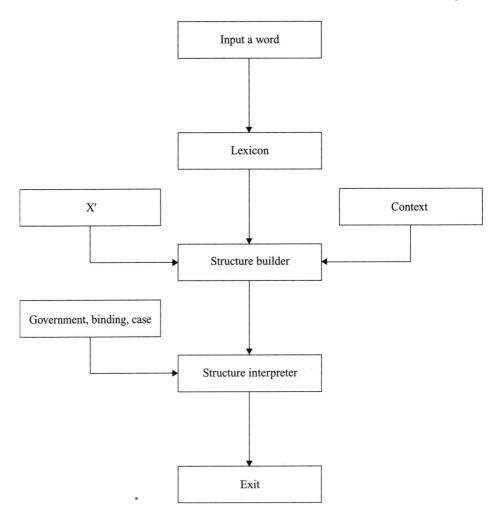

Figure 4.4
The architecture of Gorrell's parser.

(26) The horse raced past the barn fell.

the parser builds a VP-node that dominates a V-node for *raced*. In this structure, the NP precedes the VP. On processing *fell* the parser must retract this precedence relation. In the reduced relative structure, the NP-node for *the horse* dominates the node for the embedded relative clause that dominates the VP for *raced*. Since the structure builder cannot do this, conscious problem-solving mechanisms are employed, and there is a conscious garden path.

A garden path occurs as well in sentences like (27a).

(27) a. Ian told the man that he hired a story.

The parser initially constructs a complement phrase for *that he hired a*, as in (27b).

(27) b. Ian told the man that he hired a secretary.

In this initial structure, the NP-node for *the man* precedes the node for the complement phrase. Receiving *story*, however, causes reattachment of *that he hired* so that the complement phrase is not dominated by the NP-node for *the man*. Changing precedence relations is beyond the capability of the structure builder, and conscious reanalysis is required.

The principle of simplicity guides the processing of sentences with NP-movement. Examples are:

(28) a. This book$_1$ was read t$_1$ by Ian last night.
     b. Ian wants PRO to leave to planet.

In the first sentence, passive morphology (*was … by*) triggers postulation of a trace following the verb. In the second sentence, the infinitive *to leave* in triggers the postulation of PRO after the verb.

The parser handles sentences with *wh*-movement with the same principle of simplicity. In (29a) the *wh*-phrases is attached in a nonargument position.

(29) a. Which city did Ian visit?

Processing *visit* initiates construction of a NP-node, which is required for *visit*. Since the *wh*-phrase is not in an argument position, a trace is attached following *visit*.

Gorrell's parser handles more complex sentences such as (29b)

(29) b. What$_1$ did Ian say t$_1$ that Bill thought t$_1$ Fred would eat t$_1$.

in a similar fashion. Each verb leads to precomputation of an object NP, and the trace for *what* is attached. For example, *say* allows precomputation of a NP dominated by VP; if the sentence ends at *say*, the trace is attached to this NP, and the structure interpreter determines binding, case, government, and so on. When *that* is processed, the structure builder builds a complement phrase (CP); the attachment of the trace under NP remains but it is now dominated as well by CP. The trace at this point serves as an antecedent for additional traces after *thought* and *eat*. Thus, the structure analyzes the antecedent-trace relation as a series of local relations. Such sentences are not garden paths because there is no need to retract dominance or precedence relations.

Verbs with alternative subcategorization properties present special problems for processing *wh*-sentences. The following sentences from Fodor (1978) illustrate the problem:

(30) a. Which book$_1$ did Ian read t$_1$ to the children last night?
    b. Which book$_1$ did Ian read to the children from t$_1$ last night?
    c. Which child$_1$ did Ian walk t$_1$ to the office last night?
    d. Which child$_1$ did Ian walk to the office with t$_1$ last night?

Both *read* and *walk* may be transitive or intransitive. However, *read* is more often used as transitive, as in the first sentence above, while *walk* in more often used as intransitive, as in the fourth sentence above. Intuitions suggest that sentence (30a) is indeed easier than sentence (30b), while (30d) is easier than (30a). Gorrell's parser predicts that sentence (30b) produces a garden path, if it is assumed that the parser has access to information about lexical preferences. The reason is that, in sentence (30b), the parser posits a trace after the V-node and preceding the PP-node. When *from* is received, the parser must change the precedence relations and posit the trace after the PP-node. Sentence (30c) is difficult because the parser does not posit a trace after the V-node, but at the end of the sentence it becomes clear that there must be a trace after the V-node so that the *wh*-phrase can occupy an argument position. According to Gorrell (1995:155), there must be "intervention of nonsyntactic factors to prevent the parser positing the primary relations [i.e., dominance and precedence] consistent with the structurally simpler reading." Gorrell refers to eye-movement results from Altmann, Garnham, and Dennis (1992) in processing sentences with reduced relative clauses such as (31).

(31) a. He told the woman he'd risked his life for ...

The simpler structure for *he'd risked his life for* is a complement clause, as in (31b), rather than a relative clause, as in (31c) and (31d).

(31) b. He told the woman he'd risked his life for her.
    c. He told the woman he'd risked his life for that the fire was out.
    d. He told the woman that he'd risked his life for that the fire was out.

A relative clause interpretation is appropriate when there are two women and the relative clause indicates which of the two women is being referred to. In the Altmann et al. study, sentences like these were embedded in a story biased toward either the complement interpretation or the relative clause interpretation. Altmann et al. found no increase in reading times for the disambiguating region in stories that supported the relative clause interpretation. Such a result indicates to Gorrell that the NP *the woman* is immediately related to the context. If there are two women mentioned in the context, the parser builds the more complex relative clause structure.

To sum up, some of the useful ideas in Gorrell's model are the following:

1. Dominance and precedence relations are harder to change than government and binding.
2. To avoid frequent and costly reanalysis, it is necessary to use conceptual information and lexical preferences.

4.2.3 Governing Categories

Theta roles are the primary semantic functions of phrases in sentences. Theta roles include functions like agent, theme, patient, goal, proposition, and so on. It is apparent that a primary goal of comprehension is to determine the theta roles as soon as possible. It also is plausible that comprehension will be difficult if the parser must change a commitment to a particular theta role that was established earlier.

This is the central concern of Pritchett's model of parsing. The parser follows what he calls *The Theta Attachment Principle*: fill theta roles as soon as possible and find a theta role for an unassigned phrase as soon as possible. Of course, the parser may make incorrect assignments on occasion; revisions in the assignments of words to roles are easy if the reassigned word remains in the same theta domain as before the revision. A theta domain consists of an element that assigns a theta role and all of the constituents to which it assigned the theta role. For example, a prepositional phrase, consisting of a preposition and a noun phrase, is a theta domain because the preposition assigns the role of object to the noun phrase. A verb phrase, consisting of a verb and its complements, is a theta domain as well, because the verb assigns theta roles of agent, theme, goal, experiencer, proposition, and so on. Different verbs have different requirements for theta roles, and some verbs are ambiguous, in having more than one set of requirements. (See Pritchett 1992 for a review.)

There are two kinds of revisions in parsing. Revisions that maintain theta domains are unconscious and can be performed without cost; revisions that change theta domains require conscious attention and high cost. Sentences (32a) and (32b) illustrate the two kinds of revisions and how they depend on the assignment of words to theta roles:

(32) a. Without her donations to the charity failed to appear.

In (32a) the first mistaken assignment concerns *her*. In its attempt to fill theta roles as soon as possible, the parser assigns *her* to the role of theme of *without*, just as it assigns *him* to the same role in

(32) b. Without him donations to the charity failed to appear.

However, when the parser receives *donations* there is no theta role for it to fulfill if *her* has the role of theme of *without*. To provide each word with a theta role as soon as possible, the parser revises its assignment so that *donations* becomes the theme of *without* and *her* modifies *donations*. Reassignment of *her* is not costly, however, since *her* still falls within the domain of *without*.

In (32b), *to the charity* is attached as a complement of *donations*, which retains its assignment as theme of *without* until *failed* appears. *Failed* requires the external theta role of subject, but the only way to fill this role is to change the assignment of *donations* from object of *without* to subject of *failed*. Since this change involves a change in governing category from *without* to *failed*, the revision is costly, and the comprehender is aware of having been led down a garden path. While (32a) illustrates both conscious and unconscious revisions, (32b) has only an unconscious revision.

(32) c. Without her donations to the charity Bob failed to appear.

Sentence (32c) has only the cost-free revision of reassigning *her* from object of *without* to modifier of *donations*. Once *donations* is assigned to object of *without* it does not need to be reanalyzed as subject of *failed*, since *Bob* is available to occupy that role.

Pritchett's parser successfully distinguishes several cases of conscious versus unconscious garden-path sentences—for example, (33a) and (33b).

(33) a. After Todd drank the water proved to be poisoned.
     b. Susan knew her mother hated her.

Sentence (33a) is a conscious garden path because *water* changes from being assigned the role of theme by *drank* to being assigned the theme role by *proved*. Since *water* changes its theta domain, this is a conscious garden path. Sentence (33b) is not a conscious garden path. In this case, *mother* changes its role from theme of *knew* to experiencer of *hated*. However, since the clause *her mother hated her* remains as theme of *knew*, *mother* remains within the theta domain of *knew*.

The architecture of Pritchett's model is shown in figure 4.5. The central idea is that the parser attempts to maximally satisfy the theta criterion at all points during sentence processing. The strategy means that a word is assigned to any available theta role, and any available theta role is assigned a word as soon as possible.

If no word is available for a role, the parser examines the assigned tree to determine whether an assigned word may satisfy the unfilled role. If there is a word available for a role, a revision is made. If the revision does not involve a change in theta domain, the revision is cost-free and the next word is examined. If the revision

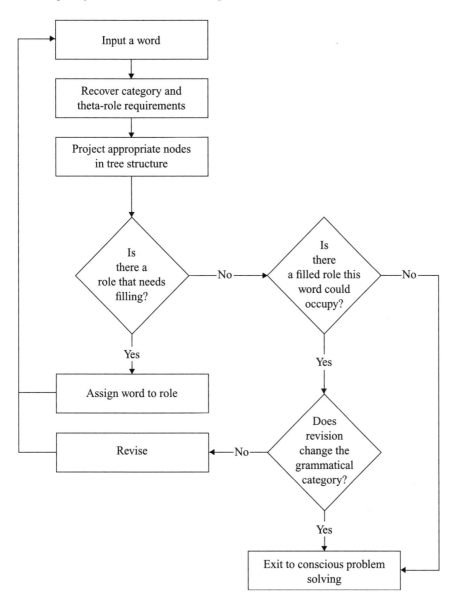

Figure 4.5
The architecture of Pritchett's parser.

does involve a change in theta domain, the revision the performed by conscious problem-solving mechanisms, which are conscious and costly.

The theta attachment principle states that the parser attempts to maximally fulfill theta-role requirements at all points. Consider the classic garden-path sentence (34):

(34) The horse raced past the barn fell.

When *raced* is processed, its maximal theta requirements are retrieved from the lexicon. Even though *raced* may simply take the theme role, it maximally requires an agent (as external subject) and a theme. The parser may adopt the active structure and assign *horse* as agent (external subject), leaving the theme role that is required for *raced* unfilled for the moment.

Alternatively, the parser may adopt the reduced relative structure by creating an empty category that has the theme role of *raced* in a relative clause, leaving the agent role that is required for *raced* unfilled. However, the parser rejects the reduced relative structure because this structure will leave *horse* without a theta role. Since the theta criterion can be satisfied more fully with the active structure, the parser assigns *horse* as the agent of *raced*. *Past the barn* is attached as the location role of *raced*. When *fell* is received, the parser looks for a NP to fill its theme role. The only possible NP to fill this role is *horse*, which already occupies the agent role for *raced*. There is substantial cost in making this revision, since *horse* must change to the new theta domain of *fell*.

Pritchett considers why some sentences that have the form of the classic garden-path sentence do not actually produce a noticeable garden path—for example, (35):

(35) The spaceship destroyed in the battle disintegrated.

The crucial difference between (35) and (34) is that *destroyed* is unambiguously transitive, while *raced* is optionally intransitive. The unambiguous cue to transitivity that *destroyed* provides prevents the violation of the theta reanalysis constraint (i.e., reanalysis that changes the theta domain is costly). When *destroyed* is processed, the active structure is adopted, the agent role is filled, and the theme role is left unfilled. When *in the battle* is received, the only way it can assign this phrase a theta role is if *destroyed* is posited as a reduced relative modifying *spaceship*. When *disintegrated* is received, *spaceship* fills its theme role. Consequently, there is no conscious garden path.

Why doesn't the reassignment of *spaceship* from subject of *destroyed* to unattached NP cost? Pritchett's answer is that it is the immediate detachment and reattachment of a phrase that is outside the capacity of the parser. When *in the battle* initiates reanalysis to the reduced relative structure, *spaceship* is detached from its role as subject of *destroyed*, but it is not reattached until *disintegrated* is received. Since the detachment and reattachment do not occur at the same time, this revision does not cost. Pritchett rejects the possibility that the parser bypasses the active analysis by filling obligatory internal arguments before optional external arguments. Thus, *spaceship* may be assigned as theme of *destroyed*, since *destroyed* requires a theme but not an agent. While this "no-misanalysis hypothesis" would fill an obligatory role early, it also would create a NP that needs a role (the head of the relative clause *spaceship*).

Some of the key ideas that emerge from Pritchett's parser are:

1. Sometimes reanalysis is costly and conscious; sometimes it is not.
2. Changing the assignment of a word to a new theta domain makes it costly and conscious.

4.2.4   Modules for Structure, Chains, Theta Roles

The structural models exhibit a range of views on how to deal with the fact that comprehension is fast, accurate, and largely effortless. One approach is to construct the parser so that it is serial and deterministic: only the correct structure is built. As we have seen, this approach requires lookahead and recoding of words into abstract categories, as in Marcus's Parsifal. A second approach is to relax the requirement of complete determinism without backtracking, but design the parser so that it can recover quickly when revision is occasionally necessary, as in Frazier's GPT (section 4.2.1). A third approach is to construct the parser so that only some aspects of structural analysis are deterministic and prohibited from participating in revision, as in Gorrell's model (section 4.2.2). Fourth, the parser may be designed so that there is no determinism: all aspects of structural analysis are subject to revision, but only certain operations of revision have a detectable cost, as in Pritchett's model (section 4.2.3).

Crocker (1996) extends this fourth approach. Crocker's parser mirrors the organization of government-and-binding theory. There are separate modules for building phrase structure, for assigning thematic roles, for constructing movement chains, and for evaluating the semantic/pragmatic function of a sentence. Each module carries out a specific function on a specific type of information. The processing system as a whole is incremental, so that as soon as a module performs its task, its results are passed on to the next module. If a later module detects an error in a previous module, the analysis is sent back for revision. Whether a revision is costly or not depends on the degree of commitment to the incorrect analysis. This in turn depends on how many modules have operated on and accepted the incorrect analysis.

Figure 4.6 shows how Crocker organizes the modules. Each syntactic processor applies the principles of corresponding components of government-and-binding theory. Based on lexical items, which include only the barest grammatical information, and X-bar theory, the phrase structure module determines sisterhood and constituency relations. The chain module establishes long distance dependencies that

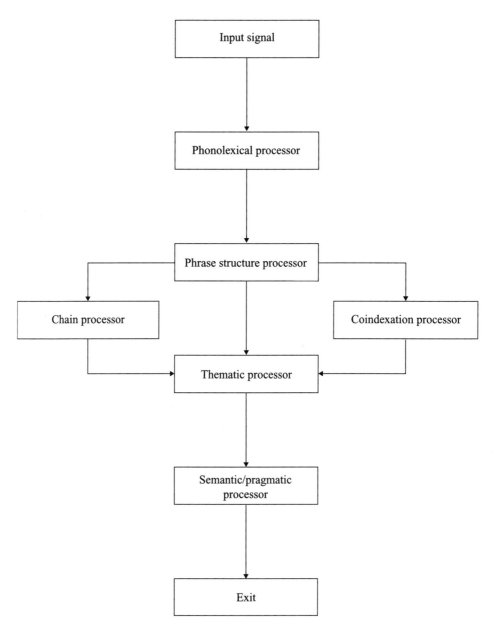

Figure 4.6
The organization of modules in Crocker's parser.

arise from movement, and the coindexation module uses binding theory to determine reference. To the information about phrase structure, chains, and coindexation, the thematic module adds subcategorization information and determines the argument structure. Based on the argument structure and knowledge about plausibility, the semantic/pragmatic processor provides a semantic representation for the general cognitive system. Thus, the various modules have access to only certain types of information.

The phrase structure module uses X-bar theory (see chapter 3) and basic lexical categories to project the phrase structure hierarchy dominating each word. Information about the basic lexical category of a word is simply N, V, and so on, and it does not include subcategorization information, such as that a particular verb is transitive or intransitive.[3] The phrase structure module uses strategies to resolve ambiguities.

A-attachment expresses the preference for attaching material into positions that potentially could receive a theta role (complements, external arguments, subject). A-attachment accounts for the preference to attach a prepositional phrase to a verb phrase to serve as an instrument, as in (36a)

(36) a. I saw the girl with binoculars.

rather than to a noun phrase to serve as a modifier, as in (36b)

     b. I saw the girl with the flu.

A-attachment expresses a preference for attaching words into licensed positions rather than potential positions, accounting for the relative ease of the first sentence below:

(37) a. While Mary was mending the sock it fell off her lap.
     b. While Mary was mending the sock fell off her lap.

And A-attachment accounts for the preference for active analysis rather than reduced relative analysis of (34), repeated here:

(34) The horse raced past the barn fell.

so that *the horse* is attached as subject (agent) of *raced* rather than receiving the patient role from *raced*.[4]

The phrase structure module also uses deep structure attachment: when it is necessary to attach to a position that does not take an argument, attach to a canonical base-generated position such as modifier, rather than to one that results from movement.[5]

The phrase structure module uses an active trace strategy: *posit a trace in any potentially vacated position*. Thus, the phrase structure module initially posits a trace at each t_1 in (38)

(38) Who$_1$ t$_1$ did you want t$_1$ Mother to make t$_1$ a cake for t$_1$?

since all of the following are grammatical:

(39) a. Who$_1$ t$_1$ left?
     b. Who$_1$ did you kick t$_1$?
     c. Who$_1$ did you want Mother to kick t$_1$?

Crocker's phrase structure module posits these traces without regard to subcategorization information, which is only available to the thematic module. According to Crocker, sentence (38) is not very difficult because the thematic module quickly rejects the chain and sends the sentence back to the phrase structure module before there is a strong commitment to it.[6]

As the phrase structure is determined, it is simultaneously passed on to the thematic module, the chain module, and the coindexation module. The thematic module uses information about the phrase structure positions of words and knowledge about theta-role requirements to assign theta roles to words. Importantly, this module does not have access to semantic features of words. Once the theta roles are determined, they are sent to the semantic/pragmatic processor. The semantic/pragmatic processor uses semantic features and the theta-role assignments to determine whether the thematic representation is plausible.

There is incremental processing. This means that as soon as a processor computes a representation, it is sent on to the next processor. The degree of difficulty in reanalysis is related to the level of commitment to an analysis—that is, to the number of processors that have accepted the analysis as well formed.

The following sentences illustrate degree of difficulty in reanalysis:

(40) a. After the child sneezed the doctor prescribed a course of injections.
     b. I broke the window with my sister.
     c. While Mary was knitting the sock fell off her lap.

In (40a), the phrase structure module attaches *doctor* as a complement of *sneeze*, but this is immediately rejected when the thematic processor tries to assign *doctor* as patient of *sneeze*. Thus, the phrase structure module needs to reanalyze. This reanalysis is neither costly nor conscious.

In (40b), the phrase structure module attaches the PP as an instrument, according to the strategy of argument attachment. Whenever possible, the phrase structure processor attaches words into potential argument positions. The thematic module assigns *sister* the role of instrument. However, the semantic/pragmatic system rejects *sister* as a plausible instrument, forcing reanalysis by both the phrase structure module and the thematic module. Reanalysis in this case is costly but unconscious because it occurs within the syntactic system.

In (40c), the phrase structure module attaches *sock* as complement of *knitting*. The thematic module assigns *sock* the role of patient. The semantic/pragmatic processor accepts these assignments as plausible. *Fell*, however, forces the phrase structure module to reanalyze *sock* as subject of *fell*. This requires the thematic module and the semantic/pragmatic processor to reanalyze as well. Since the reanalysis requires the work of three processors, it is costly and conscious.

To summarize, the key points in Crocker's parser are the following:

1. Some revisions can be performed quite easily, and others cannot.
2. Degree of commitment is related to difficulty of revision.

4.2.5   A Cost Metric for Online Computation

Some sentences are difficult not because they induce a garden path, but because their requirements for integrating words into a syntactic structure strain the limits of processing resources. This is the motivation for Gibson's Syntactic Prediction Locality Theory. The theory is unique among the contemporary structural theories we review here in that it makes clear predictions about the relative difficulty in comprehending sentences that are not garden-path sentences. (See Gibson 1998 for a review.)

Gibson developed a metric for predicting the processing difficulty of sentences. The central idea is that comprehension involves assigning words to thematic roles. Each word is stored in short-term memory until it is integrated into a syntactic structure that provides it with a thematic role. Similarly, each thematic role that is required for a predicate is stored in short-term memory until a word is found that can fulfill the role. Thus, there are two factors that increase processing difficulty. One is the number of thematic roles that have not been assigned a word. The second is the number of words that have not been assigned to a thematic role.

Gibson illustrates the cost metric with center-embedded sentences like (41a) and (41b):

(41) a. *Object relative clause*
         The reporter who the senator attacked admitted the error.
      b. *Subject relative clause*
         The reporter who attacked the senator admitted the error.

In the object relative clause, *who* has been extracted from its position as the deep structure object of the relative clause verb *attacked*. In the subject relative clause *who* has been extracted from its position as the deep subject of *attacked*.

A sentence with an object relative clause typically is harder to understand than one with a subject relative clause (see chapter 7). Gibson's explanation of this difference is that there are increased processing costs momentarily associated with unfilled syntactic commitments in a sentence with an object relative clause.

Table 4.1 shows the word-by-word processing requirements for integrating words into a syntactic structure for sentences with different types of relative clauses. The table shows how each word is attached to previous words, and what new discourse referents have been introduced since the parser received the attachment site. The integration cost $I(n)$ depends on the number of new discourse referents n introduced since the attachment site. Comparing the two types of relative clause constructions in table 4.1, we see that there is substantial cost, $I(3)$, associated with the main verb *admitted* in both constructions. However, the object relative requires that the embedded verb *attacked* be integrated in two ways while maintaining three discourse referents in memory, for an integration cost of $I(1) + I(2)$. The processing load requirement for a subject relative clause on the last word of the relative clause (*senator*) is lower, with an integration cost of $I(0) + I(1)$.

Gibson's version of simplicity is motivated by the parser's need to reduce the demands on processing resources. It follows that whenever there is a choice between alternative structures, the parser will select the one that makes fewer commitments. In cases in which alternative structures require similar commitments, both structures are retained until a definitive choice can be made. Gibson's model is an example of "ranked parallelism," in which the parser maintains alternative structures simultaneously but ranks them in terms of preference. The structure that requires the least processing resources is ranked first.

Gibson allows the parser to use plausibility and frequency information to assist in breaking a tie between alternative structures. The justification for this feature of the parser comes from evidence that information about plausibility can eliminate the garden-path effect in reduced relative clauses. For example, Trueswell, Tanenhaus, and Garnsey (1994) found that word-by-word reading times were longer during *by the lawyer* in reduced relative clauses than in unreduced relative clauses (see chapter 6):

(42) a. *Reduced relative clause*
       The defendant examined by the lawyer turned out to be unreliable.
    b. *Unreduced relative clause*
       The defendant that was examined by the lawyer turned out to be unreliable.

There was no difference in reading times for the corresponding phrase in the sentences like the following:

(42) c. *Reduced relative clause*
       The evidence examined by the lawyer turned out to be unreliable.
    d. *Unreduced relative clause*
       The evidence that was examined by the lawyer turned out to be unreliable.

Table 4.1
Integration costs in object relative and subject relative sentences

Word	How it is integrated	New referents	Cost
A. Object Relative			
The	Not integrated	None	None
reporter	Attach to *the*	None	I(0)
who	Attach to *reporter*	None	I(0)
the	Attach to *who*	None	I(0)
senator	Attach to *the*	None	I(0)
attacked	1. Attach to *senator* by assigning *attack*'s agent role to *senator*	*attacked*	I(1)
	2. Attach empty category as object and coindex with *who*	*senator* *attacked*	I(2)
admitted	Attach as main verb to *reporter*	*reporter* *attacked* *admitted*	I(3)
the	Attach as start of NP	None	I(0)
error	1. Attach to *the*	None	I(0)
	2. Attach *the error* as object of *admitted*	*error*	I(1)
B. Subject Relative			
The	Not integrated	None	None
reporter	Attach to *the*	None	I(0)
who	Attach to *reporter*	None	I(0)
attacked	1. Attach a gap in subject position	None	I(0)
	2. Attach *attacked* to its subject	*attacked*	I(1)
the	Attach as start of NP	None	I(0)
senator	1. Attach to *the*	None	I(0)
	2. Attach *the senator* as object of *attacked*	*senator*	I(1)
admitted	Attach as main verb to *reporter*	*attacked* *senator* *admitted*	I(3)
the	Attach as start of NP	None	I(0)
error	1. Attach to *the*	None	I(1)
	2. Attach *the error* as object of *admitted*	*error*	

Evidence apparently is a poor agent for *examined*, making the reduced relative interpretation more likely than in the case of the sentence with *defendant*.

According to Gibson's theory, plausibility has this effect on processing reduced relatives only because there is a small difference in processing costs between the main verb and reduced relative interpretations of *examined*. When reading *examined* in *the defendant examined* ..., the main-verb interpretation leads to a commitment for a forthcoming noun phrase for the direct object. The reduced relative interpretation leads to the prediction of a main verb (which never has a cost in Gibson's model) and an optional adverbial modifier, as in (43).

(43) The defendant examined yesterday was dismissed.

In both the main-verb and reduced relative interpretations, there is one syntactic commitment and no unassigned referents at the point of *examined*. Since the processing load for the two structures is similar, semantic information can shift the activation levels of the structures. For example, inanimate initial nouns lead to the reduced relative interpretation in *the evidence examined* ... and animate nouns lead to the main-verb interpretation in *the defendant examined....* Thus, the *by*-phrase produces an increase in reading time only for *the defendant examined by the lawyer* ..., where the main-verb interpretation is shown to be incorrect.

To recapitulate, the grains of truth in Gibson's model are the following:

1. More than one interpretation can be available at any one time.
2. Frequency and conceptual information can influence the preferred interpretation.
3. Processing load increases with the number of syntactic commitments and unattached words.

4.2.6 Comparison of Structural Theories

We began this section with several ideas due to Marcus (1980). We then sketched some of the contemporary structural theories descended from Marcus, which introduced variations on different aspects of his work. Table 4.2 summarizes variations in Marcus in the contemporary theories. We can differentiate the theories with a set of questions:

What kinds of linguistic structures are assigned?

Like Marcus 1980, Gorrell's model and Pritchett's model assign a surface structure that is annotated to indicate coreference and the location of traces. Some models develop multiple representations of linguistic structure. Frazier's model develops separate representations of phrase structure and argument structure. Gibson's model develops separate representations of phrase structure, argument structure, and discourse structure. Crocker's model develops independent representations of phrase structure, movement chains, coreference, argument structure, and pragmatic meaning.

Table 4.2
Comparison of structural theories

Issue	Marcus	Frazier	Gorrell	Pritchett	Crocker	Gibson
What structures are assigned?	Annotated surface structure	Phrase structure, argument structure	Annotated surface structure	Annotated surface structure	Phrase, chain, coreference, argument	Phrase, argument, discourse
Are candidate structures formed serially?	Yes	Yes	Yes	Yes	Yes	No
Is parsing deterministic?	Yes	No	"Yes"	No	No	Yes
What operations have a processing cost?	None	Building branches	Changing dominance or precedence relations	Changing theta domain	Changing a strong commitment	Retaining unfilled roles and unassigned words
How does reanalysis occur?	General problem solving	Visibility	Adding nodes; general problem solving	Trimming	Recycling	Reinstating an old tree
Is nonstructural information used?	Yes	"No"	Yes	No	No	Yes
How is NP movement determined?	?	Minimal attachment	Cues to traces	Theta attachment	A-attachment	Theta attachment
How is *wh*-movement determined?	?	Most Recent Filler Strategy	Subcategories; frequency	Theta attachment	Active Filler Strategy	Active Filler Strategy

Are candidate structures formed in parallel or serially?

Are two or more candidate syntactic structures generated and one selected at some point, or is the model serial, with only one structure generated? Frazier, Gorrell, Pritchett, and Crocker all follow Marcus in proposing that the parser forms syntactic representations serially. In each of these models, an initial syntactic representation is formed and modified until it "crashes." Gibson's model is the one exception to serial formation of candidate structures. In this model, all possible structures are initially computed and the computationally simpler take priority. Structures that are similar in costs are maintained until there is information that distinguishes between them.

Is the parser deterministic?

Marcus (1980) defined strict determinism to mean that once a syntactic decision is made it cannot be revoked—that is, there are no revisions. By allowing a look-ahead buffer, Marcus was able to demonstrate determinism for sentences that cause no processing difficulty. Contemporary models of human sentence processing have dropped Marcus's notion of a look-ahead buffer, and, as a result, they have changed his idea of determinism.

On the issue of determinism, Gorrell and Gibson are perhaps closest to Marcus. Gorrell proposed that decisions about dominance and precedence relations are deterministic. Other syntactic decisions are not deterministic, and the parser easily modifies these decisions. Gibson proposed that several structures are computed and maintained simultaneously. Structures may be abandoned if they are costly, or rein-troduced, but they are never modified. Frazier relinquished the idea of determinism and proposed that incorrect syntactic decisions are fairly common. To reduce pro-cessing load, the parser adopts the "minimal attachment." The cost of using this strategy is that the parser must frequently revise. Both Pritchett and Crocker aban-doned determinism. Their parsers sometimes carry out cost-free revisions when no change in theta domain is required (Pritchett), or when there is no strong commit-ment (Crocker). Otherwise, the parser carries out costly revision.

What operations have a cost in processing resources?

Structural models differ in whether syntactic operations have a measurable cost in processing resources. Operations that require conscious attention are costly; those that occur "automatically" are cost-free. For Marcus (1980) the parser's syntactic operations are cost-free; however, a grammatical problem solver operates at sub-stantial cost when the parser fails.

Contemporary structural models have introduced variations on this theme. Some models retain Marcus's idea that syntactic decisions are essentially cost-free but elaborate on the idea that revisions are costly. For example, Gorrell maintains that the parser builds structure at no cost; revisions of dominance and precedence relations can be conducted only by a grammatical problem solver and are costly. Pritchett and Crocker also suggest that basic structure building is cost-free, but in their case, the parser can carry out revisions that are costly if they involve changing a theta domain (Pritchett) or a decision with strong commitment (Crocker).

In other models, syntactic operations are costly. For Frazier, it is the cost of building structure and the need to reduce processing costs that leads to the minimal attachment strategy: rules that create more branching in the phrase structure tree are more expensive and therefore are avoided. Gibson suggests that maintaining syntactic commitments and unassigned words are both costly. A structure that is more costly than another is abandoned.

How does reanalysis occur?

Information that resolves a temporary ambiguity often occurs shortly after the ambiguity. Thus, Marcus's model was able to parse deterministically by using a three-item look-ahead buffer. For Marcus, a conscious grammatical problem solver carries out reanalysis. Contemporary models have distinguished between revisions that are easy and hardly noticeable, and those that are difficult and require conscious effort. There is general agreement on the basic facts to the explained, but there are differences in the explanation of the facts. The facts are that the first sentence in each pair of (44) is easier than the second.

(44) *Fodor and Inoue* (1998)
    a. The boy noticed *the dog* limped badly.
    b. While the boy scratched *the dog* yawned loudly.
    Pritchett (1992)
    c. Susan knew *her mother* hated her.
    d. After Todd drank *the water* proved to be poisoned.
    Sturt and Crocker (1998)
    e. The wedding guests saw *the cake* was still being decorated.
    f. While the wedding guests ate *the cake* was still being decorated.
    Sturt and Crocker (1998)
    g. Once the students had understood *the homework* was easy they quickly finished it.
    h. Once the students had understood *the homework* was easy and they quickly finished it.
    Lewis (1998)
    i. Mary forgot *her husband* needed a ride yesterday.
    j. Although Mary forgot *her husband* didn't seem very upset yesterday.

In each case, our intuitions tell us that we interpret the italicized material initially as being the object of the preceding verb, but the word following the underlined material shows that this interpretation is incorrect. The garden path is hardly noticeable in the first sentence of each pair, but it is quite striking in the second sentence. These intuitions suggest that it is easier to change the assignment from direct object to subject of a complement clause than to subject of a main clause. (Note, however, that the last pair from Sturt and Crocker 1998:395 is the only pair that controls for clause structure and verb subcategorization.) Here we consider how contemporary models explain these basic facts about ease of revision.

In Frazier's model, the parser carries out revisions when attached material conflicts with the grammar; revisions are focused at the location of the grammatical conflict (see also Fodor and Inoue 1998; Lewis 1998). The Visibility Hypothesis states that reanalysis that involves attachment to a recently postulated and uninterpreted node is relatively easy (Frazier and Clifton 1998). The Visibility Hypothesis can explain the facts, because easy reanalysis involves attachment to the recently postulated Verb node rather than to the earlier postulated Sentence node.

In Gorrell's model, reassigning the noun phrase to subject of a complement clause preserves dominance (the VP dominates the NP in both cases, although not directly for the complement structure). When the noun phrase is changed to subject of a verb in an independent clause it is no longer dominated by the VP. Since dominance must change in the second case, the revision is costly (see also Sturt and Crocker 1998). The parser can perform reanalysis that involves adding nodes, but only a general problem solver can perform reanalysis that involves destroying structure. Gorrell (1998) adds that *the horse raced past the barn fell* is difficult because there is no attachment site available for *fell* at the rightmost edge of the developing phrase structure tree once a main clause structure has been established for *the horse raced past the barn*.

In Pritchett's model, the parser carries out reanalysis by trimming the phrase structure tree. The only revision that is costly is one that requires changing the theta domain of the word. In *Susan knew her mother hated her*, the parser must change *her mother* from theme of *knew* to experiencer of *hated*, but in each case, *her mother* is within the theta domain of *knew*. In *After Todd drank the water proved to be poisonous*, the parser must change *the water* from theme of *drank* to theme of *proved*, which involves a change in theta domain. As a result, the second sentence is harder.

In Crocker's model, reanalysis occurs when a module detects an incongruity. The degree of difficulty in changing an analysis increases as the number of modules that have "accepted" the analysis increases. Crocker's model does not distinguish the sentences within pairs above. In each case, the assignment of the underlined material as direct object passes through the thematic module and the semantic/pragmatic module, and in each case, the next word signals a need for reanalysis by the phrase structure module. Reanalysis occurs by recycling through the modules.

Gibson's model makes no clear prediction about the basic facts of revision. If two alternative structures differ greatly in processing load, the more costly structure is no longer pursued. "Reanalysis" consists of reintroducing a previously abandoned structure. In the easier cases the parser must reintroduce the complement structure, and in the harder cases it must reintroduce the intransitive. If we assume that the parser drops the intransitive structure when it processes the underlined material, Gibson's model can explain the facts. However, Gibson's model provides no reason why the intransitive should be dropped while the complement clause interpretation is retained.

What is the role of nonstructural information such as conceptual representations and probabilistic information?

The structural models emphasize structural processing, and they tend to reduce the role of meaning and probabilistic information. Marcus, for example, allowed for meaning to influence the attachment of prepositional phrases, but did not specify how the relevant meaning was obtained.

Frazier departed from Marcus in stating that all initial structural decisions are made solely on the basis of syntactic category information. Plausibility and frequency of use may influence syntactic decisions in reanalysis, but these types of information do not initially influence syntactic decisions. Frazier and Clifton (1996) modified this view by acknowledging that the initial attachment decisions about nonprimary phrases involve meaning.

For Gorrell meaning has a prominent role in ensuring that dominance and precedence relations are established deterministically. The parser can use conceptual information to guide structure building. Information about frequency of use can be incorporated into the parser, but frequency of use of syntactic patterns cannot.

According to Pritchett and Crocker, the parser does not use information about meaning or lexical preferences to build structure.

For Gibson, neither frequency nor conceptual information is ordinarily accessed. These kinds of information are used only to resolve local ambiguities for which each of the readings is roughly the same complexity as the others.

How does the parser handle NP- and wh-*movement?*

While most theories provide similar treatment of *wh*-movement, the notion of NP-movement is characteristic of derivational grammatical theories. In the Marcus model, cues such as passive morphology, verbs with special properties, and *wh*-words cause the parser to attach a trace to a node and drop the node into the buffer. But *wh*-trace differs from NP-trace in that it has a special *wh*-node that moves to the first available position. NP-trace is coindexed with its referent clause by clause. Gorrell treats NP-movement such as passive and subject raising and *wh*-movement in a fashion similar to Marcus. In Frazier's model, NP-movement is handled by minimal attachment: the parser always chooses the simplest structure (at least for primary phrases). *Wh*-movement is processed with the most recent filler strategy. Pritchett,

Crocker, and Gibson treat NP-movement in similar ways. Pritchett's theta-attachment principle means that the parser adopts the structure that assigns the most roles and leaves the fewest roles unassigned. Crocker considers NP-movement indirectly through the preferences that are exhibited in A-attachment and deep structure attachment. Crocker and Gibson treat *wh*-movement using a version of the active filler strategy.

4.3   Statistical Models

Associative models that extract regularities from a complex environment are by definition learning models. Our discussion of statistical models of comprehension necessarily blends theories of inductive learning and resulting representations. Statistical models of induction face two computational questions:

• Is the information available in the input for statistically based inferences about structure? Superficially, language structures appear to be wildly varied, making it difficult to conceive of how any inductive procedure with a small amount of data could extract structurally relevant information.

• What is the inductive learning mechanism that can extract the relevant information as it goes along—even if the information is technically "in" the language, what kind of mechanism can pick it up during some kind of actual behavior?

The mathematical tools of multiple regression, multidimensional scaling, and hierarchical analysis are powerful ways to examine if there are statistically distinct factors isolable from a heterogeneous database. For example, lexical categories can be strongly differentiated and categorized just from a distributional hierarchical analysis of the contexts in which items can occur. This seems mysterious, but it is not. Words from the same lexical category tend to occur in similar environments. For example, in normal sentences a word following *the* and preceding *has* is a noun, and a word between *shall* and *a* is a verb. Any scheme that analyzes the similarities of words in terms of their immediate environments will tend to arrive at syntactic-like categories. For example, Mintz (1997) applied a cluster analysis to the words in their immediate environments, in a large sample of "motherese"—utterances by caregivers to children. He classified each word in terms of the word preceding and following it. Then, he used a clustering analysis that grouped words together based on the similarity of their environments. Words that are very similar in their environments are grouped as very low level clusters; words that differ in their environments are linked only at a very high level in the hierarchy. A hierarchical clustering model applies stepwise criteria to establish an actual single hierarchy that best fits the data. The analysis yielded a hierarchical structure in which "nouns" are well differentiated from "verbs."

A simple analysis of this kind works because of the frequency of structurally defined frames, especially in simple sentences drawing on a restricted vocabulary. At first, it might seem that this "solves" the problem of category learning with no access to meaning or prior knowledge of syntactic categories. In that view, what a language-learning child does is apply the psychological equivalent of a cluster analysis to discover the syntactic categories, and classify words into them. But how to apply a tool-like cluster analysis is not obvious. There has to be a method that intrinsically flows from ongoing behavior. This need is reflected in several important limitations, which are common to all mere demonstrations that structurally relevant information is statistically available in the input.

1. *The Grain Problem.* How do we know what size grouping to pick? Indeed, if we pick just the right level, we obtain a good separation of nouns and verbs, but this depends on the judgment of the statistician, who already knows what the goal is. Mintz suggests that there may be an optimal group size that can be maintained by a real child, which automatically determines the right level in the hierarchy. But this choice is delicately sensitive to the particular input data, and we think there probably is no single criterion that works in general.

Mitchell et al. (1995) discuss the grain problem as it applies to higher-order analyses. To use prior experiences with language to facilitate sentence comprehension, the reader or listener must record and store relevant features of those experiences and must match those features with current linguistic material during comprehension. The *grain problem* refers to the question of what level of structural features is the appropriate level to store. Consider, for example, the following sentence:

(45) Someone praised the wife of the football star who was outside the house.

In deciding whether to attach the relative clause *who was outside the house* to *the wife* or to *of the football star*, the parser might refer to information at a variety of grain sizes. From relatively coarse grain to relatively fine grain, some possibilities are:

• Decisions may be based on the relative frequency of attachment locations in sequences of the form NP-(modifying constituent)-(modifying constituent).
• There may be separate records depending on the type of initial modifier, so that the records are based on frequency of attachment locations in NP-PP-(modifying constituent) sequences.
• There may be separate records for particular types of modifying constituents that follow the PP, so that in this case the relevant records contain information about the frequency of attachment locations in NP-PP-RC ("relative clause") sequences.
• There may be separate records for experiences with NP-PP-RC sequences depending on the preposition that introduces the PP, with different records for *of, with, by,* and so on.

• There may also be different records depending on whether the structure appears early versus late in the sentence.
• There may be different records depending on the animacy of the potential noun hosts.
• There may be different records depending on the specific nouns that are potential hosts.

2. *The Category Problem.* Even if the words are strongly segregated into groups, how does the mechanism know which groups are linguistically significant and which are "noise"? This problem has two aspects.

First, the grouping system has to know what a "noun" versus a "verb" is, in order to use the grouping to establish what words fall in each. But "noun" versus "verb" is in part a linguistic differentiation that depends on their function in sentences: "verbs" require argument positions to be filled; "nouns" fill those positions. Grouping words together based on immediate contexts does not provide that definition. Rather, the category learner either has to know enough to look for specific kinds of distributional evidence about the word groups, or has to access some kind of automatic mechanism that can extract that differentiation from the input strings. It is hard to see how an automatic mechanism could word without prior knowledge of enough syntactic structure to note the differences. And, of course, postulating that the learner knows what kind of categorical information to look for is simply an example of structural "nativism."

Second, the system has to know how many other categories it is looking for. And, these too, are defined in terms of their syntactic distribution.

3. *The Dialectical Mush Problem.* Consider a world in which the word groups are learned with the hierarchical cluster analysis. Each analysis has some error in it—that is, certain actual nouns may be classified as verbs and conversely, leading to a certain degree of error. Suppose that the learner then has children: the input to the next generation will be degraded, leading to an increased amount of error. The errors will increase with each generation. To put it differently, the system works as well as it does, just because the regularity of syntactic structure guarantees that words of the same category will sometimes appear in the same environment. Without accessing an actual syntax, in which lexical categories are defined in terms of their structural distribution, the system will endure entropy with each successive learner, and lose all structure after some number of generations.

Analytic procedures like hierarchical grouping algorithms are sensitive to lexically coded regularities, but do not correspond in an obvious way to associative relations between mental entities. The cluster analyses suggest that the ecology of language provides a lot of statistically reliable information relevant to linguistic structure, but little about how to discover it. Connectionist modeling offers a mathematical technique related to multiple regression analyses, but with a transparent utilization of associative relations, and a traditional learning rule that changes strength of association. Such models can be organized to become sensitive to aspects of syntactic structure that transcend the individual lexical item category.

4.3.1   Mediation Association Theory and Connectionism

In brief, mere existence of a statistically valid structure in the language environment will not guarantee discovery or application of the structure. As we reviewed in chapter 2, Osgood postulated a learning model with an intermediate level of structure, with r-s modules connected to numerous inputs and overt outputs. But Osgood did not offer a completely explicit mathematical formula as to how the variation of connection strengths between the mediating modules and the explicit responses percolates back to vary the strength of the connections from the initial stimuli to the mediating modules. In spirit, he was drawing on Hull's (1943) fractionation of responses and goal reinforcements to allow for such backward spread of selective reinforcement, but there was no clear calculus for doing this. Thus, while intriguing, S-R mediation theory did not catch on as a major tool for the study of language acquisition and behavior. It seemed right (given the precondition of utilizing associative theory at all), but imprecise and untestable. Furthermore, the strict adherence to behaviorist-reductionist principles to account for the formation of intervening variables made the entire scheme vulnerable to classic attacks.

Recent developments in computer-based "connectionism" have offered several different kinds of schemes for learning by adjusting the weights on connections. One learning scheme called *back-propagation* requires determining the difference in the observed and desired activity of output units (Bechtel and Abrahamsen 1991; Rumelhart, Hinton, and Williams 1986). Once the difference between observed and desired activity, or "error," is computed, it is used to adjust the weights on the connections. For example, if the activity of an output unit is too high, the weight on the connection is reduced; if it is too low, the weight is increased. The error further propagates backward to adjust the weights on connections between input units and intermediate units, according to how much each intermediate unit contributes to the error. This gives an automatic and powerful scheme for training networks with intermediate levels.

Consider how this scheme would apply to Osgood's word association network (see section 2.2.2). In a learning framework, the model's task is to match as output the word and associates of the word that was given as input. Of course, with only a few words of each, and a few intermediate nodes, there is no problem, so consider a world of hundreds of words as input and output, just as Osgood did. A learning trial consists of activating an input word and examining the output. If the output is the incorrect word, the first step is to reduce the weight on that word and increase the weight on the correct word. The activation links that lead to these responses or potential responses from the intermediate layer will be adjusted according to their degree of match to the correct word. Then for each intermediate node, the weights will be adjusted as well.

This simple scheme has changed the fortunes of associative mediation psychology. It is now possible to formulate and test specific models without having to tweak the strengths of connections to the intermediate layers of connection points. We have mediation associationism without behaviorist limits on intervening structures—a decidedly liberating advance.

4.3.2 Limits of Connectionism, Same or Different?

What can this tell us about the potential effect of statistical eccentricities on the learning and use of syntactic structures? A variety of learning models have been constructed that convey a structural analysis of many aspects of syntactic structure (e.g., Rumelhart and McClelland 1986; Elman 1990). Many of these are "toy" models, in that they work only on highly tailored input. In an example pertinent for the model we present in chapter 5, Juliano and Bever (1988) explored the extent to which phrase structure segmentation can be based on statistical properties of sentence boundaries. They set up a training model with an input array for examining three words in a row, a hidden layer of nodes, and an output node. The model had a recognition vocabulary of about 200 function words, and recognized the letter length of all words. Unrecognized words were classified in terms of the distance to the nearest recognized word to its left; see (46).

(46) *3-Word Input*
The horse that
horse that was
that was raced
was raced past
raced past the
past the barn.

The model examined three-word sequences, as shown above—for example, words 1–3, then 2–4, then 3–5, and so on. Punctuation and capitalization were opaque to the model but were used after each trial to give feedback on the location of actual sentence boundaries. At each new subsequence, the model was trained on sentence boundaries to predict that the space between the second and third words is in fact a sentence boundary; the higher the output value, the more likely there is a sentence boundary. In the preceding example, only the sixth triplet would have been reinforced as positive. After training on a text of several thousand sentences, the model did a good job of predicting sentence boundaries. This reflects the fact that sentences end and begin in characteristic patterns. But the boundary between two sentences is also the boundary between two phrases. This raised the possibility that the model would generalize well in predicting where the phrase boundaries are within sentences. In fact, this is true, as shown in (47)—the numbers correspond to the value of the output.

(47) a. Who (.036) is (.020) it (.498)?
   b. We (.018) saw (.009) the (.073) children (.076) walking (.185) in (.079) the (.055) rain (.755).
   c. What (.257) did (.009) you (.057) hit (.102) that (.079) time (.333)?
   d. There's (.006) more (.131) in (.023) here (.501).
   e. We'll (.005) save (.009) this (.108) one (.186) for (.085) later (.367).
   f. What (.257) are (.009) you (.073) cooking (.101) down (.087) there (.427)?
   g. Children (.071) rain (.315), walk (095) rain (.366), yes (.875)

These values can be converted to actual segmentation by two simple interpretive rules:

1. Every local maximum corresponds to a phrase boundary. For example, a value lower than the preceding value indicates that there is a phrase boundary after the preceding word.
2. Single words are joined to the right, unless sentence final.

These rules convert the initial output of the model into phrase structured sequences, which correspond well to where linguistic boundaries would occur. Some examples appear in (48). To illustrate, in (47a) the fact that the value of .020 after *is* is lower than the preceding value of .036 indicates that there is a phrase boundary after *what*, as shown in (48a).

(48) a. [[Who] is it?]
   b. [[[We] saw the children] [walking] [in the rain].]
   c. [[[What] did you] [hit [that time]].]
   d. [[There's more] [in here].]
   e. [[We'll save this one] [for later].]
   f. [[[What] are you cooking] down there.]
   g. [[Children rain,] [Walk rain, yes].]

This is not a toy model—that is, it generalizes quite well to normal English text, not just some chosen subset. Thus it would seem to "solve" the problem of how children might discover within-sentence phrase structure segmentation, by generalizing from the patterns of sentence boundaries. But it is important to examine closely how the model really works. First, it solves the lexical decoding problem by fiat. Words are simply operationally defined as letter strings between spaces. Second, it resolves the stimulus-identification problem by having a vocabulary of fixed words of interest—the closed class—and defines other words in terms of the most recently occurring closed class item. Third, the grain and reinforcement problem is solved for it by several constraints—(1) considering only three words at a time; (2) aiming at predicting the ends of utterances; (3) focusing the prediction on the second of the three words, rather than, for example, the third. Fourth, the model generalizes well to utterance-internal phrasing only if the utterance-final boundaries are "sharpened."

Thus, the model reveals that there is a great deal of structure in utterances that can be extracted by a properly configured associative system. No doubt other pre-configurations might end up with a similar result, but each will work because it has sufficiently pretuned mechanisms designed to pick up the actual phrase structures that structurally constrain word sequences.

Several current comprehension models have been developed that attempt to use statistically valid structures as their basis. As we will see, they all share the same kind of limits and virtues.

4.3.3 The Competition Model

MacWhinney (1987:251) formulated a scheme for comprehension that centers on the attachment of roles to predicates. The system is based on lexical knowledge, "as an organizer of auditory semantic ... and role-relational (i.e., syntactic) knowledge." Possible frames associated with lexical items "compete" with each other to deter-mine the assigned information during comprehension. In general, the attempt is to base language structure on allegedly general cognitive principles. Indeed, conven-tional aspects of syntax are viewed as artifacts of linguistic theory:

Phrase structures are epiphenomena, with the core of the grammar being composed of the arguments entered on particular predicates. By relating arguments to predicates, the listener builds up something that looks like a parse tree, [but because the parse is built up out of locally statistically valid attachments] there is no need for a separate encoding of phrase structure rules, since the correct patterns emerge from the operation of predicate-argument relations. (MacWhinney 1987:268)

The kind of "phrase structure" that emerges from this scheme is a form of directed graph, with predicates having connected links to their arguments.

Consider one of MacWhinney's examples (adapted from MacWhinney 1987):

(49) The dog ate the bone
    ((the → dog) ← ate → (the → bone))

The comprehension system arrives at this structure by linking a series of roles and cues that are associated with each word as it is encountered.

The essential concept is "competition" between structures, based on the relative validity of "cues" for particular analyses. The primary kinds of cues to role relations are word order and morphology. Children learn the validity of these cues as markers of particular verb roles, and automatically weight the competing cues in ongoing comprehension. Each verb specifies a set of possible roles it can assign to nouns, and then various cues combine to specify a particular role for the nouns in its argument domain.

For example, *the* is specified as having a head that follows it, so when *dog* appears next, it can be linked to the Head position defined by *the*. *Ate* has a characteristic description of its subject (animate and preceding it), and its object (following it); these roles and associated cues then facilitate the linking of the nouns into the appropriate predicate roles.

In addition to conventional roles (e.g., subject, object, indirect object), there are a number of additional, more structural sorts of "roles" such as "exohead" and "relhead." An exohead allows for structures that take more than one argument. For example, "prepositions take two arguments, [the one separate from the head] is the verb or noun which the whole prepositional phrase modifies ... the 'exohead'.... In a sentence such as 'they discussed the dogs on the beach', the exohead of 'on the beach' could be either 'the dogs' or 'discussed'" (MacWhinney, 1987:262). (Note that this corresponds to S/VP prepositional phrase attachment ambiguities discussed in sections 4.2, 4.2.1.)

The most complex grammatical role is that of the head of a relative clause ... "relhead." Relheads allow for linking of main and relative clauses. This kind of scheme can account for garden paths in terms of the relatively strong cues for an initially misleading analysis. Thus, in reduced relative constructions, the initial cues for a main-verb analysis are so strong that it is difficult to arrive at the correct analysis. In this case, the wrong set of cues and links "compete" so effectively that they create a misleading analysis.

The competition model is an ambitious project and is quite consistent with the concept that perceptual strategies assign structure, as discussed briefly in chapter 2. The notion of relying on surface and local cue validity to assign structure is exactly the same in both theories. Furthermore, the inclusion of both morphological markers and word order "cues" supports the role of patterns distributed across lexical items. The cue $N \dots V$ is a pattern relation between lexical items in a sequence, not an intrinsic property of either lexical item.

The competition model has been elaborated and spelled out in somewhat greater detail than the strategies model. It has also sparked wide-ranging research on the acquisition of sensitivity to language-specific cues in different languages. Thus, it serves as a useful framework for proceeding with various kinds of empirical studies of the role of statistically valid cues in sentence comprehension. The model necessarily exhibits both the virtues and failings of a pure statistical model. First, it does not even address the grain problem—how to establish a natural level along which the evidence for cues is assembled. The authors often stipulate which kinds of cues are universal—for example, word order and morphology. But they do not offer a theory as to how a learning mechanism would automatically arrive at just these cues and not others (Chomsky 1959; and discussion in chapter 2).

Second, the model does not deal clearly with the question of whether syntax is prior to it, unnecessary, or mimicked by it. Over two decades of writing, the model's proponents consistently attack the notion of an autonomous syntax, yet the model itself looks very much like a variant of syntax, insofar as it works, can deal with recursive structures, and so on. The authors face a conundrum. Either the model simulates the essential features of a correct syntax or it does not. If it does, then it serves merely as a strongly equivalent structure, without guaranteeing the claim that it can be learned through independent cognitive mechanisms. If it does not, it is not adequate to the facts of a recursively rich linguistic system.

Consider the implications of the fact that language is recursive. For example, there is no principled limit on the number of relative clauses and other elaborations on an initial noun. Such elaborations intervene between the noun and the verb it agrees with.

(50) a. The evidence has proved my innocence.
     b. The evidence in the box has proved my innocence.
     c. The evidence in the box surrounded by armed guards has proved my innocence.
     d. The evidence in the box surrounded by solemn armed guards in bright uniforms has proved my innocence.

None of the preceding sentences is particularly difficult to comprehend. Even if one limited such material to ten words, the number of different constructions would be enormous. Intuitively, the reason is that the first noun phrase is treated as the head of a phrase, which includes all of the intervening material up to the verb. But accessing the abstract notion of noun phrase (and computing the correct structure and import of the intervening material) is tantamount to utilizing syntactic structure. Technically, the competition model could propose that the only aspects of syntax involved in language learning and comprehension are just those that make reliable and salient cues available enough for the language to be usable. Thus, the model might presuppose a "syntax," but not one with a derivational history for sentences, empty categories, and so on. Of course, such a syntax would be held accountable for the same kind of other behavioral facts about language, such as native speakers' intuitions. It does not seem likely that the competition model has hit on just the right scheme, where other theories have failed. However, if it did, or does, it will be a significant achievement to show that apparent syntactic structures really are functionally determined by the needs of acquisition and processing by a general-purpose learner and perceptual system.

For the moment, however, we see the usual difficulty. If a syntax is presupposed, it is clear what the cues are valid for, and the model makes sense. If syntax is not presupposed, the model has no framework to specify potential cues or to determine the significance of their validity.

4.3.4 Constraint Satisfaction

With the fundamental tools of connectionism—simple processing units whose strength of association to each other can vary over time—it should be possible to model the effects of various syntactic and semantic properties in the initial interpretation of a sentence. This section reports several attempts to model the use of associative information at the earliest points of sentence comprehension. MacDonald, Pearlmutter, and Seidenberg (1994:682) propose a lexical model of processing that indeed presupposes all the syntactic information of the kind proposed in a current generative grammar: "Both lexical and syntactic ambiguity are governed by the same types of knowledge representations and processing mechanisms." They resurrect Chomsky's (1957, 1965) traditional distinction between competence and performance and argue that performance is completely determined by local lexical knowledge, while the actual representations that build up can be abstract and rich. The main goal of their proposal is to show that even so-called "syntactic" ambiguities are actually resolved on the basis of local lexical knowledge (following Ford, Bresnan, and Kaplan 1982). For example, in (51)

(51) The witness examined by the lawyer was lying.

the garden-path ambiguity is resolved as a function of the lexical categorization of *examined*, either as a simple past or as a past participle. The garden path itself is created by the initial illusion that *examined* is the simple past, supported by the relative frequency that *examined* has been experienced as a simple past, as well as the likelihood that *witness* is an agent because of its animacy, and other factors. Thus, the constraint-based lexicalist model should contrast with models that build syntactic structure by directly accessing sentence-level grammatical information. It also should contrast with those probabilistic models that use category patterns that extend across lexical items. It is not clear that the theory successfully contrasts with either.

Their method is first to demonstrate that "syntactic"-level ambiguities have behavioral properties similar to lexical ambiguities. They are both sensitive to context information and frequency information with similar parameters. At both levels, there is an intrinsic "base" probability of a particular meaning and structure. Context influences the processing most when the "base" probabilities are low and relatively equal. This eclectic array of information can include access to adjacent [prior] words.

MacDonald, Pearlmutter, and Seidenberg (1994) illustrate the formation of syntactic structure from lexical information with the sequence in (52)

(52) John cooked.

As shown in figure 4.7. MacDonald, Pearlmutter, and Seidenberg (1994) assume a distributed representation of lexical information, so that a lexical item is "activated" when the nodes that correspond to its properties are activated. Reading the word *John* activates the semantic features associated with *John*, including the fact that *John* is animate, human, male, and so on. It also activates the lexical category information associated with *John*, including the fact that *John* is a noun and by X-bar theory *John* appears in a noun phrase. The various thematic roles in which *John* can appear are activated, and since it is animate, the agent role is strongly activated. Other factors, such as how frequently *John* appears in different roles, discourse constraints, and so on, will influence the activation of the thematic role. When *cooked* is read, information about its meaning, lexical category, voice, argument structures, and X-bar structures is activated. In each case, the level of activation of alternative interpretations is related to their frequency of use. If we assume that *cooked* most frequently appears with an ⟨agent, theme⟩ argument structure, the corresponding X-bar structure, providing syntactic slots for an agent and a theme, will be activated most strongly. When the most strongly activated X-bar structures for *John* and *cooked* correspond, as in this case, they are linked, and *John* is assigned the agent role, with the theme role needing to be filled. This example illustrates how syntactic structure emerges from lexical information.

The model developed by MacDonald and colleagues explicitly presupposes all necessary syntactic information, thereby relegating the explanation of the syntactic representations to the problem of language acquisition. This is fair enough, given the goal of accounting for details of reading comprehension. If the connectionist approach is to be a general theory of language behavior, it should provide an associative-connectionist model of acquisition that will arrive at the kinds of syntactic knowledge the reading model presupposes to be available. It should also provide a general solution to the grain problem: Which kinds of syntactic and semantic information are reinforced on each comprehension event? Attempts to solve these problems are being made, but results are not yet available (Seidenberg 1997).

The last half decade has seen the development and implementation of a number of specific, working connectionist models using the ideas of constraint satisfaction in a number of important papers. Much of this work is due to Tanenhaus and his colleagues. The remainder of this section is devoted to reviewing some of these working models. We emphasize here the models, some of their features, their uses, and what they can do. We reserve for chapter 7 discussion of the evidence from human comprehension that they have modeled.

Learning Subcategorization and Frequency Information   Connectionist models should be sensitive to statistical properties of text. Juliano and Tanenhaus (1994) constructed a connectionist model to illustrate how both verb subcategorization

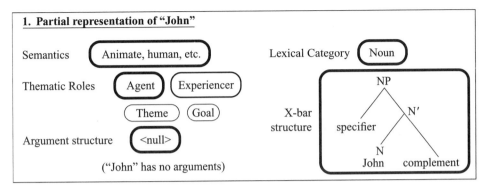

1. Partial representation of "John"

Semantics — Animate, human, etc.   Lexical Category — Noun

Thematic Roles — Agent   Experiencer

Theme   Goal   X-bar structure

Argument structure — <null>

("John" has no arguments)

NP
specifier   N'
N
John   complement

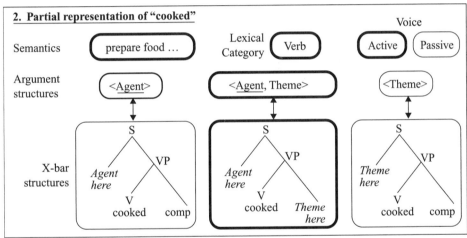

2. Partial representation of "cooked"

Voice

Semantics — prepare food ...   Lexical Category — Verb   Active   Passive

Argument structures — <Agent>   <Agent, Theme>   <Theme>

X-bar structures

S
Agent here   VP
V
cooked   comp

S
Agent here   VP
V
cooked   Theme here

S
Theme here   VP
V
cooked   comp

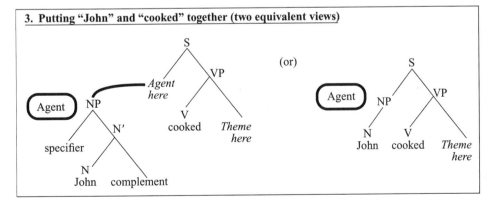

3. Putting "John" and "cooked" together (two equivalent views)

S
Agent here   VP
V   cooked   Theme here
Agent   NP   N'
specifier
N
John   complement

(or)

S
Agent   NP   VP
N   V   Theme here
John   cooked

Figure 4.7
Representations in the processing of *John cooked* (reprinted with permission from Mac-Donald, Pearlmutter, and Seidenberg 1994, fig. 3). Partial representations of lexical information appear for individual words in parts 1 and 2. Part 3 combines possible combinations of these lexical representations into a tree structure.

information and verb frequency influence reading times in sentences like (53a) and (53b).

(53) a. The student read the book was stolen.
     b. The student implied the book was stolen.

Earlier studies (Juliano and Tanenhaus 1994; Trueswell, Tanenhaus, and Kello 1993) showed that verb frequency influences reading time. For example, reading times for *the* following the verb decreases as the frequency of use of verbs that require a sentential complement increases (*hinted, implied, thought, realized*; *hinted* and *implied* are low frequency, *thought* and *realized* are high frequency). But for verbs that require an NP complement, verb frequency has little effect on reading times for the word after the verb (*invited* is low frequency; *studied* and *gave* are high frequency).

Juliano and Tanenhaus (1994) presented sentences to a simple recurrent network in a word-prediction task. The network had 214 input units, 8 hidden units, and 8 output units. The input units consisted of 156 units for each of 156 verbs, 50 units for each word than could follow the verb, and 8 units that stored the latest activation of the hidden units. The sentences were from the Brown Corpus and the *Wall Street Journal* Corpus. Training involved presenting a verb and then using back-propagation to train the network to produce the appropriate type of phrase. The network received 13,051 training trials.

The network learned. For NP only verbs (*invited, studied, gave*), the model most often predicted a noun phrase. For S-bias verbs, the model most often predicted a sentential complement.

Immediate vs. Delayed Use of Meaning   Connectionism can be used to construct detailed models of alternative theories of sentence comprehension. McRae, Spivey-Knowlton, and Tanenhaus (1998) examined the role of thematic fit between the initial noun and the initial verb in processing sentences with reduced relative clauses. In their studies, the initial noun was always animate, but in some cases, the initial noun was rated as a good agent for the verb, and in other cases a good patient.

(54) *Good agent*
     a. The cop arrested by the detective was guilty of taking bribes.

     Good patient
     b. The crook arrested by the detective was guilty of taking bribes.

Agent/patient-hood was determined by asking subjects to rate how likely is it for a cop/crook to arrest someone.

McRae and colleagues (1998) conducted two-word self-paced reading studies, and they constructed models to simulate immediate versus delayed use of thematic fit. The constraint-based model incorporated various constraints as soon as they became available:

1. Thematic fit on reading the initial verb
2. Relative frequency of the verb as past tense versus passive participle on reading the initial verb
3. The preposition *by*, which is a strong cue for a reduced relative on reading the verb + by frame (80% vs. 20%)
4. The relative frequency of main clauses versus reduced relatives on reading the initial verb (92% vs. 8%)
5. Thematic fit between the second noun and the initial verb on reading the second noun
6. The main verb, which is a definitive cue for a reduced relative on reading the main verb

The two-stage model applied the main-clause bias immediately, and the remaining constraints were applied one or two words after they conceivably could become available.

The two models were compared against actual human reading-time data. Mean reduction effects for humans closely followed the predictions of the constraint-based model and diverged from the predictions of the two-stage model. The human data showed that reduction effects were larger on verb + *by* for good patients than for good agents; there was a reversal on the second NP, and on the main verb there was a large reduction effect for good agents and no reduction effect for good patients.

The Normalized Recurrence Algorithm   Connectionism can be used to develop sophisticated quantitative models of feedback. Spivey and Tanenhaus (1998) used connectionist modeling to reproduce conflicting results of studies of reading sentences with reduced relatives. For example, they found that discourse context eliminated the processing difficulty of reduced relatives, while Murrary and Liversedge (1994) did not. We review these and related results in chapter 7. For the moment, we consider the details of how their connectionist model of sentence processing works. (Readers familiar with connectionist methods for modifying associative strength may wish to move on to the following section on hybrid models.)

Spivey and Tanenhaus (1998) assumed for convenience a localist representation of various constraints and interpretations. That is, each of several constraints was represented by one node, and each of the alternative interpretations of a syntactically ambiguous sequence was represented by one node. The model was used to predict the reading times for the ambiguous verb (*selected*) in sentences like (55).

(55) The actress selected by the director believed that her performance was perfect.

At the point of reading *selected* two interpretations are possible. *Selected* may be interpreted as a past-tense verb and function as the main verb in the sentence, or it may be interpreted as a passive participle and function as the verb in a reduced relative clause. Several constraints bias the reader toward one or the other of these interpretations.

The model determines a provisional interpretation based on the strengths of each of the constraints. The model uses an algorithm called *normalized recurrence* to modify the activation of the constraint nodes, and then recomputes the activation of the provisional interpretation nodes. The model continues this cycle—compute activation of provisional interpretations, compute feedback, normalize—until a criterion is reached that stops the model. The interpretation node with the greatest activity at that point is the interpretation that is accepted. The number of cycles that the model goes through until it reaches criterion is by hypothesis related to difficulty in reading.

The diagrams in figure 4.8 illustrate this model. Figure 4.8 shows that four constraints influence the activity of the two interpretation nodes. First, there is the frequency with which *selected* has been experienced as a past-tense verb versus a passive participle. For the sake of illustration, suppose that analysis of a corpus showed that 40 percent of the uses of *selected* in the corpus were the past tense, and 60 percent were the passive participle. The initial activation of the nodes for the past tense and the passive participle will be .40 and .60 respectively (see figure 48a).

A second constraint is the bias toward interpreting an initial noun phrase + verb sequence as a main clause versus a reduced relative. Suppose a corpus shows that 85 percent of sentence-initial sequences of noun phrase + verb are main clauses and 15 percent are reduced relatives. The initial activation of the nodes for the main clause bias will be .85 for the main clause and .15 for the reduced relative (see figure 4.8a).

Third, discourse information influences the interpretation. Discourse may bias the interpretation of the ambiguous verb toward a past tense in an active-voice main clause, or toward a passive participle in a passive-voice reduced relative clause. In this case, if there are two actresses mentioned in the preceding discourse, a reduced relative clause may be expected in order to identify which of the two actresses is being referred to (see chapter 7 for more details). Suppose that a pretest showed that subjects who read the discourse and the initial noun phrase + verb sequence in the target sentence completed the sentence as a main clause in 33 percent of the trials, and as a reduced relative clause in 67 percent of the trials. This sets the initial activation of the discourse nodes to .33 for the main clause interpretation and .67 for the reduced relative interpretation (see figure 4.8a).

The last constraint that Spivey and Tanenhaus (1998) considered was parafoveal information from the word *by*. They assumed that in this eye-movement study, subjects obtained information from the word *by* when their eyes were focused on *selected*. Suppose that analysis of a corpus reveals that *by* following a verb ending in -*ed* introduces the agent in 85 percent of the cases, and it introduces some other

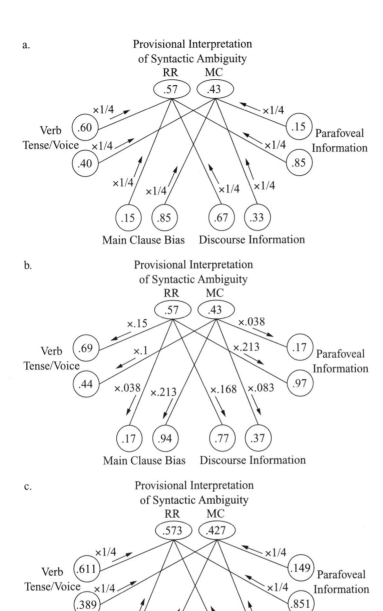

Figure 4.8
Spivey and Tanenhaus's normalized recurrence algorithm (reprinted with permission from Spivey and Tanenhaus 1998:1535, fig. 5). Part A shows how the initial activation of the reduced relative (RR) and main clause interpretations are the weighted activations of the four constraints. Part B shows that each weighted constraint is multiplied by the activation of the provisional interpretations. Part C shows the renormalization of the constraints to sum to 1.

construction, such as a locative phrase, in 15 percent of the cases. The initial activation of the parafoveal nodes will be .15 for the main clause and .85 for the reduced relative (see figure 4.8a).

Spivey and Tanenhaus assume that there are separate nodes that provisionally represent each of the two interpretations, main clause versus reduced relative. These provisional interpretations accept input from each of the four corresponding constraint nodes that support the interpretation. Because there are four constraints on each interpretation, Spivey and Tanenhaus assume that the weights on the connections between a constraint node and a provisional interpretation node are .25.

The initial activity of the provisional interpretation nodes is obtained by multiplying the weights by the initial activity of each of the constraint nodes. For example, for the reduced relative interpretation, the initial activation level is

.25[passive participle + (NP + V as reduced relative) + discourse bias toward reduced relative + *by*-bias toward passive]

.25[.60 + .15 + .67 + .85] = 0.57

as shown in figure 4.8a. For the main-clause interpretation, the initial activation is

.25[past tense + (NP + V as main clause) + discourse bias toward main clause + *by*-bias toward main clause], or

.25[.40 + .85 + .33 + .15] = 0.43

Once the initial values of the provisional interpretation nodes are determined, feedback to the constraint nodes is computed. That is, the activity of each constraint node changes to reflect the contributions of the other constraints. For example, a particular constraint node of the reduced relative interpretation (e.g., passive participle) will increase its activity level if all other constraint nodes support the reduced relative interpretation. A constraint node that supports the reduced relative interpretation will decrease its activity if all other constraint nodes support the main-clause interpretation. The amount of change in the activity of a constraint node is determined by multiplying the activity of the corresponding provisional interpretation by a weight. The weight is determined by multiplying the initial activity of the constraint by the initial weight on the connection between the constraint node and the provisional interpretation node. For example, the feedback weight for the passive-participle node is

(initial activity of constraint node) × (initial connection weight) = feedback weight

.60 × .25 = .15

as shown in figure 4.8b. The feedback weight for the past-tense node is

.40 × .25 = .10

Computing the new activity levels of the constraint nodes involves two phases. The first phase determines the amount of change in activity. The second phase normalizes this activity so that the activity levels of the two nodes for a particular kind of constraint add up to 1.0. In the first phase of feedback, the new activity level of each constraint node is determined by

[(feedback weight) × (activity of provisional node)]
+ (initial activity of constraint node)

Thus, the first phase feedback activation of the passive-participle node and the past-tense node are

$$[(.15) \times (.57)] + .60 = .69$$
$$[(.10) \times (.43)] + .40 = .44$$

as shown in figure 4.8b. Since these activation levels add to more than 1.0, the second-phase activation levels normalize the activation levels to 1.0. Normalizing the activation of the passive-participle and past-tense nodes involves the following computation:

$$(.69)/(.69 + .44) = .611$$
$$(.44)/(.69 + .44) = .389$$

as shown in figure 4.8c. These values add to 1.0, and they represent the activation of the constraints from verb-frequency information in the second cycle.

The procedure repeats so that new values of activation of the provisional nodes are computed, using the new activation levels of the constraint nodes and the weights on the forward connections. For example, the new activation levels of the reduced relative and main-clause nodes are

$$.25(.611 + .153 + .675 + .851) = .573$$
$$.25(.389 + .847 + .325 + .149) = .427$$

as shown in figure 4.8c. The activation of the reduced relative node has increased from .57 to .573, while that of the main-clause node has decreased from .43 to .427. These changes reflect the fact that three out of the four kinds of the constraints initially favored the reduced relative interpretation.

Intuitively, this interactive process captures the notion that ultimately, the winning analysis overtakes all the constraints. Furthermore, the less ambiguous or conflicted the initial analysis, the fewer cycles needed to arrive at a final interpretation. Spivey and Tanenhaus (1998) showed that this model with local representations and the normalized recurrence algorithm provided a good match with human reading-time data. In particular, the number of cycles that the model needed to reach criterion on a particular word was related to the amount of time that human participants spent reading the word. The model also matched the conflicting results from three studies

(Spivey and Tanenhaus 1998; Spivey-Knowlton, Trueswell, and Tanenhaus 1993; Murray and Liversedge 1994) when differences in materials were used to set the initial activity levels of specific constraints in different ways. Another factor that influenced the model's ability to duplicate the conflicting results was its use of differences in procedures, such as eye movement versus self-paced reading. For example, parafoveal information from *by* becomes available earlier in an eye-movement study than in a word-by-word self-paced reading study. The computations of this model are simple, yet when several potential constraints are included, its performance is impressive.

Arguments for Explicit Quantitative Models   Deciding between competing theories of sentence comprehension requires explicit quantitative models that quantify sources of constraint and specify explicit mechanisms for relating information integration to processing time. Tanenhaus, Spivey-Knowlton and Hanna (2000) illustrate the difficulties of discriminating between alternative theories with examples like:

(56) *Hard*
   a. The horse raced past the barn fell.
   b. Sally warned the lawyer was greedy.

(57) *Easy*
   a. The land mine buried in the sand exploded.
   b. Sally said the lawyer was greedy.

The difficulties that people have in understanding the hard sentences seem to support a two-stage model like the garden-path theory (e.g., Frazier 1987a). The garden path that occurs as a result of the hard sentences suggests that comprehenders assign a structure based solely on syntactic-category information in order to reduce short-term memory load. Only after initial structural assignment does the sentence-processing system use lexical properties of words such as meaning and subcategorization information to revise the initial structural assignment. However, the relative ease of understanding the structurally identical sentences in the easy group suggests that information other than syntactic-category information, such as the subcategorization information of verbs, is used to determine the initial assignment of structure. In the absence of explicit quantitative models, it is a simple matter for advocates of two-stage models to dismiss the experimental evidence from the easy sentences by claiming that the experimental measures do not tap the earliest phase of comprehension, but instead tap the revision stage.

To advance our understanding of sentence-comprehension mechanisms, it is essential that we develop explicit theories that make predictions that can be proved false. Tanenhaus and colleagues demonstrate how detailed constraint-based models lead to simulations of human sentence processing. The results of human experiments on particular sentence materials are compared with the results of computer simulations that use identical materials. To the extent that the two sets of human and model results match up, the model is supported as an explanation of human sentence comprehension.

Tanenhaus et al. (forthcoming) review experiments and simulations on the processing of sentences with reduced relative clauses:

(58) a. The witness examined by the lawyer turned out to be unreliable.
    b. The evidence examined by the lawyer turned out to be unreliable.

They identify the constraints that may operate to determine the initial structural assignment of *examined*:

1. Goodness of fit of the initial NP (*witness* vs. *evidence*) as agent or patient of the initial verb (*examined*)
2. Relative frequency of initial main clauses in English
3. Relative frequency of the initial verb (*examined*) as past tense versus passive participle
4. Relative frequency that the immediately following word (*by*) is used in an active (e.g., locative phrase) versus reduced relative construction
5. Lexical information provided by the second NP (*lawyer*)—for example, whether it is a good agent or patient of the initial verb
6. Bias from the main verb (*turned out*)
7. Whether the discourse context supports a reduced relative interpretation by mentioning two possible referents for the initial NP
8. Whether the discourse context supports a locative interpretation of the *by*-phrase in the target sentence

Tanenhaus et al. show how a constraint-based model that uses information as soon as it becomes available can mimic the results of human experiments. The model uses recurrent feedback and normalization to resolve ambiguities. The relative support that a constraint provides for a particular interpretation is related to the weight of the corresponding node. The activation of a provisional interpretation is calculated by determining the sum of its supporting constraint. The model calculates the activation of each provisional interpretation repeatedly until it settles on one interpretation. The length of time that the model requires to settle into a provisional interpretation is taken to indicate processing difficulty. The model generated results similar to those of a variety of experiments that investigated the constraints listed above (Ferreira and Clifton 1986; Hanna, Barker, and Tanenhaus 1995; Liversedge, Pickering, and Branigan 1995; Spivey-Knowlton, Trueswell, and Tanenhaus 1993; McRae, Spivey-Knowlton, and Tanenhaus 1998).

4.3.5 Dynamic Systems

Dynamic systems were developed to describe complex physical systems such as the weather or planetary systems. At any given moment, a dynamic system may be in any one of a number of states. The dynamic-systems approach uses a set of equations with several variables to describe how the system changes over time.

Tabor, Juliano, and Tanenhaus (1997) used the metaphor of dynamic systems to shed light on sentence comprehension. At any given moment, there is a preferred structural assignment for a sentence. To use the dynamic-systems metaphor, the possible structural assignments are arranged in a "representational space" that is organized according to similarity. As a sentence is heard, the system "gravitates" to a particular structural assignment, or "attractor" in the metric space. At any given moment, a number of variables influences which structural assignment or attractor is most strongly preferred. These variables include the relative frequency of a word in a particular syntactic category, the local context within the sentence, semantic information about words, discourse context, and so on. In cases of ambiguity, there is no strongly preferred assignment. That is, during temporary ambiguities, the processor is between two or more attractors. Additional information may lead the processor to move toward a particular attractor, just as a spaceship may be between planets, but some force moves the ship toward a particular planet.

Tabor, Juliano, and Tanenhaus (1997) use the sentence fragment *the insect examined ...* to illustrate the dynamic-systems metaphor for sentence comprehension. On receiving the three words in this fragment, the processor is between two attractors. For example, *examined* may have the structural role of the past tense of the main verb of the sentence, with *insect* as its subject, or it may have the role of a passive participle in a reduced relative clause. Factors that influence which of these attractors the processor is closer to include how frequently main clauses versus center-embedded reduced relatives are used, how frequently *examined* is used as a past tense versus a passive participle, and how likely it is that an insect examines something. For example, an insect may be more likely to be the object of the action *examine*, and so the processor initially may be closer to the reduced relative attractor than to the main-clause attractor. If the fragment contained a different noun that is more likely to examine something, such as *entomologist*, the processor initially might be closer to the main-clause attractor.

The researchers examined the usefulness of the dynamic-systems metaphor by conducting experiments on the processing of the word *that*, which is ambiguous between a demonstrative determiner and a complementizer, among other possibilities.

(59) *Demonstrative determiner*
    a. That cheap hotel was clean and comfortable to our surprise.
    b. The lawyer insisted that cheap hotel was clean and comfortable.

(60) *Complementizer*
  a. That cheap hotels were clean and comfortable surprised us.
  b. The lawyer insisted that cheap hotels were clean and comfortable.

Number information on the noun disambiguates *that*: if the noun is singular (*hotel*), *that* is a demonstrative determiner, but if it is plural (*hotels*), *that* is a complementizer.

Overall, *that* is used more often as a complementizer (70%) than as a demonstrative determiner (15%). However, when *that* appears at the beginning of a sentence, it is used more often as a demonstrative determiner (35%) than as a complementizer (11%). The relative usage of *that* reverses when it appears after the verb: the complementizer usage is more frequent than the determiner usage (93% vs. 6%).

Another factor that may influence the initial position of the processor in the representational space is the subcategorization requirements of the verb when *that* follows. For example, *insisted* is biased toward taking a sentential complement rather than an NP object complement, whereas *visited* is biased toward an NP object complement. Tabor et al. showed that these factors influence self-paced reading times after the disambiguating noun. They even found that reading times increased on the word *the* after verbs that require a sentential complement, suggesting that the NP object attractor exerted an influence on processing.

Tabor and Tanenhaus (1999) extend the dynamic model of Tabor, Juliano, and Tanenhaus to account for semantic effects in processing reduced relatives. They argue that syntactic structures arise as "emergent properties" of connectionist models, and that the dynamic models, which they call the *Visitation Set Gravitation* (VSG) model, demonstrate this. Thus, connectionist models induce syntactic categories from mere exposure to sentences. The VSG transforms the output of the simple recurrent network (SRN) into hypotheses about the structure of a sentence that is being parsed. The fact that the VSG model can identify the possible syntactic structures of a sentence is an advance over models that relied on a syntactically informed "oracle" to define error measures.

The VSG model can be described in terms of a representation set, metric space, attractors, starting points, trajectories, and basins of attraction. The representation set is the set of all representations that can be formed during the parse of a sentence. The metric space is the set in which distances between elements are defined; the metric space arranges states or representations according to similarity. A starting point is the position in metric space that is occupied when a word in the sentence is has been received. A trajectory is a path that the system follows over time. An attractor is a stable state that attracts trajectories that are nearby. A basin of attraction is the set of starting points that lead to a particular stable state. The change in the state of the system is described by a differential equation.

The VSG model works with a simple recurrent network that has input units, hidden units, and output units. There are recurrent connections in the hidden layer.

This SRN was trained to predict the next word of sentences. When its predictions became accurate, its weights became fixed and it was tested on new sentences. As the SRN was tested, the values of the hidden units were recorded. These values constitute the visitation set. As each word was presented, the corresponding hidden-unit states were recorded and defined as the visitation set. The hidden-unit states for each word of the sentence defined the starting points. The VSG system then changed according to its differential equation, and the system gravitated toward an attractor. The amount of time that the system took to approach an attractor was taken to correspond to human processing time.

Tabor and Tanenhaus (1999) use the VSG model to examine the distinction between semantic oddness and syntactic incongruity. The model uses both kinds of information immediately, but they have different consequences, which can be characterized as a "graded qualitative difference." The VSG model responded to syntactic violations by continuing its trajectory between attractors, whereas a semantic violation involved direct gravitation toward an attractor.

Taken together, the word of Tanenhaus and colleagues is the most impressive and empiriclly tested set of connectionist models for comprehension, at least defined as the problem of choosing between competing available analyses. The usual critical issues remain.

1. Does the model scale well, when advanced to deal with more than reduced relative sentences?
2. Does the model solve the grain problem? In particular, how is the "density" of the attractor space in Tabor and Tanenhaus constrained to form attractors that correspond to (and thereby "explain") syntactic categories?
3. Does the attractor space really replace grammatical structures and categories, and, as, in the other models we have discussed, does it "find" their behavioral doppelgängers, given that they are exposed already in the linguistic environment?

We do not wish to prejudge what can be. At the moment, the answer to each question may be negative, and seems so to us. But the inventiveness of the scheme, along with explicit recognition of the three problems, means we can also choose to be cautiously optimistic.

4.3.6 Hybrid Models

There have been recent attempts to integrate structural and associative approaches. In the models we review in this section structural information plays a central role in comprehension. This differs from the dynamic systems of the previous section, in which structure-like information allegedly emerges from the normal operation of a connectionist model.

Competitive Attachment The competitive-attachment model (Stevenson 1994) is a connectionist model that explicitly incorporates symbolic information from linguistic theory. The syntactic nodes proposed by government and binding theory are represented as processing units in a connectionist network. Figure 4.9 illustrates the processing network and the phrase structure tree for (61),

(61) The warden believes the report.

In this model each word activates the phrase structure properties that are associated with that word and potential attachments, including those that attach the word to the existing phrase structure network. For example, *believe* activates the categories V, V′, and VP, along with information about case, potential theta roles, and potential categories to be selected (e.g., object NP or sentential complement). Once attachment occurs, the activation of existing processing units is updated, and symbolic features are passed through the network. This processing continues until every processing unit in the network reaches a stable state. This stable state is either some minimum level of activation, or zero. When the activation level of an attachment node reaches zero, the node is disconnected from the phrase structure network. All possible attachments in a syntactic ambiguity are active to varying degrees until there is sufficient information to take the activation level of a potential attachment to zero. For example, receiving the word *will* after *report* establishes an attachment between the verb and a new inflection phrase, and takes the activation level of the connection between the verb and the noun phrase *the report* to zero.

Stevenson assumes that processing nodes gradually decay over time. This assumption provides several attractive properties. It allows the model to account for attachment preferences and filler-gap assignment without relying on strategies. For instance, the decay assumption explains why there is a preference for attaching *on the train* to *sleeping* rather than *saw* in the following:

(62) I saw the child who was sleeping on the train.

Since *sleeping* was attached more recently than *saw*, *sleeping* has higher activation and can compete more effectively for the phrase *on the train*. The decay assumption also provides an explanation for why attachment difficulty varies over a range of distances. For example, attachment becomes increasing harder in the order (63a), (63b), and (63c).

(63) a. I called the guy a rotten driver.
 b. I called the guy who smashed my car a rotten driver.
 c. I called the guy who smashed my brand new car a rotten driver.

The decay assumption also explains filler-gap preferences without relying on strategies. In processing a sentence like (64)

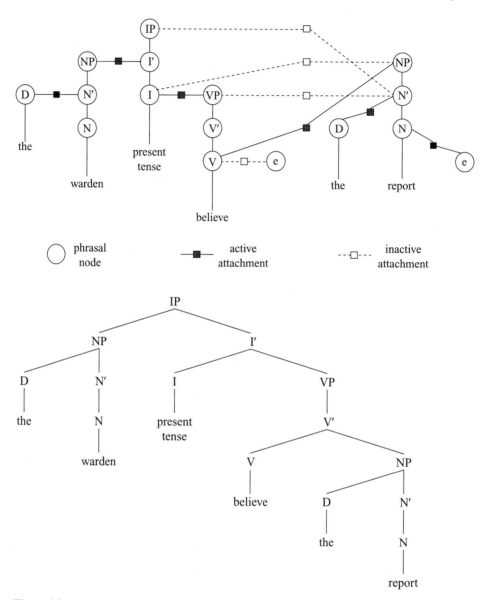

Figure 4.9
Stevenson's Competitive Attachment Model (adapted from Stevenson 1994:300, fig. 3.). Part (a) shows the network when *the report* has been attached. Part (b) shows the phrase structure tree that the network represents.

(64) a. Who did Maya kiss?

    b. Who did Sara say that Maya kissed?

the word *who* establishes a binding node that is initially unfilled. When *kiss* is received, it establishes a binding node and sends its features throughout the network, establishing the binding relationship between *who* and *kiss*. The same process operates in a sentence like (64b). The difference between (64a) and (64b) is that this one establishes a chain that links the gap after *kissed* to a binding node that is linked to a gap after *say*, which is linked to a binding node that is linked to the filler *who*.

To summarize, the competitive-attachment model is an integration of a connectionist architecture and symbolic properties of language. It provides explanations of attachment and filler-gap preferences with a single mechanism. There is no need for strategies to explain these preferences.

Structure Frequency Jurafsky (1996) presents a model of sentence comprehension that relies on frequency of occurrence of possible structures. The model entertains multiple structures in parallel, and ranks them according to their prior probability of use. Structures that have very low probability are pruned—that is, no longer considered.

Jurafsky uses probabilities to establish the relative rankings of two linguistic properties: particular constituent structures, such as a noun phrase consisting of a determine and a noun, and particular arguments for a predicate. For example, the obligatory arguments for a predicate have a probability of 1.0 of being filled, while the probability of optional arguments being filled can range from 0.0 to 1.0. The probabilities are conditioned on lexical, syntactic, and semantic information.

A "beam search" algorithm is used to determine which structures are pruned. *Beam search* means that structures that fall within a certain percentage of the highest-ranked structure are retained, while those outside that percentage are dropped. Since a garden-path sentence occurs because the appropriate structure has been pruned, this sentence sets the highest value of beam width. A sentence in which two structures are entertained sets the lowest value of beam width. Jurafsky estimated the beam width to be between 3.8 and 5.6—that is, when a structure is 4–5 times more likely than another, both are retained.

The way the parser works can be illustrated with the following garden-path sentence:

(65) The complex houses married and single students and their families.

The initial interpretation is that *complex* is an adjective modifying *house*, but the correct interpretation is that *complex* is a noun and *houses* is the verb. Probabilities account for the garden path. The accompanying table shows the probability of the application of various rules for the two structures.

Adjective-Noun		*Noun-Verb*	
S → NP ...	[.92]	S → [NP[V ...	[.48]
NP → Det Adj N ...	[.28]	NP → Det N ...	[.63]
N → ROOT *s*	[.23]	N → *complex*	[.000029]
N → *house*	[.0024]	V → *house*	[.0006]
Adj → *complex*	[.00086]	V → ROOT *s*	[.086]

Since the nonlexical nodes do not differ much, Jurafsky omits them for simplicity in calculating the conditional probabilities of the two structures. The probabilities of the two structures are:

Adj-N: $.0024 \times .00086 \times .23 = 4.7 \times 10^{-7}$
N-V: $.0006 \times .000029 \times .086 = 1.4 \times 10^{-9}$

Combining these probabilities indicates that the adjective-noun structure is 267 times more likely than the noun-verb interpretation, much greater than the beam width. Thus, the less probable noun-verb interpretation is (incorrectly) pruned, and we experience a garden-path effect.

In other cases, two alternative structures that are similar in conditional probability are retained. The structure of the following sentence is similar to that of the preceding example:

(66) The warehouse fires a dozen employees each year.

However, there is little garden-path effect (Frazier and Rayner 1987). The probabilities of the two structures are:

NN: 4.2×10^{-5}
NV: 1.1×10^{-5}

Since the ratio of these probabilities is within the beam width (3.8), both interpretations are retained, and there is no garden-path effect.

4.4   Grains of Truth

This chapter has reviewed a wide range of approaches to sentence comprehension in contemporary psycholinguistics. Despite the diversity of approaches, there are some major themes and important insights that each approach contributes. We now summarize the themes and insights of contemporary approaches to sentence processing.

4.4.1   Statistical Models
Statistical models attempt to explain comprehension in terms of cues to meaning. Cues that are highly correlated with a particular meaning have high "cue validity."

Examples of models of sentence recognition that are based on cues with high validity are Tabor, Juliano, and Tanenhaus 1997, MacDonald, Pearlmutter, and Seidenberg 1994, and the earlier work of Bates and MacWhinney (1982), Bever (1970a), and Osgood (1963). The more recent models have developed impressive quantitative methods for weighting different kinds of statistically valid cues. These cues include knowledge of the likelihood of real-world events, such as the fact that dogs bite people more often than the reverse. They include knowledge of how frequently particular subcategorization frames are used—for example, that *believe* is used more often intransitively whereas *charge* is used more often transitively, as in

(67) a. The police believed the thief picked the lock.
     b. The police charged the thief with burglary.

And they include knowledge of the frequency of use of sentence patterns or templates, such as the fact that a sequence of noun-verb-noun more often corresponds to agent-action-patient than to patient-action-agent. The probabilistic models that we reviewed showed that the comprehension system relies a great deal on statistical information.

As impressive as the probabilistic models are, though, statistical information cannot tell the whole story about comprehension. There are two senses in which statistical information falls short of a complete account of comprehension. First, statistical templates sometimes yield the incorrect meaning. For example, the simple strategy of interpreting a sequence of noun-verb-(noun) as agent-action-(patient) fails in five out of fourteen cases in the previous paragraph:

(68) a. ... that are based on cues ...
     b. ... frames are used ...
     c. ... *believe* is used ...
     d. ... *charge* is used ...
     e. ... that we reviewed ...

In each of these examples, the first noun is the patient, not the agent. By their very nature, statistical templates are guaranteed to give the incorrect meaning some of the time.

The second sense in which statistical templates fall short is that, even when they do provide the correct meaning, they do not provide a complete description of the structure of sentences. For example, in sentence (69),

(69) Several recent models have tried to integrate statistical information with comprehension.

the NVN template assigns the word *models* to the role of agent and the word *information* to the role of patient. These assignments are approximately correct, but the statistical template does not reveal that *to integrate statistical information with comprehension* is actually the object of *tried*. Nor does it describe the structure of the complex verb *have tried*, and so on. These structural details may not be necessary for a rough approximation to meaning, but they may be and can be part of the final representation of the sentence.

Statistical information provides, at best, a partial description of a sentence. Even when the most common template applies successfully, it does not provide all the details of a sentence. From the partial description that statistical information provides, the sentence-comprehension system can arrive at a complete description. The sentence-comprehension system must fill in details, just as the speech-perception system fills in details when a cough occurs at the * in (70a) to (70c) (see Warren and Warren 1970):

(70) a. The *eel was on the table.
     b. The *eel was on the orange.
     c. The *eel was on the axle.

The speech-perception system is able to provide the missing details by referring to a list of possible word patterns that fit the context (*meal, peel, wheel, deal, seal, kneel*, and so on). By referring to this list of possible word patterns, the speech-perception system can complete the rest of the pattern.

The value of this capability of filling in missing information is just as great for sentence recognition as it is for speech recognition. This becomes clear when one considers actual speech in natural settings. It is characteristic of such speech that there is noise at the level of the sentence: false starts, word substitutions, ungrammatical sentences, filled pauses, and so on (Osgood and Maclay 1967).

Pattern completion on the basis of a partial description works in the speech-perception system because the system has access to a list of possible patterns—that is, words. In the case of sentence recognition, the list of possible patterns is much larger: there is no limit to the number of possible sentences. For pattern completion to work in recognizing a sentence there has to be some way to access the list of possible sentence types. We propose that the sentence-comprehension system gains access to possible sentences through the grammar. It is the grammar that informs the comprehension system about the possible objects of perception.

4.4.2   Structural Models

There is a complementary "rock of truth" in contemporary structural models (Berwick and Weinberg 1986; Crocker 1996; Frazier and Clifton 1996; Gibson 1998; Gorrell 1995; Pritchett 1992). A parser that relies solely on knowledge of the grammar and the lexical categories of words (noun, verb, adjective, and so on) can provide much of the description of a sentence. In contrast to the statistical models, a parser equipped with the grammar and lexical categories of words may be able to provide (eventually) a complete description of a sentence. For example, various models that we reviewed in this chapter provide a description as well as a plausible explanation of the data for sentences like the following:

(71) a. The boy was kissed.
   b. The horse raced past the barn fell.
   c. Without her contributions will fail to appear.
   d. Ian knows Thomas is a fool.
   e. After the child sneezed the doctor left.
   f. The reporter who the senator attacked admitted the error.

For a structural model to provide complete description of a sentence, it must have a procedure for determining when it has obtained all possible descriptions of a sentence. It also must have a way of continuing the computation of structure even after it has obtained one analysis for the sentence, since in some cases there is more than one analysis:

(72) a. Flying planes can be dangerous.
   b. The shooting of the cowboys was disgraceful.
   c. The duck is ready to eat.

Contemporary structural models often use nonstructural information to resolve ambiguity, generally after the parser has applied grammatical principles. Depending on the particular theory, this nonstructural information includes just the kinds of information that statistical models rely on: information about word meaning such as animacy, subcategorization information, information about events in the world such as the biting preferences of dogs and people, and information about common sentence patterns.

The various structural models have emphasized several important facts about comprehension: the insufficiency of lexical-category information, the importance of basic argument structure, the parser's ability to project structure, the limitations of processing capacity, and the dependence of reanalysis on degree of commitment to an already-computed analysis. We will consider these facts in turn.

Lexical Category   Structural models agree that structural information by itself is not sufficient to produce a complete description of a sentence. The insufficiency of lexical-category information, for example, is clear in Crocker's model. In this model, a phrase structure module assembles a phrase structure using only lexical-category information. This phrase structure is checked by a thematic module, which has access to subcategorization information. This allows the phrase structure module to correct its initial error in (73).

(73) After the child sneezed the doctor left.

Basic Argument Structure   Several of the structural models emphasize the central role of basic argument structure in comprehension. Frazier and Clifton (1996) ascribe importance to basic argument structure by limiting the principle of minimal attachment to argument positions. Pritchett's (1992) model emphasizes basic argument structure in its attempt to satisfy the theta criterion at every point during processing; every NP must be assigned a theta role, and every predicate must have all its obligatory theta positions filled.

Projection   Several of the models assume that the parser can project information ahead. The nature of the projected information varies from model to model. Frazier and Clifton (1996) assume that the parser projects syntactic categories based on phrase structure rules. For example, the phrase *the boy* ... projects the minimal amount of structure necessary; in this case, the minimal structure is a verb phrase. Similarly, Gorrell (1995) assumes that verbs trigger the precomputation of syntactic categories, as when *what did Ian say* ... projects a noun phrase following *say*.

Processing Capacity   The limit on processing capacity is a driving force behind most structural theories. Gibson's (1998) model relies most clearly on this assumption, in that both noun phrases that have not been assigned to a role and project roles that have not been assigned a noun phrase, have cost-limited processing capacity. In addition, limitations of processing capacity motivate the principle of minimal attachment (Frazier and Clifton 1996).

Degree of Commitment   Most models assume some version of the idea that some kinds of reanalysis are easier than others. The central theme in predicting difficulty of reanalysis is degree of commitment to the analysis. Crocker (1996) makes this assumption most explicit, but it is apparent as well in other models. Gorrell (1995) distinguishes between a reanalysis that changes dominance and precedence relations from one that does not. Pritchett (1992) distinguishes between a reanalysis that involves reassignment to a new governing category from one that keeps an element in the current governing category.

4.5   Conclusion: Implications for an Integrated Model

We can use the grains of truth in contemporary structural models to sketch constraints on the architecture of the comprehension system. The comprehension system uses thematic requirements of verbs to project an argument structure, according to the most frequent use of a verb (as well as semantic information and plausibility).

Consider the process of understanding *He gave the dog a child*. On recognizing *gave* in *He gave* ..., the argument structure of an agent, patient, and a goal is activated. This structure is projected as the information that is needed to complete a syntactic/semantic unit.

(74) a. He gave the dog a bone.
     b. He gave the dog to the child.

On receiving *the dog* in *He gave the dog* ..., the probability of goals versus patients following immediately after *gave*, as in

(75) *Goal after verb*
     a. He gave the dog a bone.

     Patient after verb
     b. He gave the dog to the child.

(as well as plausibility) will influence the initial assignment of *dog* to patient or goal. Receiving enough noun phrases to fill all of the necessary argument roles, in this case either *a bone* or *to the child*, will trigger a process of synthesizing a syntactic representation. This syntactic representation will be compared against the input to check for grammaticality. The comprehension system will fail when the generated syntax does not match the input. For example, having assigned *dog* and *child* the roles of patient and goal respectively, in our example input sentence

(76) a. He gave the dog a child.

the grammar may generate a sequence such as

(76) b. He gave the dog to a child.

When this syntactic representation is compared against the input sentence, a mismatch is detected and the system revises its assignment of noun phrases to argument roles. Instead of *dog* being patient and *child* being goal, the system assigns *dog* the role of goal and *child* the role of patient. The grammar generates the corresponding syntactic representation

(76) a. He gave the dog a child.

which matches the input.

   As the comprehension system takes in the noun phrases to fill the projected argument roles, it must keep track of which noun phrases have been assigned to argument roles. It also must keep track of which roles are filled and which are not. Long or complex noun phrases will make it harder for the comprehension system to keep track of which argument role needs filling. Such a strain on memory capacity apparently motivates Heavy NP shift, such that long noun phrases tend to appear later in a sentence. Because of the increased demands on keeping track of which roles have been filled, the first sentence below is harder than the second:

(77) a. He gave the dog with long sharp teeth and short hair a bone.

b. He gave a bone to the dog with long sharp teeth and short hair.

These facts justify the assumption that keeping track of which argument roles have been filled can cause problems for the comprehension system. It appears that complexity of processing has greater effects on memory load than mere length. Shifting a long noun phrase to the end of a sentence does not greatly affect its difficulty. Thus, the following two sentences do not differ greatly in difficulty:

(78) a. He gave a book, a dog, a sled, and a railroad set to Bill.

b. He gave Bill a book, a dog, a sled, and a railroad set.

When an object noun phrase has a relative clause, however, processing difficulty is affected. Thus, the sentence below is harder than the two above, even though the number of words in the same:

(79) a. He gave a railroad set with an engine that produces real steam to Bill.

Shifting the complex object noun phrase to the end of the sentence makes the sentence easier, as in:

(79) b. He gave to Bill a railroad set with an engine that produces real steam.

These examples suggest that an object noun phrase with a relative clause in difficult because the relative clause triggers its own cycle of comprehension. The relative clause verb activates an argument structure, and the system searches for noun phrases that can fill those argument roles. When noun phrases have been received that can fill those roles, the grammar generates a syntax that is checked against the input to determine whether the input is grammatical based on the system's assignment of noun phrases to argument roles. It is not merely the number of noun phrases that must be assigned, but rather the completion of a semantic unit that strains the processing system. The completion of a semantic unit initiates checking of the generated syntax.

We can summarize the grains of truth of the contemporary models:

• Frequency of use of argument structures and sentence patterns influences the comprehension system's hypothesis about meaning, at least initially.
• Lexical-category information is not sufficient to produce a complete description of a sentence.
• Recognizing a verb allows the comprehension system to project the argument structure needed to complete a semantic unit.
• The grammar defines what is and what is not an acceptable sequence of words.
• It is harder to revise an analysis when the system has become more strongly committed to it.

Notes

1. It is not clear that the phrases in example 8 of (23) are accurately categorized as primary versus nonprimary. For example, Frazier and Clifton (1996) consider "purpose clauses" with a "to VERB ..." sequence as in (8a) to be arguments, and therefore subject to syntactic attachment onto the main verb phrase. They consider "rationale clauses" as in (8b) to be adjuncts, and subject to semantic association. These adverbial phrases, however, fit the usual criteria for adjunct phrases (Quirk et al. 1972):

(i) If an adverbial cannot appear initially in a negative clause, it is an adjunct.
  a. *Quickly* Nixon bought something.
  b. **Quickly* Nixon did not buy something.
  c. *Perhaps* Nixon bought something.
  d. *Perhaps* Nixon did not buy something.
  e. *To amuse us* Nixon bought something.
  f. ?*To amuse us* Nixon did not buy something.

This test suggests that *quickly* and *to amuse us* are adjuncts, *perhaps* is not.

(ii) If an adverbial can be contrasted with another adverbial in an alternative interrogation, it is an adjunct.
  a. Does he write to his parents *because he wants to* or does he write to them because he needs money?
  b. *Does he write to his parents *since he wants to* or does he write to them since he needs money?
  c. Did Nixon buy something *to amuse us* or did he by something to clean out his bank account?

This test suggests that *because he wants to* and *to amuse us* are adjuncts; *since he wants to* is not.

(iii) If an adverbial can be contrasted with another adverbial in an alternative negation, it is an adjunct.
  a. We didn't go to Chicago *on Monday*, but we did go there on Tuesday.
  b. Nixon didn't buy something *to amuse us*, but he did buy something to clean out his bank account.

This test suggests that *on Monday* and *to amuse us* are adjuncts.

2. The initial interpretation in many of these sentences is indeed governed by semantics. This fact becomes clear when we consider how the attachment preferences interact with purely syntactic phenomena. For example, there is no particular difficulty in processing the sentence depending on whether *yellow* modifies *broccoli* or *naked* modifies *John*. There is no preference for high attachment; rather, the parser appears to attach the modifier to the most plausible noun. However, when the sentence is made into a passive, there are clear differences in acceptability:

Secondary Predication, Passivized
(i) a. The broccoli was painted yellow/raw/*naked by John.
  b. The broccoli was painted by John *yellow/*raw/naked.

Serial order becomes important when the words appears in noncanonical order. In this case, the parser seems to follow the strategy of attaching the adjective to the most recent noun phrase. With active sentences, the parser is not constrained that way.

3. The separation of the processors into modules that deal with very specific kinds of information leads to difficulties for the parser. In particular, the phrase structure processor does not have access to subcategorization information. It raises the question of how the parser understands sentences when verbs like *sneeze* do take object-like constructions, as in:

(i) a. When the child sneezed his heart out ...
     b. When the child sneezed the goober into the handkerchief ...
     c. When the child sneezed his last sneeze ...

If the resolution to problem 1 is that the system is sensitive to frequency of particular subcategorizations, we are immediately on the slippery slope into a performance model that Crocker denies. Nonetheless, it would seem likely that if we compiled a list of verbs that can take objects but do so with differential probability, we would also find "graded" degrees of complexity at the garden-path site.

Second, the claim that subcategorization information is not accessed in assigning phrase structure may result in inconsistencies anyway. Consider:

(ii) a. The boy pushed the cat the ball.
     b. The boy pushed the cat to us.

Intuitions suggest that the first sentence above involves a small garden path at *the ball*. That is, intuitively, *the boy pushed the cat* is a complete sentence. But *the cat* has been initially miscategorized as the direct object. The subcategorization information in *pushed* will not resolve the local ambiguity, because *push* does not require an indirect object, and hence the direct-object assignment of *the cat* can end a well-formed sentence. Only when *the ball* is encountered is there information that *the cat* was miscategorized.

So far, Crocker could claim that this is all okay with his theory since the treatment of

(iii) a. The boy pushed the cat the ball.

is like that of

(iii) b. After the child sneezed the doctor ...

Notice, though, that Crocker ought to predict that the *sneeze* sentence is less of a garden path than the *pushed* sentence. This is because the *pushed* sentence cannot be noticed as a small garden path until arriving at the final phrase. The *sneeze* sentence, however, can be corrected right at the next word, based on subcategorization information in *sneeze*. Hence, the incorrect object assignment of *the cat* is more entrenched by the time recoding has to occur.

But now consider a verb that must have two arguments—for example, *give*. Why is the first sentence below no harder than the second?

(iv) a. The boy gave the cat the ball.
     b. The boy gave the cat to us.
     c. The boy donated the cat to us.

Crocker's model has the phrase structure processor making the same initially incorrect assignment, which also cannot be known to be incorrect until the words after the object, just as in *the boy pushed the cat the ball*. So, there ought to be the same kind of small garden path. But these isn't.

4. However, the patient-argument position, for example,

(i) The boy was hit.

is needed more than the agent argument position, for instance,

(ii) ? The boy hit.

This means that Crocker has no way of explaining the relative difficulty of passive.

5. Regarding subject raising, the deep structure attachment strategy is relevant. Crocker's theory incorrectly predicts that

(i) John seemed to be happy.

is harder than

(ii) John wanted to be happy.

since *John* in the *seemed* sentence does not occupy the deep structure position of *seem*. The *seemed* sentence, therefore, would require reanalysis.

6. The following examples show that subcategorization information is used in positing traces:

(i) Which cat did Bill push the ball?

(ii) Which cat did Bill push to us?

(iii) Which cat did Bill give the ball?

(iv) Which cat did Bill give to us?

Sentence (i) is harder than (iii). There is closure at *push* in (i) since *push* only requires a patient (*cat*), and hence a garden path when *the ball* is received. This garden path does not occur in (iii), because *give* requires a recipient. This suggests that the parser accesses subcategorization information.

(v) In what house$_1$ did you know Bill lives t_1?

(vi) In what house$_1$ did you say Bill lives t_1?

(vii) In what house$_1$ did you say t_1 Bill knows Enstein?

Crocker says that a trace is posited as soon as possible. So, for (vi) Crocker there is a trace posited at *say*. This is revised on receiving *lives*, so there should be a garden path ((vi) actually seems quite easy). The fact that semantics determines acceptability without any observable garden path is a problem for Crocker.

Chapter 5

Embedding the Grammar in a Comprehension Model

At last, we come to our own approach to comprehension. In chapter 3 we outlined some essential features of grammars relevant to the problem of comprehension. In chapter 4, we sketched how various contemporary models treat comprehension. Our conclusion is that any viable and behaviorally adequate model must have both an associative and a syntactic component. This chapter presents an architecture for the integration of the two kinds of information during comprehension.

5.1 Syntactic Derivations and Probabilistic Information in Comprehension

The syntactic component of a grammar represents the formal computational steps involved in defining the representation of sentences. We have outlined several enduring properties of syntactic structures and processes that are relevant for processing models:

- Lexical items are categorized syntactically. For example, there are nouns, verbs, and so forth.
- Lexical sequences are grouped hierarchically into categorized phrases, such as noun phrases and verb phrases.
- Syntactic operations can operate on phrasal categories.
- Syntactic operations include movement or computation of distant configurations of syntactic elements such as features and phrases.
- Syntactic operations are ordered and occur cyclically.

Consider the implications of these properties for models of comprehension. Our primary question is whether a syntactic structure can be constructed by direct left-to-right application of a grammar. We will conclude that it cannot. This conclusion motivates consideration of a model that "reconstructs" the syntactic derivation.

The first three syntactic properties above set constraints on any comprehension model. First, a comprehension model must quickly access the lexical category of each lexical item and the phrase type of each phrase. Ordinarily, both of these processes

/ are thought of as "bottom up." In such a model lexical items are stored and recognized by matching. Based on the category of their content words, phrases are then "projected." In sentence (1), the first phrase—*the horse*—would be recognized in the following kinds of stages:

(1) The horse races.

1. Recognize *the* as initial noun phrase.
2. Recognize *horse* as a noun.
3. Construct the noun phrase (*the horse*).

Such processes can be compiled to build up a labeled phrase structure representation by proceeding from left to right. Having assigned *the horse* status as a noun phrase, the system can assign "verb" and "verb phrase" status to *raced* and put the whole hierarchy together as a syntactically well-formed sentence as the words are heard. Thus, the orderly application of syntactic knowledge seems adequate for at least the surface phrase structure involved in sentence comprehension.

However, it is often noted but rarely attended that lexical items in speech are not neatly segregated for auditory recognition. For example, the pronunciation of *the horse* might be something like *thuoarse*, with no pause and the /h/ dropped. Thus, recognition of words even in a simple phrase can involve much more than simple linear processing. Suppose sentence (2a) has the rough pronunciation of (2b):

(2) a. The horse races and wins.
     b. Thuoarserayseznwinz.

A listener might initially code *thuoarse* simply as an unrecognized noun phrase, based on the fact that it begins the sentence and the initial sequence *thu* is a reasonable pronunciation of *the*. This would allow for further processing. But then the *raysez* could either be a continuation of the noun phrase or the verb, requiring further suspension of a final analysis. In fact, the structure of the initial phrase is not really clear until the sequence *winz*, along with the fact that that is the end of the utterance. In certain instances, even the word *horse* may not be recognized until near the end of the sentence. Even worse, the sequence *winz* might be heard as the noun *winds*, in which case the entire sequence would be incorrectly analyzed as a noun phrase until its very end.

Simple cases like this show that the comprehension mechanism for auditory input cannot always work as the mere mechanical application of syntactic categories and frames from left to right. Rather, there must be a set of procedures for dealing with temporarily indeterminate information even at the acoustic level and using projected phrase and content information to guide comprehension both prospectively and retrospectively. That is, there must be a set of templates and processes that can predict likely sequences and structures from incomplete information.

This kind of information is partially structural, partially probabilistic. It is a structural fact that *the* introduces a noun phrase. But it is a probable fact that horses *race* more often than they *raise* or *ease*. Thus, in fast speech, sentence (3a) may be mistaken more often as (3b) than the reverse.

(3) a. The pony erased the competition.
    b. The pony raced the competition.

Because *horse* is animate, it is more likely an agent for a verb than not. And finally, it is more often the case that the initial noun phrase of a sequence is the subject of the verb than not. It would be functional for a comprehension system to utilize all these kinds of information during comprehension.

A second homely fact relevant for sentence comprehension is that normal speech is often defective. There are frequent mispronunciations, slips, false starts, and outright ungrammatical sentences. Any model that depends on completely recognizable well-formed units will not be adequate to the normal task of comprehension. Probabilistic knowledge may be important in dealing with this problem as well.

Thus, prima facie, it appears that the probabilistic modelers are right: Comprehension models must include devices that can quickly apply many kinds of probabilistic knowledge as well as assign syntactic structure. Such models might be able to account for the rapid assignment of some syntactic structures as sentences are heard. Indeed, we saw in the previous chapter that connectionist models are excellent at "pattern completion" when there is only partial input. Thus, an adequate comprehension model includes both an implementation of rule-based grammar and an implementation of associative information.

However, this kind of "hybrid" model is not sufficient by itself. Syntax not only involves left-right orderings arranged into hierarchical structures, it also involves cyclic, successive upward movement and other computational relations between distant elements. Therefore, each sentence has a derivational history that ranges over its entire structure. How are we to recover the cyclic stages involved while computing sentences from left to right?

The computational problem is that if the movements are ordered and cyclic, recovering the initial input form by "reversing" the derivation presents too many computational paths. Of course, if traces had actual phonetic form and wore their indexes in their pronunciation, recovering the source trees of a sentence would be a great deal easier. But traces are inaudible and generally have no phonetic effect. Even when they are explicitly instantiated in pronouns, they do not intrinsically indicate how they are coindexed. Thus, the comprehension system has to recover the source sequence of structures by undoing operations and moving phrases back to their source positions without having any explicit marks that locate the source positions or the relations to their particular derived positions. To compute this would require an inverse system to keep track of multiple possibilities, which expand exponentially with each level of embedding. It cannot be proved that this is *impossible*, only that it is computationally overwhelming with even fairly simple sentences.

5.2 Analysis by Synthesis

We perceptually organize speech as made up of discrete sounds and higher-order units. But the process of talking obscures the boundaries between the units. Producing speech is like taking an ordered lineup of different kinds of eggs, breaking them so each overlaps with its neighbors, then scrambling them up a bit so there is a continuous egg belt, and then cooking them. Comprehension is analogous to the problem of figuring out how many eggs there were originally, exactly where each was located, and what kind it was. This is a hard problem for any template-matching system that is ordered as below:

(4) Input → sequence of sounds → words → phrases

The problem of acoustic analysis is even harder. Each physical speech sound is perceived in the context of a particular speaker with a particular vocal tract. This means that certain sounds are perceived differently depending on who utters them. For example, Ladefoged and Broadbent (1957) demonstrated that a vowel sound acoustically between /i/ and /e/ is perceived clearly as one or the other, depending on who the speaker is that introduces it. This deepens the importance of an active perceptual model.

Of course, the problem is made somewhat easier by the fact that in language the units are not lined up in arbitrary ways. Each language has phonetic, phonological, lexical, and syntactic constraints that severely limit the possible sequences. But the problem remains of how to bring such grammatical knowledge to bear on the input signal.

Theories of the perception of phonemes—speech sounds at the most elementary level—offer a model for our consideration. Two distinct kinds of proposals converge on the same idea. In a long series of theoretical and research papers, the Haskins Laboratory group has outlined a "motor theory" of the perception of speech sounds (for example, Liberman et al. 1967). Separately, Halle and Stevens (1964) suggested that speech perception could proceed in an "analysis-by-synthesis" framework. The essential feature of both proposals is that an initial preliminary analysis of the input is used to trigger the mechanism that generates grammatically possible forms in the language. The candidate output of the grammar is compared with the speech input. When there is a match, the system assigns the grammatical representation used to provide the match. Figure 5.1 shows the Halle and Stevens model.

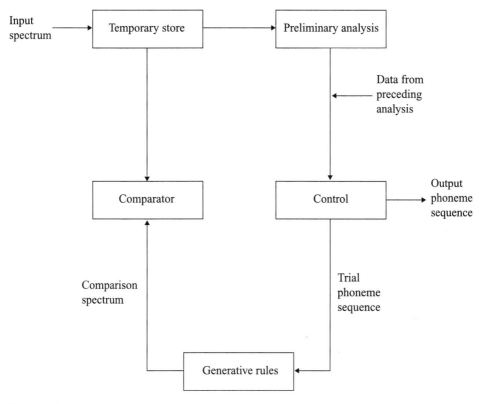

Figure 5.1
Halle and Stevens's analysis-by-synthesis model for speech recognition (from Halle and Stevens 1964:608).

It is clear how such a scheme approaches the scrambled-egg problem. In terms of our scrambled-egg analogy, the analysis-by-synthesis model starts with a particular hypothetical egg sequence, scrambles and cooks them in a virtual kitchen, and then compares the resulting virtual omelet with the actual input. When the virtual omelet matches the actual omelet, the input and cooking sequence producing the virtual omelet is confirmed as the correct analysis. The analysis-by-synthesis model has considerable appeal at the phonetic level. One reason is that the physical basis for speech production ensures that phonemes are realized in different ways, depending on their context. Thus, /k/ between two /i/s is made with the tongue farther forward in the mouth than between two /a/s; /a/ between two /k/s is made with quite a different tongue shape than /a/ between two /t/s. Hence it is difficult to find constant acoustic features for many speech sounds. The analysis-by-synthesis model solves the problem by generating the surface from an input sequence, which is not ambiguous initially.

The analysis-by-synthesis model can also apply at higher levels of analysis (see Neisser 1967 for further examples). Consider the word-level recognition of the sentence-initial phrase, assuming for the moment that a phonetic analysis has been performed:

(5) Thuoarse ...

The preliminary sounds *Thu* can be recognized as a potential instance of *the*, which is also recognized as a noun phrase initial word, with a head noun somewhere:

(6) [[the]$_{Det}$[oarse]$_N$]$_{NP}$

The problem now is to find a noun corresponding to the monosyllable *oarse*, but there is no such noun. Enlarging the search to monosyllabic nouns that end in *oarse* reveals a few: *course, horse, Norse, force, source,* and so on. Trying to fit each of these candidates to the input phonetic sequence, the grammar would generate:

(7) a. the Norse ...
    b. the force ...
    c. the course ...
    d. the source ...

Each of those cannot match the input because of the initial consonant. But in trying *the horse*, and optional process of rapid speech in American English can drop initial /h/, as in:

(8) a. If /h/ is internal to a sequence, then /h/ → 0.
    b. But he found his bat ... → buteefoundizbat

Thus, one of the derivable pronunciations of *the horse* is, in fact, *thuoarse*, creating a match to the input.

This simple example clarifies the importance of grammatical derivations in motivating an analysis-by-synthesis scheme. Suppose perception proceeded entirely by recognition schemes: such a scheme might recognize *thu* as *the*, but *oarse* does not occur anywhere in the lexicon. Only after application of the /h/-dropping rule is there a match to the input.

One could list all such alternate pronunciations of each word, but this would create massive duplication of information. Maintaining a normal lexicon and having a framework in which normal grammatical processes can apply both represents and greatly simplifies the role of grammatical constraints in recognition.

Such information duplication might be conceivable at the lexical level, but it would be intractable at the phrase and sentence levels, because there are too many of them. Figure 5.2 represents how the entire analysis-by-synthesis architecture might look at the clause level.

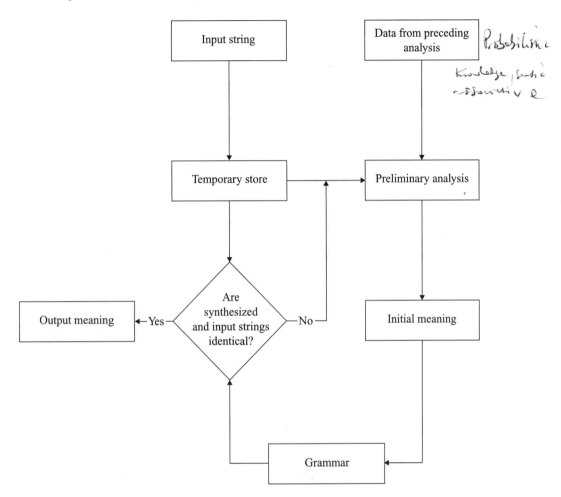

Probabilistic

Knowledge, Symbolic
associative

Figure 5.2
An analysis-by-synthesis model at the sentence level.

According to the model shown in figure 5.2, a quick-and-dirty parse is initially elicited, assigning major phrases and setting them in conceptual relation to each other. This preliminary analysis uses a variety of surface schemata in conjunction with verb argument and control information to organize an initial hypothesis about meaning. From that, a complete parse may be accessed that computes a derivation and fills in the remaining syntactic details. In this view, one purpose of assigning a complete syntactic parse is to make sure that the initial statistically and lexically based initial meaning is consistent with a syntactically well-formed parse. The model articulates three major steps in comprehension:

1. Assign a likely meaning.
2. Map that onto a syntactic structure and derive a surface structure.
3. Check the output of step 2 against the input.

This model also resolves the major difficulty in how to interrelate syntactic structures with processing models. Put crudely, an initial structural and associative system isolates a candidate analysis based on surface cues, and syntactic processes check that the analysis can derive the sequence. The difficulty for such models is to limit the initial hypothesized search space of potential syntactic structures. If the input to that stage included a specification of the thematic roles of the words and phrases, it would limit the generated hypotheses to sentences that have the indicated words with just those underlying structure roles that typically correspond to the conceptual thematic roles. It is a subsidiary result of that claim that the syntactic parse usually follows the initial semantic analysis. We suggest further that if the parse characteristically follows an initial semantic analysis, this solves the problem of limiting the search space.

The idea that a sentence may be initially "understood" before a complete and correct parse is assigned sets one limit on how the formation of levels of representation might be integrated. Of course, there may be natural situations in which the initial pass at assigning the meaning is incorrect, or simply not complete enough to constrain the syntactic parse. Under those circumstances, assignment of the syntactic parse may actually precede the correct semantic representation; thus, our most basic claim is that the two levels of representation are computed independently. Before turning to some examples of how the model works out, we review the different components in some detail. First, the model assigns a likely meaning and form. The initial stage of assigning a likely meaning/form involves what we call *pseudosyntax*. This component assigns lexical categories, segments major phrases, isolates their heads, and assigns likely argument relations between the heads of major phrases. Pseudosyntax is largely passive and bottom up. Since it relies on statistical properties of the ecology of language and specific lexical information, it is a probabilistic analysis of the meaning and form. Its ultimate output is:

• A list of likely lexical items
• A list of likely heads
• An arrangement of heads into a syntactic structure that relates arguments to predicates

On the basis of this pseudosyntax, a likely candidate meaning or conceptual structure is assigned.

Second, the model forms a candidate real syntax. This process takes the candidate meaning/form from pseudosyntax and maps it onto a corresponding set of structures that serve as the input to a syntactic derivation. The mapping principles are partly statistical, applying first the most likely syntactic structures corresponding to the output of the pseudosyntax. The mapping principles are also partly structural, constrained by lexical subcategorization information and syntactic well-formedness constraints.

Third, the model generates and matches the syntax. This stage derives a complete surface structure from the input and compares it to the stored sequential input.

Now consider each stage in even more detail.

1. *Assign a likely meaning.* This process involves isolating lexical items and phrases, relating them in a likely syntactic structure, and assigning a meaning to that. As a largely passive process, there is no principled reason why the different aspects of this kind of structure cannot be assigned partially in parallel. But for expository purposes we discuss the different aspects of structure as though they were ordered bottom up.

a. *Lexical recognition.* As we discussed above, sometimes lexical pronunciation is distinct and unique enough to allow for immediate segregation and recognition. At other times, there is no segmentation, and local encoding effects may obscure and blur isolated word recognition, so that it depends on a larger context. A salient part of that context is the phrase.

b. *Phrase segregation.* Not only is isolation of phrases an important aid to recognition of individual words, it is a logical prerequisite to assignment of arguments to predicates. All languages include a small number of function words and morphemes that give some cues to phrase boundaries and phrase types. In English, such words tend to begin phrases. For example, if we segmented and categorized each phrase in the sentence before last, using a simple strategy of segmenting before each function word, we would see:

(9) a. All languages ...
   all = quantifier
   quantifier phrase
   b. can include ...
   can = modal
   verb phrase
   c. a small number ...
   a = determiner
   determiner phrase
   d. of function words ...
   of = preposition
   prepositional phrase
   e. and morphemes ...
   and = conjunction

f. which give ...
   which = relative pronoun
   relative clause
g. some cues ...
   some = quantifier
   quantifier phrase
h. to phrase boundaries ...
   to = preposition
   prepositional phrase
i. and word types.
   and = conjunction

Once a skeletal segmentation of this sort occurs, isolation of individual lexical items becomes simpler. The typology of each phrase based on its leading function word also constrains identification of its head. Furthermore, many local phonetic encoding processes that obscure words are contained within major phrases. Thus, the initial segmentation of phrases, identification of phrase types and heads, and recognition of words all are mutually supportive, and all can rely in large part on simultaneous passive recognition processes.

   c. *Assign a configurational syntactic structure.* Meaning is compositional and depends on some structural form that specifies possible arguments in relation to possible predicates. Isolated phrases must be integrated within a higher-order framework to arrive at a candidate conceptual interpretation of sentences. This, too, can in part depend on passively accumulated and applied statistical generalizations. The most salient example is that a noun phrase preceding and agreeing in number with a verb is taken as the subject of that verb—that is, the noun phrase has the subject relation in a phrase structure tree. Similarly, a noun phrase following a verb is taken to be the object of the verb; in other words, it falls within the same verb phrase. Assigning a configurational syntactic structure to the sample sentence above would yield:

(10) (All languages) ((can include) (a small number)) ...

Prepositional phrases, conjuncts, and relative clauses can be initially interpreted as locally attached, yielding:

(11) (All languages) ((can include) (a small number (of function words and
     phrases))) (that give cues (to phrase boundaries and word types))

   So far, we have developed quite a rich structure based entirely on superficial cues and likely phrase organizations with no appeal to meaning. The logically final operation of this stage is to project a likely conceptual interpretation onto the hypothesized syntactic configuration. A well-grounded set of generalizations accounts for a large proportion of such hypothesized structures:

(12) N...(V...(N...) (N...)) = agent, action ((patient) (recipient))

(13) HEAD (adjunct) = adjunct modifies head

2. *Forming the syntax.* So far so good. But as the reader is sure to have thought, the system cannot count on always being presented with statistically dominant structures and meanings. There has to be some mechanism to check that the initially hypothesized meaning is correct, and if not, a system for generating additional guesses. This is the function of the next step, which is to generate a syntactic structure based on the initial analysis, and check its output against the original input sequence. The hypothesized meaning-form input to the syntax-formation process includes the actual inflected lexical items, the head-marked and categorized phrases, the initial syntactic framework, and the hypothesized conceptual structure. (Henceforth, we refer to this representation as the *initial meaning-form hypothesis.*) This sets many constraints on the possible initial syntactic structures selected by a grammar.

Within the current Minimalist Program (Chomsky 1995), the inflected lexical items provide the initial numeration as part of the input to a derivation. The conceptual structure adds information on likely functional relations. For example, patients of verbs and prepositions are likely to be accusative (in English), agents are likely to be nominative, verbs agree with their agent/subjects, and so on. The result is a numeration that meets the basic input requirements for a derivation, which can then proceed.

3. *Syntax generation and matching.* The derivation of a syntactic surface sequence proceeds in the normal manner of a grammar. The result yields as a fully specified syntactic description, a derivational analysis together with a complete surface phrase structure, word order, agreement markings, and so on. This is matched to the original input, and if it provides a match, the computation is terminated. If there is not a match, the computation starts again at various points. In later chapters, we discuss specific examples of initial misanalyses and strategies for recovery.

5.3   A Case Study: The Passive

Consider how this system works on simple declarative sentences, as in (14):

(14) Athens was rich.

The first logical stage is to segregate the phrases:

(15) [Athens]$_{np}$, [was]$_{copula}$, [rich]$_{adj}$

While the dominant NVN = agent, action, patient pattern does not apply here, an immediately subordinate canonical sequence and category template can apply to this sequence to postulate an initial meaning. That is, (16a) corresponds to (16b):

(16) a. NP, BE[inflected to agree with NP], ADJ
       b. Adjective is predicated of NP

In this case,

(17) Rich:Athens (that is, *rich* is predicated of *Athens*)

This conceptual structure in turn constrains the possible grammatical structures that can express it, relying on conceptual to structural mapping regularities, in this case:

[adj]:np → NP is dominated by S

(18) ADJ is dominated by VP
      insert BE as Verb
      dominated by S

This regularity between conceptual structure and components of grammatical structure specifies a list of lexical items, their case and tense, and functional relations. All this is tantamount to an initial input of words and functional structures to the synthetic component. This initial structure in turn has as one of its most direct surface expressions, the exact input sentence, thus completing the parse analysis of the input.

Now consider how this sequence of processes applies to a more complex structure such as a transitive sentence:

(19) Sparta attacked Athens.

The first phase is isolation of the major phrases, based on lexical cues and surface morphology:

(20) [Sparta]$_{np}$, [attacked]$_v$, [Athens]$_{np}$

The next phase is to assign a canonical structure to the sequence, relying on surface order cues. In this case, the simple canonical order NVN can be taken as corresponding to agent-action-patient following the formula in (12), leading to the initial, and correct, hypothesis that the meaning of the sentence is:

Sparta = agent
attacked = action
Athens = patient

This along with the lexical items can then serve as input to the syntactic generator, using the following sorts of regularities:

Agent → the NP in construction with an agent-assigner
Action → verb that assigns agent and patient roles
Patient → verb-internal argument

These regularities between conceptual and functional organization specify a particular initial structure.

The generation of that structure and checking it against the original input constitute the final stage of applying a parse within the framework of analysis by synthesis. Thus, in both these cases, the sentence is initially correctly "understood" via surface regularities, and then an exact parse is applied using the initial conceptual analysis as a constraint on possible initial derivational structures.

 This is all a straightforward implementation of the model. But consider now how the same sorts of processes apply to a passive construction such as:

(21) Athens was attacked by Sparta.

The first stage again is to isolate the phrases and their order and apparent morphological agreement:

(22) [Athens]$_{np}$ [BE]$_{copula}$ [[attacked]$_{adj}$ [by]$_{prep}$ [Sparta]$_{np}$]$_{modifier}$

The initial schema outlined for simple predications can apply to the initial part of this sentence to interpret the apparent adjective as a modification on the initial NP that agrees with the copula:

(23) [[attacked] [by Sparta]]:Athens

This analysis is conceptually correct, as far as it goes. That is, it is correct that *Athens is attacked*, and that *by Sparta* serves as a special modifier on the nature of the attack. However, it is part of the lexical meaning of a morphologically passive nonlexical adjective like *attacked* that it entails a passive concept. In other words, lexical information in *attacked* specifies that *Athens* is not the agent of the corresponding predicate but the "patient," as in:

(24) a. NP   = agent
    b. attacked by Sparta = predicate
    c. Athens   = patient

A default strategy is to fill in the one extra NP into the missing position for it. This default strategy yields a conceptual structure:

(25) a. by Sparta = agent
    b. attacked = predicate
    c. Athens   = patient

Combining the conceptual information and the order information, and using the kind of conceptual–to–functional structure mappings described above, part of the initial input to the synthetic component of the system is:

(26) NP attacked Athens; by Sparta

This underlies a derivation that corresponds at the surface structure exactly to the original input passive sentence, which would thus complete the parse and be confirmed against the input during syntax checking.

This example is important in several ways. First, it shows that in certain cases, a preliminary incorrect parse can lead to a correct initial conceptual organization and hypothetical meaning, and thence a correct initial syntactic input derived from the conceptual organization. That is, the system first interprets a passive sentence as an active copula sentence with a complex adjectival predicate. Since the lexical meaning of the "adjective" is itself morphologically marked as passive, the correct conceptual interpretation is assigned. This in turn is the basis for reconstituting the correct deep structure and thence the correct surface parse.

A second feature of this analysis is that it depends critically on lexical morphology. For example, it is crucial that *attacked* is assigned a "passive" conceptual status with its argument assigned patient status. This is the basis for then assigning a deep structure with the argument noun phrase placed in the usual patient position. This is consistent with the fact that *attacked* is not an adjective within the permanent lexicon.

Contrast a true passive like *Athens was attacked by Sparta* with a superficially parallel structure such as (27):

(27) Athens was surprised by Sparta.

In this case, the immediate conceptual analysis accesses *surprised* correctly as a lexical adjective rather than a morphologically passive deverbal adjective. This is consistent with the differentiation of apparent "passive" constructions into those that are truly syntactic and those that are lexical in source. Some typical bases for differentiating lexical from syntactic passives are the distributional facts showing that lexical passive words can appear in adjectival locations:

(28) a. The surprised city
      b. *The attacked city
      c. Athens looked surprised.
      d. *Athens looked attacked.

Accordingly, the conceptual structure of this sentence is:

(29) Surprised[by Sparta]: Athens

Since *surprised* is a lexical adjective, this is conceptually identical to *rich:Athens*. Hence, the initial structure it relates to is:

(30) Athens BE surprised [by Sparta]

This has the consequence that the same apparently passive surface sequence is assigned a deep structure passive analysis in one case, with noun phrase movement.

But in another case it is treated as an adjectival construction, for purposes of both initial conceptual analysis and syntactic structure. We return below to some empirical confirmation of this distinction.

The active or passive morphology of the verb then signals the actual argument structure. In the case of the passive, this occasions a reassignment of patient role to the surface subject. At this point, there is available for syntactic analysis the surface string, an initial segregation into major phrases, and a conceptual representation of those phrases and how they are related. The goal of the syntactic parser is to take these structures as input and construct a derivation of intermediate syntactic structures consistent with them.

The cases in which the correct conceptual interpretation is derived from an initially incorrect parse are particularly interesting. These appear to include all cases of NP-movement in English, in which a noun phrase is removed from the position that assigns it its theta role, but it has case assigned by its surface position. These cases include passive (31a), raising (31b), and perhaps tough-movement (31c):

(31) a. Athens was attacked t by Sparta.
     b. Athens was likely t to attack Sparta.
     c. Athens was tough to attack t.

In each of these cases, our hypothesis is that the initial conceptual interpretation is arrived at on the basis of an incorrect and incomplete organization into a complex predicate that modifies the subject noun. The incorrect organization in the case of passive establishes an adjective with modifier, in the case of raising a "double-verb" construction, and in the case of tough-movement a complex adjective, as below:

(32) a. Athens, was, [attacked-by-Sparta]$_{adj}$
     b. Athens, was, [[likely-to-attack]$_v$, Sparta]$_{adj}$
     c. Athens, was, [tough-to-attack]$_{adj}$

These cases of movement are distinct from apparent movement, in which the noun phrase is coindexed with another but receives its theta role and case from its deep structure position. *Wh*-movement is in this latter category: the acceptability of /whom/ versus /who/ reveals the case-marked patient role.

(33) a. Who are they; He hit whom; *Whom are they
     b. Whom did Sparta attack t

Such cases show that, like other NP-movement, the *wh*-word [whom] acquires its patient role from its source position during the derivation. In addition, its inflected case is assigned by a nonfinal derivational position. Another reflection of this is that despite the fact that it is in superficial preverbal subject position [at least ordinally], the verb agreement is determined by the agent noun phrase.

The implications of these facts is that the initial assignment of conceptual structure to such sentences with movement must first treat the *wh*-word as moved back into its source position. This movement allows the comprehension system to meet the requirement that the input have the appearance of a well-formed sentence. Until the *wh*-word is related to its source position, it does not have an assigned case relation. That is, the first stage of comprehending sentences such as (34a) is to assign the *wh*-word to its source position as in (34b) and the surface subject *Sparta* to its preverbal position so each can receive case.

(34) a. Who$_1$ is Sparta attacking t$_1$
     b. Sparta$_1$ is attacking who$_1$

The conceptual analysis of this sentence then proceeds as for a regular transitive active sentence. We discuss some implications of the difference between NP- and *wh*-movement below and in the next chapter.

These considerations require a revision of the order of decoding events during comprehension. The first stage includes carrying out the minimal "syntactic" operations that yield a superficially well-formed sentence. In English (and we expect universally) what this comes down to is moving *wh*-marked main-argument phrases back into their source positions before applying the canonical template strategies to provide an initial meaning/form analysis.

5.4   Pseudosyntax, Real Syntax, and the Grain Problem

This sketch outlines the framework and stages of the model. There are several additional general points that put the model into perspective.

5.4.1   Cycles, Online Comprehension, and Dummy Variables

The first point concerns computations and comprehension during sentences. We have presented the model as a "whole-sentence" cyclic process. Through a strictly literal interpretation of what we have said so far, one could conclude that comprehension does not "really" occur until the end of each sentence. We have presented the model that way to simplify the discussion; but in fact, the essential idea that initial meanings are hypothesized before their full syntactic analyses can apply at many levels and subsequences simultaneously. To return to example (1), as the initial NP is assigned and regenerated to analyze it syntactically as *(the horse)np*, it can also trigger the NVN template in (12) to yield a complex construction as in (35):

(35) (the horse)np
     N = agent (V (N (N)))

The initial lexical cycle has correctly assigned the phrase, while it also is assigned the initial component of the larger template. With slow speech, or in a context of many simple sentences with *the horse* as agent and subject, this could also trigger a syntactic cycle. This would be based on treating the V and N as dummy elements, yielding a derivation that glosses as (36):

(36) The horse V_i-es (some NP_i (some NP_j))

Thus, it is appropriate to think of the comprehension process as potentially a simultaneous cascade of analysis-by-synthesis cycles. If such overlapping cycles are rampant, indeed it could be difficult to empirically disentangle the analysis-by-synthesis model from certain "syntax-first" models: difficult, but not impossible in principle. First, it remains the case that meaning is initially assigned at each level. Thus, in principle we should be able to show that meaning precedes structural assignment in each case, even if it is not clear how to show that with current methods. But, most important, the model is constrained to work in real time, not abstract computational space. In empirical fact, auditory input may come too fast for complete synthetic cycles to occur at intermediate points.

5.4.2 Pseudosyntax and the Grain Problem

Our model suggests that the initial comprehension of a sentence depends on lexical and surface cues that have built up inductively with experience and time. We learn to associate particular lexical items with particular categories, and sequential frames with particular conceptual relations, based on the frequency of those pairings in our experience. This is a classic associationistic claim, and if we do not elaborate it, it is subject to the classic rejoinder, namely, that there is no obvious solution to the problem of independently defining the units that are to be associated. This critical weakness of associationism was first pointed out by Chomsky in his review of Skinner's S-R treatment of language and all behavior (see section 2.2.1), and has been reborn in modern psycholinguistics as the "grain problem" (see section 4.3). In a simple declarative sentence

(37) The jockey rode a horse and . . .

how do we know that the relevant associations to reinforce are between *jockey* and *rode*, and *rode* and *horse*, and not between *The* and *rode* or *rode* and *a* or between *horse* and *and*? How do we know where to delimit a higher-level structure for reinforcement? For example, it is relevant at the level of word-association pairs that jockeys ride, and that horses get ridden; but how do we define the structure that reinforces the concept that *jockeys ride horses* in particular? It cannot be merely an accumulation of the separate NV and VN associations, because there are many counterexamples:

(38) The jockey rode his bicycle.

(39) The horse rode the train to Kentucky.

(40) The cowboy rode the horse.

Thus, there must also be a superordinate level, roughly corresponding to the proposition, available for a reinforcing relation to the lexical sequence. To form the appropriate associations, there must be a skeletal analysis that delimits the relevant units.

The classic proposal is that syntax provides the required skeletal information about sentences. Indeed in the introduction to this book, we noted that sentence-level grammar makes a critical contribution to any associationistic treatment of language behavior. Sentence-level grammar defines the objects over which associations can be learned. Most structurally minded linguists would agree that this is what makes grammar acquisition a prerequisite to the accumulation of inductive language habits. That is all well and good. But while it is logically sufficient to make the claim against mere associationistic treatments of language, it is more productive to show how the grammar might provide the needed skeletal information, and the units among which the associations are formed. Somehow we must envisage a theory that maintains the grammar and associative components distinct enough from each other, so that they each can inform the other during comprehension. The impasse that we otherwise face is that associationistic enterprises will be tempted to exclude any role for grammatical structures, and grammatical theories will be distorted by attempts to build frequency information into the grammars themselves. We have seen some of each in the current theories reviewed in chapter 4.

The analysis-by-synthesis model segregates the two kinds of information, placing associative templates in the "analysis" component, and syntactic structures in the "synthesis" component. The relation between the two components offers two points of information and constraint that reduce the intractability of the grain problem. First, pseudosyntax provides the synthetic grammar with a lexical and grouping analysis, along with an initial-meaning hypothesis that can map onto functional-category relations. Second, the syntax meets the analytic component by giving a full syntactic analysis and checking the literal form of the sentence. Both points of contact set constraints on the units available for associative processes.

• Most obviously, the grammatical syntactic analysis provides a repertoire of units over which associations might be selected. That is a specific formulation of the linguist's traditional answer to the grain problem: The grammar provides the units, while experience forms associative relations between them.
• Along with an initial-meaning hypothesis, the pseudosyntax must provide just those structures required to trigger a potential syntactic derivation. Thus, the relevant units for associative learning out of those the syntax makes available, are just those that are critical at the input stage of a grammatical derivation. In the minimalist framework, this set includes the inflected lexical items, grouped sequences, and functional-category information that plays a role in relating the groups in terms of predicates and argument positions.

Thus, the analysis-by-synthesis framework and minimalist syntax together offer a particular architecture that can resolve the grain problem. The units over which associations can be confirmed are drawn from those that the syntax provides, and the particular subset are just those units and kinds of information the grammar needs to start a derivation.

5.4.3 Formation of Canonical Templates

The processes that create templates in the pseudosyntax automatically give greatest associative strength to those aspects of analysis that occur most frequently. This has the consequence that broad-ranging canonical sentence patterns will be most strongly confirmed. Almost every instance of English clauses and most sentences have the superficial form, "NV((N)N)"; most of those correspond to "agent action ((patient) recipient))". Thus, while there are many variations in finer sentence details, almost every experience with an English clause or sentence confirms the association expressed in the canonical "NVN = agent action patient" template. It is likely that this will in fact be the most strongly confirmed abstract pattern available to the pseudosyntax.

In the following chapters, we will expand on the explanatory role of the NVN template. It is truly astounding how much of the existing experimental literature it describes. In light of the possibility of shorter (and longer) analysis-by-synthesis cycles, it is important that the analysis-by-synthesis model actually predicts that the canonical sentence-level template will be the most pervasive. Consider the different kinds of information primed in the pseudosyntax:

1. Initial segmentation and phrase-category assignment
2. Assignment of subcategorization information
3. Assignment of thematic relations between phrases

Each of these components has both a categorical and an associative component. That is, phrase segmentation can be locally influenced based on frequent patterns (see the discussion of Juliano and Bever in chapter 4), and it can be determined by function word classification. Verbs carry with them subcategorization information about the arguments they take, but this information itself can be graded with different subcategorization patterns having different strength, unique to each verb (see the discussion of Tanenhaus et al. in chapter 4). Finally, the thematic relations assigned to the segmented phrases as required by the verb frames can be influenced by the statistical properties of the verbs and the noun phrases as potential fillers of those arguments.

All this information can be locally coded. It has been argued by some (see sections 4.3.4 and 4.3.5) that it is entirely lexically based and best modeled within a framework that sets up spreading activation strengths only between pairs of lexical items. We agree that this is one of the important grains of truth to be found in the associative approach to comprehension. But we see that the analysis-by-synthesis model predicts a special status for sequences of words that comprise a potential complete proposition. This follows from the fact that in the model, the synthetic component usually applies to assign a complete syntactic structure to complete clauses. If the language has a favored "canonical" form, a natural outgrowth of the application of the synthetic component will be special importance attached to an apparent "perceptual strategy." In the case of English, this is (41):

(41) N V (N (N)) = Agent Action (Patient (Recipient))

In the subsequent three chapters, we will focus mostly on the extraordinary range of supporting evidence and explanatory power of this schema.

5.4.4 Pseudosyntax Is Associative and Real Syntax Is Categorical

The analysis-by-synthesis model segregates the role of associative information in the pseudosyntax, and of categorical information in the synthetic component, the grammar. This offers a specific architecture that resolves the question of how to integrate associative and categorical information while preserving each separately. Pseudosyntax is couched in terms of associative frequencies between surface forms and associated structures and meanings, as articulated by the grammar. This may seem circular, since it is not possible to form associations within a sentence without already knowing its grammatical structure, yet the model proposes that the first comprehension step in forming the structure is based on associations. For the moment, we will assume that the two kinds of knowledge have accumulated by the time the language learner is proficient at language understanding. As recognized by many of the more modest connectionists (e.g., Seidenberg 1997), this recasts the problem as one of acquisition. We answer it in chapter 9, where we briefly address the learning problem.

Theorists of many different stripes are willing to postulate that both the syntactic category and meaning of individual words and perhaps major phrase patterns may be recognized by overlearned templates. The watershed between associative and structural theories involves higher-order associations between words and phrases and associations to compositional meanings. In our view, pseudosyntax relies on such associations to form initial meaning-form hypotheses. This has an important implication for understanding what pseudosyntax does and does not do. Pseudosyntax does activate particular structures and meanings using associative relations between cues, structures, and concepts. It does *not* provide a "preliminary syntactic analysis." Another way of clarifying this is to distinguish the mental operations available to pseudosyntax from those available to the grammar. The *lingua mentis* of pseudosyntax is "spreading activation" (that is, it is associative); the *lingua mentis* of the grammar is "symbolic manipulation" (that is, it is categorical). Thus, in theory, what looks like the same information about a sentence actually can be represented in two ways mathematically. For example the notion that *horse* is a noun and that *the horse* is a phrase is expressed associatively as follows ("/" indicates grouping boundary):

horse—(strength H) → noun
the—(strength D) → determiner
the noun—(strength DP) → /the noun/

The corresponding information is expressed syntactically as:

[horse]$_n$
[the]$_{det}$
[[the]$_{det}$ [horse]$_n$]$_{DP}$

Similarly, subcategorization information about a verb with different options like *want* can be represented, for example, as

want—(strength O) → want [noun](patient)
want—(strength C) → want [compS](patient)

while syntactically it is represented as:

((want)$_v$ NP)$_{VP}$
((want)$_v$ CompS)$_{VP}$

Finally, sequential information bearing on conceptual relations can be represented as:

/det noun/$_1$ verb /det noun/$_2$ → noun$_1$—(strength Nvn) = agent of verb
                          noun$_2$—(strength nvN) = patient of verb

while syntactically it would be:

(((det)(N))$_{NP}$ ((verb)(det(N))$_{VP}$)$_S$)

This distinction is important at all levels of analysis. If it is not understood and respected, the reader (especially the syntax-first theorist) will be inclined to interpret pseudosyntax as a distillation of just those syntactic structures needed for comprehension. It is a short distance from there to arguing that pseudosyntax invalidates the need for a full syntax, and hence the role of the synthetic component. We have noted that pseudosyntax differs critically from real syntax in that it can actually prime an initial structure that would correspond to the *wrong* syntactic analysis. We strengthen the independence of pseudosyntax and real syntax by noting that they use entirely distinct kinds of computational relations.

In our discussions, we generally explicate the processes involved in pseudosyntax serially, and sometimes use terms that sound categorical. This is purely a descriptive convenience that is sometimes necessary for clarity. There is no principled reason why all types activation processes in pseudosyntax could not be effective simultaneously, with cross-connections between them.

5.4.5 Relation of Pseudosyntax to Prior Models

The initial stage of pseudosyntax corresponds historically to the "perceptual-strategies" model (Bever 1970a; Fodor and Garrett 1967; Fodor, Bever, and Garrett 1974; see chapter 2). Most salient is the fact that the strategies have as input surface sequences, and have grammatical organization as their output. In addition, the strategies were allegedly learned inductively and could apply simultaneously. However, there are numerous critical differences between the perceptual-strategies approach and our current understanding of pseudosyntax. First, perceptual strategies were themselves couched in a full set of syntactic categories. Second, the perceptual-strategies model had as a goal, mapping surface structure onto a complete and accurate deep structure that would feed into a conceptual representation (following the *Aspects* model of syntax; see section 3.4.1). Always having to get the analysis ultimately correct, or to mimic human failures to do so, created an unbearable burden on the set of strategies. This is an important reason that the strategies approach lost currency; working out the details of a zillion strategies and substrategies seemed daunting and never-ending. While the details remain numerous, the current model is consistent with connectionist spreading-activation implementations, which at least provide a calculus with considerable power. In addition, the current model offers a theoretical motivation for the unique strength of certain sentence-level canonical forms. Finally, the current model depends critically on the synthetic component, both to fill in derivational syntactic details and to provide a separate check on the entire proposed meaning.

Thus, it is important that the operation of pseudosyntax is consistent with contemporary proposals about nongrammatical activated structures. These include Tanenhaus and Carlson's (1989) notion of lexical thematic grids, as well as proposals by Frazier (1978), Marcus (1980), Steedman (1996), and Kaplan and Bresnan (1982). Each of these authors is arguing (for different reasons) that the linguistic input must be initially organized in part by principles outside the actual grammar. Most important for the current intellectual milieu is that as an inductive associative activation mechanism, the pseudosyntax is appropriately modeled within connectionist frameworks.

5.4.6 Relation of the Model to Minimalist Syntax

The analysis-by-synthesis model sets the syntactic parsing problem in a somewhat different light than currently fashionable. However, the model is entirely consistent with the minimalist syntactic model. The Minimalist Program in syntax integrates with this model in interesting ways (see section 3.4). In the Minimalist Program, a derivation starts with a numeration of the actual lexical items in their surface morphological form, marked for case where relevant. Thus, an important component of the initial part of a syntactic derivation is already available from the first-pass analysis of a sentence. In addition, the semantic analysis of the verb can specify aspects of the derivation that are not immediately apparent from the actual words. For example, a verb's action type (e.g., "telicity") can require a particular kind of movement (chapter 3): *attack* is an activity verb, with a specific action and point in time. Accordingly, it must be delimited by a patient or in some other way, in verb phrase–internal position. A natural way to achieve this in the syntactic passive case is to postulate a copy of the surface subject that can then be attached in patient position, as one of the initial subtrees of a derivation.

This formulation allows for a rather compelling model. The initial analysis based on pseudosyntax provides the lexical groupings and an initial conceptual interpretation. The lexical items comprise part of the numeration input to a derivation. The semantic interpretation in turn sets further constraints on the particular trees, including the specification of missing elements that ultimately correspond to traces. Clearly, we need to work out and test a variety of examples to explore the limits on this formulation. But it appears to be a quite promising reunification of psychological modeling with linguistic theory. This is significant, because such unification has been lacking generally, since the formulation of the *Aspects* model in the mid-1960s. Later syntactic architectures, especially government and binding, provided a hodgepodge of theoretical systems of constrains, each of which might correspond to psychological operations (as, e.g., in the minimal attachment model; see chapter 4). But it was not clear how to set up an architecture of the behavioral application of these different sets of constraints, other than the free form provided by the grammar itself. In the present case, we can now develop specific hypotheses about the actual sequential operations involved in building subtrees, checking features, and so on. Of course, in the limiting case, we may have to accede to the notion that the relation between formal syntax and actual instantiated derivations is "abstract," in which the behavioral operations are not directly mapped from the syntactic operations. But at least we can now attempt a coherent search for what the mapping might be.

Hope springs eternal: perhaps a new "derivational theory" of the psychological operations involved in assigning syntactic derivations is at hand.

5.4.7 Pseudosyntax in Other Kinds of Languages

The model may seem to depend on peculiarities of English. For example, English inflection and agreement systems are sparse, leaving much of the information dependent on explicit function words and word order. Languages with freer word order generally have correspondingly rich inflections and agreement systems. In those languages, the associative component of the pseudosyntax can converge on the inflections as reliable cues (Bever 1970a; Bates and MacWhinney 1987; see section 4.3.4). Indeed, inflections often seem to be more reliable cues to grammatical relations than order constraints are.

Verb-final languages may also seem to present a special problem for the model, especially the phrase-segmentation component. Many verb-final languages have inflection and function words at the end rather than the beginning of words and phrases. However, so long as the inflections are consistent and the function words consistently located, phrase segmentation proceeds as easily as in English.

5.5   Some Basic Facts Consistent with the Model

The next chapters review a range of largely experimental facts in support of the analysis-by-synthesis model we have just sketched. But first we turn to some more traditional kinds of linguistic facts and one enduring behavioral fact. We consider the implications of the stages of the comprehension model for the acceptability of different kinds of sentences.

5.5.1   Linguistic Phenomena

In this section we examine various linguistic phenomena in terms of stages of the Late Assignment of Syntax Theory (LAST). We consider the processing of sentences without function words, reduced relative clauses, *wh*- and NP-trace, and ungrammatical sentences that initially appear acceptable.

No Function-word Cues   The most elementary process of comprehension involves the isolation of function words and the segregation and categorization of phrases based on that. This process predicts that sentences devoid of explicit function words should not only be odd, but that they are often unacceptable to the point where they might be thought of as ungrammatical. Thus, (37a) is grammatical but very odd and almost incomprehensible because of the lack of function words:

(42)   a.   Sheep sheep butt back butt.
       b.   Some sheep that other sheep butt back do butt.

Reduced Relative Clauses   We have invoked canonical sentence-level strategies as crucial in providing an initial organization and meaning for sentences. The most significant of these is the so-called NVN strategy, which assigns agent-predicate-patient to such sequences. A significant problem arises if a sentence has sequences that superficially conform to a simple declarative NVN structure, as in (43):

(43)   The horse raced past the barn fell.   (the horse fell)

This specific sentence and general construction have occupied a considerable portion of the psycholinguistic experimental litrature, which we review in detail in chapter 7. But, prima facie, sentences like (43) simply seem ungrammatical. It is often virtually impossible to convince nonlinguists that they are grammatical, even after exposure to a set of comparative sentences with similar structures that do not run afoul of the NVN strategy. The sentences in (44) are all easier than (43) because they weaken the NVN strategy in various ways. The final NV sequence may be implausible, as in (44a):

(44) a. The horse raced past the barn panted.
     b. The horse raced near to the barn fell.
     c. The horse ridden past the barn fell.
     d. The horse that was raced past the barn fell.

There may be no apparent object, as in (44b). The morphology on the verb may be unambiguously a passive participle (see 44c). Or the initial verb may be signaled as subordinate, as in (44d).

***Wh*- vs. NP-Movement** We have argued that *wh*-trace and NP-trace are computed differently in comprehension (section 5.3). In particular, *wh*-trace is moved back into its source argument position before (or simultaneous with) the application of sentence-level strategies like the NVN strategy. This is necessary since *wh*-movement can yield noncanonical structures that are not otherwise instantiated in the grammar. Support for this distinction between NP-trace and *wh*-trace can be found in cases involving the interaction of the NVN comprehension strategy with subcategorization information.

Note that a sentence like (45a) has an intuitive very small garden path, in which the NVN strategy assigns the second noun status as a patient, while (45b) does not show this effect.

(45) a. ?Harry pushed the cat the bone.
     b. Harry handed the cat the bone.

The reason is that *hand* requires two objects, while *push* does not. Simultaneous access to this information along with the NVN pattern facilitates premature closure with *push*, incorrectly assigning *cat* direct-object status, as in (46):

(46) a. Harry pushed the cat.
     b. *Harry handed the cat.

This mistake is inhibited with *hand* since the proposition cannot end with one object, as in (46b). The effect goes away when the preposition explicitly marks the indirect object ((47a) and (47b)).

(47) a. Harry pushed the bone to the cat.
     b. Harry handed the bone to the cat.

Now consider the facts when one of the objects is *wh*-piped to the front of the sentence:

(48) a. ?This is the cat that Harry pushed t the bone.
     b. ?This is the bone that Harry pushed t the cat.

Both (48a) and (48b) seem relatively bad compared with (48c) and (48d).

(48) c. This is the cat that Harry handed t the bone.
     d. This is the bone that Harry handed t the cat.

We can explain the relative unacceptability of (48a) and (48b) on the same basis as (46a). If *that* is moved to its source position first, the same principles will apply that contrast (45a) and (45b). The NVN pattern can apply but will be inhibited from closure in the case of *hand* because of the fact that it requires two objects to be a complete proposition. Notice that the difficulty of (48a) and (48b) is not due to the salience of *Harry pushed the bone/cat* at the end of the sentence. This is shown by the fact that (48a) becomes completely acceptable when the correct non-direct-object location of *cat* is marked, as in (48e).

(48) e. This is the cat Harry pushed the bone to [t].
     This is the cat to whom Harry pushed the bone [t].

Now consider corresponding constructions with NP-trace in the passive:

Direct object topicalized, single object
(49) a. ?The bone was pushed the cat by Harry.

Indirect object topicalized, single object
(49) b. The cat was pushed the bone by Harry.

Direct object topicalized, double object
(49) c. ?The bone was handed the cat by Harry.

Indirect object topicalized, double object
(49) d. The cat was handed the bone by Harry.

Each of these examples is middling bad, with no particular difference between sentences with *push* and *hand*. These facts follow from the syntax-last model, in which passive sentences are first understood by the application of a complex predicate analysis strategy, as in (50):

(50) The bone was [pushed by Harry]$_{adj}$

Such a strategy applies equally well to *push* and *hand* and does not immediately reconstitute an NVN sequence. Hence, no difference is predicted between the two verbs.

    Rather, in both of these cases, the versions with the indirect object topicalized ((49b) and (49d)) are noticeably easier than with the direct object topicalized ((49a) and (49c)). This is consistent with other cases, in which the [V + ed by NP]$_{adj}$ is treated as a separately moved constituent. For example, as an adjunct to a noun phrase, an adjective phrase is acceptable, as in (51a); with passive pseudoadjective phrases, this is acceptable when the noun is the indirect object ((51b) and (51c)), but not the direct object ((51d) and (51e)).

(51) a.   Happy about the bone, the cat purred.
     b.   Pushed the bone, the cat purred.
     c.   Handed the bone, the cat purred.
     d.   *Pushed the cat, the bone disappeared quickly.
     e.   *Handed the cat, the bone disappeared quickly.

Apparently, when explicit in a small clause, the V + NP sequence must be Verb + Object as in *pushed the bone* in (51b), and (51c). (It is not clear at the moment whether this is a grammatical or perceptual constraint.) This is true even when semantic support for the indirect object interpretation is overwhelming, as in (51f):

(51) f.   *Given the charity, the money was no longer tainted.

Note that the corresponding full passive is acceptable, albeit more awkward than the alternative with the indirect object topicalized and the direct object as part of the apparent VP. We can explain the difference as a function of the fact that passives are perceptually analyzed initially as though actually a predicate construction. This initial analysis briefly gives the V + NP phrase-segmented status, which contributes to the difference in acceptability, based on the fact that when fully separate, the construction with the direct object is ungrammatical.

Really Odd Sentences That Make You Shake Your Ears   We have argued that the initial comprehension of a sentence is based on the elicitation of sentence templates. If they lead to an incorrect sequence, the system tries again with subordinate templates. This leaves open the possibility that the system could run out of statistically supported templates and be left with an incomprehensible but arguably grammatical sequence. When the system runs out of templates, and the ones that seem to apply conflict with each other, sentences indeed become impossible to grasp.

Consider the following sentence, which is unacceptable, though it seems grammatical at first glace.

(52) The shopkeepers were unsatisfied by midnight.

Trace your intuitions as you consider this sentence. At first, it seems acceptable, but then you realize that it does not really have a stable meaning that you can rest on. There is no obvious grammatical reason this is unacceptable, as shown by the acceptability of several kinds of parallel constructions.

(53) a.   The shopkeepers were still unsatisfied by midnight.
     b.   The shopkeepers were unhappy by midnight.
     c.   The shopkeepers were unsatisfied at midnight.
     d.   The shopkeepers were dissatisfied by midnight.
     e.   The shopkeepers were unsatisfied by the price.

It may be that the first sentence runs afoul of a conflict between a salient sentence template based on the apparent passive morphology, and the fact that *unsatisfied* is a lexical passive (i.e., an adjective that looks like a syntactic passive). The apparent local applicability of the NVN template requires that *unsatisfied* be derived from an agentive verb, which it cannot be. At the same time, the temporally delimiting quality of the final phrase *by midnight* requires that there have been a change of state. A change of state ordinarily is expressed as a verb if one is available. And *unsatisfy* apparently is available. But then, it is not really a verb. Thus, the initial templates in the pseudosyntax elicit competing initial representations of the sentence without a grammatical resolution.

Finally, there are intuitions that are neatly explained if people first apply sentence templates to a sequence, form an initial meaning, and then check its syntax. Consider (54a):

(54) a. *That's the first time that anyone sang to me like that before!
     b. That's the first time that anyone sang to me like that.
     c. No one sang to me like that before.

In fact, (54a) is an ungrammatical blend of two grammatical sentences. But what is important is the sequence of introspective events you go through when trying to understand it. First, it seems fine because it triggers well-oiled sentence templates with roughly the same meaning. Then it gradually starts to rattle as you realize that it does not quite compute into an actual sentence. The following sentence is even more marked because, while it triggers plausible sentence templates, they do not add up to a coherent initial meaning.

(55) a. More people have gone to Russia than I have.

This sequence works its way into the system at first, by triggering two templates:

(55) b. More people have gone to Russia than I ... (could believe).
     c. ... people have gone to Russia [more] than I have ...

But then, when synthesizing it into a surface sequence, nothing coherent emerges.

One might argue that these curios are insignificant ephemera at the boundaries of legitimate linguistic investigations. Similar objections have been raised against the use of visual illusions as tests of visual theories. But we find that the importance of illusions is critical in both the study of vision and language. Thus, the oddity of such examples and intuitions about the sequence of mental events they trigger are testament to the theory that predicts and explains them.

5.6 Conclusion: The Heightened Clarity of Grammatical Speech

The study of language comprehension has been the subject of hundreds of reported experiments since the 1950s. But the original report by Miller and Isard (1963) remains a puzzle: words that form a sentence simply sound clearer, and are more resistant to interference than the same words in a list or in an ungrammatical sentence. Fifty years of research on the detailed steps involved in sentence comprehension leave this profound fact unexplained (see chapter 2).

The analysis-by-synthesis model offers an explanation that has been largely unnoticed, but that we highlight here as a conclusion to this chapter. Consider the architecture of the system as shown in figure 5.2. When a sentence is understood, it involves a derivational synthesis of its surface form for comparison to the stored input. Thus, the process of assigning a syntactic structure creates *an extra representation of the surface form*. Many of the models we reviewed in chapter 4 presuppose that there is a store for the input, while comprehension processes are underway. But only the analysis-by-synthesis model requires that there be two simultaneous surface representations. It is the presence of two representations that explains the relative perceptual clarity: words in sentences sound clearer because they have two mental resonances, not one.

We take this as the first serious confirmation of the basic premise of the model—that comprehension involves comparison of stored and synthesized surface representations. The following chapters review other evidence in support of the model.

Chapter 6
Basic Evidence for the Model

This chapter presents facts that bear specifically on the comprehension model that embeds a grammar in an analysis-by-synthesis architecture. Various other models can account for some of the individual facts that we consider here, but the facts in aggregate uniquely support the architecture we are proposing.

The chapter is organized in terms of the approximate progression of activities that occur during comprehension. We first consider evidence on the initial application of low-level syntactic structure, which we call "pseudosyntax." Then we consider evidence on early behavioral access to meaning, followed by evidence on late behavioral access to "real syntax." We conclude with a discussion of the model's explanation of rapid judgments about sentence acceptability.

6.1 Pseudosyntax

Pseudosyntax consists of the immediate initial processes that isolate major phrases, differentiate lexical categories, and assign initial thematic relations. Pseudosyntax involves recognition of function morphemes and lexical categories, which segregate and distinguish phrases and verbs. Assignment of words to syntactic categories and major phrases coincides with the application of frequent sentence patterns that assign these phrases to thematic roles. The sentence patterns that are appropriate for a particular sentence depend on subcategorization properties of verbs. The review of other comprehension models in chapter 4 highlighted several kinds of syntactically relevant information that can be extracted from statistically supported patterns. For example, Juliano and Bever (1988) verified that a simple connectionist model with a moving three-word window can learn to predict utterance boundaries and, thereby, phrase boundaries. Mintz (1997) showed that a three-word window provides sufficient information to differentiate the lexical category of the middle word. Many models invoke the priority and cue validity of the statistically dominant thematic pattern: NVN = actor action patient. Each of these investigations with formal models

Box 6.1
The monitoring task

In the word-monitoring paradigm, subjects receive a cue word to listen for. A stimulus sentence or sentences is then presented. In critical cases, the stimulus material contains an instance of the cue word. This instance of the cue word in the stimulus material is called the *target*. For example:

Cue word: ONLY
Stimulus: "The owner rented only to older couples"
Target word: only

The measure of performance is either accuracy or speed of detecting the target word. If speed is measured, a timing tone is usually placed on tape to coincide with the target word. The timing tone triggers a timer, which stops when the subject makes a response. The subject's response may be a key press or a vocal response. It is assumed that as response times decrease, the amount of effort needed to recognize the target word decreases.

Monitoring tasks have used a variety of other targets. In many studies, subjects monitor for a particular phoneme, such as /k/. Sometimes the target is a synonym of a cue word, such as a synonym of *old*. Subjects sometimes monitor for category label targets, such as an "age descriptor," or for nonsense word targets ("respond when you hear a nonsense word"). Box 9.1 describes a monitoring task in which the subject listens for a change of speaker (e.g., "respond when you hear a word spoken by someone of another gender"). See Foss 1969; Marslen-Wilson and Tyler 1980; Marslen-Wilson, Tyler, and Seidenberg 1978.

---

supports the claim that surface sequence cues and patterns provide a great deal of reliable information relevant for initial syntactic analysis.

6.1.1 Early Access to Function Words

Friederici (1985) demonstrated that comprehenders access function words more rapidly than content words. Subjects monitored two-sentence texts for a particular target word. The two sentences were semantically unrelated. The target word was either a function word (article, demonstrative, or quantifier) or a content word (noun or adjective). After hearing the target word, subjects heard the text material, and pressed a response key as soon as they recognized the target word in text (see box 6.1). Some example materials appear below (with target word italicized):

Function-word target, unrelated context

(1) Die Kommandos beim Wenden   eines Segelbootes sind oft   sehr knapp.
    the commandos in-the putting-about of a sailboat   are often very close

(2) Der Besitzer vermietet *nur* an ältere Ehepaare.
    the owner   rented   only to elderly couples

Table 6.1
Mean word-monitoring times (ms) for function words and content words in short discourses

Target	Related	Unrelated
Function word	319	328
Content word	338	369

Source: Adapted from Friederici 1985, table 1

Function-word target, related context

(3) Die Auflagen   beim   Anmieten einer Wohnung sind oft   sehr strikt.
    the restrictions on-the renting   of-a   home   are   often very strict

(4) Der Besitzer vermietet *nur*   an ältere   Ehepaare.
    the owner   rented   only to elderly couples

Content-word target, unrelated context

(5) Der verliebte Student entschloss sich,   ins   Grüne   zu fahren.
    the lovesick student decided   himself into-the country to drive

(6) Der Mann hoffte, *Geld*   zu gewinnen.
    the man   hoped money to win

Content-word target, related context

(7) Der verarmte   Spieler entschloss sich,   ins   Kasino zu gehen.
    the impoverished player decided   himself in-the casino to go

(8) Der Mann hoffte, *Geld*   zu gewinnen.
    the man   hoped money to win

Response times were faster for function words than for content words, especially
for unrelated contexts (table 6.1). A context sentence semantically related to the
second sentence reduced response times by 31 ms for content-word targets but only
9 ms for function-word targets. In addition, semantic context reduced monitoring
times for function words that carried optional information unrelated to the main-
verb arguments, such as prepositions that introduce locations. Semantic context did
not affect monitoring time for function words that carried structural information,
such as prepositions that introduce obligatory arguments.

6.1.2   Function Words and Low-Level Phrases

Accessing function words early could enable comprehenders to determine quickly the
words that fill major thematic roles. If one hears *the*, one knows to search for a head
noun. In fact, O'Seaghdha (1997) has shown that determiners prime nouns. He used a
cross-modal naming task in which subjects heard sentence fragments followed by a

Box 6.2
The cross-modal naming task

> The cross-modal naming task requires subjects to "name" or say aloud a visually presented word while listening to speech. The task is called *cross-modal* because two modalities are used: the stimulus is presented in speech, but the word to be named (i.e., the target) is presented in print. The spoken stimulus may end when the target appears, or it may continue. For example,
>
> Stimulus (speech): "The message of that"
> Target (print): LETTER
>
> Typically, the relatedness of the target to the linguistic stimulus is varied. Speed of naming the target is measured by starting a timer at the point at which the target word appears. It is assumed that faster response times indicate that less processing effort is needed to recognize the target word because of expectations induced by the linguistic material. See Tyler and Marslen-Wilson 1977.

target word to say aloud (see box 6.2). The sentence fragments were consistent with the next word being either a noun or a verb. Some sample materials appear here:

(9) *Grammatically consistent, semantically related*
   a. the message of that LETTER
   b. the message that was SENT

(10) *Grammatically consistent, semantically unrelated*
   a. the nose and the LETTER
   b. the nose that he SENT

(11) *Grammatically inconsistent, semantically related*
   a. the message of that SENT
   b. the message that was LETTER

(12) *Grammatically inconsistent, semantically unrelated*
   a. the nose and the SENT
   b. the nose that he LETTER

The target word was either consistent or inconsistent with the syntactic context in the sentence fragment. For example, *the message for that* is consistent with a noun target, while *the message that was* is consistent with a verb target. The target word was also either related to a content word in the sentence fragment (*message-letter, message-sent*) or not related. The sentence fragments consistent with a following noun ended with determiners (*the, a, this, that, her, many, its, those*) and in some cases they ended with prepositions (*of, from, in*). The sentence fragments consistent with a following verb ended with pronouns or proper names (*she, they, he, John*), modal verbs (*would,*

Table 6.2
Mean naming times (ms) for noun versus verb targets

Target	Context bias		Bias effect
	Noun	Verb	
Related			
Noun	470	492	22
Verb	498	494	4
Unrelated			
Noun	480	499	19
Verb	505	498	7

Source: Adapted from O'Seaghdha 1997, fig. 2

should, could), or adverbs (*just, often, first*). In fact, the sentence fragments above are only "disposed" to a following noun or verb. For example, a noun-disposing context *the message of that* can precede a noun or an adjective (e.g., *the message of that long letter*). Similarly, a verb-disposing context like *the message that was* can precede a passive participle (*sent*), an auxiliary verb (*being*), an adverb (*quickly*), an adjective (*long*), a determiner (*a mistake*), or even a noun (*ear-piercing*). On this basis, the noun contexts were more constraining than the verb contexts.

Response times to name the target were faster when the syntactic category of the target was consistent with the syntactic context (table 6.2). This effect was stronger for noun than verb targets. The syntactic context effect was similar for semantically related and semantically unrelated targets. These results demonstrate that comprehenders attend to function words, and these can help them identify nouns in particular.

6.1.3 Number Morphemes

Pseudosyntactic structures are assigned by templates triggered by superficial cues. Attending to explicitly recognizable function morphemes attached to words can also assist in comprehension (Friederici 1985). Plural number on the end of a noun is such a function morpheme. In English, singular nouns are unmarked, but plural nouns are marked, as in *speech-speeches, author-authors*, and so on. Therefore, we can expect that a plural morpheme on a noun will lead the comprehender to expect plural marking on a following verb. At the same time the unmarked singular ending does not trigger a local pattern as strongly.

Behavioral evidence for comprehenders' sensitivity to plural morphemes on nouns comes from Nicol, Forster, and Veres (1997). In a subject- or self-paced whole-sentence reading task (see box 6.3), they varied factorially the number marking on two preverbal nouns and the verb. A portion of their design and materials appears below:

Box 6.3
The subject-paced reading task

In a subject-paced or self-paced reading task, linguistic material is presented segment by segment on a computer screen. The subject reads the material at his or her own pace by pressing a key on the keyboard. Each key press removes the previous segment, measures and records the amount of time the subject spent on the previous segment, and displays the next segment. The display unit may be any size. The most frequently used display units are words, phrases, and whole sentences (see box 6.4 for more details about the word-reading task). These three display units are illustrated below with a separate line for successive displays:

Word: The
                       army
                relentlessly
                 attacked
                   the
                   city.
Phrase: The army
           relentlessly attacked
              the city.
Sentence: The army relentlessly attacked the city.

Sometimes a single sentence is displayed, and the subject's task then is to press a key when the subject feels that he or she understands the sentence. Response times decrease as processing load decreases. See Aaronson and Scarborough 1976; Just, Carpenter, and Woolley 1982.

(13) *Singular head noun, singular local noun*
The author of the speech was subsequently well rewarded.

(14) *Singular head noun, plural local noun*
The author of the speeches was subsequently well rewarded.

(15) *Plural head noun, singular local noun*
The authors of the speech were subsequently well rewarded.

(16) *Plural head noun, plural local noun*
The authors of the speeches were subsequently well rewarded.

Table 6.3 shows that when the head noun was singular (*author*), reading times were longer when the local noun was marked as plural (2044 ms) than when it was singular (1920 ms). When the head noun was plural (*authors*), there was only a 1-ms difference in reading time depending on the local noun. The failure to find elevated reading times when the local noun is singular and the head noun is plural demonstrates the early use of overt number information, which appears on plural nouns but not on

Table 6.3
Mean sentence-reading times (ms) depending on number of head noun and local noun

	Head noun	
Local noun	Singular	Plural
Singular	1920	1994
Plural	2044	1995
Difference (P–S)	124	1

Source: Adapted from Nicol, Forster, and Veres 1997, table 2

singular nouns. Nicol and colleagues replicated these results with a two-choice word-by-word selection task (see section 6.4.2).

In the study by Nicol, Forster, and Veres, the explicit marker to plural number on a local noun primes plural marking on the following verb. Reading times may be elevated when the head noun is singular and the local noun is plural because the comprehension system incorrectly assigns the local noun as the subject of the verb. This simple result reflects the power of local syntactic patterns in assigning an initial pseudosyntax.

6.1.4   NVN Is a Canonical Word Order in Pseudosyntax
Further evidence for early pseudosyntax comes from a large body of research on the comprehension of sentences that violate the canonical pattern NVN = agent-action-patient (see chapter 2). We discuss the recent literature in detail in chapters 7 to 9 when we consider various applications of the model to comprehension and acquisition. In this section, we present some highlights of this research.

The purpose of isolating words into major phrases is to fill thematic positions. The most common pattern of thematic roles in English sentences is the NVN pattern. In this pattern, the initial noun phrase is the agent, the verb corresponds to the action that the agent performed, and the first postverbal noun phrase is the patient or theme of the action. The difficulty of sentences with a surface order of phrases not in the canonical pattern is evidence for the early application of the NVN template.

A well-attested fact in psycholinguistics is that a passive sentence is harder to process than the corresponding active. Thus, in matching sentences to pictures, it is harder to match a passive sentence than an active (Slobin 1966):

(17) *Active*
     The dog is chasing the cat.

(18) *Passive*
     The cat is being chased by the dog.

In judging the grammaticality of sentences, passives are harder than actives (Forster and Olbrei 1974). In measures of sentence reading time, passive sentences take longer than actives as in (19) and (20), which are adapted from Davison and Lutz (1985):

(19) *Active*
    A man in California raised a twenty-five-year-old dachshund.

(20) *Passive*
    A 25-year-old dachshund was raised by a man in California.

Similar processing differences appear in other pairs of canonical/noncanonical sentences. For example, children have more difficulty acting out object-cleft sentences than subject-cleft sentences (Bever 1970a). Object-cleft sentences violate the canonical order.

(21) *Subject cleft*
    It was the dog that chased the cat.

(22) *Object cleft*
    It was the cat that the dog chased.

Memory load, as measured by difficulty of recall of unrelated names presented during the sentence, is greater when processing object relative clauses (Wanner and Maratsos 1978), which violate the canonical order:

(23) *Subject relative with interpolated word list*
    The witch who despised JOHN GEORGE SAM BILL HANK sorcerers frightened little children.

(24) *Object relative with interpolated word list*
    The witch whom sorcerers JOHN GEORGE SAM BILL HANK despised frightened little children.

The syntax that is assigned initially in each of these cases is rudimentary. This pseudosyntax is based on simple matching of major phrases to the canonical sentence patterns in order to assign argument roles. For example, in a subject relative clause the phrases match up with the canonical template as follows:

who   =   initial NP   =   agent
despised   =   verb   =   action
sorcerers   =   second NP   =   patient

An object relative clause is more difficult because its phrases do not match the canonical sentence pattern:

whom   =   initial NP   =   patient
sorcerers   =   second NP   =   agent
despised   =   verb   =   action

Argument roles are assigned as a concomitant of the matching of major phrases to common sentence patterns.

6.1.5 Syntactic Categories

The *syntactic category* of a word refers to its categorical role in a sentence. These roles include noun, verb, adjective, and so on. In the Late Assignment of Syntax Theory (LAST), syntactic category is assigned as a concomitant of the organization of words into major phrases that fill thematic roles. Homographs such as *duck*, *train*, and *fire* are ambiguous with regard to syntactic category. LAST predicts that if a word can fill a thematic role, it is assigned to the corresponding syntactic category. Assignment of a word to a needed syntactic category, however, will be harder if the word is rarely used as that category.

Boland (1997b) examined the influence of a variety of probabilistic factors in the initial assignment of syntactic category. She studied sentences that contained a homograph like *duck*:

(25) *Possessive pronoun, noun*
     She saw her duck and chickens near the barn.

(26) *Accusative pronoun, verb*
     She saw her duck and stumble near the barn.

In these sentences, the appropriate syntactic category of *duck* as a noun or a verb cannot be fully determined until the sixth word (*chickens* or *stumble*). The frequency of use of a word as a noun or verb influences its immediate assignment. For example, *duck* is used more often as a noun than as a verb and tends to be assigned initially the category of noun, all other factors equal. In actual sentences other factors, such as local context, are usually not equal. Based on O'Seadgha's (1997) results, we would expect that when the preceding pronoun is possessive, *duck* will be assigned the category of noun, and when the pronoun is accusative, *duck* will be assigned the category of verb:

(27) *Preceding possessive pronoun*
     She saw his duck.

(28) *Preceding accusative pronoun*
     She saw him duck.

Since *her* may be either possessive or accusative, it does not establish with certainty the category of *duck*. However, we can expect that the frequency with which *her* is used as a possessive versus accusative will influence its initial case assignment as well, and also influence the immediate assignment of *duck*.

Another potential factor in assigning a syntactic category is the ambiguity of the main verb *saw*. This verb may take a noun phrase object as a transitive verb, or a sentential complement as an object control verb, as in:

(29) *Noun phrase object*
She saw her.

(30) *Object with sentential complement*
She saw her stumble.

If the main verb subcategorizes only for a noun phrase object, *her* will initially be assigned the accusative case, yielding an initial meaning that corresponds to (31).

(31)   She hit her.

(32) *She hit her stumble.

Other verbs, such as *think*, however, require additional cases depending on the subcategorization frame, as in:

(33) *Sentential complement*
I think she left.

(34) *Noun phrase object*
I think her thoughts.

(35) *Object with sentential complement*
I think her a fool.

(36) *Pronoun object*
*I think her.

   The possible subcategorization frames and their frequency of use can influence the assignment of syntactic category to a homograph as well. Boland used a moving-window reading task to examine the effects of frequency of use of a homograph and discourse context on the initial assignment of words to syntactic categories (box 6.4).
   The target homograph appeared in sentences such as one of the following:

(37) *Unambiguous possessive pronoun, noun*
She saw his duck and chickens near the barn.

(38) *Unambiguous accusative pronoun, verb*
She saw him duck and stumble near the barn.

The target sentences were preceded by a context sentence such as the following:

(39) *Context bias toward possessive pronoun, noun*
As they walked around, Kate looked at all of Jimmy's pets.

(40) *Context bias toward accusative pronoun, verb*
As they walked around, Kate watched everything that Jimmy did.

Box 6.4
The moving-window reading task

> The moving-window reading task is a variant of subject-paced reading, discussed in box 6.3. As discussed in box 6.3, single-word presentation often displays one word at a time in the center of the screen. In the moving-window paradigm, each screen contains information about punctuation, spacing, and the length of the words, but the letters of only one word are displayed. For example, the lines below represent successive displays:
>
> The **** ************ ******** *** ****.
> *** army ************ ******** *** ****.
> *** **** relentlessly ******** *** ****.
> *** **** ************ attacked *** ****.
> *** **** ************ ******** the ****.
> *** **** ************ ******** *** city.
>
> Each key press replaces the previously displayed word with asterisks, records the time that the previous unit was displayed, and shows the next word together with asterisks corresponding to the remaining words on the line. The amount of time the subject spends reading a word is taken to indicate the processing load needed for that particular word. See Just, Carpenter, and Woolley 1982.

The first discourse context highlights Jimmy's possessions, while the second highlights things Jimmy did. If discourse context influences the initial assignment of syntactic category, reading times for the pronoun *his* ought to be faster when the discourse context is biased toward the possessive, and reading times for *him* ought to be faster when it is biased toward the accusative. If syntactic category assignment depends on frequency of use of the noun-versus-verb meanings of the homograph, reading times in possessive contexts ought to decrease as the noun meaning of the homograph increases in frequency.

Discourse context did not have a significant effect on reading times on any word (see table 6.4), though its effect approached significance on the disambiguating word (*stumble, chickens*). This result indicates that discourse context does not play a role in the immediate assignment of syntactic category.

On the other hand, Boland did find that homograph bias was related to reading time. Contingent homograph bias was determined by asking subjects to complete fragments such as *she saw her duck* ... Homographs that more often produced completions with a noun usage of the homograph are "noun biased," while those that produced more completions with verb usage are "verb biased." The size of the difference between noun and verb completions indicates the strength of homograph bias. Boland found a significant correlation ($r = .75$) between strength of homograph bias and reading times for the word following the homograph (i.e., *and*). When the pronoun was the accusative *him*, which allows a following verb, reading times for *and*

Table 6.4
Mean word-reading times (ms) depending on discourse context and local context

	Word			
	him/his	duck	and	stumble/chickens
Him				
Poss discourse	340	350	385	425
Acc discourse	345	355	350	405
Discourse effect	−5	−5	35	20
His				
Poss discourse	335	345	400	400
Acc discourse	330	375	395	430
Discourse effect	5	−30	5	−30

Note: Acc refers to accusative contexts; *poss* refers to possessive contexts.
Source: Adapted from Boland 1997b, fig. 1

decreased as the homograph became more verb dominant. When the pronoun was the possessive *his*, which allows a following noun, reading times for *and* decreased as the homograph became more noun dominant. The effects of contingent homograph bias do not appear until the word after the homograph.

Boland's research shows that frequency of use and local context of the alternative meanings of a homograph influence its immediate assignment to a syntactic category, but discourse context does not. The central question from the standpoint of LAST is, does this assignment occur as a by-product of assigning words to major phrases that correspond to thematic roles? There is no research of which we are aware that examines this question. The simplest test of this question would compare processing difficulty on the last word in sentences like the following (from Frazier and Rayner 1987; MacDonald 1993):

(41) The desert trains crashed.

(42) The desert trains soldiers.

The NVN template predicts that a sequence like *desert trains* that can be assigned the categories of NV will be assigned those categories, assuming that the noun and verb interpretations of *trains* are equally probable overall. This would make the initial assignment incorrect in the first sentence above, since *crashed* indicates that *trains* is in fact a noun, not a verb.

6.1.6 *Wh*-Trace

Wh-movement leaves behind a trace to indicate its original structural position. Here are some examples of *wh*-movement (Frazier, Clifton, and Randall 1983; Nicol and Swinney 1989):

(43) Wh-*movement*
      Which book₁ did the teacher show t₁ to the children?

(44) The policeman saw the boy₁ that₁ the crowd at the party accused t₁ of the
      crime.

In the first sentence, *which book* moves from the position of object of *show* to the
front of the sentence. It leaves behind a trace in the object position where it originally
received the role of patient from *show*. In the second sentence, *boy* occupies the object
role of *accused* in D-structure. In the form of *that*, *boy* moves to the front of the
object relative clause to modify *boy* in the main clause, again leaving behind a trace
that corresponds to the D-structure position of the moved element.

When *wh*-movement has occurred, there is usually an overt marker in the sentence.
In the examples of *wh*-movement above, these markers are *which* and *that*. We can
expect that the comprehension system may use these markers to immediately establish the trace for the moved element. The presence of overt markers for *wh*-movement
distinguishes it from NP-movement, as we will see later in the section on NP-trace.
However, there is another property of *wh*-movement that influences sentence processing, namely, that *wh*-movement destroys canonical structure and creates types
of phrase sequences that do not correspond to any simple untransformed sentence.
In chapter 5, we outlined how LAST accommodates to the unique surface phrase
sequences that *wh*-movement creates. We proposed that very early *wh*-return strategies apply to activate a representation of the moved phrase in its original position.
This restores a canonical surface phrase order, to which the early syntactic pattern
strategies can apply. This is equivalent to using sentence pattern templates that are
specific to cases of *wh*-movement.

Priming from *Wh*-trace   The early reactivation of *wh*-trace correctly predicts that
the *wh*-trace location primes its antecedent immediately. Swinney et al. (as reported
in Nicol and Swinney 1989) used a cross-modal lexical decision task to examine the
activation of *wh*-words at the location of traces (see box 6.5). Subjects heard sentences like the following and saw a test probe at a pretrace point, at the *wh*-trace, or
at a posttrace point:

(45) The policeman saw the boy₁ that₁ the crowd at the party [pretrace test point]
      accused t₁ [*wh*-trace test point] of the [posttrace test point] crime.

The probes were either related or unrelated to *boy* (the antecedent of the trace) or to
crowd.

Swinney et al. found significant facilitation in lexical decision for *boy* at the *wh*-
trace and at the posttrace point, but not at the pretrace point (table 6.5). In contrast,
there was facilitation for probes related to *crowd* at the pretrace point but not at the

Box 6.5
The cross-modal lexical decision task

> The cross-modal lexical decision task involves visual presentation of a sequence of letters as the subject listens to speech. The subject's task is to indicate by voice or key press whether or not the sequence of letters spells a real word. The probe item may be related to the meaning of part of the spoken linguistic stimulus. For example,
>
> Stimulus (speech): "The policeman saw the boy₁ that₁ the crowd at the party accused t₁ [T] of the crime"
> Related Target (print): SON
> Unrelated Target (print): HAM
>
> One of the target words appears at a particular point in the spoken sentence—for example, at the location indicated by *T*. Typically, response times to correctly indicate that a target is a word are faster for related targets (SON) than for unrelated targets (HAM). Such an outcome is taken to show that the related word in the sentence is activated at the time of the lexical decision.
>
> In some cases, the lexical-decision task is used with only unrelated targets to indicate processing load. In this case, a target unrelated to any word in the sentence, such as HAM for the above sentence, is presented at one of several points during the sentence. The point at which response times to make the lexical decision are longer is taken to indicate a point of increased processing load during comprehension. See Swinney 1979.

Table 6.5
Mean priming scores at three test points relative to the location of *wh*-trace (in ms, differences in lexical decision times to unrelated and related probes)

	Test point		
	Pre	*Wh*	Post
Antecedent (*boy*)	12	27	27
Control (*crowd*)	44	19	8

Source: Adapted from Nicol and Swinney 1989, table I

wh-trace or the posttrace point. The significant priming of probes related to *boy* at the *wh*-trace indicates that the *wh*-trace primes its antecedent immediately. (But see Mckoon and Ratcliff 1994 as well as McKoon, Allbritton, and Ratcliff 1996 for a different interpretation; see Nicol, Fodor, and Swinney 1994 for a reply.)

6.1.7   Subcategorization Frames

Because it appears so frequently, the NVN template is the default template. The comprehension system uses the NVN template unless there is overt and reliable contrary information. An alternative subcategorization frame of a verb can modify the application of the NVN template, particularly if the alternative frames for the verb are used frequently.

Jennings, Randall, and Tyler (1997) demonstrated the role of frequency of use of subcategorization frames with verbs that optionally take either a noun phrase (NP) object or a sentential complement (SC):

(46) *NP object with a preferred NP verb*
The cheerful author denied the allegations.

(47) *SC with a preferred NP verb*
The cheerful author denied (that) the allegations were true.

(48) *NP object with a preferred SC verb*
The leading chemist concluded the experiments.

(49) *SC with a preferred SC verb*
The leading chemist concluded (that) the experiments were important.

Although both *deny* and *conclude* may take either type of complement, Jennings, Randall, and Tyler found that with *deny* people prefer to use a noun phrase object. With *conclude* they prefer a sentential complement.

Jennings and colleagues used the cross-modal naming task to determine whether comprehenders use subcategorization preferences online (see box 6.2). In this task, sentence fragments were presented auditorily and a target word (capitalized below) was presented visually:

(50) *Object NP target with preferred SC verb*
The leading chemist concluded ... THEM

(51) *Subject NP target with preferred SC verb*
The leading chemist concluded ... THEY

(52) *Object NP target with preferred NP verb*
The leading chemist denied ... THEM

(53) *Subject NP target with preferred NP verb*
The leading chemist denied ... THEY

The target word plausibly can be integrated with the preceding material depending on whether the main verb (*concluded* or *denied*) is interpreted as taking a noun phrase object or a sentential object. For example,

(54) The leading chemist concluded they were inert.

(55) The leading chemist denied them laboratory space.

Subjects apparently do attempt to integrate the visually presented word with the auditorily presented sentence fragment, since their naming times for targets such as

Table 6.6
Mean naming times (ms) depending on preference for use of the verb in NP object vs. sentential complement frames

Preference	Type of target	
	Object	Subject
NP object	378	388
SC	391	377

Source: Adapted from Jennings et al. 1997, fig. 2

kindly versus *kindness* were significantly faster when the target completed a grammatical sentence (421 ms):

(56) My cousin always behaves kindly.

than when it did not (434 ms):

(57) My cousin always behaves kindness.

Table 6.6 shows that naming response times were shorter numerically when the target was consistent with the subcategorization preference, but the interaction between type of target and preference was not significant. Jennings and associates did find, however, that response times to object (*them*) versus subject (*they*) targets were correlated with degree of verb preference for a sentential complement versus object noun phrase complement, as determined by pretest. For example, *indicate* shows a slight preference for object noun phrase complement, and response times to fragments with *indicate* were slightly faster for *them* than for *they*. *Accepted* strongly prefers to take an object noun phrase complement, and response times to fragments with *accepted* were much faster for *them* than for *they*. Response times were faster for *they* for verbs that prefer to take a sentential complement, and the size of this advantage for *they* increased with the strength of preference for sentential complements. Thus, comprehenders are immediately sensitive to subcategorization information, and the availability of different interpretations is related to usage preferences.

We can extend this conclusion about early sensitivity to subcategorization properties of verbs with noun phrase versus sentential objects. Similar results are found with verbs that may subcategorize for noun phrase objects versus no object. Branigan, Pickering, and Stewart (discussed in Branigan et al. 1995) report that a sentence context activates a particular subcategorization frame. They measured reading times for early-closure sentences that contained a verb that was ambiguous between transitive and intransitive (58) when another early-closure sentence preceded it (59) versus when a late-closure sentence preceded it (60). Branigan and colleagues found that reading times were faster for the early-closure target sentence when preceded by an early-closure sentence. Similarly, late-closure targets were read faster when the context sentence was late-closure rather than early-closure.

(58) *Target sentence, early closure*
Although the film was frightening the young child enjoyed the plot.

(59) *Context sentence, early closure*
While the woman was eating the creamy soup went cold.

(60) *Context sentence, late closure*
While the woman was eating the creamy soup the pudding went cold.

This effect may involve priming of the transitive versus intransitive subcategorization frames. The early-closure context sentence primes the intransitive interpretation, which enhances the strength of a similar interpretation of *frighten* in the target sentence. This is further evidence that the comprehension system has early access to subcategorization information.

6.2   Meaning

The comprehension system uses the pseudosyntactic structure as the basis for an initial meaning. This initial meaning-form hypothesis rests on the organization of words into major phrases, the assignment of lexical categories, retrieval of likely subcategorization frames and application of canonical sequence templates. The initially accessed meaning, however, precedes the assignment of real syntax. This predicts that people are sensitive to meaning information before a complete syntactic

 structure.

6.2.1   Pragmatic Information Comes Before Verb Morphology
There is evidence that pragmatic violations are detected earlier than syntactic violations. Fodor et al. (1996) recorded eye movements as subjects read sentences with pragmatic violations, syntactic violations, or no violations (see box 6.6), as in the sentences below (slashes indicate the five scoring regions):

(61) *Pragmatic violation*
It seems that cats / won't usually / bake the / food we / put on the porch.

(62) *Syntactic violation*
It seems that cats / won't usually / eating the / food we / put on the porch.

(63) *No violation*
It seems that cats / won't usually / eat the / food we / put on the porch.

Table 6.7 shows first-pass residual reading times over five critical regions, depending on type of violation.

Box 6.6
The eye-tracking task

> The eye-tracking task uses a camera to record the exact point on which a subject is focusing moment by moment while reading a sentence.
>
> The eye-tracking equipment also records the amount of time that the eye rests on each point during the initial, left-to-right scan through a sentence. This time is called *first-pass fixation time* and is assumed to measure processing load at the point of initially fixating on a word.
>
> Trueswell, Tanenhaus, and Garnsey (1994) have noted that first-pass fixation times tend to be longer for scoring regions that have more characters. However, since this correlation is not linear, it is recommended either to use scoring regions of constant length, or to correct for nonlinearity. If scoring regions are not of constant size, Trueswell and colleagues recommend correcting for nonlinearity by using *residual reading times*. Calculating residual reading times requires two steps. First, one calculates the linear regression equation that predicts first-pass reading times from length of scoring region. Second, one subtracts the predicted reading time from the actual reading time. A negative residual reading time indicates that actual reading times for a region of given length were faster than predicted, while a positive residual reading time indicates that actual reading times were slower than predicted. An alternative approach for dealing with the nonlinear relation between length of region and fixation time is to compute a quadratic function.
>
> The eye-tracking equipment is also able to record "regressions" or backtracking. The number of regressions and amount of time spent on them are taken to indicate reanalysis and its difficulty. A third measure that the eye-tracking task yields is total processing time.
>
> The eye-tracking procedure has some advantages and disadvantages over subject-paced word-by-word reading. The eye-tracking task does not require the subject to make a response after each word, but instead allows for more natural presentation of the reading material. However, the eye-tracking procedure does require that the subject's head be stationary, usually through the use of a chin bar on which the subject's chin rests, or a bite bar. See Carpenter and Daneman 1981; Frazier and Rayner 1982.

Table 6.7
Mean residual first-pass eye-fixation times in five scoring regions for different types of violations

| Type of Violation | Region | | | | |
	1	2	3	4	5
Pragmatic	57	2	19	−20	−22
Syntactic	79	2	8	−63	−70
None	79	11	13	−52	−66

Source: From Fodor et al. 1996, fig. 1

Table 6.8
Percent of eye-movement regressions in five scoring regions for different types of violations

Type of Violation	Region				
	1	2	3	4	5
Pragmatic	· 5	11	12	16	29
Syntactic	7	9	19	28	20
None	8	9	6	9	15

Source: From Fodor et al. 1996, fig. 2

There was no difference in reading times in the region that contained the verb (*bake*, *eating*, or *eat*) and the following determiner (region 3). Over regions 4 and 5 (*food we* and *put on the porch*), reading times were longer for the pragmatic violations than for sentences with no violation. Reading times for sentences with syntactic violations did not differ from reading times in the sentences with no violation in any region. Thus, there was an effect of pragmatic anomaly, but not syntactic anomaly, on first-pass reading times. (Incorrect) progressive tense morphemes apparently are ignored on the first pass.

Fodor et al. found that regressive eye movements were more frequent for syntactic violations than for pragmatic violations, as shown in table 6.8. Regressions were elevated for syntactic violations in region 3 (verb + det) and in region 4 (*food we*). Finding evidence for detection of syntactic violations on regressions but not first-pass reading is problematic for syntax-first theories. Since these theories maintain that syntactic decisions are made before pragmatic decisions, we would expect the opposite, namely, effects of syntactic violations on first-pass reading, and effects of pragmatic violations on regressions. Thus, the results suggest that there is early access to pragmatic violations, and somewhat later, access to syntactic violations.

Fodor et al. also used the same materials in a cross-modal lexical decision task (see box 6.5). The same materials were presented in speech compressed to about half its normal rate. A lexical decision probe that was unrelated to the meaning of the sentence appeared at one of five points. The test points were 81 ms before the verb, at the verb, 81 ms after the verb, 162 ms after the verb, or 243 ms after the verb. Subjects indicated as quickly as possible whether or not the probe was a word. Fodor et al. interpreted slower response times on this task as evidence of increased processing load. In one condition, subjects were required to paraphrase the sentence after it was completed. Mean response times for the paraphrase group appear in table 6.9.

At the point of the verb, lexical decision times were longer for both syntactic and pragmatic violations than for no violation. In fact, at the verb and immediately after, pragmatic violations are more disruptive than syntactic violations. Only at the last

Table 6.9
Mean lexical decision times (ms) for paraphrase group at five test points depending on type of violation (test points identified by time in ms before (−) or after (+) the verb)

	Test point				
Type of Violation	−81	0	+81	+162	+243
Syntactic	794	803	770	802	810
Pragmatic	795	817	812	796	763
None	794	746	802	822	749

Source: Fodor et al. 1996, note 10

test point did lexical decision times become substantially greater for syntactic violations than for pragmatic violations.

We can understand these results in terms of LAST. The verbs *eat* and *bake* are potentially intransitive. Based on the NV pattern, the pseudosyntax presents a complete proposition, the grammar generates a candidate syntax, and the system checks it against the memory representation of the input (see figure 5.2). At the point of the verb, assigning the initial meaning draws attention away from the surface form. Hence, responses to the lexical decision task at the verb are slow. Right after the verb, the initial meaning hypothesis is available, which can then slow processing if there is a pragmatic violation. The elevated response times for syntactic violations at the end of the sentence reflect detection of a mismatch between the candidate syntax and the input. The sentences with pragmatic anomalies and no anomalies also produce syntax checking at this point, but do not produce an incorrect syntax, and hence do not result in slowed reaction times.

6.2.2 Accessing Semantic Before Syntactic Aspects of Arguments

Subcategory information provides the major syntactic category frames that a predicate requires. Some predicates require an object noun phrase, some require two object noun phrases, some an object noun phrase and a prepositional phrase, some a sentential complement, and so on. Subcategory information indicates what arguments are needed to make a complete unit of meaning. LAST therefore proposes that subcategory information and associated thematic roles are available early in order to assign major phrases to thematic roles. The question at hand is, does the semantic information become available prior to the syntactic information?

Boland (1997a) used cross-modal naming and lexical decision tasks immediately after hearing a sentence to examine the integration of a probe item with subcategorization information and argument requirements (see boxes 6.2 and 6.5). Boland used sentence fragments that contained a verb that was ambiguous between taking two or three arguments (*toss*). Other sentence fragments contained a verb that unambiguously takes two (*inspect*) or three arguments (*describe*). (Some readers may feel *describe* can take only two arguments, as in *Nancy described the necklace.*) Sample materials appear below, with the probe item in capital letters:

(64) *Ambiguous, two-argument*
     Which salad did Jenny toss BILL

(65) *Ambiguous, three-argument*
     Which baseball did Jenny toss BILL

(66) *Unambiguous, two-argument*
     Which necklace did Nancy inspect SAM

(67) *Unambiguous, three-argument*
     Which necklace did Nancy describe SAM

The subcategorization and thematic requirements of these verbs allowed Boland to examine the availability of semantic and syntactic information. Semantically, the verb *toss* may take either two arguments (agent, patient) or three arguments (agent, recipient, and patient):

(68) Jenny tossed the salad.

(69) Jenny tossed Bill the ball.

Syntactically, the subcategorization frame of *toss* is ambiguous between

toss $\langle$NP$\rangle$

toss $\langle$NP NP$\rangle$

where the material inside the angle brackets indicates phrases that are required inside the verb phrase (i.e., omitting the subject, which is always required).

In Boland's (1997a) analysis, *inspect* semantically takes exactly two arguments (agent, patient), and *describe* takes three (agent, patient, and goal):

(70) Nancy inspected the necklace.

(71) Nancy described the necklace to Sam.

Syntactically, the subcategorization frames of these verbs are:

inspect $\langle$NP$\rangle$

describe $\langle$NP PP$\rangle$ *put i wt sthjschny 3 argts for describe*

Since the subcategorization frame of *inspect* does not allow it to take a second argument inside the verb phrase, we expect that it will be difficult to integrate the probe *Sam* into the sentence. However, the subcategorization frame of *describe* does allow it to take an additional argument, but, syntactically, it must be in the form of a prepositional phrase, not a noun phrase, since neither of the following is grammatical:

Table 6.10
Mean naming times (ms) for ambiguous and unambiguous verbs depending on the number of arguments they allow

	Arguments		
	2	3	Mean
Ambiguous	609	608	609
Unambiguous	627	625	626

Source: Adapted from Boland 1997a, table 2

(72) *Nancy described the necklace Sam.

(73) *Nancy described Sam the necklace.

Thus, *describe* can take a goal as well as an agent and patient, and, on semantic grounds, Sam is a plausible goal, but the third argument must be in the form of a prepositional phrase, not a noun phrase.

Boland used the naming task as a measure of sensitivity to syntactic constraints and the lexical decision task as a measure of sensitivity to semantic constraints (see Boland 1993). Because of the differences in subcategorization and thematic requirements, sentences with different verbs will produce differences in performance on these tasks. Consider first the naming task, which other studies have shown to be sensitive to syntactic constraints (see box 6.2). If all subcategorization frames are momentarily and indifferently accessed, there will be no difference in naming times for the two ambiguous sentences with *toss*. Since neither *inspect* nor *describe* subcategorizes for a third NP, there also will be no difference in naming times for *inspect* and *describe*. Since the syntactic requirements of *inspect* and *describe* do not include a third NP, naming times for these sentences will be slower than naming times for the ambiguous *toss*, which does subcategorize for a third NP. The results for the naming task appear in table 6.10.

Boland found that naming times were faster for ambiguous sentences than for unambiguous sentences. This shows that both subcategorization frames of the ambiguous verb are available for integration with the probe. Boland also found that response times did not differ between the ambiguous two-argument condition (*toss* with *salad*) and the ambiguous three-argument condition (*toss* with *baseball*). If plausibility influenced the availability of subcategorization frames, one might expect that *salad* would rule out the three-argument frame. Because response times did not differ for the two- and three-argument ambiguous conditions, Boland concluded that all syntactic subcategorization frames possible for a verb are activated, regardless of semantic context. However, we could as easily conclude that the syntactic frames are

Table 6.11
Mean lexical decision times (ms) for ambiguous and unambiguous verbs depending on the number of arguments they allow

	Arguments	
	2	3
Ambiguous	659	643
Unambiguous	699	666
Mean	679	655

Source: Adapted from Boland 1997a, table 3

not accessed at all in a way that influences the naming time—that is, the differential effects of syntactic complexity do not have an immediate effect.

Boland's evidence unequivocally shows that the semantic aspects of the argument structure are immediately accessed. Consider the lexical decision task, which is sensitive to semantic constraints (see box 6.5). If meaning is accessed initially, lexical decision times will be faster for the three-argument verbs than for the two-argument verbs, since in the three-argument cases the probe can be interpreted with the sentence fragment to complete the argument requirements of the verb. Thus, response times ought to be faster for the *toss* sentence with *baseball* and the *describe* sentence than for the *toss* sentence with *salad* and the *inspect* sentence.

The results for the lexical decision task appear in table 6.11. Boland found that lexical decision times were faster for three-argument sentences than for two-argument sentences. This result suggests that the probe item is integrated semantically with the three-argument sentences, which is not possible with the two-argument sentences. Based on the argument requirements of subcategorization frames, the probe item is incorporated whenever possible into an initial representation of meaning, regardless of the detailed syntactic requirements of the verb.

6.3   Real Syntax

Up to this point, we have highlighted experimental facts consistent with an early formulation of a meaning-form hypothesis, prior to a complete syntax. We now turn to evidence for the regeneration of a complete syntactic description from constraints set by the formulation of the initial meaning. The real syntax of a sentence refers to the entire derivation and annotated phrase structure tree for the sentence. The output of real syntax differs from pseudosyntax in two ways. First, real syntax includes detailed phrase structure within major phrases, whereas pseudosyntax includes the segregation of words into major phrases based on function words and major lexical categories. Second, real syntax includes the linking of NP-traces and antecedents.

The grammar generates a real syntax for a sentence based on an initial guess about meaning. This initial meaning-form hypothesis includes the thematic roles that have been associated with major phrases.

6.3.1   Well-Formedness Constraints Apply After Meaning and Pseudosyntax

Semantic information appears early enough to influence performance on a sentence matching task (see box 6.7). As subjects performed the sentence matching task, Murray and Rowan (1998) measured first-pass fixation times in an eye-tracking task (see box 6.6). The matching sentences were designed so that the initial noun phrase/ verb pair was either plausible or implausible, and so that the verb/second noun phrase pair was either plausible or implausible. Examples of their materials appear below:

(74) *Plausible NP₁-V, plausible V-NP₂*
      The hunters stacked the bricks.

(75) *Plausible NP₁-V, implausible V-NP₂*
      The hunters stacked the tulips.

(76) *Implausible NP₁-V, plausible V-NP₂*
      The bishops stacked the bricks.

(77) *Implausible NP₁-V, implausible V-NP₂*
      The bishops stacked the tulips.

The basic measure of interest in this version of the sentence-matching task was first-pass reading time on the initial noun phrase in the first sentence. The results are most interesting, and appear in table 6.12. For the initial noun phrase in the first sentence, first-pass reading times were 15 ms/word faster for plausible NP₁-V sequences than

Box 6.7
The sentence-matching task

In the sentence-matching task, the subject sees one whole sentence, then presses a key to display a second sentence so that both sentences appear simultaneously. In some experiments, the second sentence appears after a certain time, such as 2 sec, without the subject pressing a key. The two sentences appear together centered and on adjacent lines, as in

The hunters stacked the bricks.
The hunters stacked the bricks.

The subject's task is to indicate whether the two sentences contain the same words in the same order. The dependent variable typically is response time to make this judgment, measured from the onset of the second sentence. See Forster and Olbrei 1973.

Table 6.12
Mean first-pass reading times (ms/word) on the initial noun phrase (NP_1) in the first sentence

NP_1-V	V-NP_2		
	Plausible	Implausible	Mean
Plausible	244	238	241
Implausible	252	260	256
Difference	8	22	15

Source: Adapted from Murray and Rowan 1998, table II

for implausible NP_1-V sequences. This difference was significant despite the fact that subjects were not required to understand the sentences, only to match them physically. The results suggest that semantic information becomes available quickly and mandatorily, indicating that meaning is an early part of comprehension. Murray and Rowan argue that the semantic-plausibility effect is due to computation of the semantic relation between the initial noun phrase and the verb, which does not occur early according to LAST. The effect, however, may have occurred because of immediate access to associative information, such as residual associations between the noun and the verb or the plausibility of the initial noun as an agent, both of which are elicited early according to LAST. If *hunters*, for example, is a more plausible agent than *bishops*, a sequence that begins with *hunters* conforms more strongly to the initial noun = agent template (see also section 7.1.1). Thus, we would expect faster processing time on *hunters* than on *bishops*, regardless of the verb. Supporting this interpretation was a significant semantic effect on fixation times for the initial noun phrase *before* the verb had been fixated.

Freedman and Forster (1985) showed that some aspects of syntax are accessed in the sentence-matching task. These aspects of syntax include the organization of words into major phrases that correspond to arguments, subject-verb agreement, and quantifier placement—that is, those features marked by pseudosyntax. Their materials included acceptable and unacceptable sentences, and their unacceptable sentences involved violations of phrase structure, agreement, and quantifier placement rules. The phrase structure violations consisted of either two noun phrases or two verb phrases from two different acceptable sentences. Some sample materials are:

(78) *Acceptable phrase structures*
    a. The girl behind you reminds me of your sister.
    b. The subsequent discussion soon got boring.

(79) *Phrase structure violations*
    a. The girl behind you the subsequent discussion.
    b. Reminds me of your sister soon got boring.

Table 6.13
Mean sentence-matching times (ms) for three violations of pseudosyntax

	Phrase structure	Agreement	Quantifier
Acceptable	1432	1385	1274
Violations	1555	1427	1340
Difference	123	42	66

Source: Adapted from Freedman and Forster 1985, tables 5 and 6

(80) *Acceptable agreement*
Mary was writing a letter to her husband.

(81) *Agreement violation*
Mary were writing a letter to her husband.

(82) *Acceptable quantifier placement*
The baby ate his cereal all up.

(83) *Quantifier placement violation*
The baby ate his cereal up all.

As in the sentence-matching task (box 6.7), Freedman and Forster presented two lines of text on a screen. In the critical positive trials in which the lines matched, the lines were either acceptable or unacceptable sentences. Freedmen and Forster recorded response times to judge whether the two lines were identical. No judgment of acceptability was required. The results appear in the table 6.13. For each type of material, response times were significantly longer for violations than for the corresponding acceptable sentences. These results suggest that constraints on phrase structure, subject-verb agreement, and quantifier placement become available quickly and mandatorily.

While meaning and pseudosyntax are available early, certain syntactic information becomes available only at a late stage of comprehension. This late syntactic information includes well-formedness constraints that block the grammar from allowing certain kinds of movement. Consider the examples below from Freedman and Forster 1985:

(84) *No movement, no specified subject*
The duchess sold a portrait of her father.

(85) *Movement, no specified subject*
Who$_1$ did the duchess sell a portrait of t$_1$?

The examples above show that English syntax allows movement of a *wh*-word that refers to *father*. In these examples, the movement crosses a nonspecific subject, *a portrait*. However, the corresponding movement across a specific subject, *Turner's portrait* in the examples below, produces an ungrammatical sentence:

(86) *No movement, specified subject*
The duchess sold Turner's portrait of her father.

(87) *Movement, specified subject*
*Who$_1$ did the duchess sell Turner's portrait of t$_1$?

Since the grammar must allow movement of the object in some cases but not others, there must be a filter that rules out certain cases. The relevant difference between the grammatical and ungrammatical cases is that sentences in which the movement crosses a specific subject such as *Turner's portrait* are ungrammatical. Crossing a nonspecific subject (*a portrait*) is allowed. This constraint is called the *specified-subject constraint*.

Another example of a violation of a well-formedness constraint is subjacency. The grammar allows movement across one S-node, indicated below with left bracket, since there are acceptable sentences such as the following (Freedman and Forster 1985):

(88) *No movement, no subjacency constraint*
It is hard to trust Ann.

(89) *Movement, no subjacency constraint*
Ann$_1$ is hard [to trust t$_1$].

But moving an element across two NP- or S-nodes produces an ungrammatical sentence:

(90) *No movement, subjacency constraint*
It is hard to trust rumors about Ann.

(91) *Movement, subjacency constraint*
*Ann$_1$ is hard [to trust [rumors about t$_1$]].

The subjacency constraint therefore prohibits sentences in which there has been movement of an element across two NP- or S-nodes.

Freedman and Forster (1985) used the sentence-matching task to examine sensitivity to violations of the specified subject and subjacency constraints (see box 6.7). The distractor trials were pairs of sentences of similar construction in which the sentences differed in just one word.

In order to assess sensitivity to well-formedness constraints on movement, it was necessary to compare the effects of movement with violations of a constraint and the effects of movement without violation of a constraint. If subjects are sensitive to these constraints in the sentence-matching task, there should be greater effects of movement on matching times for sentences with violation of a constraint than for sentences without violation a constraint. The results for critical "same" responses

Table 6.14
Mean sentence-matching times (ms) for specified subject constraint and subjacency

	No violation	Violation	Difference
Specified subject			
Movement	1268	1549*	281
No movement	1199	1511	312
Difference	69	38	
Subjacency			
Movement	1198	1498*	300
No movement	1050	1350	350
Difference	148	148	

Note: Asterisks indicate the ungrammatical cases.
Source: Adapted from Freedman and Forster 1985, tables 1 and 3

appear in table 6.14. For both specified subject and subjacency constraints, there was no difference in the effect of movement on response times whether a constraint was violated or not. These results suggested that subjects can perform the sentence-matching task without accessing knowledge about the specified subject and subjacency constraints.

However, subjects do access these constraints late in comprehension. An unspeeded test—that is, allowing subjects to take their time—showed that subjects judged sentences with movement that violated the specified subject constraint to be odd or bad in 82 percent of the cases, compared to 33 percent for sentences with movement that did not violate this constraint. Thus, the specified subject constraint is accessed late, after the response is made on a speeded sentence-matching task.

The results of this set of studies show that meaning and pseudosyntax appear early enough to influence judgments on the sentence-matching task, but constraints on movement do not. The sentence-matching task requires comparison of two sentences based *only* on lexical items. Nevertheless, certain higher-level properties of sentences influence matching performance. These properties include the organization of words into major phrases such as noun phrases and verbs and the local plausibility of the subject phrase and the verb. What does not influence matching are high-level constraints on movement, even though they do influence unspeeded judgements of grammaticality. The sentence matching results provide clear evidence that certain aspects of syntax are accessed late.

6.3.2 Early Access to Major Phrase Segmentation, Late Access to Complete Phrase Structure

A series of studies on the mislocation of brief sounds (clicks) presented during sentences supports the view that major phrases are isolated early but detailed phrase

Box 6.8
Response bias in the click-location task

In early click-location tasks, the subjects listened through headphones to a spoken sentence in one ear and a click in the other ear. They then wrote down the sentence and marked where the click had occurred. Errors in locating the click were attributed to processes that occur during the perception of the sentence. An alternative "response bias" interpretation is that errors in click location occur because of the subject's use of phrase structure as a cue to where misperceived clicks must have occurred.

Bever, Hurtig, and Handel (1975) addressed the problem of response biases directly. In their procedure, subjects listened to the sentence and click. They then turned the page of a booklet to reveal the sentence already printed, with a "window" of location for the click, as marked by slashes below.

Along with /his wives the prince/ brought the court's only dwarf.

The subject's task was to mark the subjective location of the click within that window. The window was always centered on the objective click location, which was either one word before the clause break, in the clause break, or one word after the clause break. However, in some trials with experimental sentences, the click was absent. Bever, Hurtig, and Handel prepared subjects for this by including nonexperimental sentences with clicks of varying loudness. This gave the subjects the information that the clicks varied in loudness and sometimes were hard to hear. In addition, to keep subjects vigilant about encoding the entire sentence, the page revealed for occasional nonexperimental sentences was blank, and subjects had to write down the entire sentence and locate the click in it.

This procedure allows direct comparison of the pattern of mislocations when the click was present versus absent. Bever and associates found significantly different patterns in the click-present and click-absent trials. In the click-absent trials, the position just before the clause break attracted the most responses. In the click-present trials, many more responses were located in the phrase break than either preceding or following it. Thus, the mislocation pattern to actual clicks is perceptually mediated. See Bever 1973; Garrett, Bever, and Fodor 1966.

---

structure is assigned late. The paradigm is described in box 6.8. Fodor and Bever (1965) reported that clicks are mislocated towards clause boundaries. The characteristic response pattern was that clicks objectively prior to or after the clause-break position [O] were reported as having occurred in the clause break [R]:

Along with his wives the prince brought the court's only dwarf.
　　　　　　　O R

Correspondingly, clicks objectively in the clause-break position were accurately located more often than clicks in other positions.

Along with his wives the prince brought the court's only dwarf.
　　　　　　　OR

Fodor and Bever initially proposed that "surface phrase structure" was assigned immediately during comprehension and that phrase units tended to resist interruption, thus accounting for the displacement of clicks to points between clauses. They argued that their data justified the claim that the entire phrase structure is assigned immediately, because assigning the clause break logically occurs as a function of that, but only if the complete structure is assigned. In LAST, the assignment of clause segmentation occurs as a consequence of assigning basic thematic relations to arguments of verbs. A complete surface phrase structure is not necessary for that.

Bever, Lackner, and Kirk (1969) examined the question of whether surface phrase structure segmentation or underlying thematic roles affect click location. They contrasted sequences that differed in their "deep" structure but not in their surface structure:

(92) The corrupt police can't force criminals [to confess].

(93) The corrupt police can't bear [criminals to confess].

The phrase structure relation between the main verb (*bear*, *force*) and the following noun phrase (*criminals*) is the same in these two sentences. However, in the first sentence the noun phrase is the patient of the main verb and the agent of the complement verb. In the second sentence the entire complement is the patient of the main verb, while the noun phrase is still the agent of the complement verb. Thus, the only difference is whether or not the noun phrase is isolated as the patient of the verb. Bever, Lackner, and Kirk found that clicks objectively located in the main verb were more often misplaced into the position between the verb and the noun phrase in the second sentence (80%) than in the first sentence (40%). This result is consistent with the view that the argument structure and associated segmentation can govern click mislocation.

Bever, Lackner, and Kirk also examined whether all structural details are initially assigned or just the phrases that correspond to the complete set of thematic roles. In one experiment, they used materials like:

(94) When he stood up my son's book fell off the table.

Clicks were objectively located within one of the two words preceding the clause boundary (*stood*, *up*) or within one of the two words following the clause boundary (*my*, *son's*). Bever and colleagues classified the mislocations in terms of whether or not they were toward larger breaks in the phrase structure tree. The relevant structural details here are that *stood up* constitutes a phrase structure unit, but *he stood* does not. Thus, if detailed phrase structure is assigned immediately, clicks within *stood* will be mislocated more often before *stood* than after it.

Bever, Lackner, and Kirk found that less than 42 percent of the mislocations supported the within-clause phrase structure hypothesis. Thus, while clicks objectively in words tend to be reported as having occurred between words in general, there was no effect of minor phrase boundary differences.

These results created a conundrum:

1. Clicks within words are subjectively reported between words.
2. Only major phrases that correspond to the required arguments of a verb affect click location.

That is, words are units relevant for click mislocation, and major phrases are also relevant, but minor phrase structure that rests between the level of words and major phrases is not relevant. This conundrum either invalidates the idea that the entire surface phrase structure determines subjective click location, or it invalidates syntax-first theories. However, it is entirely consistent with LAST. The system simultaneously assigns arguments to verbs, which requires at least isolating major phrase heads. At the same time, to map an initial meaning-form hypothesis, it must isolate as many content words as possible. Thus, the system accesses words and major phrases as an initial part of its computation.

The initial assignment of major argument relations requires that they be identifiable in the surface sequence. This process of idenifying major argument relations involves an initial process of segmentation of lexical sequences into likely major phrases, based on superficial structural cues such as the location of function words. This in turn depends on segregating and representing separately function words and content words. These early steps in comprehension are supported by the systematic mislocation of clicks while listening to sentences. Clicks are systematically mislocated as occurring between words, and also between major argument-bearing phrases.

These results would also be consistent with a full phrase structure–building component, of the sort presupposed by most syntax-based comprehension theories. But clicks are not perceptually attracted to phrase structure breaks intermediate between word- and argument-phrase level. The failure initially to assign a complete structure is consistent with the LAST. But it is also a prediction of the LAST that the complete structure *is* assigned late, as part of the grammatical synthesis of the sentence for comparison with the input. Thus, the prediction is that minor variations in phrase structure will affect click mislocation, but only after some time, not as an immediate perceptual effect.

Bever and colleagues tested this using a standard click-location paradigm but requiring subjects to wait a few seconds after hearing the sentence and auditory click before locating it. With this paradigm, minor variations in phrase structure do have the predicted systematic effect on click mislocations, suggesting that the entire phrase structure is now mentally represented. It might be argued that all the effects of structure on click location *must* be a response bias, since locating a click clearly necessitates postperceptual process. This is not logically required and should be subjected to the same kind of test as the mislocation of clicks to major boundaries

(Bever, Hurtig, and Handel 1975). If future research shows that nonexistent clicks are "located" at minor phrase boundaries a few seconds after hearing the sentence, this will demonstrate that some kind of postperceptual process is at issue. Of course, LAST claims that this postperceptual process is specifically the reconstitution of the entire syntactic derivation including the surface phrase structure, so even if it were a response bias the systematic pattern is consistent with the model.

6.3.3 NP-Trace

The properties of NP-movement provide further evidence that the details of syntax are assigned after meaning. We noted in chapter 4 that NP-movement differs from *wh*-movement of major arguments. NP-movement does not leave explicit markers of movement, and it preserves canonical order. This allows NP-trace sentences to be understood initially by (mis)application of the initial template. These two properties of NP-movement suggest that the comprehension system establishes NP-traces in their original location *after* assigning a meaning, rather than before as it does in the case of *wh*-movement (see section 6.1.6).

Here are some examples of NP-movement (from McElree and Bever 1989):

(95) *NP-movement*
   a. The judge$_1$ is certain t$_1$ to argue the appeal.
   b. The lawyer$_1$ was suspected t$_1$ by the judge.

In the first sentence above, *judge* occupies the subject position in front of the verb *argue*, where it receives its thematic role as agent of *argue*, When *judge* is moved to its surface position at the beginning of the sentence, it receives nominative case assignment. Because of the grammatical requirement in government and binding theory that thematic roles are projected at all levels of structure, the movement operation leaves behind a trace t_1. The common subscript indicates that *t* and *judge* refer to each other.

In the second sentence, *lawyer* occupies the object position following *suspected* in D-structure, where it receives the role of patient of *suspected*. There is movement to the front of the sentence, leaving behind a trace following the verb. Once again the common index indicates coreference.

NP-movement creates sequences similar to base-generated sequences. Consider the following pair of sentences:

(96) *NP-movement*
   a. The judge$_1$ is certain t$_1$ to argue the appeal.

   PRO
   b. The judge is eager PRO to argue the appeal.

The first sentence above has NP-movement. However, the sequence of major phrases in the first sentence corresponds to those of the base-generated sequence in the second sentence. The deep subject of *is eager* is *judge*, but the deep subject of *is certain* is *the judge to argue the appeal*. The following pattern of acceptable and unacceptable sentences confirms that this pair of sentences has different main subjects:

(97) a.   It is certain that the judge will argue the appeal.
     b.   *It is eager that the judge will argue the appeal.
     c.   For the judge to argue the appeal is certain.
     d.   *For the judge to argue the appeal is eager.

Similar differences occur in the following pair, with the first sentence but not the second having NP-movement:

(98) a.   The lawyer$_1$ was suspected t$_1$ by the judge.
     b.   The lawyer was unsatisfied by the decision.

In the first sentence above, *lawyer* is the deep object of *suspected*, but in the second sentence it is not the deep object of *unsatisfied* because *unsatisfy* is not a transitive verb. The following pair confirms that *lawyer* is the deep object only in the first sentence above:

(99) a.   The judge suspected the lawyer.
     b.   *The decision unsatisfied the lawyer.

In the case of sentences with NP-movement the comprehension system may initially assign an incorrect syntactic structure while accessing an almost correct meaning. The similarity of surface patterns between sentences with NP-movement and other base-generated patterns may lead to an initial meaning-form hypothesis that is based on canonical sentence patterns that have different meanings. For example, the following sentence pattern may elicit an initial meaning-form hypothesis for predicate adjective sentences:

(100) NP + BE + ADJ ⇒ Experiencer + BE + state

Applied to the sentence

(101) The lawyer was unhappy with the decision.

the template yields the following meaning assignments:

lawyer   =   Experiencer
unhappy with the decision   =   State

Applied to a passive sentence, the same template yields corresponding meaning assignments:

(102) The lawyer was suspected by the judge.

lawyer   =   Experiencer
suspected by the judge   =   State

Because of the similarity in surface patterns between passive and predicate adjective sentences, a passive sentence is interpreted initially as a stative (adjectival) sentence like *the lawyer was unhappy*. This hypothesis about the meaning serves as the basis and constraint on what the grammar generates as a corresponding syntactic derivation. The grammar attempts to generate the syntax for a stative based on grammatical information associated with the specific lexical items that have been recognized. However, the grammatical information associated with *suspect* includes the fact that it is a transitive verb, which requires an object (patient) and, optionally, a subject (agent). Thus, the grammar will be unable to generate an adjectival structure, and will block the analysis, disposing of the initial meaning-form hypothesis. The comprehension system receives the information that the grammar failed to generate an adjectival structure, and accessing the subcategorization frames allowed by the verb derives the hypothesis that the meaning is

judge   =   agent
suspect   =   action
lawyer   =   patient

Based on this meaning, the grammar generates the correct syntax.

Thus, sentences with NP-movement will be processed differently than sentences with *wh*-movement. Special strategies for developing a conceptual representation for *wh*-sentences lead to generation of the correct syntax. The similarity of sentences with NP-movement to other canonical sentences leads to generation of an initially incorrect syntax. Since the initial hypothesis about meaning for sentences with NP-movement leads to the incorrect syntax, LAST assigns the correct syntax of such sentences late.

Priming from NP-Trace   Experimental evidence supports the prediction that the correct syntax for sentences with NP-movement is assigned late. McElree and Bever (1989) used a probe recognition technique with sentences like those below (see box 6.9):

(103) *NP-movement*
      The dazed cabbie$_1$ who drove the beat-up taxi was resented t$_1$ (P1) constantly (P2).

(104) *Predicate adjective*
      The dazed cabbie who drove the beat-up taxi was resentful (P1) constantly (P2).

P1 and P2 indicate the points at which the probe items appeared. The first sentence has a passive structure, with a trace indicating the deep position of *the dazed cabbie*. The second sentence has a predicate adjective structure, which has no movement and

Box 6.9
The probe-recognition task

In the probe-recognition task, the subject hears or reads linguistic material. At some point the material stops and the subject hears or sees a probe item. The subject's task is to indicate as quickly as possible whether or not the probe had appeared in the sentence. Timing usually begins with the onset of the probe item, and ends with the subject's vocal or manual response. For example, subjects might hear

Though Pete called up his aunt each night at [P] nine, he rarely called his grandmother.

and see a probe such as UP at the point corresponding to P (Townsend and Bever 1978). By presenting the probe task at different test points during the sentence, it is possible to determine accessibility to the target item at different points. Rapid response times are taken to indicate that the target is easily accessed at that test point. See also Caplan 1972.

Table 6.15
Mean probe recognition times (ms) in passive vs. adjectival sentences at two test points

	Test point relative to NP-trace	
Sentence	Trace	Posttrace
Passive	901	932
Adjectival	909	1008

Source: From McElree and Bever 1989, table II, exp. 5

no trace. While reading such sentences, subjects received a probe word such as DAZED at the point of P1 or P2. The results appear in table 6.15.

McElree and Bever (1989) found no difference in response times at the first probe position for adjectival and passive sentences. At the second probe position, however, response times were faster for passive sentences than for adjectival sentences. These results indicate that the correct syntax of a passive sentence, including the trace, is not assigned immediately. The initial interpretation of a passive sentence corresponds to that of a predicate adjective sentence.

In a separate experiment, McElree and Bever (1989) tested for antecedent activation in NP-raising sentences. Example sentences are:

(105) *NP-raising*
   The conceited actor$_1$ who worked with the leading lady was sure t$_1$ to (P1) rehearse for the entire evening (P2).

(106) *PRO*
   The conceited actor who worked with the leading lady was eager PRO to (P1) rehearse for the entire evening (P2).

Table 6.16
Mean probe recognition times (ms) in three sentence types at two test points

| | Test point | |
Sentence	P1	P2
NP raising	882	922
PRO	909	986
Adjectival	905	1022

Source: From McElree and Bever 1989, table II, exp. 2

(107) *Adjectival*
   The conceited actor who worked with the leading lady was rude to (P1) the rehearsers in the evening (P2).

The results appear in table 6.16. A NP-trace had no immediate effect on probe recognition response times, but it did have an effect at the end of the sentence. Response times for the three sentence types did not differ at the NP-trace position, but they were faster at a later point for NP-raising sentences than for either PRO or adjectival sentences.

The results show that NP-trace does not activate its antecedent at the trace position, but it does so considerably later. This suggests that the initial interpretation of NP-raising is similar to a predicate adjective sentence. Later, the comprehension system has assigned the correct syntax of *the conceited actor* as subject of *rehearse*.

Osterhout and Swinney (1993) confirmed the late effect of a NP-trace in passive sentences with a cross-modal lexical decision task. They presented a single item for lexical decision during a spoken sentence such as

(108) *Passive*
   The dentist$_1$ from the new medical center in town was invited t$_1$ by the actress to go to the party.

(109) *Active*
   The dentist from the new medical center in town invited the actress to go to the party.

A lexical decision probe related to the meaning of *dentist*, such as *tooth*, occurred immediately at the point of the trace (t$_1$), 500 ms later (in the passive sentence, near the beginning of *actress*), or 1000 ms later (in the passive, near the end of *actress*). Unrelated probe words such as *flood* appeared at the same points. The results appear in table 6.17.

In passive sentences, only at 1000 ms did related probes produce significantly faster response times than unrelated probes. In active sentences there was no significant

Table 6.17
Mean lexical decision times (ms) in passive and active sentences at three test points

	Test point relative to NP trace		
	0 ms	500 ms	1000 ms
Passive			
Related	589	637	615
Unrelated	607	661	661
Difference	18	24	46
Active			
Related	592	657	645
Unrelated	600	654	653
Difference	8	−3	8

Source: Adapted from Osterhout and Swinney 1993, table III

difference between related and unrelated probes at any of the three test points. These results support LAST. NP-trace primes its antecedent, though this priming does not occur immediately. The mechanism for priming occurs after the formation of an initial guess about meaning and after generation of the incorrect syntax, at the stage of revising the syntax.

Word-priming results like these could, of course, be due to factors other than the syntax. For example, the passive construction in English characteristically gives discourse focus to the surface subject, deep patient. In that view, it is not surprising that there is selective priming to the subject. Of course, this does not explain the lack of priming for noneventive passives, which also focus the surface subject and it does not explain why NP-traces are primed late. But it is useful to explore NP-trace priming with other constructions that might control for some of the potential artefacts. Bever and Sanz (1997) did this in Spanish. Sanz (1996) noted that unaccusative intransitive verbs in Spanish are syntactically raising verbs (verbs such as *fall, arrive*). This follows from the fact that such verbs are telic, and must be delimited by a verb phrase–internal argument, but unergative intransitive verbs do not exhibit evidence of raising (verbs such as *speak, sleep*). Thus, Bever and Sanz (1997) could contrast priming for the initial noun phrase in sentences like the following:

(110) *Unaccusative*
El apuesto critico ... llego [np]. ...

(111) *Unergative*
El apuesto critico ... hablo. ...

In critical cases, Bever and Sanz (1997) found more priming for unaccusative than unergative verb constructions. This result is important because the initial noun phrase position has the same discourse role in Spanish for both types of verbs.

6.3.4 Synthesis Based on Conceptual Representation

LAST relies on a generative component to synthesize a detailed syntactic representation. The input to the synthetic component—that is, the grammar—has available a representation of meaning, words, and bits of a structural representation. This component of the model resembles the computation of syntactic representations in sentence production, in which the speaker begins with an intention to utter some conceptual representation and must then formulate the structure of a sentence that expresses it. However, unlike sentence production, the representation that the syntactic synthesis supplies for comparison with the input is itself internal, not an actual utterance.

The synthetic component of comprehension provides an internal syntactic representation of a sentence, based on a conceptual representation and the actual words. When we memorize a sentence for later recall, the possibility arises that it is encoded abstractly and is fleshed out into an actual utterance only when actively recalled. The classic studies of sentence memory by Miller and his students (chapter 2) suggested that sentences are coded in terms of basic propositions. Consistent with this view, Lombardi and Potter (1992; Potter and Lombardi 1990, 1998) proposed the *regeneration hypothesis* for sentence recall: When a sentence is recalled verbatim, the recall is based on a conceptual representation, including an abstract representation of the verb and its argumetns, and activated lexical items. The recalled sentence is generated from this conceptual representation using the rules of grammar.

Lombardi and Potter (1992) used a RSVP recall task following a list of distractor words (see box 6.10). The duration of the words was 200 ms, and the sentence was followed by a sequence of five distractor words. In the critical cases, the list of distractors contained a word related to a target word in the sentence. Their procedure involved presenting a sentence in RSVP (200 ms/word) followed by a sequence of five words, and then a probe item. The subject must indicate whether the probe item was in the sequence of five words, and then recall the sentence as accurately as possible. The critical sentences contained alternating datives, which can present the recipient as a prepositional phrase or as a noun phrase:

(112) *NP-PP*

   The rich widow is going to give a million dollars to the university.

(113) *NP-NP*

   The rich widow is going to give the university a million dollars.

Box 6.10
The RSVP recall task

In the Rapid Serial Visual Presentation (RSVP) task each word of a sentence is displayed for a brief amount of time, one after the other. The word-presentation times typically are constant within a sentence, and they range from durations as short as 20 ms in studies of unconscious word priming to durations as long as 250 ms. Participants typically are asked to recall immediately as many words as possible. In some uses of this paradigm, the sentence is followed by a sequence of distractor words, and then the instruction to recall the sentence appears. The distractor words prevent the participants from recalling the last words of the sentence out of a short-term memory buffer. See Forster 1970.

The sequence of five words contained a lure such as *donate*. The lure is a non-alternating dative that can appear only with the recipient in a prepositional phrase. Lombardi and Potter assume that if the surface structure is stored, the lure will intrude more in sentence recall when it matches the surface frame of the sentence to be recalled. If a conceptual representation is stored, lure intrusions will not differ for the two types of sentences.

Lombardi and Potter (1992) found no significant difference in intrusions of the lure in the two types of sentences. For NP-PP sentences the intrusion rate was 11 percent, and for NP-NP sentences it was 7 percent. Furthermore, when the lure did intrude in recall of NP-NP sentences, the grammatical form of the sentence was changed to fit the grammatical requirements of the lure. For NP-PP sentences, changes in grammatical form occurred in only 7 percent of the cases.

In a second experiment, subjects read a sentence in RSVP, then read a probe word, and had to say whether the probe could replace a word in the sentence without changing anything else in the sentence, including the meaning. When the subjects said yes, they then had to report the sentence as it would appear with the probe word. The sentences were alternating datives in either NP-PP or NP-NP form:

(114) *NP-PP*
    The agent will send his report to the government when his mission ends.

(115) *NP-NP*
    The agent will send the government his report when his mission ends.

The probe words were either alternating datives (*mail*) or nonalternating datives (*transmit*).

The results appear in table 6.18.

When the probe word was an alternating dative, the probe could fit into either type of sentence. In this case, accuracy was high and response time fast. When the probe word was a nonalternating dative, accuracy was high for NP-PP sentences but not for

Table 6.18
Percentage of correct responses and mean RTs (ms)

	% Correct	RT
Alternating probe		
NP-PP sentence	88	1460
NP-NP sentence	88	1434
Nonalternating probe		
NP-PP sentence	91	1379
NP-NP sentence	33	1829

Source: Adapted from Lombardi and Potter 1992

NP-NP sentences. The correct response for the NP-NP sentences is no, since substituting the probe into the sentence would yield an ungrammatical sentence:

(116) *The agent will transmit the government his report when his mission ends.

Since accuracy was so low for trials with NP-NP sentences and nonalternating probes, the subjects must not have stored the surface structure. The percentage of actual changes in the sentence confirms this conclusion. When subjects incorrectly said yes, their recall of the sentence with the probe verb involved a change to restore grammaticality in four times as many cases as when they said no.

While almost tautological, the Lombardi and Potter 1992 study gives some empirical force to an existence proof for corresponding processes in the synthetic component of comprehension. To put it in terms relevant to the work of Potter and Lombardi: If sentence comprehension involves mechanisms of literal recall, the recall process involves a synthesis of the surface form from conceptual representations together with specific content words, verbs, and their arguments. Garrett (1999) has generalized this notion, arguing that many component processes of speech production are involved in assigning structure during comprehension.

6.4   Introspection and Sentence Processing

Linguistic theory relies largely on intuitions about well-formedness of sentences, independent of their processing complexity. Accessing an acceptability intuition calls on the native speaker's direct knowledge of whether a sentence initially appears to be computable as a sentence. While such intuitions can be refined by experience or theoretical expectations and are sometimes more variable than one would like in data, there is a bedrock of stable intuitions underlying syntactic theory. There is a sense in which grammaticality intuitions involve examination of the language, not of the speaker's attitude toward or behavior with the language. This contrasts with intu-

itions about relative complexity, which are sometimes used to initiate or buttress processing theories. To render an intuition about comprehension complexity, a speaker
must imagine perceiving the sentence (or be presented with it for comprehension),
and then introspect about how difficult it seemed to be to arrive at an interpretation. In the end, results from such investigations require verification with more
objective paradigms, but they have held up remarkably well (e.g., Haviland and
Clark 1974).

In this chapter our focus is on the specific question of how the interpretation of
a semantic representation is ordered in relation to the assignment of a syntactic
analysis. The corresponding question for introspection is: Do we make judgments
about meaning before we make judgments about the structure, or do we access intuitions about these levels of representation in the opposite order? Trying to answer
this question by direct introspection is like trying to use introspection to answer any
question about internally interdependent processes. In vision, for example, do observers recognize an object in a scene first by isolating its contours and then recognizing what it is, or do they first formulate a hypothesis about what it is and then use
that hypothesis to check the contours? One cannot ask observers such questions
directly. But it is possible to construct indirect questions that probe the underlying
issue.

This example from vision is germane to our present concern. In vision, it was long
taken for granted that object recognition must follow identification of object contours, since they delimit the stimulus to be recognized. This apparently logical point
is like that of the many theorists who argue that the perception of meaning must
follow that of syntax because syntax assigns a particular configuration between words
and phrases that delimits the domain of the meaning. Yet, while it may seem logically necessary, in the case of vision it is not true. Recent research has shown that
a preliminary local hypothesis about what an object is can guide decisions about
where the figure-ground contours lie (Peterson 1994).

In the case of vision it is possible to manipulate the salience of local object
versus figure-ground cues and study the resulting shifts in reported location of the
figure. In studying the corresponding question in sentence processing, it is less clear
what manipulations and measures to use. Sentences are superficially highlighted
from their background by a combination of location, voice quality, and continuity.
Closure around clause boundaries may offer a corresponding way of studying sentence perception in ways similar to vision.

Sentences offer a feature that visual stimuli do not. Unlike visual stimuli, sentence
components are presented in a particular order. This feature of sentences offers a
possibility of studying the effects of distortions introduced at specified points. The
distortions can be either syntactic or semantic errors, thereby creating a method of
studying whether syntax or semantics is accessed first.

A strong assumption underlies the use of introspection to bear on processing order of different kinds of information. This assumption is that the order of appearance to the introspective array corresponds to the order of unconscious assignment during initial processing. This assumption is startlingly redolent of failed nineteenth-century introspectionism. But a past failure is not a principled reason to reject a current attempt, so we must examine the venture on its own terms.

Consider how introspection might work on a behavior with an explicit derivation, such as finding one's way from point A to point B. Suppose further that, while every choice point in the path has landmarks, the directions are a mixture of instructions to make particular directional turns (formal instructions, or "quasi-syntax"), and to go toward particular landmarks (instructions with content, or "quasi-semantics"). Finally, suppose that we contrive an experimental situation so that errors do occur (for example, by making either the turn points or the landmarks somewhat ambiguous). The experimental question is, do people process the landmarks or the turn choices first? The introspective method would be to wait until the end of each complete path. At that point, subjects must introspect on whether they made the right sequence. The relevant question is, in trying to figure out if something went wrong, do subjects *prospectively* retrace their path from the beginning, or *retrospectively* work backward from the end? If it is the former, we might conclude that the data also reveal something related to the original processing; but if the search is retrospective, it would be perverse to conclude that the introspective order corresponds to the processing order. Rather, we might conclude that it corresponds to the posttrip salience of different parts of the just-completed trip.

The same is true of introspection on any process that involves a sequence of operations. Depending on the task structure, the introspection can be prospective (first I did this, then that) or retrospective (I just did that, before that I did this). There are corresponding models of introspection about sentences. Is an introspection prospective or retrospective in terms of processing? According to the prospective model, sensitivity to different sentence features proceeds in the same order as they are actually assigned in comprehension. In the retrospective model, sensitivity is governed by how recent, and therefore how salient, different features are.

6.4.1 Predictions Made by LAST

Consideration of LAST suggests that the relative salience of acceptability violations depends on when the probe event occurs. The expected order corresponds to the hypothesized order of computations during comprehension:

• Basic phrase-level segmentation (i.e., pseudosyntax), including assignment of syntactic category and movement of *wh*-argument gaps into their source location—for example, violations like the following:

(117) *The mouse that I like ate a rarely.

· Meaning violations, as in

(118) *The mouse that I like ate a decision.

· Subcategorization violations, as in

(119) *The mouse I like squeaked a cheese.

· Discontinuous syntactic phenomena, as in

(120) *It's the cheese that I like the mouse who ate.

Each of the above sequences becomes definitively ill-formed on the last word. LAST clearly makes opposite predictions about which kind of ill-formedness will be easiest to detect depending on whether the introspective probe occurs during the sentence processing or after it is complete. If the search is prospective, elementary syntactic and semantic violations should be noted before configurational syntactic violations. On the other hand, if the search is retrospective and occurs after the sentence is complete, the surface sequence and related syntactic structures are more salient immediately following the application of the grammatical synthesis and surface examination during syntax checking.

6.4.2 Prospective Search

The experimental literature does not offer systematic exploration of introspection with acceptability violations. Most incongruity-based tasks presented during a sentence involve comprehension, such as effects on word-reading time, or on overall comprehension success or rate. Nicol, Forster, and Veres (1997) used an online lexical choice task that required comparison of alternative sequences for their relative acceptability at each point. This task is called the *verbal-maze* task (see box 6.11).

Nicol, Forster, and Veres explored the power of local number marking on nouns in controlling agreement with the main verb of a sentence. (We described the reading-time data of Nicol and colleagues on number information in section 6.1.3.) They varied the number on both the head noun of a complex noun phrase and the number on an adjunct noun that immediately precedes the verb. Table 6.19 shows sample materials and the results. The decision times for correctly choosing *is* showed that if the immediately preceding noun is plural, it can slow down reading time. However, an immediately preceding singular noun did not slow down the correct choice of *are*.

There are a number of interpretations for this asymmetry. Nicol, Forster, and Veres argue that plural nouns are marked with an explicit morphological unit, which can then be mistaken as dominating the number of the entire noun phrase. Singular nouns lack an explicit morphological number, and hence cannot dominate the inter-

Box 6.11
The verbal-maze task

In the verbal-maze task, two words are presented at the same time, and the subject has to choose the one that best fits with a continuing sentence. For example, the subject reads one line at a time below, and for each line after the first, must select one of two words that best continues the sentence, in this case obtaining *The author of the speeches is here now*.

The
by   author
boy   of
the   ran
slowly   speeches
is   dog
here   laughed
funny   now

Response times for selecting the appropriate word at any particular point are assumed to indicate the operation of syntactic and semantic constraints at that point. For example, at the point of deciding between *is* and *dog*, the difficulty of selecting *is* reflects both the requirement that a verb appear next rather than a noun, and the number information on the preceding noun (*speeches*). See Nicol, Forster, and Veres 1997.

Table 6.19
Mean lexical choice decision times (ms) for main verb

Is *Targets*	
SS: The author of the speech is here now.	669
SP: The author of the speeches is here now.	739
Mean for *is*	704
Are *Targets*	
PP: The authors of the speeches are here now.	724
PS: The authors of the speech are here now.	724
Mean for *are*	724

Note: S = singular, P = plural; the first letter refers to number information on the head noun, the second to number information on the adjunct noun.
Source: From Nicol, Forster, and Veres 1997, table 1

Box 6.12
The "stops making sense" task

The "stops making sense" task uses subject-paced word-by-word reading combined with an explicit acceptability task. As each word appears, the subject decides whether it makes sense in the sentence up to that point. If the sentence makes sense at that point, the subject presses one key (e.g., *Y* for yes), which records the response and the reading time on that word, removes the word, and displays the next word in the sentence. If the sentence does not make sense at that point, the subject presses a different key (e.g., *N* for no). This task can be interpreted as tapping online momentary introspections about acceptability. See Boland, Tanenhaus, and Garnsey 1990.

pretation of the number on the noun phrase. This interpretation is consistent with the early phase of pseudosyntax in LAST. It is in the early phase of pseudosyntax that explicit function words and morphemes are quickly recognized and used to create segmentation of major phrases. Overt function morphemes can trigger segmentation. Furthermore, a likely template for quickly determining the number of a noun phrase is to look at the number it carries on its final noun. Thus, as we noted earlier in this chapter, a plural morpheme explicitly marks the end of a noun phrase and also the number it carries.

Another example of prospective search in introspecting about sentences comes from Boland et al. 1995. Boland et al. utilized an online word-by-word "stops making sense" task (see box 6.12). They used a range of sentence constructions. The elegance and clarity of their design and results suffice to stand for a much wider range of research, so we go through their study in some detail. Their ultimate goal was to investigate whether sensitivity to semantic factors could precede the full syntactic analysis that supports the semantic analysis.

The first step was to verify that a semantically implausible object is introspectively detected in the object *wh*-position in object relative clauses. The dependent variable is the cumulative number of "no longer makes sense" responses that subjects generate at each point. We present difference scores, subtracting at each point, the score for the plausible (b) from the corresponding implausible cases (a) (from Boland et al. 1995, fig. 1):

(121) *% Implausible – % Plausible*
      a. Implausible: Which prize ...
      b. Plausible: Which client ...
      did the salesman visit _ while in the city?
            0   14   40 57

The implausibility of *prize* as an object of *visit* produces a 14 percent difference in "no longer makes sense" judgments on the verb. This result makes several points for us. First, it shows that the *wh*-phrase is immediately moved to the object location, even while reading the verb. Second, it shows that the semantic analysis is arrived at very quickly—immediately in some cases. However, the object position also coincides with the end of the clause, so this result could also be consistent with the view that meaning is not determined until that point.

Boland et al. included a second pair of sentences that controls for this and also explores the effect of subcategorization options (from Boland et al. 1995, fig. 1):

(122) *% Implausible − % Plausible*
    a. Implausible: Which movie ...
    b. Plausible: Which child ...
    did your brother remind _ to watch the show?
          0   2   14   37

The fact that the implausibility of *movie* is clearly noticed after *remind* suggests that subjects can immediately access the subcategorization frames of the verb. (Note that the "makes no sense" task is too slow to provide conclusive evidence on the immediate use of subcategorization information; see section 6.1.7.) This allows the expectation that *remind* will be followed by a direct object, as in

(123) Which movie did your brother remind *us* to watch?

Thus, the subject suspends the conclusion that the sentence is implausible until reading *to watch*, at which point there is no further choice.

Boland et al. note that this result could be accommodated by a filtering model in which all category-based alternatives are entertained at the verb and then filtered out by subsequent information (Frazier 1987; Mitchell 1989). They rule out this filtering interpretation by using the "filled-gap" effect (Fodor 1978; Stowe 1986) to show that only one alternative structure is chosen even when more than one exists. The filled-gap effect is the difficulty caused by having a noun phrase immediately after an empty *wh*-object position (e.g., *us* in the sentence below).

(124) Which movie$_1$ did your brother watch *t$_1$ us make t$_1$.

The presence of a noun phrase in this position can impede comprehension as measured by reading time and other techniques (e.g., Crain and Fodor 1985; Stowe 1986). The filled-gap effect is taken to reflect the immediate attempt to fill the gap with the available filler, even when it turns out to be inappropriate.

Boland et al. verified the filled-gap effect for their introspective task with simple object relatives versus declarative sentences. In this case, we present the accumulated "no sense" responses for the filled-gap sentence minus the second sentence from Boland et al. 1995, fig. 3):

(125) *% Filled gap – % Declarative*
    a. Filled gap: Which star did the assistant watch _ ...
    b. Declarative: I wonder whether the assistant watched ...

                                        0   1

    them photograph last week.
     6   16

It is striking that there is even a small effect (a 6% difference) on "makes sense" judgments as a function of the filled gap, since in fact the filled-gap sentence is perfectly sensible. This small effect is further evidence for the automaticity of filling an object argument position with an available unattached *wh*. (We discussed evidence for the early filling of *wh*-gaps in section 6.1.6.)

Boland et al. then showed that the filled-gap effect occurs with verbs like *remind*, which explicitly take different kinds of objects. In this case, we subtract the plausible potential *wh*-filler from the implausible potential *wh*-filler case (from Boland et al. 1995, fig. 2):

(126) *% Implausible – % Plausible*
    a. Implausible: Which movie ...
    b. Plausible: Which child ...
    did Mark remind _ them to watch?
                1   5   12   14

Boland et al. found that the filled-gap effect occurs more strongly with a plausible than an implausible *wh*-object filler. This would not occur on a filtering model, since the plausibility would have no relative effect until the filtering process itself.

As a final examination of the immediate effects of verb subcategorization, Boland et al. examined the interaction of plausibility and dative verbs. Unlike object control verbs such as *remind*, dative verbs can have animate or inanimate objects. Boland et al. used dative verbs to meet the possibility that the effects with object control verbs were strictly mediated by the animate/inanimate variable as opposed to verb subcategorization. A dative verb can have the double-object frame

⟨NP NP⟩

(127) The maid delivered suite 304 some towels.

that encodes arguments in the order goal and patient. A dative verb can also present just the patient in a transitive frame,

⟨NP⟩

(128) The maid delivered some towels.

or it can have the indirect-object frame

⟨NP PP⟩

(129) The maid delivered some towels to suite 304.

that encodes arguments in the order patient and goal. The data appear below (from Boland et al. 1995, fig. 4):

(130) *% Implausible – % Plausible*
      a. Implausible: Which suite ...
      b. Plausible: Which towels ...
      did the maid deliver _ after she was reprimanded?
          0   2   17 25

The fact that there is very little effect on the verb itself suggests that subjects immediately adopt the indirect-object interpretation when the direct-object frame is implausible. Boland et al. (1995:794) summarize their results thus far as follows: "The word position where plausibility effects occur ... depends on the argument structure of the verb; when [it] provides only one possible gap site, [it] is posited and interpreted.... If [there are] alternative gap sites, the filler will be assigned the thematic role with ... the most semantic overlap."

With this as background, Boland et al. tackled the question of whether the semantic plausibility effects of a filler can occur before any possible gap is actually encountered. That is, in terms of LAST, they asked whether the semantic analysis can proceed before syntactic assignment. To explore this, they used nonalternating dative verbs like *distribute*, which do not alternate between an indirect-object/direct-object frame

⟨NP NP⟩

and a direct-object/indirect-object frame

⟨NP PP⟩

but rather have only the latter frame, as shown by the following pair:

(131)   Harriet distributed the exams to the students.

(132)   *Harriet distributed the students the exams.

Boland et al. constructed examples in which there is a plausible and implausible indirect object. The results showed that subjects recognize the implausibility of the sentence well before the actual *wh*-gap location following the preposition.

(133) *% Implausible – % Plausible*
      a. Implausible: Which car salesmen ...
      b. Plausible: Which uneasy pupils ...
      did Harriet distribute the science exams to?
         1   3   17   40

The striking fact here is that the introspection that the sentence is implausible emerges well before the syntactic evidence is present to integrate the implausible object with its verb/preposition. These results suggest that comprehenders can access the meaning directly via the subcategorization frame information, a conclusion consistent with LAST.

So far, so good. But what evidence is there for the immediate application of *wh*-object movement to create NVN structures? Boland et al. (1995) report little if any evidence that NVN governs the recognition of implausible sequences. In particular, there were no clear plausibility effects on the verb for object control verbs (*remind*) or dative verbs (*read*), except for the straightforward object relative clause cases. But data from Boland et al. 1989 with similar paradigms show clear reading-time effects that suggest that the *wh*-filler is at first moved to the direct-object position and that the NVN pattern continues to operate, even if masked by the introspective reports themselves. The data below show differences between response reading time to implausible and plausible cases (from Boland et al. 1989, fig. 1; we subtract the plausible reading times from the implausible reading times, measured in ms):

(134) *Transitive verb*
      Implausible reading times – Plausible reading times (ms)
      a. Implausible filler: Which stone ...
      b. Plausible filler: Which star ...
      ... did the assistant watch _ all through the night?
          10 65   170   120

(135) *Object control verb*
      Implausible reading times – Plausible reading times (ms)
      a. Implausible filler: Which movie ...
      b. Plausible filler: Which girl ...
      ... did the woman remind _ to watch the show?
          5   40   30   100

(136) *Dative verb*
      Implausible reading times – Plausible reading times (ms)
      a. Implausible filler: Which baby ...
      b. Plausible filler: Which poem ...
      ... did the babysitter read _ in a funny voice?
          10   55   70 70

Each case shows some elevation associated with the implausible fillers at the verb, even when the structure would not support it. This is consistent with the postulation in LAST that *wh*-movement and the NVN template applies prior to accessing subcategorization information and meaning. These results suggest that *wh*-movement and the NVN template are subsequently squelched by the subcategorization information. Whether this is limited to paradigms that require explicit word-by-word judgments remains to be seen.

This concludes our discussion of online prospective introspection. The studies indeed lend support to the proposal that during sentence comprehension, introspective tasks reveal sensitivity to various aspects of pseudosyntax, verb categorical structure, and initially hypothesized meanings.

6.4.3   Context and Introspective Search

Considerable attention has also been given to postsentence judgments. In this case, we expect a different pattern of results. After a sentence, the grammar has generated a complete description and the system has checked it against a memory representation of the input. Thus, the syntax and surface structure should be the most salient sentence features.

A study by Forster and Olbrei (1974) involves a well-formedness judgment paradigm that we think can be manipulated to be either prospective or retrospective, depending on the kind of contrasting ill-formed sentences. They had subjects respond positively to well-formed sentences that varied along two dimensions: semantic reversibility of subject and object, and active versus passive construction. Their goal was to investigate carefully the claim started by Slobin (1966) and echoed by others, that computational effects of syntactic operations such as the passive are neutralized in sentences that are semantically irreversible. Slobin showed that irreversible sentences are matched to corresponding pictures equally fast in the passive and active, while reversible sentences show the expected effect of greater matching time for the passive.

(137) *Nonreversible*
    a. The boy liked the ball.
    b. The ball was liked by the boy.

(138) *Reversible*
    a. They boy liked the girl.
    b. The girl was liked by the boy.

Such results suggested that the syntactic component of comprehension might be circumvented by an apparently more direct perception of meaning based on semantics. Indeed, some took this to show that syntactic computation only occurs as a last resort when semantic analysis is indeterminate. Nonetheless, Gough (1966) showed that the same effects occur when the picture is delayed several seconds after hearing the sentence, thereby suggesting that the effects have to do with accessing the meaning for purposes of picture matching rather than online processing. Gough's result

Box 6.13
The sentence-acceptability task

In the sentence-acceptability task, a whole sentence is displayed on a screen. The subject's task is to press one of two keys to indicate whether the sentence is a meaningful and acceptable sentence. A timer starts when the sentence appears, and it stops when the subject presses a key. Distractor sentences are unacceptable for semantic or syntactic reasons. The nature of these distractors will influence the use of different kinds of information for the acceptability judgment. See Haviland and Clark 1974.

had surprisingly little impact, and many continued to believe that Slobin had shown that semantic analysis proceeds first when it can.

In several studies, Forster and colleagues took another tack. They attempted to show that whether or not a sentence is reversible, plausible, or even implausible, the relative processing load is determined by the syntactic structure. Forster and Ryder (1971) compared semantically irreversible-plausible, irreversible-implausible, and semantically anomalous sentences, each with twenty different syntactic structures. In a comprehension paradigm, the complexity effects of variation in the syntactic structure were strongly correlated across all three semantic conditions. This implicates a constant role for syntax, but it does not demonstrate that semantics is irrelevant to comprehension—there could still be an interaction between the two.

To attack this question more directly, Forster and Olbrei (1974) used a sentence-acceptability task (see box 6.13). They created semantically irreversible sentences in two ways, in half the sentences by varying the animacy of the apparent subject, and in the other half by varying the apparent object. Although they do not comment on this part of their design, it manifestly dealt with the possibility that "reversibility" effects are actually only a function of whether or not the patient is the only varied noun, as in Slobin and many other studies of semantic reversibility. To make it possible to vary the animacy of agents, they used "psych" verbs (e.g., *surprise*), which can have both animate and inanimate "agents." (We use *R* to refer to "reversible" and *N* to refer to "nonreversible.")

Actives
(139) Subject-varying (psych verbs)
    a. R: The agent surprised the model.
    b. N: The idea surprised the model.

(140) Object-varying
    a. R: The boy liked the girl.
    b. N: The boy liked the smell.

Passives

(141) Subject-varying

    a. R: The girl was liked by the boy.

    b. N: The smell was liked by the boy.

(142) Object-varying (psych verbs)

    a. R: The model was surprised by the agent.

    b. N: The model was surprised by the idea.

Forster and Olbrei used two paradigms that differed only with respect to the ill-formed distractor sequences. In one study the distractors were "almost sentences"; in the other they were "word salad," easily recognized as ill-formed.

(143) *Almost-sentences*

    a. *The reporters printed the senator.

    b. *The workers were repaired by the priest.

(144) *Word salad*

    a. *A poor substitute the amused

    b. *The number light under side

Each test sequence was presented all at once on one line. The subjects were asked to respond positively if the sentence was acceptable, and not to respond at all if it was ill-formed in some way. The results appear in table 6.20.

The quality of the fillers had dramatic effects on the decision-time data. First, the almost-sentence contexts elicited much slower overall response times than the word-salad contexts (188 vs. 257 ms/word). Presumably, this reflects the fact that the word-salad distractors reduced the care with which the sequences must be read to weed out the ungrammatical cases. In addition, there were marked qualitative differences. The almost-sentence contexts elicited both the predicted reversibility effect (63 ms) and the predicted effect of passive (290 ms). The word-salad contexts elicited a similar active/passive difference (166 ms), but showed a weak reversal of the reversibility effect itself (significant in one experiment): nonreversible sentences were actually judged more slowly than reversible sentences (by 35 ms).

Consider first the almost-sentence distractor contexts. Sentences in this paradigm require careful consideration of the details, since analysis in terms of lexical categories, or even coherence of phrases, will not weed out the ill-formed sequences. This explains the slow reading/decision times. It also explains why both reversibility and sentence construction have recognizable effects. In LAST, the checking for grammaticality is carried out during the stages of synthesis and comparison, and confirmation of the initially postulated meaning. At that point, the relative difficulty of the passive construction has accumulated as a function of several stages of processing. The passive violates the NVN template at the initial stage, it involves more computations

Table 6.20
Mean sentence-acceptability decision times for correct *yes* responses

	Nature of distractors	
	Word-salad	Almost-sentence
OVERALL MS/WORD	188	257
Total decision times		
Active		
Rev	1030	1436
Nonrev	1065	1361
Rev effect	−35	+85
Passive		
Rev	1196	1709
Nonrev	1230	1668
Rev effect	−34	+41
Passive-active		
Rev	+166	+273
Nonrev	+165	+307
Overall	+166	+290
MEAN REV EFFECT	−35	+63

Note: Rev = reversible/reversibility, nonrev = nonreversible
Source: Word-salad data from table 2, almost-sentence data from table 3, Forster and Olbrei 1974

during the synthesis, and it takes longer at the syntax checking stage. The much more modest effect of reversibility is an unequivocal factor only after the final meaning is confirmed (see below for discussion of why it is neutralized in the early stages of processing).

Many comprehension models are consistent with the results from the almost-sentence context. Since the decision time is quite slow, even theories that postulate an early stage at which meaning is computed can accommodate the continuing difference between passive and active constructions. But the results from the word-salad contexts more uniquely confirm LAST and other theories that postulate an early stage of computing meaning. In the case of LAST, this difference follows from the fact that subjects can make their decision very quickly, based on a check of the initial meaning. If the sequence has a recognizable meaning, it is well-formed in the context of word-salad distractor trials, and later stages may be ignored in the process of making a decision.

Following our theoretical sketch of the earliest phases of processing actives and passives, the initial application of the NVN template is blocked by the morphology and replaced by the N + be + Pred template. The sequence then is reinterpreted lexically to arrive at the hypothesized meaning for the passive. The active goes directly from NVN to a hypothesized meaning. This difference in initial computation accounts for the quickly appearing relative difficulty of passives in general (albeit with a somewhat smaller effect than in the almost-sentence context, perhaps because that also includes the syntactic regeneration differences).

The surprising effect in the word-salad context is that reversible sentences are easier than nonreversible sentences, not harder. Most theories of comprehension cannot explain this counterintuitive result. The explanation for the relative ease of reversible sentences in relation to LAST lies in how the reversibility was implemented. Consider actives first. They are subject to the application of the NVN template. This goes through for both reversible and nonreversible object-varying sentences. Since there is no strategy that is affected by the animacy of verb objects, there is no difference predicted for those two active cases. However, the subject-varying actives present a different feature. In subject-varying actives the apparent object of psych verbs can be semantically an agent of some kind. This is reflected in the fact that the object must be sentient. If the apparent agent is animate, the sentences are ambiguous as to whether the primary mental activity is on the part of the apparent subject (145) or apparent object (146):

(145) *Subject agent, active*
  a. The agent surprised the model by going "boo."
  b. *The agent surprised the model by going "boo," but he didn't know it.

(146) *Object experiencer, active*
  The agent surprised the model by being so simple, but he didn't know it.

(147) *Subject experiencer, passive*
  a. *The model was surprised at the idea by going "boo."
  b. The model was surprised at the idea by its being so simple.

It is clear that it is the apparent object of (146), not the apparent subject, that is some kind of experiencer. But the simple interpretation of NVN, in which the initial noun is an agent, is consistent with the sequence, reinforced by its animacy. This is sufficient to determine that the sequence is a grammatical sentence when close attention to grammatical details is not needed for the decision.

Psych-verb sentences with inanimate subjects raise several problems for the initial stages of meaning formation. First, the sentences are not ambiguous, but force an interpretation like (146) above on which the apparent object actually is the only active intentional actor in the situation.

(148) a. *The idea surprised the model by going "boo."
  b. The idea surprised the model by being so simple.

The correct interpretation of the preceding example requires blocking the NVN template assignment of agent status to the initial noun. It also requires reconfiguring the object from being assigned patient to being assigned some kind of agent or experiencer status. All these lexical reinterpretations of "nonreversible" psych actives explain why they are actually more complex to judge than the corresponding "reversible" versions. Since the object-varying sentences do not differ, or differ only slightly, the net effect for all active constructions is in favor of reversible actives.

Now turn to the passive constructions. In all cases, the morphology blocks NVN, and they are then interpreted as $N + be + Pred$:

(149) a. The girl/smell was [liked by the boy].
      b. The model was [surprised by the agent/idea].

In the case of simple transitive verbs, there may be an initially stronger attempt to apply NVN with an initial animate noun, before the morphology triggers the $N + be + Pred$ template. However, after that, the lexical mapping takes the noun from the *by*-phrase and labels it as agent in both cases, hence no further difference as a function of reversibility. So, in this case, LAST predicts a slight superiority for nonreversible sentences.

The opposite is strongly the case for psych-verb passives. At first, the NVN template strongly labels the initial animate noun as an agent. Then the morphology triggers the $N + be + Pred$ template, which unmarks the sentence subject as agent and marks it as experiencer of the predicate phrase. At that point, the same lexical mapping leads to a correct interpretation of the reversible sentences with animate *by*-phrase nouns. That is, as in (145) above, the *by*-phrase animate noun is indeed interpretable as an active intentional agent. But this interpretation is blocked if the *by*-phrase noun is inanimate, since in that case, the only likely interpretation is one like (146) and (147), in which the model is now remarked as the experiencer-agent and the *by*-phrase is unmarked as agent and marked as some kind of patient. Thus, there are several additional computational steps involved in comprehending the nonreversible passives, which accounts for the surprising reversal in the effect of reversibility.

The detailed analysis of the passives suggests that nonreversibility with psych verbs can actually lead to several more miscodings and recodings than does reversibility with simple transitive verbs. Thus, in this set of materials, the net difference is in favor of reversible passives being easier to compute.

Those with connectionist proclivities will be tempted to model these effects as a compound of distinct associative connections—for example, initial nouns are agents, the object of psych verbs are agents, and so on. The results can probably be made to come out the same. This makes sense to us, since our point is that in the word-salad context, all subjects have to do is discover *some* meaning to determine grammati-

cality. This allows the process to rest on the initial stages of meaning formulation, which in LAST is largely probabilistic in nature, and therefore naturally simulated in a connectionist framework.

We conclude that Forster and Olbrei's two paradigms actually tap two different stages of comprehension and introspection. The word-salad contexts tap comprehension and introspection during the apprehension of an initial meaning; the almost-sentence contexts tap these processes after completion of synthesis and checking the output of the grammar against the memory of the linguistic input.

6.4.4 Retrospective Search

Other studies of introspection have arguably concentrated more clearly on postsentence processes, examining the different time course of recognizing semantic versus syntactic violations. Consider the following unacceptable examples from McElree and Griffith 1998:

(150) *Syntactic-configurational*
 *It was the essay that the writer scolded the editor
 [who admired _].

(151) *Syntactic-verb subcategorization*
 *It was the essay that the writer knew
 [the editor had gloated _]

(152) *Semantic-distant*
 *It was the essay that the writer knew
 [the editor had amazed _]

The syntactic-configurational error is related to a grammatical sentence:

(153) The writer scolded the editor who admired the essay.

Syntactic-configurational errors violate a constraint that restricts raising an object from an adjunct relative clause across a *wh*-expression. The meaning of McElree and Griffith's syntactic-configurational errors may be clear, but the syntactic structure is not allowed, perhaps because of a universal constraint on movement out of "islands" (Ross 1974).

The syntactic-verb subcategorization error is related to an ungrammatical sentence:

(154) *The writer knew the editor had gloated the essay.

The error here is in the use of a direct object for a verb that cannot ordinarily take one. Again, a meaning might be imputed—for example, "the editor gloated about the essay."

The semantic-distant error also is related to an ungrammatical sentence:

(155) *The writer knew the editor had amazed the essay.

The semantic-distant error violates a semantic constraint in that the intended syntactic structure and meaning are clear, but it postulates the impossible fact that a person had amazed an essay.

McElree and Griffith studied the question of which kind of violation is explicitly noticed more quickly when people are asked to judge whether sentences are acceptable. In a postsentence judgment task, they recorded the time it takes to note the fact that sequences like these are unacceptable (see box 6.13). They found that response times increased in the order syntactic-configurational (1.14 sec), syntactic-verb subcategorization (1.36 sec), and semantic-distant (1.46 sec).

In a second experiment, McElree and Griffith used a response-signal speed-accuracy tradeoff paradigm, as described in box 6.14. McElree and Griffith found that the intercept (δ) increased in the same order as RTs in the earlier experiment: syntactic-configurational (10 ms), syntactic-verb subcategorization (374 ms), and semantic-distant (435 ms). At the earliest interruption point (14 ms), they found that the d' measures were above chance for the syntactic-configurational sequence, but near chance for the syntactic-verb subcategorization and semantic-distant sequences.

McElree and Griffith take it as obvious that the order of discovering the ungrammaticality of the strings corresponds exactly to the original order of processing. Hence, they conclude that their study supports the conventional view that complete syntactic structures are assigned prior to meaning. We think there are reasons for an alternative interpretation that is consistent with LAST, in which representations are formed in the order pseudosyntax, pseudomeaning, real syntax, real meaning.

First, McElree and Griffith required that subjects did not render their judgments until after they were sure the sentence was over, as cued by the response signal. Making judgments after the sentence is complete is maximally likely to inculcate a retrospective process of introspection. Thus, the subject tries to understand the sentence and gets an initial report from the comprehension system that something is odd. Then to be sure, the subject checks it against the sentence to confirm what is in fact odd about it. According to LAST, at the end of a sentence the grammar has just generated a complete syntax. Thus, at the time of the acceptability judgment, syntactic features are most salient. If the most recently assigned representation is the most salient, this accounts for the immediate ease of noticing the surface violation of the island constraints, next the assignment of the subcategorization structure, and finally the entire meaning of the proposition. At the point of the acceptability judgment, the generative system will have just crashed in the case of the syntactic-configurational violation, since no superficially similar sentence can be will formed. The subcategorization violation takes somewhat longer to be sure about, since super-

Box 6.14
The response-signal speed-accuracy trade-off task

The response-signal speed-accuracy trade-off task is designed to overcome interpretative problems that may arise in response-time tasks. The problem is that since faster responses tend to yield more errors, it is difficult to interpret faster responses as indicating conclusively that the relevant information is available earlier. The response-signal speed-accuracy trade-off task solves this interpretive problem by requiring subjects to make their judgment of acceptability at particular times. This procedure explicitly varied speed and allowed clearer examination of accuracy at different speeds of responding (McElree and Griffith 1995).

In McElree and Griffith 1998, the words of a stimulus sequence were presented visually one after the other for a duration of 250 ms per word. After the end of the stimulus sequence, there was a variable processing interval. A 50-ms, 1000-Hz tone was presented 14, 100, 243, 500, 800, 2000, or 3000 ms after the beginning of the final word of the stimulus sequence. Subjects were instructed to make their judgment of sentence acceptability only on hearing the tone, and within 300 ms of the tone. With a one-hour practice session, subjects were able to make their response within the specified time interval. The subjects were then tested in ten 1-hour sessions that each contained a mixture of sentence types and response lags.

In this paradigm, unbiased measures of accuracy (d') are plotted against response time (including the response lag). The d' measure corrects for guessing by combining the rate at which subjects correctly say that an unacceptable sentence is unacceptable ("hits") with the rate at which subjects incorrectly say that an acceptable sentence is unacceptable ("false alarms"). A speed-accuracy trade-off (SAT) curve is fitted to the d' measures at the various response lags according to

$$d'(t) = \lambda(1 - e^{-\beta(t-\delta)}), \quad t > \delta \text{ else } 0$$

This SAT curve initially shows no recognition of unacceptability (i.e., d' = 0), followed by a rapid rise in recognition of unacceptability (β), and ending with a leveling off of recognition of unacceptability at a maximum level of accuracy (λ). The time δ at which the SAT curve begins to rise from d' = 0 is the intercept, and is taken to indicate the point at which information becomes available during comprehension.

---

ficially this sequence corresponds to a possible surface form (as in *It was the essay that the writer knew the editor had admired*). Finally, the semantic-distant sequence is recognized as ill-formed, based on returning to attend to the meaning.

Second, the reaction time to identify the ill-formed sequences was slower than the time to identify well-formed sequences. Faster response times for well-formed sequences would not be expected if the recognition of ill-formedness was proceeding as the sentence is understood. With that strategy, well-formed sentences would require an exhaustive search to be sure they are well formed, while ill-formed sentences could be identified as soon as the ill-formed feature is encountered. Thus, online recognition of ill-formedness would produce faster response times for ill-formed sequences.

Since ill-formed sequences were in fact judged slower than well-formed sequences, introspective judgments must not have occurred "online," but after the sentence ended.

Third, the order of recognition of the different syntactic violations does not clearly conform to the order of processing the corresponding syntactic information. In particular, in many models, these sequences contain an early trigger of a search for a gap. In the syntactic-verb subcategorization sentences, the subcategorization of the final verb is encountered immediately on recognizing the verb. Since the sentence ends at that point, marked by a period presented simultaneously with the verb, the subject can immediately identify ill-formedness (because *gloated* cannot take an object). This judgment is computationally more complex at the corresponding point of the syntactic-configurational sequence because the system has to check whether the potential gap position after *admired* is a legal gap for the unassigned filler (*essay*), and it is not. Prima facie, configurational violations should be recognized more slowly than the corresponding subcategorization violations, but the opposite is the case, as predicted by LAST, for tasks that can be carried out retrospectively.

There is a strategic interpretation of the order of noticing ill-formedness in McElree and Griffith's materials. In this view, the comprehension system reports that a sentence is odd, and then the subject searches back through it to check on that. In the case of configurational violations, the subject needs to look only at the last two words (*who admired*) to note that no sentence could end in that way. Subcategorization violations in the same materials require a span of eight words to be sure that they are ill-formed. (Subjects have to scan back far enough to locate the relative pronoun *that* and then conclude that the subcategorization of the final verb cannot take an object.) Semantic violations require checking back to determine whether the head of the *wh*-phrase (*essay*) is inanimate to make sure there is no interpretation possible. This "strategic" interpretation is consistent with LAST, but more mediated than our first interpretation. That is, to be sure about the ill-formedness of the syntactic violations, reference has to be made implicitly to the syntactic possibilities, which will be enhanced if the syntax is most fresh in mind. Counterfactually, if semantic violations were still easier to find, that would have definitely clinched the claim that they are most salient.

6.5   Conclusion

In this chapter we reviewed a wide range of experimental data. We cited several kinds of evidence that we took to demonstrate an early phase of pseudosyntax. Function words are rapidly accessed, and they prime their syntactically relevant content words. Disruptions in processing that occur because of violations of canonical word order suggest that canonical sentence patterns are applied early during comprehension.

Syntactic category and subcategorization information have immediate effects on reading. *Wh*-traces in argument position immediately prime their antecedents.

Recent studies also suggest that semantic information becomes available early on in sentence comprehension. Violations of semantic constraints influence first-pass reading, but violations of syntactic constraints do not. The argument structure of verbs has early effects on reading.

Several studies suggest that certain syntactic properties have late effects on processing. Higher-level constraints on movement do not influence speeded sentence matching, though they do influence off-line judgments of acceptability. In addition, properties of pseudosyntax and meaning do influence speeded sentence matching. Major phrase and word boundaries attract judgments of click location, but minor phrase boundaries do not, at least immediately. NP-traces prime their antecedents but only relatively late.

We reviewed several studies that suggest that access to semantic and syntactic information depends on when the access task is performed. If it is performed online, semantic information is available more rapidly than syntactic information. If it is performed after a sentence has been understood, syntactic information is accessed more quickly.

Of all the experimental results we have presented in this chapter, there is no single result that critically confirms LAST over all the other theories we reviewed in chapter 4. In fact, there are different theories that can explain various subsets of the results we have cited. For example, the results on rapid identification of function words are compatible with structural theories such as Crocker's or Frazier's, and with constraint-based theories such as Tanenhaus's or MacDonald's. The evidence on *wh*-trace is compatible with theories that adopt an active-filler strategy. Several theories probably could account for the data on introspection by making use of different decision criteria. There also are individual theories that can account for much of the data we have cited. Other than LAST, however, no current theory can directly explain all these facts. There may be a way to amend one of the current theories we reviewed to account for all the results in this chapter. But no theory other than LAST can do so in a way that follows naturally from the architecture of the theory.

Chapter 7
Canonical Sentence Templates

In this chapter, we review some of the evidence that supports the pervasive use of canonical sentence templates during an early stage of comprehension. These templates include roughly:

NVN   =   agent-action-object
NV   =   agent/experiencer-action
NVNN =   agent-action-patient-recipient/location

Rather than using the cumbersome NV(N(N), we refer to sentence templates generically as the NVN template, with the assumption that argument-requiring properties of the verb stimulate alternative sentence-level templates.

First, we compile many of the studies on reduced object relative clause constructions, such as (1).

(1) *Reduced object relative passive clause*
    The horse raced past the barn fell.

An enormous number of experiments have explored the parameters that control the strength of the italicized misleading parse in reduced relative constructions. From our standpoint, these studies offer information on the kinds of cues that elicit sentence templates. Most of these have been devoted to the question of whether semantic factors have an immediate impact on parsing, or whether the garden path is strictly controlled by the sequence of syntactic categories. We review many of these studies with more attention to how they bear on the analysis-by-synthesis model than to their success or failure at revealing online semantic effects. We outline what factors should influence the processing of reduced relatives, according to LAST.

After reviewing studies on the processing of reduced relatives out of context, we review recent research on the question of how discourse contest influences the comprehension of reduced relatives. The general question is, to what extent is the garden-path interpretation dependent on pure structure-assigning processes? Conversely, to what extent can the garden-path interpretation be modulated or even negated by strong counterindicative lexical, semantic, or discourse information? There are many studies on such questions, often producing orthogonal and sometimes apparently conflicting results. We will see that the architecture of LAST explains the wide-ranging data on reduced relatives.

The reduced relative constructions can reveal the power of the entire NVN template, since it involves both the subject-verb relation and the verb-object relation. But other constructions have been studied, which concentrate on the isolated tendency to treat the initial noun as agent, as in the contrast between subject and object relative sentences:

(2) *Subject relative*
The horse that raced the dog fell.

(3) *Object relative*
The horse that the dog raced fell.

Correspondingly, other studies have explored the tendency to take a verb-noun sequence, as action-patient, as in the contrast between direct object and complement constructions:

(4) *Direct object*
The horse knew the trainer.

(5) *Complement*
The horse knew the trainer is nice.

In addition, we summarize other garden-path examples of the role of sentence templates in comprehension. Overall, it is startling to see the explanatory power of this simple formulation. It accounts for data in several hundred published articles and conference presentations. But given our theoretical scheme, that is exactly what one would predict.

7.1 Reduced Relative Clauses out of Context

The main-clause/relative clause (MC/RC) ambiguity is the classic garden-path sentence, and it plays an important role in virtually all theory development (e.g., Crocker 1996; Frazier and Clifton 1996; Gibson 1998; Gorrell 1995; MacDonald et al. 1994; Marcus 1980; Pritchett 1992). The following sentence from Bever 1970a illustrates the MC/RC ambiguity:

(6) The horse [raced past the barn] fell.

This sentence is particularly tough to interpret, but is grammatically acceptable, as revealed by the corresponding

(7) The classes [scheduled for next Tuesday] are canceled.

From the viewpoint of LAST, it is instructive to consider the factors that make sentences like (6) difficult and those like (7) easy.

In chapter 6, we reviewed evidence that the comprehension system uses pseudo-syntax to establish an initial meaning-form hypothesis. Pseudosyntax is sensitive to grammatical morphemes and function words, lexical information such as the relative strength of subcategorization requirements, and sentence-level templates. We also reviewed evidence that the comprehension system uses this initial representation of meaning to generate a detailed syntax, which it then compares with a representation of the linguistic signal. According to LAST, sentence-level templates, lexical category information, grammatical morphemes, and subcatgorization and other lexically based strategies will play important roles in producing the garden path in reduced relatives. What should not play a role in the immediate processing of reduced relatives is conceptual information that requires syntactically precise combinatorial processing of phrases within the sentence, because LAST claims that the initial meaning-form hypothesis is based on statistical patterns and lexical-associative information only.

7.1.1   The NVN Pattern in Reduced Relatives

As a rough approximation to LAST's processing of (8), the initial meaning-form hypothesis is based on the fact that the sequence *the horse raced past the barn* elicits an NVN template.

(8) The horse raced past the barn fell.

The horse is assigned the agent role, the intransitive *raced* is assigned as the action, and *past the barn* is assigned the role of a locative prepositional phrase.

The subcategorization properties of the verb define what counts as a complete semantic unit. In this case, the verb *raced* may be transitive, intransitive, or a passive participle, as in

(9) *Transitive*
     The horse raced the turtle.

(10) *Intransitive*
     The horse raced on Tuesday.

(11) *Passive*
     The horse was raced by the jockey.

All other things being equal, we assume that whenever pseudosyntax accumulates enough information to form a complete semantic unit, it does so. However, it may be that NVN represents a canonical sentence pattern more than other sequences, such as NV.[1] That is, although *the horse raced* forms a complete semantic unit in the intransitive sense of *raced*, the comprehension system may still assume that the verb is used transitively and expect a second noun phrase immediately after the verb. In the case of (8), the sequence of words *the horse raced past the barn* completes a semantic unit based on the intransitive interpretation of *raced*. The comprehension system uses this meaning to generate a candidate syntax.

(12) [[The horse] [raced [past the barn]]]

The comprehension system finds that this candidate syntax matches the surface sequence up through *barn*. The match between the candidate syntax and the surface sequence confirms the syntax and the corresponding meaning is stored. *Fell*, however, indicates that the candidate syntax is incorrect, and the previously accepted parse is now inhibited. Therefore, the pseudosyntax elicits a less strongly primed meaning-form hypothesis for the grammar to generate a new candidate syntax. Thus, in general, the garden path occurs because of faulty application of the NVN template, which assigns the initial noun as agent of the embedded verb.

Several experimental demonstrations are consistent with the view that the comprehension system presents an initial meaning-form hypothesis based on the NVN pattern, Rayner, Carlson, and Frazier (1983) found that eye-fixation times were greater in reduced relative clauses (13) than in unreduced relative clauses (14).

(13) *Reduced relative*
    The florist [sent the flowers] was very pleased.

(14) *Unreduced relative*
    The florist [who was sent the flowers] was very pleased.
This difference persisted even when the initial noun was an implausible agent, as in

(15) *Reduced relative*
    The performer [sent the flowers] was very pleased.

(16) *Unreduced relative*
    The performer [who was sent the flowers] was very pleased.

Ferreira et al. (1996) examined the processing of reduced relative clauses in speech. They used the auditory moving-window technique, in which listeners control the rate of presentation of spoken words. The results showed that listening times on *agreed* were greater for reduced relatives such as (17) than for active sentences such as (18).

(17) *Reduced relative*
    The editor [played the tape] agreed the story was important.

(18) *Active*
    The editor played the tape and agreed the story was important.
    The classic example of the MC/RC ambiguity is a particularly powerful garden path. People typically have great difficulty in detecting that the sentence is gram-

matical when they first examine it. As we noted earlier, reduced relatives differ widely in their ease of processing, and it is instructive to examine the factors that influence the strength of the MC/RC garden path. Depending on their associative strength, these factors increase or decrease the strength of the NVN template, and thus how easily the garden path can be overcome.

7.1.2 Grammatical Morphemes

The reduced relative construction works as a garden path only insofar as the interpretation as a simple past declarative sentence is supported. Morphological cues associated with the initial verb can strengthen or weaken this interpretation. The garden-path effect depends on the use of a verb in the relative clause that is morphologically homonymous with a past tense. Thus, a variety of studies have shown that if the embedded verb is morphologically distinct from a simple past, it will not elicit a garden-path interpretation, as in:

(19) The horse [ridden past the barn] fell.

Since the -*en* ending on *ridden* makes it unambiguously a passive participle, the unambiguous passive morphology inhibits the NVN template.

7.1.3 Subcategorization Properties

According to LAST, embedded verbs that do not have the potential interpretation of the intransitive but are ambiguous between past tense, transitive, and passive participle should still produce a garden path. In this case, however, the garden path should be far less compelling. The reason the garden path will still occur is that pseudosyntax at first assigns the initial noun as the agent of the embedded verb. The reason the garden path will be less compelling is that without the intransitive interpretation being possible, the comprehension system will not detect an initial meaning-form hypothesis, will not initiate synthesis of a surface form, and will not check the synthesized form against the input.

Consider the following example from Pritchett 1992 (see section 4.2.3):

(20) *Transitive embedded verb*
      The spaceship [destroyed in the battle] disintegrated.

Sentence (20) is much easier than one such as (21) in which the embedded verb is potentially intransitive.

(21) *Potentially intransitive embedded verb*
      The spaceship [disintegrated in the battle] destroyed many enemy ships.

Technically, both sentences could have a direct object somewhere after the embedded verb. But the placement of the prepositional phrase *in the battle* intervenes, and would make the ultimate appearance of an object rather awkward, in (22) and (23).

(22) *Transitive-only verb + prepositional phrase + direct object*
The spaceship destroyed in the battle all of the enemy cruisers and several of the enemy battleships.

(23) *Potentially intransitive verb + prepositional phrase + direct object*
The spaceship disintegrated in the battle all of the enemy cruisers and several of the enemy battleships.

The NVN template is inhibited because the canonical location for the object noun phrase is directly after the verb. We return to this issue in more detail later in this section.

Nonetheless, a past tense verb form that does not have an intransitive sense still elicits a much weaker garden path even when the object phrase is ultimately presented. The potentially intransitive *disintegrated* allows the formation of a complete semantic unit before the actual main verb, as in *The spaceship disintegrated in the battle*. This complete initial meaning-form hypothesis leads to syntax generation and checking and to readiness for a new analysis-by-synthesis cycle. On the other hand, the past form *destroyed*, which does not have an intransitive sense, does not allow the comprehension system to form a complete semantic unit before the actual main verb, as in *the spaceship destroyed in the battle*. Thus, pseudosyntax does not present an initial meaning-form hypothesis for it. This greatly weakens the lure of the garden-path NVN.

The importance of homonymy with an intransitive main verb is made even clearer when an agentive *by*-phrase is present:

(24) *Potentially intransitive verb with* by-*phrase*
The spaceship [disintegrated by the enemy] disappeared.

(25) *Transitive-only verb with* by-*phrase*
The spaceship [destroyed by the enemy] disappeared.

When a verb such as *destroyed* cannot be intransitive, the presence of the clear agentive phrase appears intuitively to completely neutralize the garden path available with potentially intransitive verbs.

MacDonald (1994) systematically investigated the impact of several of these factors that govern the strength of the garden path. First, she contrasted self-paced word reading times for reduced relatives with embedded verbs that are potentially intransitives (PI) such as *fought*, verbs that are transitive-only (TO) such as *capture*, and verbs that are unambiguously passive participles such as *overthrown*. The unambiguous passive participles were half from potentially intransitive verbs such as *drawn*, and half from transitive-only verbs such as *overthrown*.

(26) *Potentially intransitive*
The ruthless dictator fought in the coup was hated.

(27) *Transitive only*
   The ruthless dictator captured in the coup was hated.

(28) *Unambiguous passive participle verb*
   The ruthless dictator overthrown in the coup was hated.

Note that since *fought* is potentially intransitive, the NV template applies, and pseudo-syntax detects the acceptable surface form in (29), which matches the input.

(29) *Intransitive*
   The ruthless dictator fought in the coup.

Thus, at the point of *coup*, the comprehension system has generated a complete meaning-form hypothesis and matched it to the input. The system is then ready for another analysis-by-synthesis cycle.

   MacDonald (1994) used a self-paced moving-window paradigm to examine ambiguity effects in potentially intransitive versus transitive-only verbs. In table 7.1, we show the difference in reading times for ambiguous and unambiguous trials, in which the relative clause morphology *that was* appears after the initial noun (*dictator*). When there is a garden path, this difference is large and positive, and it is called an *ambiguity effect*. For the data reported in table 7.1, reading times were adjusted for differences in phrase and word length in each region. The results clearly show that the ambiguity effect on the main verb (*was hated*) is larger for potentially intransitive verbs (a 40-ms difference) than for transitive-only verbs (a 15-ms difference). MacDonald (1994) supported this conclusion further by contrasting potentially intransitive verbs that have an intransitive bias (e.g., *move*) with those having a transitive bias (e.g., *push*). The corresponding data for this study appear in parentheses in table 7.1. These results suggested to MacDonald that the transitive-bias embedded verbs tend much less to create the classic garden-path elevation of reading times at the main-verb disambiguation point.

Table 7.1
Ambiguous – unambiguous word reading time (ms) for potentially intransitive (PI) and transitive-only (TO) verbs by region

	Relative clause	Main verb
PI (IB)	−14 (0)	40 (32)
TO (TB)	−2 (−8)	15 (4)
Difference	−16 (−8)	+25 (+28)

Note: Ambiguity effects for intransitive bias (IB) vs. transitive bias (TB) in parentheses
Source: From MacDonald 1994, exp. 1, fig. 1, collapsed across goodness of cue; exp. 3, fig. 4, intransitive bias vs. transitive bias

7.1.4   Lexical-Category Effects on the Strength of NVN

Information that supports the NVN template should increase the garden-path effect. As we noted earlier, lexical-category information that follows the verb but decreases the likelihood that there is a direct object for the verb weakens the strength of the NVN pattern. LAST maintains that lexical-category information is part of pseudo-syntax, and hence, available for eliciting an initial meaning-form hypothesis.

MacDonald (1994) explored the effect of postverbal evidence for a transitive (NVN) interpretation. She varied the first word following the verb so that it either was or was not consistent with a possible direct object following it:

(30) *Initially implausible direct object (~DO)*
      The dictator [fought in the coup] was hated.

(31) *Initially plausible direct object (DO)*
      The dictator [fought just after dawn] was hated.

In the sentences in which a direct object is initially implausible (~DO), the presence of *in* immediately after *fought* indicates that the embedded verb (*fought*) is not likely to be transitive. In the sentences with an initially plausible direct object (DO), the word *just* immediately after the verb conceivably may be part of a direct object, as in *just one soldier*, and so the ambiguous verb may have a transitive interpretation.

Using optionally intransitive verbs, MacDonald (1994) found no ambiguity effect within the relative clause for sentences like (30). However, there was a highly significant ambiguity effect on the main verb for sentences like (31). In sentences like (31), the adjunct phrase prolonged the possibility of a transitive garden-path interpretation of the embedded clause.

MacDonald argued from this that what makes reduced relatives garden-path is not just the tendency to interpret the embedded verb as a simple past intransitive, but also the tendency to interpret it as a simple past transitive. That is, *any* information that supports the inappropriate assignment of NVN of some kind can increase the garden-path effect. This interpretation is puzzling, however, since the garden path with transitive-prolonging cues is much larger for optionally intransitive verbs than for the transitive-only verbs. It would seem that the availability of a potential intransitive still plays an important role in eliciting the garden path.

Another postverbal lexical category cue that can affect the strength of the garden path is the word *by*. The word *by* following a verb that is ambiguous between past tense and passive participle is strong but not decisive evidence that the verb is being used as a passive participle. In (32) the *by*-phrase may be interpreted as the agent of *moved*, suggesting that *moved* is a passive participle and the construction is a reduced relative interpretation.

(32) *Potentially intransitive verb* + by
   The cattle moved by the cowboys.

Alternatively, the *by*-phrase may be interpreted as a locative phrase, suggesting that *moved* is a past-tense intransitive verb and the construction is a main clause. Frequency counts of the use of *by* following a verb indicate that it is used much more frequently as an agent phrase than as a locative phrase. Unfortunately, several studies on the processing of reduced relatives have acknowledged but failed to appreciate fully the possibility that a postverbal *by*-phrase can weaken the NVN interpretation, and hence the garden path. (See Clarke, Townsend, and Bever 2000, who systematically show that the preposition *by* does tend to inhibit the garden-path interpretation, compared with other prepositions.)

7.1.5 Animate vs. Inanimate Initial Nouns
Another factor that influences the strength of the NVN pattern is animacy of the initial noun. When the initial noun is animate, it is likely that it is the agent of the verb. When the input contains a initial animate noun and words and phrases that correspond to N + V + N, pseudosyntax likely will assign the meaning sequence agent + action + patient. If an animate initial noun increases the garden-path effect, this is evidence that semantic factors can be integrated during processing.

   While it is not intuitively controversial that semantic factors should have such an effect, the scene about it was set confrontationally by Ferreira and Clifton (1986). They studied eye-fixation patterns when reading reduced relative clause sentences with animate and inanimate initial nouns with materials like the following:

(33) *Animate initial noun, reduced relative*
   The defendant [examined by the lawyer] turned out to be unreliable.

(34) *Animate initial noun, unreduced relative*
   The defendant [that was examined by the lawyer] turned out to be unreliable.

(35) *Inanimate initial noun, reduced relative*
   The evidence [examined by the lawyer] turned out to be unreliable.

(36) *Inanimate initial noun, unreduced relative*
   The evidence [that was examined by the lawyer] turned out to be unreliable.

For both animate and inanimate subject nouns, Ferreira and Clifton (1986) reported the same degree of increase in reading time for the *by*-phrase when the relative pronoun and past tense were deleted. They concluded that the animacy of the noun did not control the garden-path effect, consistent with their theoretical viewpoint that the garden path is itself the result of a syntactic attachment process, not influenced by semantic factors (see section 4.2.1). In their view, "minimal attachment" gives a higher priority to the NVN interpretation of reduced relatives than to the correct reduced relative interpretation. Thus, this study served as a strong argument in favor of the notion of an independent process of assigning surface phrase structure.

The challenge from Ferreira and Clifton (1986) launched a number of counterstudies by researchers promoting the nonmodular connectionist view of parsing. In that view, semantic and syntactic factors commingle during every stage of parsing, and thus semantic factors should show an immediate effect (see section 4.3.4).

MacDonald (1994) investigated the question of whether the animacy of the initial noun influences the effectiveness of the garden path. She contrasted animate and inanimate initial nouns in combination with postverbal information that makes a direct object plausible or implausible, as in:

(37) *Inanimate subject, direct-object plausible*
     The shipment [transported almost two thousand miles] would help ...

(38) *Inanimate subject, direct-object implausible*
     The shipment [transported to the polluted beaches] would help ...

(39) *Animate subject, direct-object plausible*
     The workers [transported almost two thousand miles] would help ...

(40) *Animate subject, direct-object implausible*
     The workers [transported to the polluted beaches] would help ...

MacDonald (1994) measured self-paced word-reading times in sentences like these, as well as in control sentences with unreduced relative clauses, as in *the shipment that was transported* ...

MacDonald (1994) predicted that animate subjects would elicit larger differences in reading time between reduced and unreduced relative clauses. Table 7.2 shows the average reduced minus unreduced differences in word-reading time. On the disambiguating main verb, sentences with an animate initial noun showed a larger ambiguity effect than sentences with an inanimate initial noun. When the initial noun was animate, plausible-direct-object sentences showed a 26-ms ambiguity effect on the main verb. But when the initial noun was inanimate the corresponding ambiguity effect was only 11 ms. The implausible-direct-object sentences showed a 10-ms ambiguity effect on the main verb for animate initial nouns, but only a 4-ms ambiguity effect on the main verb for inanimate initial nouns. These results demonstrate that animacy of the initial noun, as well as the beginning of a potential patient noun phrase after the embedded verb, support the NVN pattern, and therefore increase the strength of the garden path.

MacDonald's reading time data within the relative clause supports this interpretation. Sentences with an animate initial noun actually have smaller ambiguity effects

Table 7.2
Adjusted ambiguous–unambiguous word-reading time by region

| | Region | |
	Relative clause	Main verb
Direct object (DO)		
Animate	10	26
Inanimate	29	11
DO overall	20	19
Not direct object (~DO)		
Animate	18	10
Inanimate	24	4
~DO overall	21	7

Source: From MacDonald 1994, fig. 3, exp. 2

during the relative clause compared to sentences with inanimate subjects. That is, the difference in reading time between reduced and unreduced relative clauses is smaller when the initial noun is animate than when it is inanimate. For plausible-direct-object sentences, the ambiguity effect within the relative clause was 10 ms for animate initial nouns and 29 ms for inanimate initial nouns. This result suggests that the animate nouns facilitate the NVN interpretation. This interpretation is further strengthened by the fact that the facilitation is much larger for plausible-direct-object sentences than for implausible-direct-object sentences. Clearly, this difference occurs because the postverbal material in the relative clause of plausible-direct-object sentences prolongs the possibility of a direct object. Unfortunately, in this experiment (MacDonald's experiment 2) the reported results collapse across equal numbers of optionally and obligatorily transitive verbs. Since MacDonald's other studies show that there are considerable differences in strength of the garden path with these kinds of embedded verbs, we must be cautious in interpreting the results.

Trueswell, Tanenhaus, and Garnsey (1994) responded directly to Ferreira and Clifton (1986). Trueswell and colleagues first noted that Ferreira and Clifton's materials had a number of flaws. In particular, a number of sentences had embedded verbs that could serve as good predicates for inanimate nouns, as in *the trash smelled.* In other cases, the verb could allow an instrumental interpretation of the inanimate subject of the embedded verb, as in *the car towed.* Trueswell and associates reckoned that about half of Ferreira and Clifton's materials had such properties that would allow good garden-path continuations for their inanimate nouns. Trueswell et al. also noted that Ferreira and Clifton presented the sentences with the embedded verb as the final word of the first line of print. This might independently trigger segmentation regardless of the subject noun's animacy.

Table 7.3
First-pass reading times (ms) for reduced (R) and unreduced (U) relatives

	Region			
Sentence type	NP	V + *ed*	*by*-phrase	MV
Animate noun				
Reduced	390	350	625	490
Unreduced	400	350	500	490
R − U	−10	0	125	0
Inanimate noun				
Reduced	420	350	520	450
Unreduced	440	320	490	440
R − U	−20	30	30	10

Source: From Trueswell, Tanenhaus, and Garnsey 1994, fig. 3, exp. 2

Trueswell, Tanenhaus, and Garnsey ran a set of redesigned studies with reworked materials and a presentation format that had the complete sentence on a single line. They used the eye-tracking procedure, and measured first-pass reading times. Their results appear in table 7.3. They reported a significant effect of the animacy of the initial noun. In fact, the only ambiguity effect was for reduced relatives with animate subject nouns. This effect occurred on reading the *by*-phrase.

7.1.6 Conceptual Fit

We have seen that the garden path in a reduced relative occurs because of the incorrect detection of a NVN pattern, which elicits assignment of the initial noun as agent of the embedded verb. The independent pattern that an initial animate noun is the agent of the verb can compound the garden path. We have suggested that pseudosyntax accesses noun animacy immediately on recognition of the word, but that local associations between particular nouns and verbs come into play only after they are set in conceptual relation to each other. In this section, we examine conceptual fit and its interactions with subcategorization properties of verbs. We will see that the immediate effect of conceptual fit is not as strong as that of animacy, and that its effect depends greatly on the argument requirements of the embedded verb.

Several researchers have investigated the role of local associations in the effectiveness of the garden path. It has been noted that nouns may differ in their appropriateness as an agent for verbs independently of their animacy. For example, both (41) and (42) contain animate initial nouns, but these nouns differ in their plausibility as agents/recipients of the action of sending a bouquet of flowers:

(41) *Implausible agent/plausible recipient*
     The performer sent the bouquet was very pleased.

(42) *Plausible agent/implausible recipient*
     The florist sent the bouquet was very pleased.

A florist is more likely to send a bouquet of flowers compared to a performer, and less likely to receive a bouquet of flowers. Thus, comprehenders may be more likely to misinterpret the reduced relative clause in the second sentence as actually being a main clause. The question arises whether this type of plausibility information influences the initial meaning-form hypothesis, and hence the strength of the garden path.

Trueswell and associates followed up their work on animacy, which we reviewed in the previous section, with additional work on "conceptual fit." They performed a post hoc analysis on the conceptual fit of the inanimate nouns as good patients of the embedded verb. They acquired ratings to such questions as:

(43) *Goodness-of-patient questions*
     a. How typical is it for evidence to be examined by someone?
     b. How typical is it for a power plant to be attacked by someone?

(44) *Goodness-of-agent questions*
     a. How typical is it for evidence to examine someone?
     b. How typical is it for a power plant to attack someone?

These ratings showed, for example, that *evidence* is a better patient than *power plant* in the following sentences:

(45) The evidence examined by the lawyer turned out to be unreliable.

(46) The power plant attacked by the terrorists suffered heavy losses.

The mean patient-goodness rating for *evidence* was 6.3 out of 7, and for *power plant*, 4.4 out of 7.

Trueswell and colleagues then determined the correlation between the size of the ambiguity effect and the rating of the initial inanimate nouns as good patients. The correlation between patienthood of inanimate nouns and first-pass ambiguity effect on the verb was $r = -.42$, $p = .12$, while the corresponding correlation on the *by*-phrase was $r = -.51$, $p < .05$. The results showed a nonsignificant negative correlation at the embedded verb, but a significant negative correlation on the *by*-phrase.

Trueswell et al. (1994) then isolated the inanimate noun + embedded verb sequences that had a simultaneous good conceptual fit as patients and poor conceptual fit as agents of the embedded verb, as determined by the ratings described above. Ambiguity effects on reading time for poor patients, good patients, and animate nouns appear in table 7.4. The data show showed that the garden-path effect is entirely absent for sequences with inanimate nouns that are good patients for the embedded verb. This result follows from the view that the good patients were interpreted immediately as patient of the embedded verb because they do not serve well as agent of the embedded verb.

Table 7.4
Ambiguity effect for animate nouns, and for inanimate nouns divided into those that are good
patients/poor agents and poor patients/good agents of the embedded verb (RT for reduced
relative minus unreduced relative)

	Region	
Sentence type	verb + *ed*	*by*-phrase
Inanimate noun		
Poor patient	44	46
Good patient	7	−9
Animate noun	5	100

Source: After Trueswell, Tanenhaus, and Garnsey 1994, fig. 5

Table 7.5
Mean reading times (ms) for the initial noun phrase and verb depending on animacy of the
initial noun

	Region	
	Initial NP	Embedded verb
Reduced relative		
Inanimate	420	345
Animate	380	345
I − A	40	0
Unreduced relative		
Inanimate	435	320
Animate	390	345
I − A	45	−25

Source: Adapted from Trueswell, Tanenhaus, and Garnsey 1994, fig. 3, exp. 2

Before going further, we consider these kinds of data in light of LAST. According
to LAST, associative information in the form of statistical regularities, common
sentence patterns, and global associations to lexical items such as animacy immediately elicits an initial meaning-form hypothesis. Local relations between words
that require computation will not appear immediately. The distinction between the
immediacy of global information and the delay in local relations makes several predictions. First, the effects of animacy on reading time may appear very quickly. For
example, in experiment 2 of Trueswell et al. the reading time for the initial animate
noun phrase itself was about 40–45 ms faster than for the inanimate noun phrase (see
table 7.5). Yet the reading time for the embedded verb was actually about 25 ms
faster for the inanimates than animates in the unreduced constructions, while there

was no difference in the reduced constructions. As we noted in the previous section, the animate-noun/agent association may combine with the initial noun/agent association to facilitate rapid reading and agent assignment of an initial animate noun phrase, compared with an inanimate noun phrase. Thus, inanimate nouns like *evidence* are read more slowly than animate nouns like *lawyer*. But in the reduced relative construction, there is not time for the difference between the plausibility of the two nouns as patients of *examine* to have an effect on reading time. Second, if patienthood has any influence on the size of the ambiguity effect at the embedded verb, it should occur because of faster reading times in unreduced constructions, which allow sufficient time for the noun and verb to be set into conceptual relation. In the unreduced case, pseudosyntax may establish a relatively complete proposition for the relative clause, corresponding to *the defendant was examined*, with the agent unspecified.

(47) *Unreduced*

The defendant [that was examined] ...

N	=	agent	=	defendant
[N	=	agent	=	?]
V	=	action	=	examined
N	=	patient	=	defendant

But for a reduced relative such as (48), there are not enough cues to overcome the NVN pattern and establish the corresponding proposition for the relative clause:

(48) *Reduced*

The defendant examined ...

N	=	agent	=	defendant
V	=	action	=	examined

Thus, any difference in the conceptual fit between the initial noun and the verb can emerge at the verb, but primarily in the unreduced sentences, which enable the system to present a meaning-form hypothesis for the relative clause. This will establish the conceptual fit between the noun and the verb.

Table 7.6 contrasts the effect of a good patient on verb reading time for reduced and unreduced relative clauses in a number of studies (McRae, Spivey-Knowlton, and Tanenhaus 1998; Pearlmutter and MacDonald 1992; Tabossi et al. 1994). The table presents mean reading times for good-agent initial nouns minus mean reading times for good patient initial nouns. As predicted by LAST, these studies show that reading times for the embedded verb are faster for good patients than for good agents primarily in unreduced relative clauses. They also show that the goodness of the patient has the predicted reduction in reading time on reading the *by*-phrase. This follows from the fact that by that time, there is sufficient time and information

Table 7.6
Reading-time effects of conceptual fit (good agent − good patient word-reading times in ms)

	Region		
Sentence type	Verb	*by*-phrase	Main verb
Pearlmutter and MacDonald 1992:			
Unreduced	2	25	25
Reduced	−50	−2	82
	Verb + *by*	det + NP	Main verb
McRae, Spivey-Knowlton, and Tanenhaus 1998:			
Unreduced	20	35	−10
Reduced	−17	47	40
Tabossi et al. 1994:			
Unreduced	22	47	23
Reduced	6	35	77

Source: From Pearlmutter and MacDonald 1992, fig. 1; McRae, Spivey-Knowlton, and Tanenhaus 1998, fig. 5; Tabossi et al. 1994, table 24.1

to extract the noun-verb conceptual relations. Note that none of these studies reports data with the same effect of patient goodness on verb reading time in reduced constructions.

The point at which goodness-of-patient has an effect distinguishes LAST from more global spreading activation models. Spreading activation models predict that the effect of goodness-of-patient will occur on the verb, but LAST predicts that it will come at the completion of an analysis-by-synthesis cycle. Consider first the predictions of spreading activation models and the evidence for these predictions. In unmodified versions of spreading activation models, all kinds of information are accessed immediately, and good patients should immediately squelch the garden-path interpretation. Spreading activation models predict that for good-patient nouns, there will be little difference in reading time for reduced versus unreduced relative clauses. If a good-patient noun immediately establishes the initial noun as patient of the verb, additional information provided by the relative clause morphology *that was* cannot increase the strength of that interpretation. But for poor-patient nouns, spreading activation models predict a large garden-path effect. Indeed, Trueswell and colleagues found that the correlation between patient goodness and the size of the ambiguity effect on the embedded verb was negative, so that as the goodness of the initial noun as a patient increased, the size of the ambiguity effect decreased. However, in both of their experiments that examined the relation between goodness-of-patient and ambiguity effect, Trueswell and associates failed to find that this correlation was significant.

Table 7.7
Ambiguity effects (ms) in four experiments on goodness of patient (ambiguous − unambiguous word reading times)

Patienthood	Region		
	Verb	*by*-phrase	Main verb
Pearlmutter and MacDonald 1992:			
Good patient	30	25	20
Poor patient	−20	−5	75
	Verb + *by*	det + NP	Main verb
McRae, Spivey-Knowlton, and Tanenhaus 1998, fig. 5:			
Good patient	61	35	0
Poor patient	25	44	60
Tabossi et al. 1994, animates only:			
Good patient	39	47	18
Poor patient	21	21	73
McRae, Spivey-Knowlton, and Tanenhaus 1998, fig. 2:			
Good patient	66	0	10
Poor patient	60	44	9

Source: From same studies as in table 7.6, with the addition of MacRae, Spivey-Knowlton, and Tanenhaus 1998, fig. 2

Several studies explicitly varied goodness-of-patient of the initial noun in order to examine ambiguity effects in various regions of the sentence. Table 7.7 summarizes the ambiguity effects in these studies by presenting the ambiguous minus unambiguous reading-time differences at various regions. The specific regions vary across experiments because of procedural differences in the studies. The four studies summarized in table 7.7 agree that good patients do not eliminate the garden-path effect on the initial verb. In these studies, the ambiguity effects on the initial verb for good patients ranged from 30 to 66 ms. It is only on the following noun phrase or even later that a good-patient initial noun eliminates the garden path. Of the four studies in table 7.7, only MacRae, Spivey-Knowlton, and Tanenhaus (1998, fig. 2) found that good patients eliminated the garden path as early as the *by*-phrase.

There is a consistent feature across these experiments. The ambiguity effect for reading time on the verb (or verb + *by*) is actually larger for good patients than for poor patients. It is not until the main verb that the studies generally demonstrate the predicted result of poor patients showing a larger ambiguity effect than good patients. Close examination of actual experimental sentences used in the studies reveals a clue to this puzzle. In short, the obtained effects of patienthood depend on subcategorization properties of the verb, and hence, when an analysis-by-synthesis

Table 7.8
Percentage of sentences with potentially intransitive (PI) embedded verbs used in studies of reduced relative garden paths

Study	Percent PI verbs
1. Ferreira and Clifton 1986, exp. 1	31
2. MacDonald 1994, exp. 2	28
3. McRae, Spivey-Knowlton, and Tanenhaus 1998	20
4. McRae, Ferretti, and Amyote 1997	10
5. Pearlmutter and MacDonald 1992	100
6. Tabossi et al. 1994	31
7. Trueswell 1996, low PP condition	70
high PP condition	0
8. Trueswell, Tanenhaus, and Garnsey 1994, exp. 1	13
exp. 2	25

Note: Potentially intransitive verbs in the above studies: attacked, burned, cooked, dissolved, entertained, exploded, helped, hunted, interviewed, investigated, kicked, lectured, lifted, listened, moved, paid, painted, popped, poured, read, ripened, scratched, searched, served, shattered, sketched, smelled, stalked, studied, surrendered, taught, visited, washed, watched, widened, worshipped

cycle is to be completed. Recall MacDonald's (1994) finding that garden-path effects are more reliable when the embedded verb is potentially intransitive. It turns out that almost all studies both before and after MacDonald (1994) used more purely transitive than potentially intransitive embedded verbs. Table 7.8 shows the proportion for each of the studies we have discussed. This is a startling state of affairs. How could four years of research continue to study reduced relative garden-path effects with a preponderance of transitive-only embedded verbs, when MacDonald actually found no ambiguity effect for them, especially at the main-verb disambiguation point? In most spreading activation models, constraints are additive. While there may not be an overall garden-path effect for transitive-only embedded verbs, such models still predict that transitive-only verbs will show a larger ambiguity effect for poor patients than for good patients. Thus, within the spreading activation framework, it should be possible to study the effect of the independent effects of patient fit regardless of verb type. The imbalance in favor of pure transitive verbs in most experimental materials may be an instance in which a theory has driven researchers to ignore their own work.

7.1.7   Interactions of Conceptual Fit and Subcategorization

In this section, we examine the issue of whether conceptual fit effects depend entirely on the argument requirements of verbs. We will find evidence that they do. In short,

Table 7.9

Ambiguity effects depending on conceptual fit for sentences with potentially intransitive embedded verbs

Noun	Region		
	Verb + *by*	Det + noun	Main verb
Good agent	68	97	208
Good patient	2	16	34
Difference	66	81	174

Source: Reanalysis of Tabossi et al. 1994 data

at the point when a verb requires an agent to form a complete proposition, good agents have an effect. Similarly, when a verb requires a patient to form a complete proposition, good patients have an effect. This evidence establishes that semantic compositional information influences processing only at a later stage of comprehension, in contrast to lexically specific semantic information, which influences the initial meaning-form hypothesis.

Tabossi et al. (1994) examined conceptual fit between the initial noun and the embedded verb. The study by Tabossi and colleagues is particularly useful because it included a detailed appendix with data for each individual sentence. Since there were thirty-two experimental sentences with animate subjects, it is possible to contrast differences between sentences that allow for an intransitive reading of the embedded verb, and those that do not. We did this, finding that about a third of their sentences have potentially intransitive embedded verbs. Consider first the ambiguity effects for sentences with potentially intransitive verbs that appear in table 7.9.

These results are quite striking. Good agents show noticeably larger ambiguity effects compared to good patients. A large ambiguity effect for good agents appeared even on the embedded verb + *by*. This result limits MacDonald's (1994) finding of greater ambiguity effects for intransitive verbs than for transitive verbs to those that appear with good agents.

Both the standard connectionist models and LAST predict greater ambiguity effects for good agents than for good patients when the verb is intransitive, but for different reasons. In the standard connectionist model, a good agent should stimulate more activity for the main-clause garden-path interpretation.

(49) *Good patient*
   The performer applauded by ...

(50) *Good agent*
   The audience applauded by ...

The word *by* presented at the same time as the verb to some extent triggers the passive even in the reduced relative construction, making the passive interpretation more consistent with a good-patient initial noun. Hence, the word *by* following the verb in a sentence with a good-patient initial noun works against the main-clause garden path. This greatly reduces the ambiguity effect for good-patient nouns. An initial main clause proposition on the NV pattern is complete at the intransitive embedded verb. A good agent supports the main-clause interpretation, but a following *by* interferes with this interpretation, making the ambiguity effects larger for good agents than for good patients.

The two theories may be differentiated by their predictions for the transitive-only embedded verbs. On the standard connectionist version, the same relative effect should occur for transitive-only versus potentially intransitive verbs. Good patients should be more consistent with the correct reduced relative assignment and therefore show smaller ambiguity effects on the embedded verb. This is not the case, as table 7.10, with transitive-only verbs, shows when compared with table 7.9, with potentially intransitive verbs. Tables 7.9 and 7.10 clearly show that conceptual fit has *opposite* effects on processing the embedded verb for transitive-only versus potentially intransitive verbs.

Before turning to an explanation of tables 7.9 and 7.10 within the framework of LAST, consider for a moment how confusing these results are for interpreting the several dozen major experiments with reduced relatives. Most of the published materials show more than half of the sentences to use embedded verbs that are only transitive. This may explain why the reported impact of conceptual fit on ambiguity effects at the embedded verb is so variable. The two kinds of sentences appear to have opposite effects at that point.

Why should conceptual fit interact with verb subcategorization type? To explain this, we must examine additional syntactic and semantic properties of the two kinds of verbs. There are two importantly different kinds of passives, which we will call agent-requiring verbs and patient-requiring verbs.

Table 7.10
Ambiguity effects depending on conceptual fit for sentences with transitive-only embedded verbs

	Region		
Noun	Verb + *by*	Det + noun	Main verb
Good agent	4	−38	32
Good patient	58	63	10
Difference	−54	−101	22

Source: Reanalysis of Tabossi et al. 1994 data

(51) *Agent-requiring*
   The performers were applauded by the audience.

(52) *Patient-requiring*
   The thief was captured by the cop.

Agent-requiring verbs always require an agent, at least implicitly (see Mauner et al. 1995; Mauner and Koenig 1999; Melinger and Mauner 1999), or something else such as an adverb that can mark them as an event, whereas patient-requiring verbs do not. Hence the relative oddness of (53) and (54) compared to (55) to (58).

Agent-requiring
(53) ?The performers were applauded.

(54) ?The applauded performers ...

Agent-requiring
(55) The performers were applauded at the end.

(56) The loudly applauded performers ...

Patient-requiring
(57) The thief was captured.

(58) The captured thief ...

The fact that verbs like *applaud* require agents may also allow them to appear intransitively with only an agent. But (59) to (62) show that patient-requiring verbs like *capture* may not appear intransitively with only an agent:

Agent-requiring
(59) The audience applauded.

(60) The audience's applauding was unexpected.

Patient-requiring
(61) *The cop captured.

(62) *The cop's capturing was unexpected.

The requirement that agent-requiring verbs have an agent also explains why these verbs can be ambiguous when they appear as a deverbal nominal as in (63) and (64).

Agent-requiring
(63) The applauding of the audience was unexpected.

(64) The audience's applause was unexpected. (either interpretation)

Sentences (65) and (66) show that the corresponding deverbal nominals with patient-requiring verbs allow only a patient interpretation of the noun.

Patient-requiring

(65) The capturing of the thief was unexpected.

(66) The thief's capture was unexpected. (patient only)

The ambiguity of the agent-requiring verbs in (63) and (64) depends on the fact that they can be interpreted as transitive or as intransitive. If there is a patient, the verb is interpreted as transitive, but if not, it is interpreted as intransitive. On the other hand, patient-requiring transitive-only verbs must have a patient in all their various constructions, either explicitly or implied, but they can often lack an agent. According to LAST, lexically specific information is accessed only after the obligatory argument positions are filled. Thus, LAST predicts that the primary effect of conceptual fit will be for good agents with potentially intransitive embedded verbs and for good patients with transitive-only verbs. This is exactly the obtained pattern of results.

LAST makes a further prediction. The early ambiguity effect with transitive-only verbs will be due primarily to an asymmetry in the unreduced constructions. At the auxiliary and passive participle, unreduced constructions explicitly mark the initial noun as object and a potential patient. When the verb is patient-requiring, it requires a patient and not an agent, and so its required arguments are filled and the specific fit of the initial noun as a patient with a particular verb will have an immediate effect.

(67) *Patient-requiring, good patient*
     The thief [that was captured by ...]

(68) *Patient-requiring, good agent*
     The cop [that was captured by ...]

Thus, for unreduced patient-requiring verbs reading times will be faster with a good patient as in (67) than with a good agent as in (68). Conversely, agent-requiring verbs are potentially intransitive, and should show no effect of conceptual fit on unreduced constructions, because their required agent argument has not yet been encountered:

(69) *Agent-requiring, good patient*
     The performer [that was applauded by ...]

(70) *Agent-requiring, good agent*
     The audience [that was applauded by ...]

Thus, for unreduced agent-requiring verbs reading times will be similar with good patients and good agents.

The data from Tabossi and colleagues confirm both of these predictions. Table 7.11 shows the difference in reading time between good agents and good patients within the relative clause, beginning with the embedded verb. For transitive-only verbs, the reading time for unreduced constructions was consistently longer during

Table 7.11
Reading-time difference between good agents and good patients for unreduced relative clauses
(good agent − good patient)

Type of verb	Good agent − good patient
Potentially intransitive	−29
Transitive only	93

Source: From Tabossi et al. 1994

Table 7.12
Ambiguity effects within relative clauses for primarily transitive-only verbs (reading times for
reduced − unreduced)

Study	Region		
	Verb + *by*	Det + noun	Main verb
Spivey-Knowlton, Trueswell, and Tanenhaus 1993:			
Exp. 1	46	110	50
Exp. 2	34	55	26
McRae, Ferretti, and Amyote 1997	63	24	10

Sources: Spivey-Knowlton, Trueswell, and Tanenhaus 1993 (exps. 1 and 2, tables 2 and 4, 1
referent condition only) and McRae et al. 1997 (exp. 3, fig. 2)

the relative clause with good agents than with good patients. There was no such difference for potentially intransitive verbs.

Tabossi et al. did not design their study to distinguish between the two types of verbs, so we need to look for independent confirmation of the pattern shown in their results. As we noted earlier, several studies of reduced relatives (it appears by chance) use a preponderance of one or the other kind of verb (see table 7.8). First, Spivey-Knowlton, Trueswell, and Tanenhaus (1993) and McRae, Ferretti, and Amyote (1997) used almost all transitive-only verbs in self-paced reading time studies. In both sets of studies, the initial noun was an acceptable patient. Like Tabossi et al. they both report more ambiguity effect during the relative clause than at the main verb, as shown in table 7.12.

A few studies contrasted potentially intransitive with transitive-only verbs. As we noted earlier in this section, MacDonald (1994) pointed out that the classic main-verb reading-time elevation occurs only with potentially intransitive verbs. But her data also show the *reverse* effect for the transitive-only verbs (see table 7.4). That is, transitive-only verbs show more relative garden-path elevation of reading time during the relative clause.

Table 7.13

Relative clause ambiguity effects for potentially intransitive (PI) vs. transitive-only (TO) verbs (combined into mean word reading time for two-word regions)

Verb type	Region		
	Verb + *by*	Det + noun	Main verb
PI	−4	49	85
TO	22	25	5

Source: Trueswell 1996

Finally, in two different studies Trueswell (1996) contrasted single-word self-paced reading of materials that contained almost entirely potentially intransitive verbs in one study with materials that had almost entirely transitive-only verbs in the other. The initial nouns were acceptable as both an agent and patient of the critical verb. The ambiguity effects for transitive and intransitive verbs appear in table 7.13. The results neatly contrast the two kinds of verbs in the same way as in Tabossi et al. (1994).

Trueswell's results are a striking within-study confirmation of the pattern of data from Tabossi and colleagues. However, Trueswell was interested in showing that what controls the strength of the garden path is the relative frequency with which the particular passive participle is used in the passive. He predicted that the garden-path effect would be larger for verbs that appear in the passive form relatively infrequently. It is obvious that the relative frequency of the past being used as a passive is likely to be a function of the total number of constructions the verb can appear in. Thus, potentially intransitive verbs have relatively fewer appearances in the passive because they can appear in a larger number of different construction types. Indeed, Trueswell's materials group with mostly potentially intransitive verbs was his "low passive participle frequency" group. The frequency distinction is almost completely confounded with the verb-type distinction in his materials, so further research is needed to untangle the variables.

This complex of results is generally consistent with LAST, but of course, must be taken cautiously. First, as we noted earlier, these studies were not designed explicitly to differentiate the effects of potentially intransitive versus transitive-only embedded verbs. This variable needs to be embedded within several replications of various studies that we have discussed. Second, there remains the systematic confound of the distinction between the two kinds of verbs and the relative frequencies of the passive participle. In principle, this can be teased apart by using verbs of only one type and varying the relative frequency of the passive participle within that type. If the relative frequency of the passive participle accounts for the variance within each verb type, that would argue strongly for it as the overall cause, depending on the strength of the effect. Third, we can imagine a variety of implementations of spreading activation models that might make the same propositional structure–dependent predictions as made by LAST. We predict that such models will turn out to be either explicit or happenstantial implementations of the critical features of LAST. That too remains to be seen.

7.1.8 Unergative vs. Unaccusative Verbs

We have noted that the transitive-intransitive distinction is critical in producing a garden path. Research by Stevenson and Merlo (1997) suggests that within the class of potentially intransitive verbs the unergative-unaccusative distinction is important in processing sentences with reduced relatives. Intransitive verbs can take only one argument, which is either agent or experiencer. Intransitive verbs typically are differentiated into verbs such as *melt*, which are *unaccusative*, and verbs such as *race*, which are *unergative* (see section 6.3.3). The action depicted by an unaccusative verb typically "happens to" its subjects and cannot be intentional, while the converse is true of an unergative verb.

(71) *Unaccusative verbs*
    a. What happened to the butter was it melted
    b. *The butter intentionally melted

(72) *Unergative verbs*
    a. *What happened to the horse was it raced
    b. The horse intentionally raced.

In addition, both unergative and unaccusative verbs alternate between intransitive and transitive uses, but these types are distinguished in terms of whether the agent of the intransitive verb and the patient of the transitive verb causes an action. In both uses of the unergative *raced*, for example in (73) and (74), *horse* in some sense causes the action of racing.

(73) *Unergative, intransitive*
    The horse raced past the barn.

(74) *Unergative, transitive*
    The rider raced the horse past the barn.

This is not true for *butter* in (75) and (76), which have an unaccusative verb.

(75) *Unaccusative, intransitive*
    The butter melted in the pan.

(76) *Unaccusative, transitive*
    The cook melted the butter in the pan.

Stevenson and Merlo (1997) argued that unergative verbs as a class are intuitively more susceptible to gardens path in sentences with a reduced relative clause, compared to unaccusative verbs. Thus, (77) seems harder than (78).

(77) *Unergative, reduced relative*
     The horse raced past the barn fell.

(78) *Unaccusative, reduced relative*
     The butter melted in the pan was lumpy.

Filip et al. (1997) presented survey data that suggested that unergative and unaccusative verbs overlap in their difficulty in sentences with reduced relatives. Since there have been no online studies reported comparing unergative and unaccusative verbs, the relevance of this distinction as a syntactic versus semantic dimension needs clarification. It may well turn out that these properties of verbs interact with sentence-level units, just as the argument-requiring properties of verbs do. In addition, it seems likely that verb features such as telicity may underlie the unergative-unaccusative distinction (see sections 3.4.1 and 5.4.7). Such semantic features translate directly into functional syntactic categories, and thus have immediate effects during formation of the initial meaning-form hypothesis.

To conclude our discussion of the comprehension of reduced relatives out of context, we find early effects of available propositional analyses based on subcategorization and thematic properties of verbs. Most notably, garden-path effects are greater for potentially intransitive verbs than for transitive-only verbs. Conceptual fit between the initial noun and the embedded verb interacts with subcategorization properties of the verb. Thus, good agents increase the garden path with potentially intransitive verbs by increasing the salience of the agent-action interpretation. In contrast, good patients decrease the garden path with transitive-only verbs in reduced relatives by increasing the salience of the patient-action interpretation in the unreduced version. The results attest to the compelling perceptual salience of any initial sequence that corresponds to a declarative sentence with an inflected verb. The results appear to be consistent with LAST and to present some challenges to spreading activation models insofar as structural assignment mediates the effects. The fact that different kinds of verbs have superficially opposite garden-path interactions with goodness-of-agent and goodness-of-patient requires that many studies be redone. Finally, the research has been totally dependent on reading and reading-time measures. It is high time to apply various measures of auditory processing load and auditory attention to the problem in ways that do not destroy the natural intonational structure of spoken sentences (see Ferreira et al. 1996; O'Bryan, Townsend, and Bever 2000). Intuitively we know that reduced relatives are quite as bewildering auditorally as visually, possibly more so. But it remains to be seen how the auditory processing system goes about recovering from them when it does, and what variables facilitate that.

7.2 Reduced Relative Clauses in Context

LAST relies in part on the argument requirements of verbs to elicit an initial meaning-form hypothesis. The grammar uses this initial meaning-form hypothesis to generate a candidate syntactic structure for the sentence. The comprehension system then checks the candidate syntax against the input. If the candidate syntax matches the input, the meaning of the sentence is integrated conceptually; if it does not, there is a second analysis-by-synthesis cycle.

On this model, attention to the meaning and structure of a sentence is cyclic. There is initial attention to pseudosyntax, then to its associated meaning, followed by attention to the derived syntax and then attention to meaning again when the sentence meaning is integrated into a higher-level conceptual representation. In this architecture, context can exert an effect in two ways. First, context may prime words (e.g., Forster 1981; Seidenberg et al. 1982). The associated lexical structure, such as subcategorization information, may then influence the initial meaning-form hypothesis. Second, context may prime propositions. This information is most available at the point of integrating the sentence meaning into a discourse representation (Bransford and Franks 1971). A topic of intense research effort during the 1990s was the question of whether the parser can use discourse context to resolve syntactic ambiguities. Multisentence discourses typically connect the sentences with a focused topic—that is, what the sentences are "about." This kind of connection can make sentences with a reduced relative clause more acceptable by emphasizing the importance of the relative clause as a modifier. Altmann and Steedman (1988) pointed out that a noun phrase often is modified by a relative clause when it is necessary to identify which of two referents the speaker is talking about. Thus, a context that requires distinguishing between potential referents for a noun phrase could eliminate the processing complexity of reduced relatives.

The debate on the role of discourse context in processing sentences with reduced relative clauses has been fueled by some studies that support one position, and by others that support the opposite position. Unlike all other current models, LAST accounts for results both for and against the view that the parser uses contextual information to resolve temporary ambiguities. Briefly, studies that demonstrate contextual resolution of garden-path sentences involve the activities of the comprehension system at the point of integrating sentence meaning with discourse context. Studies that demonstrate little effect of context involve cases in which the comprehension system has presented an incorrect meaning-form hypothesis that must then be revised. In the remainder of this chapter we show how LAST accounts for the data on garden paths of the main clause/reduced relative. We return to discourse-context effects in chapter 8.

7.2.1 Potentially Intransitive Verbs Yield No Context Effect

Studies that show little effect of context on resolving main-clause/reduced relative garden paths have used embedded verbs that primarily are potentially intransitive, as in (79).

(79) *Potentially intransitive*
    The wolf [hunted by the ranger] was rabid.

Since *the wolf hunted* satisfies the required arguments of *hunt*, the embedded verb elicits an initial meaning-form hypothesis when the comprehension system receives it. The initial meaning-form hypothesis leads to generating a candidate syntactic structure, checking the syntax, and recoding. Therefore, we expect that studies that used embedded verbs that are potentially intransitive will show strong evidence of a garden path when the main verb is received, regardless of contextual support. Another way of putting this is that potentially intransitive verbs elicit such a strong garden path that supportive or conflicting context is usually overshadowed.

Studies that show that context eliminates the garden-path effects have used mostly embedded verbs that are only transitive, as in (80).

(80) *Transitive verb*
    The wolf [captured by the ranger] was rabid.

As we have seen, transitive-only verbs minimally require a patient. Studies that have shown that the garden path disappears in supportive discourse typically have shown the context effect on the embedded noun (e.g., *ranger*). Hence, the garden path in such studies tends to be resolved at the end of the embedded clause, and there is little difference in the processing of the main verb in reduced and unreduced constructions.

The critical issue distinguishing current approaches to the processing of sentences in context is the point during the sentence when context has an effect. Thus, it is essential to pinpoint the location at which there is processing difficulty. For this purpose we can divide a sentence with an embedded reduced relative clause into several processing regions: the initial noun phrase (NP1), the embedded verb plus preposition (EV + P), the embedded noun phrase (NP2), the main verb (MV), and the remainder of the sentence (REST). The various studies on processing reduced relatives in context differ in which of the regions they examine.

Table 7.14 summarizes the materials of six studies that investigated the effects of discourse context on the processing of sentences with reduced relative clauses. The table shows the percentage of embedded verbs that are used only in a transitive sense, and the argument role of the initial noun phrase in the preceding context sentence. It is clear that the garden-path effect disappears in context when the embedded verb is transitive-only and when the context primes a patient role for the initial noun.

Ferreira and Clifton (1986) measured eye tracking while reading sentences with MC/RR ambiguities such as (81) versus control sentences such as (82). The target

Table 7.14
Summary of studies on the role of discourse context in processing sentences with reduced relatives

Study	Garden path	Context role of NP1	%TO
Ferreira and Clifton 1986	Yes	Recipient Patient Agent	50
Britt et al. 1992	Yes	Agent	13
Rayner, Garrod, and Perfetti 1992	Yes	Patient	13
Murray and Liversedge 1994	Yes	Agent	0
Spivey-Knowlton, Trueswell, and Tanenhaus 1993	No	Patient	100
Trueswell and Tanenhaus 1991	No	Patient Agent	75

sentences appeared in contexts that supported either the reduced relative interpretation or the main-clause interpretation. In both target sentences, the word *agreed* establishes the structure of the sentence unambiguously. Accordingly, Ferreira and Clifton (1986) recorded fixation times on the word *agreed.* The target sentences were presented in one of three contexts.

(81) *Reduced relative target*
     The editor [played the tape] agreed the story was a big one.

(82) *Main-clause target*
     The editor played the tape and agreed the story was a big one.

One of the target sentences followed a three-sentence preamble (83) and a priming context sentence, either (84), (85), or (86). The context sentence biased the interpretation of the garden-path sentence. In one case, the context sentence supported the reduced relative interpretation by mentioning two editors in the sentence that preceded the target sentence as in (84). Thus, a relative clause would be appropriate for distinguishing which of the two editors the writer is referring to. In a second case, the context sentence supported the main-clause structure by mentioning only one editor in the preceding sentence as in (85), and in a third case, the context sentence was neutral between the reduced relative and main-clause biases as in (86).

(83) *Preamble*
     John worked as a reporter for a big city newspaper. He sensed that a major story was brewing over the city hall scandal, and he obtained some evidence that he believed pretty much established the mayor's guilt. He went to his

Table 7.15
Mean first-pass fixation times (ms/character)

	Region		
Context-target	NP1 + EV + NP2	MV	REST
RR-RR	26	32	29
N-RR	24	32	28
MC-MC	24	30	24
N-MC	25	27	24

Source: Adapted from Ferreira and Clifton 1986, fig. 2

editors with a tape and some photos because he needed their approval before he could go ahead with the story.

(84) *Context sentence with reduced relative bias*
He ran a tape for one of this editors, and he showed some photos to the other.

(85) *Context sentence with main-clause bias*
He gave a tape to his editor and told him to listen to it.

(86) *Context sentence with neutral bias*
He brought out a tape for one of his editors and told him to listen carefully to it.

The average fixation times in the ambiguous region (NP1 + EV + NP2, *the editor played the tape*), the disambiguating word (MV, *agreed*), and the remainder of the sentence (REST, *the story was a big one*) appear in table 7.15 (RR = reduced relative, MC = main clause, N = neutral). Inspection of table 7.15 shows that fixation times were longer on *agreed* (region MV) and the remainder of the sentence (region REST) when the target sentence was a reduced relative. Ferreira and Clifton (1986) found that fixation times were significantly longer in the relative clause sentence than in the main-clause sentence, and that there was no interaction with context.

About 50 percent of the embedded verbs in this study were potentially intransitive (*played, taught, raced, sued, served, paid, read, asked*). As we noted earlier, an embedded verb that is potentially intransitive initially may elicit a meaning hypothesis that corresponds to the intransitive interpretation at the point of the embedded verb. Thus, *the editor played* constitutes a complete semantic unit following the NV pattern. In addition, the sequence *the editor played the tape* constitutes a complete semantic unit following the NVN pattern. The predominance of both patterns conspires to induce a garden path.

Britt et al. (1992) found that supportive contexts did not eliminate the garden-path effect in reduced relatives. Of the eight test sentences that Britt et al. used, seven contained embedded verbs that were potential intransitives, as in:

(87) *Reduced relative*
The woman / rushed to the hospital / had given birth safely.

(88) *Main clause*
The woman / rushed to the hospital / without taking her laundry.

The slashes indicate viewing windows in self-paced reading. There were three viewing windows: NP1, EV + P + NP2, and MV + REST. The contexts supporting the reduced relative were discourses in which the antecedent for *the woman* was no longer in focus:

(89) *Relative clause bias*
Harry had driven taxis for many years but he still really enjoyed it. Today there was all kinds of excitement. His first call involved rushing a pregnant woman to the hospital and at one moment he expected to have to deliver the baby himself. He then had to take a special package to the airport and only just arrived in time. On the way back he turned on his radio. They said that the woman rushed to the hospital had given birth safely ...

(90) *Main-clause bias*
John had just received the news that their mother was seriously ill in the hospital. His initial thought was to rush to the hospital as quickly as possible. But then he realized that he needed to get in contact with his sister Mary. Her roommate thought that she might be in the laundromat, so john called and described her to them. They said that the woman rushed to the hospital without taking her laundry ...

Since *the woman* in the relative biasing context is no longer in focus at the time of the target sentence, a relative clause modifying *the woman* was needed to clarify its referent. If the comprehenders establish a referent for *the woman* as soon as possible, they should interpret *rushed to the hospital* as a reduced relative clause identifying *the woman*. In this case, the sentence with a reduced relative clause should be no harder than the one with the main-clause interpretation. Table 7.16 shows the results.

Britt et al. (1992) found that reading times for the disambiguating region (MV + REST) were longer in reduced relative sentences than in main-clause sentences. The reduced relative effect occurred in both the no-context condition and in the biasing-context condition. Thus, discourse context does not eliminate the garden path.

Rayner, Garrod, and Perfetti (1992) tested the hypothesis that discourse focus influences the processing of reduced relatives. In an eye-tracking study, they used sentences with verbs that primarily are potentially intransitive (13/15), like the following:

Table 7.16
Mean first-pass fixation times (ms/character) (0 refers to no discourse context)

Context-target	Region		
	NP1	EV + P + NP2	MV + REST
RR-RR	61	70	80
MC-MC	69	68	65
0-RR	72	93	126
0-MC	69	89	105

Source: Adapted from Britt et al. 1992, table 7

(91) *Reduced relative*
     The coffee / spilled on the rug / was difficult / to conceal.

(92) *Main clause*
     The coffee / spilled on the rug / and even marked / the new wallpaper.

The viewing windows were NP1, EV + P + NP2, MV, and REST. The contexts that supported the relative clause interpretation were of two types:

(93) *Reduced relative bias, focus*
     Anne didn't know what to say to her parents when they came home. She had thrown a party and the house was in a terrible state. Her friends had spilled coffee on the rug and scratched her mother's new table. The coffee spilled on the rug was difficult to conceal ...

(94) *Reduced relative bias, nonfocus*
     Anne didn't know what to say to her parents when they came home. She had thrown a party and the house was in a terrible state. Her friends had spilled coffee on the rug and scratched her mother's new table. She tried to do her best to clean things up a bit. Then she heard her parents at the front door. As they entered she tried to distract their attention. The coffee spilled on the rug was difficult to conceal ...

(95) *Main-clause bias*
     Anne had spent a fortune decorating the living room and fitting an expensive new rug. So when her friends came round for coffee she really enjoyed being able to show it off to them. Imagine her embarrassment when she tripped over the table with a tray in her hand. The coffee spilled on the rug and even marked the new wallpaper ...

Table 7.17 shows the results. For the three context conditions, the only significant effect was an interaction between region and context. Fixation times on the main

Table 7.17
Mean first-pass fixation times (ms/char)

	Region		
	NP$_1$	EV + P + NP$_2$	MV
Context			
RR-bias, nonfocus	34	31	34
RR-bias, focus	34	30	36
MC-bias	33	31	28
No context			
RR	33	34	39
MC	33	33	34

Source: Adapted from Rayner, Garrod, and Perfetti 1992, table 4

verb were faster for the main-clause condition than for the two reduced relative conditions. The two reduced relative conditions did not differ.

Murray and Liversedge (1994) investigated the role of discourse context in processing sentences with reduced relative clauses. An example of their materials contains a potentially intransitive verb (they did not report all of their materials):

(96) *Reduced relative*
The man / dressed as a woman / looked quite ridiculous.

(97) *Unreduced relative*
The man / who was dressed as a woman / looked quite ridiculous.

(98) *Main clause*
The man / dressed as a woman / and looked quite ridiculous.

The viewing windows were NP1, EV + P + NP2, and REST. The contexts differed in whether there was one entity, or two, to which the initial noun phrase could refer:

(99) *Double context (reduced relative bias)*
After the auditions two people had been chosen to perform in a local village pantomime. One was a man who was playing the prince and the other was a man who was playing an old witch ...

(100) *Single context (main-clause bias)*
After the auditions two people had been chosen to perform in a local village pantomime. One was a woman who was playing the prince and the other was a man who was playing an old witch ...

Since the double contexts contain two possible referents for the initial noun phrase in the ambiguous target sentence, they support a reduced relative interpretation of the

Table 7.18
Mean reading times (ms/word) depending on type of context and type of sentence

Context-target	Region	
	EV + P + NP2	MV + REST
MC-UR	238	256
MC-RR	210	280
MC-MC	197	271
RR-UR	223	259
RR-RR	213	279
RR-MC	210	256

Source: Adapted from Murray and Liversedge 1994, tables 15.4 and 15.5

target. Murray and Liversedge (1994) measured eye-fixation times in the disambiguating region. The referential theory of Altmann and Steedman (1988) predicted that the double context would eliminate the garden path, since this context requires a relative clause to distinguish the referent of *the man*.

Murray and Liversedge (1994) found that fixation times in the initial region (*the man*) were faster in double contexts. The results for the ambiguous and disambiguating regions appear in table 7.18. Fixation times in the ambiguous region were shorter for reduced relatives than for unreduced relatives. Fixation times in the disambiguating region were longer for reduced relatives than for unreduced relatives. Context, however, had no effect on fixation time, and did not interact with sentence type.

Four studies showed that contexts in which there are two potential referents for the initial noun did not eliminate the processing difficulty of the reduced relative. All four studies found that reading times were longer for the reduced relative sentence at the point of reading the main verb, regardless of biasing contexts. The proportion of reported relative clause verbs that were potentially intransitive were 8/16, 7/8, 13/15, and 1/1. These verbs lead the comprehension system to present an initial meaning-form hypothesis that is based on an intransitive interpretation:

(101) The woman rushed to the hospital.

(102) The coffee spilled on the rug.

(103) The man dressed as a woman.

The comprehension system generates a syntax, which it then checks against the input, and accepts. The appearance of a second verb causes reanalysis.

7.2.2 Transitive-Only Verbs Yield a Context Effect
Other studies that have examined the role of context in processing reduced relative clauses have used predominantly verbs that are only transitive. Since these verbs

minimally require a patient, the comprehension system searches for a plausible patient (see section 7.1.7). Contexts that enhance the likelihood that the initial noun is a patient will decrease the effect of the reduced relative garden path. However, these effects appear most clearly on the noun at the end of the embedded clause.

Spivey-Knowlton, Trueswell, and Tanenhaus (1993) used self-paced reading to examine the effect of discourse context on processing reduced relatives. They used embedded verbs that were transitive. An example target sentence is:

(104) The prisoner / (who was) / removed by / the guard / fought violently / to break / free of / the guard's grip.

The sentence was presented two words at a time, and the critical viewing windows were NP1, EV + P, NP2, MV, and REST. The goal of Spivey-Knowlton and colleagues was to test the referential theory. Spivey-Knowlton, Trueswell, and Tanenhaus (1993) further tested the referential theory with contexts like these:

(105) *Two-referents context*
       In the visiting room, two prisoners began yelling at each other. To prevent a fight, the guard removed one of the prisoners from the room but not the other . . .

(106) *One-referent context*
       In the visiting room, a prisoner and a visitor began yelling at each other. To prevent a fight, the guard removed the prisoner from the room but not the visitor . . .

The referential theory predicts that the two-referent context will eliminate the difference in reading reduced versus unreduced relative clauses in the target sentence:

(107) *Reduced vs. unreduced target sentence*
       The prisoner (who was) removed by the guard fought violently to break free of the guard's grip.

If contextual information is used early to resolve the ambiguity, context effects should appear on the embedded verb.

Spivey-Knowlton, Trueswell, and Tanenhaus (1993) reported reading times for two-word segments as shown in table 7.19. Reading times were faster for the unreduced sentences than for the reduced sentences, faster for the two-referent context than for the one-referent context, and the interaction between sentence type and context was significant. For the Verb + *by* region, the interaction between sentence type and context was not significant. However, the 46-ms ambiguity effect on Verb + *by* in the one-referent context was significant by items, but not by subjects. Spivey-Knowlton and colleagues concluded that the two-referent condition did eliminate the ambiguity effect on the embedded verb + *by*. These results appear to support the claim that the comprehension system uses discourse information to immediately resolve the garden

Table 7.19
Mean reading times depending on number of referents in context (ms/word)

Sentence type	Region			
	Det + N	Verb + *by*	Det + N	MV
One referent				
RR	612	462	494	509
UR	596	416	384	459
RR − UR	16	46	110	50
Two referents				
RR	547	410	422	472
UR	572	403	410	443
RR − UR	−25	7	12	29

Source: Adapted from Spivey-Knowlton, Trueswell, and Tanenhaus 1993, table 2

path. Three aspects of their results, however, suggest that we interpret them cautiously: the marginal significance, the longer reading times overall for one-referent contexts, and the differences in reading times for the initial noun. Spivey-Knowlton, Trueswell, and Tanenhaus (1993) attributed the longer reading times overall for one-referent contexts than for two-referents contexts to the infelicity of using a relative clause modifier when there is only one possible referent. But the infelicity of a relative clause in the one-referent contexts cannot account for the wide variation in reading times for the initial noun phrase. Since the initial noun appears before the relative clause is read, the comprehender has no way of knowing whether the material that the sentence that he or she is reading is going to be infelicitous.

How can we account for the faster reading times on the initial noun phrase in the two-referent contexts? One possibility is that these contexts prime the initial noun phrase by referring to it more often (see Murray and Liversedge 1994). The two-referent context refers to a prisoner three times: *two prisoners, one of the prisoners*, and *the other (prisoner)*. The one-referent context refers to prisoner only twice: *a prisoner* and *the prisoner*. Thus reading times may be faster in the two-referent context than in the one-referent context because of more references to the initial noun phrase.

In a second experiment Spivey-Knowlton and associates compared reading times for morphologically unambiguous passive participles (*taken*) as a baseline for ambiguous verbs (*removed*), as in

(108) *Unambiguous embedded verb*
The prisoner taken by the guard fought violently to break free of the guard's grip.

Table 7.20
Mean reading times in ambiguous vs. unambiguous sentences (ms)

Sentence type	Region			
	Det + N	Verb + *by*	Det + N	MV
One referent				
Ambiguous	691	532	543	594
Unambiguous	702	498	488	568
U − A	−11	34	55	26
Two referents				
Ambiguous	660	476	468	529
Unambiguous	635	487	470	545
U − A	25	−11	−2	−16

Source: Adapted from Spivey-Knowlton, Trueswell, and Tanenhaus 1993, table 4

(109) *Ambiguous embedded verb*

The prisoner removed by the guard fought violently to break free of the guard's grip.

The results appear in table 7.20. There was a marginal effect of ambiguity in the one-referent condition. Again, the reading times were faster overall in two-referent contexts and there was variability in reading times for the initial noun. It appears that the two-referent contexts serve to increase the salience of the initial noun and therefore to reduce generally the reading time for the entire sentence. Still unexplained, however, is why there is no effect on verb + *by* in the two-referent case, as we would expect with a standard spreading activation architecture.

With single-word presentation, Spivey-Knowlton et al. (1993) found no interactions between context and ambiguity. The failure to find such an interaction on the verb in single-word presentation indicates that context does not have an immediate effect. Spivey-Knowlton et al. did find an effect of ambiguity on the embedded noun such that reading times were longer for the embedded noun in ambiguous sentences than in unambiguous sentences. These results again show that discourse context does not eliminate the garden-path effect of a reduced relative clause. The ambiguity functionally disappears at the end of a relatively complete semantic unit, for example when *the prisoner removed by the guard* yields the semantic unit *the prisoner was removed by the guard*. The processing of the reduced relative sentence appears to be influenced primarily by the subcategorization requirements of verbs and little by discourse context.

Trueswell and Tanenhaus (1991) examined the role of temporal context in resolving main-clause/reduced relative ambiguities. They noted that a main clause that introduces a new event must maintain the tense that has appeared earlier in the discourse. Thus, a story told in the past tense will introduce a new event in the past tense. A reduced relative clause with an ambiguous verb, however, is ambiguous concerning tense, so that (110) is ambiguous between (111), (112), and (113).

(110) The student spotted by the proctor ...

(111) The student who was spotted by the proctor ...   (past)

(112) The student who is spotted by the proctor ...   (present)

(113) The student who will be spotted by the proctor ...   (future)

These observations suggest that the comprehension system may use temporal information in the discourse context to resolve the temporary ambiguity of a sentence with a reduced relative clause. In particular, processing reduced relatives should be easier when the context is in the future tense than when it is in the past tense. This is because it is infelicitous to introduce a new event with a main clause containing a past-tense verb, as in *The student spotted X*, when the context is future tense, as in (115).

Trueswell and Tanenhaus used discourse contexts that were in either past tense as in (114) or future tense as in (115), followed by a target sentence that had either a reduced or unreduced relative clause (116):

(114) *Past context*
       Several students were sitting together taking an exam yesterday. A proctor came up and spotted one of the students cheating ...

(115) *Future context*
       Several students will be sitting together taking an exam tomorrow. A proctor will come up and spot one of the students cheating ...

(116) *Target sentence*
       a. The student spotted by the proctor received a warning ... (reduced, past)
       b. The student who was spotted by the proctor received a warning ... (unreduced, past)
       c. The student spotted by the proctor will receive a warning ... (reduced, future)
       d. The student who was spotted by the proctor will receive a warning ... (unreduced, future)

The embedded verbs were mostly transitive-only verbs (about 75%). Participants read the texts two words at a time. The results appear in table 7.21.

The results showed the following effects:

$V + by$:   There was an ambiguity effect: reading times were faster for unreduced relatives. There was no interaction of context and sentence type. How-

Table 7.21
Mean reading times depending on tense in context (ms)

Sentence	Region		
	Verb + *by*	Det + N	MV
Past context			
RR	485	490	520
UR	460	470	505
RR − UR	25	20	15
Future context			
RR	475	455	480
UR	460	450	475
RR − UR	15	5	5

Source: Adapted from Trueswell and Tanenhaus 1991, fig. 1.b

ever, the ambiguity effect was significant in past contexts but not in future contexts.

Det + *N*: There was an ambiguity effect for past contexts but not for future contexts.

MV: There was a context effect: reading times were faster for future contexts than for past contexts.

The fact that the ambiguity effect appears on the Det + N for past contexts but not for future contexts shows that temporal information is used at the end of the relative clause. It is at that point that the comprehension system presents an initial meaning-form hypothesis, and semantic context is integrated with the meaning that the comprehension system has presented.

The two studies that report that context can influence early decisions of a reduced relative clause have used predominately transitive-only verbs (16/16 and 12/16). They have found the clearest effect of context on the embedded noun, as in *guard* and *proctor* in:

(117) The prisoner removed by the guard . . .

(118) The student spotted by the proctor . . .

The results of both studies support LAST. It is on the embedded noun that a complete proposition is explicitly formed, and hence, integration with context is most natural. Discourse context thus has relatively little effect on the formation of the initial meaning-form hypothesis, but a relatively large effect at the point of integrating the derived meaning-form into a memory representation of discourse. The studies of discourse context support the importance of a propositional unit in initiating the synthesis stage.

7.3 Full Relative Clauses

In this section, we examine additional evidence for the sentence template especially with reference to subparts of it, NV = agent + action, and VN = action + patient, by considering how the first portion of the template applies to subject-first and object-first active relative clauses. Then we consider evidence that nonsequential information, such as noun animacy, information from long-term knowledge, and information from recent context, can influence the initial meaning-form hypothesis.

The following sentences illustrate subject and object relative clauses:

(119) *Subject relative*
      The boy [who pushed the ball] ran home.

(120) *Object relative*
      The boy [who the dog bit] ran home.

The default application of the initial position of the NVN template primes the agent interpretation for the first noun in the sentence, *boy*. But then the relative pronoun *who* (or *that*) signals the beginning of a new clause, which triggers its own fresh application of the NVN template to *who*, now treated as a noun. Thus, we can expect that the NVN template will favor subject relative sentences over object relative sentences. The obvious explanation for this is that a subject relative such as (119) matches the initial portion of the template, as in:

Template matching for subject relative

The boy	=	N	=	agent
who	=	"N"	=	agent
pushed	=	V	=	action
the ball	=	N	=	patient

Consider this in more detail. The first portion of the NVN template, in which *who* functions as initial noun, allows the pseudosyntax to prime a preliminary assignment of agent, immediately confirmed by the following verb, *pushed*. In contrast, the same agent assignment for *who* is wrong within an object relative clause such as (120).

Template matching for object relative

The boy	=	N	=	agent
who	=	"N"	=	agent?
the dog	=	N	=	agent
bit	=	V	=	action
ran	=	V	=	?

First, *who* elicits agent status, but then the following noun does not confirm that assignment. The remaining portion of the object relative, *the dog bit*, does conform to the initial portion of the NVN pattern, and the pseudosyntax can correctly assign agent status to the noun phrase *the dog*. But then, this application of the entire template runs afoul when the main verb *ran* appears. The system now has no patient for *bit* and must find one, which requires undoing the agent status of *who* and reassigning it patient status. Accordingly, we can expect that object relative clauses will be harder than subject relative clauses and that the relative difficulty will be most apparent near the end of the relative clause.

Several experimental studies show that object relative sentences are indeed harder than subject relative sentences. For example, Wanner and Maratsos (1978) interrupted subjects' word-by-word reading of a sentence containing a relative clause with a random list of five proper names such as *John George Sam Bill Hank* (see section 6.1.4). The instructions were to read the sentence and recall as many of the names as possible. The names were presented at one of four points within the sentence (indicated by a slash below):

(121) *Subject relative*
     / The witch who despised / sorcerers frightened / little children./

(122) *Object relative*
     / The witch whom sorcerers / despised frightened / little children./

Wanner and Maratsos (1978) found that errors in name recall were greater for object relatives like (122). However, this difference was significant only in the middle of the relative clause, at the second test point (after *sorcerers*). Holmes and O'Regan (1981) found that question answering is poorer for object relatives than for subject relatives, and regressions in eye movements are greater for object relatives than for subject relatives.

These results are generally consistent with the view that the comprehension system responds to the NVN template. In addition, there is considerable evidence that the critical difficulty is most apparent in the latter portion of the object relative clause.

7.3.1 Assignment of Patient Role

King and Just (1991) measured word-reading times with a moving-window reading task (see box 6.4) in subject and object relative sentences, as in

(123) *Subject relative*
     The reporter [that attacked the senator] admitted the error.

(124) *Object relative*
     The reporter [that the senator attacked] admitted the error.

Mean reading times for various regions within the critical sentences appear in table 7.22. King and Just found that reading times were longer for object relatives than for

Table 7.22
Mean reading times (ms) in regions of sentences with subject relative (SR) and object relative (OR) clauses

Subject relative			
... reporter that attacked the	*senator*	*admitted*	*the error*
530	630	650	590
Object relative			
... reporter that the senator	*attacked*	*admitted*	*the error*
500	720	790	580
SR – OR difference			
30	−90	−140	10

Source: Adapted from King and Just 1991, fig. 1

subject relatives on the final word of the relative clause—that is, *attacked* in (124) versus *senator* in (123)—and on the main verb (*admitted*).

King and Just (1991) also compared reading times for subjects with high reading span versus low reading span. They found a significant difference between these subject groups only on the main verb of object relative sentences (*admitted*). High-span subjects read the main verb of object relatives more than 200 ms faster than low-span subjects. The difference between people with a large verbal memory capacity occurs at the point where the comprehender is looking for a word to fill the object role of the relative clause verb. To do this, the comprehender must recall the initial noun and use it to fill the gap.

Several other methodologies support the conclusion that an important difficulty in processing object relative clauses involves the assignment of patient role. Baird and Koslik (1974) found that recall of the action-patient relations was poorer in object relatives than in subject relatives. Frauenfelder, Segui, and Mehler (1980) found that phoneme-monitoring times for targets immediately after a relative clause were longer for object relative clauses than for subject relative clauses (see box 6.1). For targets before the end of a relative clause, however, monitoring times did not differ for subject versus object relative clauses. Cohen and Mehler (1996) confirmed both of these patterns with a click-detection methodology (see box 6.8), but no difference in click-detection times early in object versus subject relative clauses. Using a cross-modal lexical decision task (see box 6.5), Swinney, Ford, Frauenfelder, and Bresnan (as reported in Nicol and Swinney 1989) found that response times to target words that were similar in meaning to the patient were reduced after the relative clause verb, but not before it. Ford (1983) found that word-by-word lexical decision times in a reading task were longer for object relatives than for subject relatives only on the last word of the relative clause and on the main verb. The differences occur at the point at which the patient role must be assigned for the relative clause verb. If the system recorded the sequence *the dog bit* in (120) as the beginning of an NVN pattern, we would expect slower processing times in just that region.

7.3.2   Moving the Start of a Sentence Template

Center-embedded relative clauses interrupt the NVN pattern of the main clause. We know that this interruption by itself does not present comprehenders with difficulty. Holmes (1973), Baird and Koslick (1974), and Hakes, Evans, and Brannon (1976) have shown that sentences with a single center-embedded relative clause on the main-clause subject as in (125) are no harder than ones with a right-branching relative clause on the main-clause object as in (126).

(125) *Subject relative on main-clause subject*
      The dog [that bit the boy] likes the girl.

(126) *Subject relative on main-clause object*
      The girl likes the dog [that bit the boy].

Pseudosyntax can start a new application of the sentence template when the relative pronoun *that* (or *who*) signals a new clause and hence a new NVN sequence:

The dog		=	N	=	agent
	that	=	"N"	=	agent
	bit	=	V	=	action
	the boy	=	N	=	patient
likes		=	V	=	action
the girl		=	N	=	patient

Processing object relatives such as (127) and (128) does not work so smoothly because the relative pronoun is followed by another noun phrase (*the dog*) rather than a verb.

(127) *Object relative on main-clause subject*
      The boy [that the dog bit] ran home.

(128) *Object relative on main-clause object*
      The girl likes the boy [that the dog bit].

Consider below how sentence (127) activates the NVN template. Sentence templates activated by neither *the boy* nor *that* are completed. At the same time, *the dog* activates another NVN pattern that is confirmed immediately by the following verb, *bit*:

the boy			=	N	=	agent
	that		=	"N"	=	agent?
		the dog	=	N	=	agent
		bit	=	V	=	action
		ran	=	V	=	?

These observations suggest the surprising conclusion that the presence of the explicit relative pronoun actually disrupts the processing of object relatives more than its absence, since its absence as in *the boy the dog bit ran home* produces fewer incorrect activations of the sentence template:

The boy	=	N	=	agent
the dog	=	N	=	agent
bit	=	V	=	action
likes	=	V	=	action?

Intuitions suggest that an object relative clause without a relative pronoun is not particularly hard to understand, and may even be easier than one with a relative pronoun.

There is experimental support for this intuition. Hakes, Evans, and Brannon (1976) used a paraphrase task to examine the effects of deleting the relative pronoun in sentences like:

(129) *Object relative on the main-clause subject*
       After the final curtain on opening night, the director [(that) the repertory company had hired] praised the star performer.

(130) *Subject relative on the main-clause subject*
       The children [(that were) playing in the hayloft] startled the farmer's wife when she went to gather the eggs.

(131) *Object relative on the main-clause object*
       After the final curtain on opening night, the star performer praised the director [(that) the repertory company had hired].

(132) *Subject relative on the main-clause object*
       The framer's wife startled the children [(that were) playing in the hayloft] when she went to gather the eggs.

Table 7.23 shows the proportion of sentences that were paraphrased correctly. Hakes and colleagues found that for object relative clauses, paraphrase performance was more accurate when the relative pronoun was absent than when it was present. For subject relative clauses, there was no difference in paraphrase performance for sentences with the relative pronoun present versus absent.

The results reported in Hakes, Evans, and Brannon confirm that a relative pronoun contributes to the difficulty of processing object relative clauses. We can explain this result in terms of the relative pronoun activating a new NVN pattern and analysis-by-synthesis cycle, which must immediately be turned off and started over again when the noun phrase *the repertory company* is received.

Table 7.23
Proportion of correctly paraphrased sentences with relative clauses depending on whether a relative pronoun is present or absent

Sentence type	Relative pronoun	
	Present	Absent
Subject relative		
On main subject	.679	.646
On main object	.625	.628
Average	.652	.637
Object relative		
On main subject	.451	.514
On main object	.409	.460
Average	.430	.487

Source: From Hakes, Evans, and Brannon 1976, tables 1 and 2

7.3.3 Plausibility and Agency

In our discussion of reduced relatives, we observed that the pseudosyntax is sensitive to semantic information such as the fact that animate nouns frequently fill the agent role of a verb (see section 7.1.5). This information can counteract to some extent the misapplication of the NVN pattern in reduced relatives.

The pseudosyntax is sensitive to semantic information in the initial assignment of argument roles in other constructions. In the study mentioned earlier, Frauenfelder, Segui, and Mehler (1980) showed that phoneme-monitoring times were longer after object relative clauses than after subject relative clauses when the relative clauses were reversible. They also showed that plausibility could eliminate the processing difficulty of object relative clauses. Frauenfelder and colleagues examined the effect of type of relative clause following nonreversible relative clauses as well. Examples of materials in all conditions appear below:

(133) *Reversible subject relative*
Le savant [qui connait le docteur] travaille dans une université moderne.
(The scientist [who knows the doctor] works in a modern university.)

(134) *Reversible object relative*
Le savant [que connait le docteur] travaille dans une université moderne.
(The scientist [who the doctor knows] works in a modern university.)

(135) *Nonreversible subject relative*
L'éditeur [qui publie la revue] demande beaucoup de reigueur dans les articles.
(The editor [who publishes the journal] requires much precision in the articles.)

Table 7.24
Phoneme monitoring times (ms) in reversible and nonreversible sentences with subject vs. object relative clauses

	Type of relative clause	
	Subject	Object
Reversible	421	485
Nonreversible	456	446

Source: Adapted from Frauenfelder, Segui, and Mehler 1980, fig. 2

(136) *Nonreversible object relative*
Les articles [que publie la revue] demandent une lecture attentive.
(The articles [that the journal publishes] require attentive reading.)

In French the relative pronoun *que* is the only syntactic cue to an object relative structure. Frauenfelder and associates found that phoneme-monitoring times for the initial phoneme of the final noun of the relative clause were longer for object relative clauses than for subject relative clauses (see table 7.24), confirming that object relative clauses are harder to process, even with an unambiguous object relative pronoun. The materials for nonreversible relative clauses, however, vary the plausibility of the initial noun of the sentence as fulfilling potential argument roles of the embedded verb. It is more likely that editors publish journals than that journals publish editors, and it is more likely that journals publish articles rather than that articles publish journals. Frauenfelder, Segui, and Mehler (1980) found no difference in monitoring times for main-verb targets (*demande, demandent*) between subject and object relatives when the relative clause was nonreversible. The results suggest that pseudo-syntax is sensitive to information about plausibility in filling the patient gap in an object relative clause. This can reduce the processing complexity of subject versus object relative clauses (but see Holmes 1979).

   Weckerly and Kutas (as reported in Kutas 1997) examined brain responses to animate versus inanimate nouns during the processing of object relative clauses. They used materials that had an inanimate initial noun and an animate noun in the relative clause, I(A), or an animate initial noun and an inanimate noun in the relative clause, A(I):

(137) *Inanimate initial noun, animate embedded noun*
The poetry [that the editor recognized] depressed the publisher of the struggling magazine.

(138) *Animate initial noun, inanimate embedded noun*
The editor [that the poetry depressed] recognized the publisher of the struggling magazine.

Weckerly and Kutas found a reading-time difference starting on the noun in the relative clause. For the relative clause noun and for each of the next four words, reading times were faster in I(A) than in A(I). This result suggests that animate nouns are more readily interpreted as agents. Weckerly and Kutas also measured event related potentials (ERPs) when the words were presented visually and sequentially for 500 ms each. These results showed an effect of animacy on the initial noun and on the noun in the relative clause. There also was an animacy effect on the main verb, which is just at the point when comprehenders would expect a noun to fill the patient role of the relative clause verb. These results suggest that the animacy of the initial noun elicits assignment of it to the agent role of the embedded verb, which must then be corrected at the verb.

7.4 Direct-Object/Sentential Complement

Several theorists have discussed the direct-object/sentential complement (DO/SC) ambiguity (Crocker 1996; Frazier and Clifton 1996; Gorrell 1995; MacDonald, Pearlmutter, and Seidenberg 1994; Pritchett 1992; Tabor, Juliano, and Tanenhaus 1997; see chapter 4). An example of a DO/SC ambiguity is:

(139) *Direct-object/sentential complement ambiguity*
       John knew⌐the answer was wrong.⌐

Some demonstrations show that there is a tendency to take the first noun after the verb (*the answer*) as patient, consistent with the NVN template, rather than immediately assigning the noun as the beginning of a complement.

The theoretical discussion has centered on two questions: What causes the garden path, and when is it noticed? Several researchers have found that the DO/SC ambiguity has behavioral effects, yet both Pritchett (1992) and Gorrell (1995) have noted that it is not a *conscious* garden path. Nevertheless, the local DO/SC ambiguity is both behaviorally and intuitively easier than the MC/RC ambiguity that is created by a reduced relative clause even though both ambiguities appear to involve equally complex revisions in phrase structure. For example, the MC/RC ambiguity involves changing assignment of a main verb to a verb in a subordinate clause that modifies the initial noun. The DO/SC ambiguity involves changing the direct object of a verb to the subject of a subordinate clause that is a complement of the verb. Thus, the ease of the DO/SC ambiguity is a puzzle, especially for many syntax-first models.

In terms of LAST, (139) elicits the following initial meaning-form hypothesis:

John	=	N	=	agent
knew	=	V	=	action
the answer	=	N	=	patient

Then the verb *was* is encountered, immediately requiring an agent, and forcing recoding *the answer* as the beginning of a complement, itself in the patient role.

part of the patient, not the whole patient —

According to Pritchett (1992), so long as *the answer* remains part of the patient of the same verb, reanalysis is not conscious. We do not have enough cases of this kind to support the broad claim, but it is tempting to agree with the spirit of Pritchett's proposal that recodings are hard to detect if they maintain an argument in the same general thematic relation to a verb. In terms of LAST, however, plausibility, verb preferences, and their interactions with the NVN template may contribute to the ease of assigning the noun phrase to the patient role and recoding it as a complement when needed.

So first N is only part of the complement of V is & not the whole patient —

7.4.1 Plausibility

Several studies have established that the direct-object interpretation is preferred over the sentential-complement interpretation. The plausibility of the postverbal noun as a patient of the verb may have a weak effect on the DO/SC garden path at the syntax-checking and semantic integration stage. Pickering and Traxler (1998) examined eye-movement patterns while reading sentences such as:

(140) *Sentential complement, plausible direct object*
      The criminal confessed his sins that upset kids harmed too many people.

(141) *Sentential complement, implausible direct object*
      The criminal confessed his gang that upset kids harmed too many people.

If plausibility of a noun as direct object influences fixation times, *his sins* and its modifying relative clause *that upset kids* should be read faster than the corresponding regions in the second sentence. When *harmed* is read, however, reading times should increase in the first sentence, relative to the second, since *his sins* turns out to not be the direct object of *confessed*, but rather a sentential complement. Pickering and Traxler found no interaction of this sort in first-pass reading times. However, they did find an interaction in number of regressive eye movements between the relative clause region and the disambiguating verb. Regressions were relatively more frequent for the sentences with an implausible direct object within the relative clause, but relatively more frequent for the sentences with a plausible direct object on the disambiguating verb.

Garnsey et al. (1997) examined eye-fixation times and self-paced reading times in sentences such as:

(142) *Equal bias, plausible direct object*
      The senior senator regretted (that) the decision had ever been made public.

(143) *Equal bias, implausible direct object*
      The senior senator regretted (that) the reporter had ever seen the report.

Counts of frequency of usage show that verbs like *regretted* are used equally often with a noun phrase direct object versus a sentential complement. For these verbs,

Garnsey et al. found a trend toward the plausibility of the postverbal noun phrase as a direct object influencing the size of the ambiguity effect. The ambiguity effect was numerically greater when the noun phrase was a plausible direct object (*decision*) than when it was an implausible direct object (*reporter*). The marginal effect of plausibility for balanced verbs is consistent with LAST. Pseudosyntax elicits the meaning-form hypothesis corresponding to NVN = agent-action-patient. At the checking stage, plausible direct objects are integrated into a complete meaning, while implausible direct objects are not.

7.4.2 Verb Preferences

Garnsey et al. (1997) also examined reading times when the verb showed a strong preference for use with a direct object versus a sentential complement. An example sentence with a verb that is more often used with a noun phrase direct object is

(144) *Direct-object bias, plausible direct object*
      The art critic wrote (that) the interview had been a complete disaster.

The results appear in table 7.25. For direct-object bias verbs, Garnsey et al. (1997) found that reading times were longer in the region of disambiguation (*had been*) when the complementizer *that* was omitted than when it was present (361 vs. 346 ms.) When *that* is omitted, pseudosyntax finds an NVN pattern and presents the meaning hypothesis:

The art critic   = N = agent
wrote   = V = action
the interview   = N = patient

Table 7.25
Mean first-pass fixation times (ms) in the disambiguating region depending on verb bias and DO-plausibility

	Verb bias		
	DO	Equal	SC
Plausible DO			
No *that*	364	352	337
That	343	335	338
Ambiguity effect	21	17	−1
Implausible DO			
No *that*	357	345	347
That	349	344	340
Ambiguity effect	12	1	7

Note: DO = direct object; SC = sentential complement
Source: Adapted from Garnsey et al. 1997, table 6

The comprehension system generates a syntax that matches the input up through the word *interview*. The word *had*, however, signals that this analysis is incorrect. For direct-object bias verbs, Garnsey et al. even found a 17-ms ambiguity effect when the second noun was implausible as a direct object:

(145) *Direct-object bias, implausible direct object*
      The art critic wrote (that) the painting had been a clever forgery.

For direct-object bias verbs, the system presents the guess that the postverbal noun phrase is patient of the verb regardless of plausibility.

    Garnsey et al. (1997) found a different pattern of results with verbs such as *confessed* that are used more frequently with a sentential complement. They used sentences like (146) and (147).

(146) *Sentential-complement bias, plausible direct object*
      The bank guard confessed (that) the robbery had been his own idea.

(147) *Sentential-complement bias, implausible direct object*
      The bank guard confessed (that) the vault had been left open intentionally.

There was no effect of plausibility in sentences with verbs like *confessed* that frequently are used with a sentential complement. They also found no effect of the complementizer *that* in sentences with sentential-complement bias verbs (see also Holmes, Stowe, and Cupples 1989). This result suggests that the subcategorization preferences of verbs automatically influence the initial meaning-form hypothesis. A subcategorization preference for a sentential complement triggers special patterns that allow the system to project the information that is required of the verb.

    Trueswell, Tanenhaus, and Kello (1993) used a naming task to show that there is immediate use of verb-subcategorization preferences. The technique relies on the fact that *him* is appropriate as a direct object for a verb, whereas *he* is appropriate as subject of a sentential complement for a verb. Trueswell and colleagues used materials like the following:

(148) *Sentential-complement bias*
      The old man insisted (that) ... HIM/HE

(149) *Direct-object bias*
      The young boy observed (that) ... HIM/HE

Subjects heard the lowercase material. After either the verb or *that* depending on the condition, subjects saw a printed version of *him* or *he*. Their task was to read aloud the printed word as fast as possible. The results appear in table 7.26. Without *that* present, naming times were faster when the pronoun was congruent with the bias. With sentential-complement bias, *he* was faster than *him*, but with direct-object bias, *him* was faster than *he*. This result suggests that the subcategorization information

Table 7.26
Mean naming times (ms) depending on complementizer, target pronoun, and verb bias

	Verb bias	
	DO	SC
he *target*		
No *that*	532	519
That	499	486
Ambiguity effect	33	33
him *target*		
No *that*	492	532
That	533	539
Ambiguity effect	−41	−7

Note: DO = direct object; SC = sentential complement
Source: Adapted from Trueswell, Tanenhaus, and Kello 1993

primes the appropriate sentence template and projects different patterns depending on this information. With *that* present, naming times were faster for *he* than for *him* for both types of verbs. This result shows that the complementizer provides a local cue that can override the lexical preferences for subcategorizing verbs.

Trueswell and Kim (1998) have obtained further evidence that the use of sub-categorization information of verbs can be primed. In a self-paced word-by-word reading task, a priming word was presented visually for 39 ms immediately before the main verb. At this duration, the prime is perceived as a flicker. Trueswell and Kim found that briefly displaying an ambiguous priming verb that is strongly biased toward taking a sentential complement (e.g., *realized*) significantly reduced the pro-cessing difficulty of a sentence that contains a main verb that is strongly biased toward a direct object (*accepted*).

7.4.3   Interactions of NVN
Holmes, Stowe, and Cupples (1989) demonstrated how the NVN pattern interacts with subcategorization information. They varied the length of a potential direct object by presenting a simple noun phrase (*the teacher; the woman*) or a noun phrase modi-fied by a relative clause (*who walked past; who had arrived*), as in (150) and (151).

(150) *Sentential-complement bias*
       The principal knew (that) the teacher (who walked past) had already been working.

(151) *Direct-object bias*
       The reporter saw (that) the woman (who had arrived) was not very calm.

Table 7.27
Mean reading times (ms) in the disambiguating region depending on complementizer, length, and verb bias

	Verb bias	
	DO	SC
Long NP		
No *that*	520	510
That	480	470
Ambiguity effect	40	40
Short NP		
No *that*	555	455
That	475	470
Ambiguity effect	80	−15

Note: DO = direct object; SC = sentential complement
Source: Adapted from Holmes, Stowe, and Cupples 1989, fig. 3

As shown in table 7.27, Holmes and colleagues found that increasing the length of the potential direct object increased reading times on the two words of the disambiguating auxiliary verb (*had already*) for sentential-complement bias verbs without *that* (from 455 to 510 ms). For direct-object bias verbs (e.g., *saw*), reading times in the disambiguating region were greater without *that* than with *that* regardless of length.

These results demonstrate the interactions of the NVN pattern with verb subcategorization. The verb *knew* might take a noun phrase object, or it might take a sentential complement. At the point of reading *teacher* the NVN applies. The strength of this meaning-form hypothesis, however, is relatively weak since *know* is used more frequently with a sentential complement. If the next word is part of a verb phrase, such as *had*, the system relinquishes the NVN analysis of *the principal knew the teacher*, and the NVN template is elicited again with *teacher* as the first noun and *had* as the verb or part of the verb. If instead the next word after *teacher* is *who*, the NVN analysis of *the principle knew the teacher* is accepted and the sentence template reapplies with *who* as the first noun and *walked past* as the verb (intransitive). By the time *had already* is received, the NVN pattern has been fulfilled twice, and consequently reanalysis is difficult. This interaction does not occur with direct-object bias verbs, since the direct-object bias leads the system to accept the initial NVN analysis whether or not there is a potential relative clause modifying the noun phrase.

7.4.4 NVN Interactions in DO/SC vs. MC/RC
As we noted above, recovery from the direct-object misanalysis in a DO/SC ambiguity is intuitively much easier than recovery from a MC/RC ambiguity. Apart from

any statistical differences in the frequency of occurrence of particular sentence-level patterns, this difference may occur because of the extent to which the system must give up previous meanings based on the NVN pattern (see Pritchett 1992).

In the DO/SC ambiguity, the NVN template applies in both the mistaken analysis and the correct analysis. The system must change the analysis from the first meaning below to the second, in which system assigns the sentence pattern N + BE + Pred corresponding to *the tree is tall* to the material after the main verb to serve as the object of the main verb:

Direct-object interpretation

John	= N	= agent
knew	= V	= action
the answer	= N	= patient

Sentential-complement interpretation

John		= N	= agent
knew		= V	= action
	the answer	= N	
	was	= V	
	wrong	= Pred	

Thus, the initial direct-object analysis needs only slight modification.

In the MC/RC ambiguity, however, the application of the NVN template must be undone in the embedded relative clause. That is, for (1), repeated here, *raced* must be disconnected from *horse* as agent, with the role of *horse* in the main clause undetermined.

(1) The horse raced past the barn fell.

In addition, *raced* must be reinterpreted as an action that happens to the patient *horse*:

Main-clause interpretation

The horse	= N	= agent
raced	= V	= action
past the barn	= PP	= location

Reduced relative interpretation

The horse		= N	= agent
	raced	= V	= action
	[the horse	= N	= patient]
	past the barn	= PP	= location
fell		= V	= action

The role of the NVN template in recovering from a MC/RC ambiguity is shown by the fact that embedding this ambiguity as a complement clause reduces the impact of the ambiguity. For example, the MC/RC garden path is reduced greatly in

(152) *Embedded MC/RC ambiguity*
He knew the horse raced past the barn fall.

The reason appears to be that *horse* is initially assigned the role of patient of *knew*. This weakens the strength of the NVN template for the sequence *the horse raced*, producing a weaker garden path. This corresponds to our intuitions, but needs empirical support.

7.5 Sentential Complement/Relative Clause

We observed in the discussion of reduced relative clauses that appropriate sentence context may play a role in motivating a relative clause as a selective modifier, thereby facilitating its correct interpretation. We can study this in relative clauses on main-clause objects by contrasting the processing of sentential complement/relative clause (SC/RC) garden-path sentences. In (153) the preferred interpretation of *that he was having trouble with* is a sentential complement of the verb *told*.

(153) The psychologist told the wife that he was having trouble with ...

Thus, comprehenders experience a garden path when the sentence continues *to leave her husband*. In this case, the sequence *that he was having trouble with* must be a relative clause.

As we discussed in section 7.2, the referential theory (Altmann and Steedman 1988) proposed that a relative clause interpretation may be appropriate for the above sentence when there are two wives, one of which the psychologist was having trouble with. Thus, the garden-path sentence may not present difficulty if it appears in an appropriate discourse context.

Crain and Steedman (1985) tested whether referential context influences the processing of SC/RC garden paths. Subjects read discourses in Rapid Serial Visual Presentation at a rate of one word every 550 ms. Following a tone, a target sentence appeared. The subjects' task was to judge whether the target sentence was grammatical. Examples of target sentences are:

(154) *Sentential complement*
The psychologist told the wife that he was having trouble with her husband.

(155) *Relative clause*
The psychologist told the wife that he was having trouble with to leave her husband.

Table 7.28
Percentage judgments of ungrammaticality

	Clause in target sentence	
Contextual support	Complement	Relative
Complement	12	50
Relative	54	22

Source: Derived from Crain and Steedman 1985

The relative-supporting context implied that there were two wives, while the complement-supporting context implied only one:

(156) *Complement-supporting context*
A psychologist was counseling a married couple. One member of the pair was fighting with him but the other one was nice to him . . .

(157) *Relative-supporting context*
A psychologist was counseling two married couples. One of the couples was fighting with him but the other one was nice to him . . .

The results appear in table 7.28. Judgments of ungrammaticality were more common when the context did not match the structure of the target sentence. This result supports the referential theory: a context that requires differentiating between two possible referents facilitates comprehension of a garden-path sentence in which the less preferred interpretation is appropriate.

Further studies have examined the role of discourse context in the online processing of SC/RC ambiguities. Mitchell, Corley, and Garnham (1992) examined self-paced reading times for groups of words in sentential-complement/relative clause garden-path sentences. The following sentence is temporarily ambiguous between sentential complement and relative clause up through the word *with*:

(158) *Object relative*
The taxi driver told the woman that he / had been / arguing with / that she wouldn't miss her train.

The slashes mark the boundaries of displays in the study by Mitchell, Corely, and Garnham, so that in this sentence there were four displays. In our application of LAST, the preference is to interpret *that he had been arguing with* as the patient or theme of *told* and *the woman* as its recipient. The system presents this initial meaning-form hypothesis, confirms a correct syntax, and stores a meaning for the sentence. When the second *that* appears, it is apparent that *that he had been arguing with* is a relative clause, and reanalysis must occur. This reanalysis produces longer reading times on the material after *arguing with* compared to either of the following sentences

(159) *Subject relative*
   The taxi driver told the woman that / had been / arguing with him / that she
   wouldn't miss her train.

(160) *Sentential complement*
   The taxi driver told the woman that he / had been / arguing with / the
   councilors about the bus lane.

LAST predicts that reading times for *had been* will be shorter in the object relative
and sentential-complement sentences, since the preceding *he* in both of these cases
allows the interpretation of *had been* as part of the theme of *told*. The lack of an
explicit subject of *had been* in the subject relative sentences rules out this interpretation. Mitchell and associates did find that reading times for *had been* were longer in
subject relatives than in the other two cases. They dubbed the faster reading times on
object relatives than on subject relatives the *object relative advantage*.

   Mitchell et al. (1992) also examined the role of discourse context in processing
these garden paths. The relative-supporting context mentioned two women, while
the complement-supporting context mentioned only one. Importantly, the relative-
supporting context supported the subject and object relative sentences equally by not
establishing either *taxi driver* or *woman* as agent or patient:

(161) *Relative-supporting context*
   A taxi driver dropped two women off at the station. On the way they had run
   into a traffic jam. The taxi driver and one of the women had been arguing but
   the other remained calm . . .

(162) *Complement-supporting context*
   A taxi driver dropped a man and a woman off at the station. On the way
   they had run into a traffic jam. The taxi driver and the woman had been
   arguing but the man remained calm.

   The referential theory predicts that a relative-supporting context will eliminate the
differences in reading time for *had been*. Mitchell and colleagues, however, found that
reading times on *had been* were longer for the subject relative sentence regardless
of context. The results appear in table 7.29. In this table, display 2 refers to *had
been*, display 3 refers to *arguing with* (object relatives and sentential complements)
or *arguing with him* (subject relatives), and display 4 refers to the remainder of the
sentence. The results in table 7.29 suggest that pseudosyntax initially assigned *that
he had been arguing with* to the role of theme. Further indication of this initial
assignment comes from comparing reading times for the disambiguating region (display 4) in the relative-supporting contexts: reading times are longer for the object
relative cases than for the subject relative cases. The longer reading times on display 4

Table 7.29
Mean reading times depending on context (ms/word)

Sentence	Region		
	D2	D3	D4
Relative context			
OR	600	621	2561
SC	602	681	2561
SR	773	915	1995
Complement context			
OR	604	651	2396
SC	652	612	2245
SR	729	774	2158

Notes:
D1 = OR: The taxi driver told the woman that he ...
     SC: The taxi driver told the woman that he ...
     SR: The taxi driver told the woman that ...
D2 = ... had been ...
D3 = OR: ... arguing with ...
     SC: ... arguing with ...
     SR: ... arguing with him ...
D4 = OR: ... that she wouldn't miss her train.
     SC: ... the councilors about the bus lane.
     SR: ... that she wouldn't miss her train.
Source: From Mitchell, Corley, and Garnham 1992, table 4

for object relatives compared to subject relatives indicates that pseudosyntax had presented the theme interpretation for the object relatives.

To summarize, Mitchell, Corely, and Garnham found an object relative advantage on reading times for the embedded verb in SC/OR garden-path sentences, compared to the embedded verb in subject relative sentences. They attributed this difference to an initial preference for the minimally attached complement clause. In terms of LAST, the object relative advantage occurs because *told* activates a template with the theme role. In the object relative case, the theme interpretation is possible through the ambiguous region, but in the subject relative case, the lack of an explicit subject for *had been* rules out the theme interpretation.

Altmann, Garnham, and Henstra (1994) suggested that measuring processing load on the embedded verb is too late to find the immediate effect of context, since the earlier appearance of the embedded subject in the SC/OR sentences has already ruled out the subject relative interpretation. Accordingly, they compared fixation times for *that had been* (subject relative) and *that he'd been* (object relative).

Altmann et al. (1994) used an eye-tracking methodology to examine the processing of SC/RC ambiguities like the following:

(163) *Object relative*

He told / the woman / that he'd been / waiting / for *that they* were both very lucky.

(164) *Subject relative*

He told / the woman / that *had been* / waiting / for him that they were both very lucky.

The italicized portion indicates the disambiguating region, and slashes indicate the scoring regions. The object relative example is ambiguous between a complement clause and an object relative until the disambiguating region. Altmann and colleagues also used contexts like these:

(165) *Object relative supporting context*

A firefighter was talking to two women after a fire at their house. He was telling them how serious the situation had been. The firefighter had been waiting to speak to one of the women about it. He thought that the other woman had been too shocked by the fire to talk about it . . .

(166) *Subject relative supporting context*

A firefighter was talking to two women after a fire at their house. He was telling them how serious the situation had been. One of the women had been waiting to speak to him about it. The other woman had been too shocked by the fire to want to talk about it . . .

The results appear in table 7.30. When the target sentences were presented out of context, Altmann, Garnham, and Henstra (1994) found that fixation times for *that he'd been* (object relative) were shorter than those for *that had been* (subject relative) (29.2 vs. 35.2 ms/character). In contexts that support the relative clause structure of the target sentence, there was no difference in fixation times for this region depending on type of relative clause (23.6 vs. 23.3 ms/character). Altmann and associates concluded that appropriate referential contexts can resolve the ambiguity of *that* as a relative pronoun versus complementizer.

When interpreting the effect of discourse context, it is important to distinguish the use of conceptual information and lexical sequence. The essence of this difference is captured in the priming of *maybe* from a prior occurrence of *perhaps* (conceptual) versus a prior occurrence of *maybe* (lexical). The Altmann et al. result that the object relative advantage disappeared when the target sentence was presented in context likely is due to priming of particular lexical sequences. To illustrate this point, notice that the object relative context-target pairs consisted of (167) and (168), while the

Table 7.30
Mean first-pass fixation times (ms/character) in the disambiguating region depending on context

| | Structure of target sentence | |
Contextual support	OR	SR
None	29.2	35.2
OR/SR supportive	23.6	23.3

Source: Adapted from Altmann, Garnham, and Henstra 1994, table 1

subject relative context-target pairs consisted of (169) and (170). In (167) to (170), corresponding subscripts indicate corresponding lexical prime-target pairs.

(167) *Object relative–supporting context*
The firefighter$_1$ had been$_2$ waiting . . .

(168) *Object relative target sentence*
that he$_1$'d been$_2$ waiting for . . .

(169) *Subject relative–supporting context*
one of the women$_1$ had been$_2$ waiting . . .

(170) *Subject relative target sentence*
the woman$_1$ that had been$_2$ waiting . . .

Each context-target pair presented the coreferring noun and auxiliary verb in the same order. The equivalent reading times for *that he'd been* and *that had been* may occur simply because the two contexts primed the specific sequence of noun and auxiliary verb. The contexts in the studies by Altmann and colleagues may have primed specific sequences of subject noun phrase and auxiliary verb.

7.6 Direct Object/Subject

An example of local Direct Object/Subject (DO/S) ambiguity is

(171) *Direct-object/subject ambiguity*
While Mary was mending the sock fell off her lap.

Crocker (1996), Frazier and Clifton (1996), and Pritchett (1992) have all discussed this type of garden-path sentence. We can explain the garden path simply in terms of LAST model. The system matches the NVN pattern to *Mary was mending the sock* and assigns *Mary* as the agent, *was mending* as the action, and *the sock* as the patient. Based on this initial meaning-form hypothesis, the comprehension system generates a syntactic structure, and checks it against the input sequence. Since the candidate syntax matches the input sequence, the meaning is stored. When *fell* is received, the system cannot match an initial verb with any common sentence pattern, and so an error is detected. In this case, the assignment of *the sock* as patient of *was mending* is replaced by accessing a different subcategorization of the verb (as an intransitive) and reassigning *the sock* as an "agent" of *fell*.

7.6.1   A Classic Demonstration

Frazier and Rayner (1982) measured eye movements while reading sentences in which a noun phrase could be interpreted as direct object of a verb or as the subject of a second clause. In early-closure sentences, the verb does not take the following noun phrase as direct object, and in late-closure sentences it does. Frazier and Rayner also varied the length of the potential direct object, as in (172) to (175).

(172) *Early closure, short*
       Since Jay always jogs a mile seems like a short distance to him.

(173) *Early closure, long*
       Since Jay always jogs a mile and a half seems like a short distance to him.

(174) *Late closure, short*
       Since Jay always jogs a mile this seems like a short distance to him.

(175) *Late closure, long*
       Since Jay always jogs a mile and a half this seems like a short distance to
       him.

The results appear in table 7.31. Early-closure sentences with a long potential direct object required more time to read than the other sentences. These results support LAST. Each of these sentences elicits the NVN template, but correctly only in the case of late-closure sentences. Why is it easier to recover from the incorrect assignment of NVN in the early-closure cases when the potential direct object is shorter? The NVN template may be activated less strongly for a shorter noun phrase (see

Table 7.31
Mean first-pass fixation times (ms/letter) in the disambiguating region depending on sentence type and length

Sentence type	Length of second NP	
	Short	Long
Early closure	41	54
Late closure	47	40

Source: Adapted from Frazier and Rayner 1982, table 2

Crocker 1996). When the next word after the noun is a verb, the incorrect analysis is discovered more quickly. When the next words begin a conjoined noun phrase, this has the effect of maintaining the NVN analysis longer, and makes it harder to reclassify the complex noun phrase as the start of a new NVN pattern.

7.6.2 Interactions of NVN

Evidence from Ferreira and Henderson (1991, 1995) shows that potential NVN patterns interact to predict other examples of garden-path sentences with the DO/S pattern. Ferreira and Henderson (1991) used a grammaticality judgment task with rapid serial visual presentation at 250 ms/word and self-paced reading to examine the effects of length and complexity of the potential direct object in DO/S ambiguities. Some examples of early-closure and late-closure sentences with a relatively short second noun phrase (NP_2) are:

(176) *Early closure, short NP_2*
       When men hunt the birds typically scatter.

(177) *Late closure, short NP_2*
       When men hunt the birds the deer typically scatter.

In general, Ferreira and Henderson found that sentences were correctly judged grammatical more often in late-closure sentences than in early-closure sentences (81% versus 63% for sentences with a short NP_2 in experiment 1). This supports the view that the system relies greatly on the NVN pattern.

Ferreira and Henderson (1991) also examined the ability to make grammaticality judgments depending on the length and complexity of the second noun phrase:

(178) *Early closure, long NP_2 with relative clause*
       When men hunt the birds that cheetahs eat typically scatter.

(179) *Early closure, long NP_2 with prepositional phrase*
       When men hunt the birds with bright plumage typically scatter.

(180) *Late closure, long NP_2 with relative clause*
       When men hunt the birds that cheetahs eat the deer typically scatter.

(181) *Late closure, long NP_2 with prepositional phrase*
       When men hunt the birds with bright plumage the deer typically scatter.

The results appear in table 7.32. Ferreira and Henderson (1991) found that sentences were correctly judged grammatical more often when the potential direct object was short as in (176) and (177) rather than long as in (178) and (181). Their explanation of the length effect is in terms of the distance between the head of the second noun phrase and the disambiguating material. When this distance is short, it is easier to make the grammaticality judgment. Ferreira and Henderson found no difference in

Table 7.32
Percentage of sentences judged grammatical

Sentence type	Nature of second NP		
	Short	Long with RC	Long with PP
Early closure	63	35	34
Late closure	81	67	69

Source: Adapted from Ferreira and Henderson 1991, fig. 5

grammaticality judgments when the potential direct object contained a relative clause modifier as in (178) and (180) or a prepositional phrase modifier as in (179) and (181), which were both harder than the short version.

In the case of both the relative clause and the prepositional phrase, there are three words between *birds* and the potential disambiguation point on *typically*. In a later experiment, Ferreira and Henderson (1991) found that lengthening the potential direct object with pre-nominal adjectives produced only slight difficulty. For example, the early-closure sentence with pre-nominal adjectives was nearly as easy as the one with a short noun phrase. The percentage of judgments of grammaticality were 61 percent for short NP_2 as in (182), 24 percent for long NP_2 with relative clause as in (183), and 51 percent for long NP_2 with pre-nominal adjectives as in (184).

(182) *Early closure, short NP_2*
While the boy scratched the dog yawned loudly.

(183) *Early closure, long NP_2 with relative clause*
While the boy scratched the dog that is hairy yawned loudly.

(184) *Early closure, long NP_2 with prenominal adjectives*
While the boy scratched the big and hairy dog yawned loudly.

These results are consistent with LAST. In terms of this model, the real factor is amount of commitment to the NVN analysis. When the commitment lasts longer, reanalysis is harder. Thus, (183) is harder than (184) because *that* initiates a new analysis-by-synthesis cycle. This has the effect of increasing the commitment to assigning *dog* as patient. For (178) to (181), both the relative clause and the prepositional phrase modifiers increase the commitment to *birds* as patient.

7.6.3 Plausibility

Christianson et al. (forthcoming) have reported evidence that the temporarily incorrect assignment of the noun following a verb as the patient of the verb can influence the ultimate interpretation. After reading sentences such as the following (185) or (186), subjects answered questions about meaning such as (187).

(185) *Potentially intransitive verb followed by NP*
      While the grocer hunted, the rabbit ran into the woods.

(186) *Intransitive-only verb followed by NP*
      The rabbit ran into the woods, while the grocer hunted.

(187) *Meaning question*
      Did the grocer hunt the rabbit?

Subjects were more likely to report that the grocer hunted the rabbit in response to (185) than to (186). Christianson and colleagues argued that this result shows that *the rabbit* is temporarily assigned patient status, but only when it immediately follows the verb *hunted*. This intriguing fact shows two things. First, it reflects the local organizing power of the NVN template and immediate access to a conceptual representation. Second, it shows that the initial meaning-form representation persists, despite the later incompatible syntactic information that forces the patient of the first verb to be changed to the agent of the second. In this case, the premature semantic information is compatible with the final interpretation.

7.6.4 Prosodic Patterns

Prosodic patterns can influence the initial meaning-form hypothesis. These prosodic patterns can reduce the effect of DO/S garden paths in speech.

Kjelgaard and Speer (1999; Speer, Kjelgaard, and Dobroth 1996) established that prosodic information can eliminate DO/S garden paths. Subjects listened to tape recordings of early-closure and late-closure sentences in three conditions: cooperating, conflicting, and baseline. In the cooperating condition, the sentences were recorded so that prosodic boundaries had a lengthening and a drop in pitch on the final word of the phrase, as in (188) and (189), which originally are from Slowiaczek (1981) and published in Carroll and Slowiaczek (1987). The / indicates a syntactic clause boundary, and the % indicates a prosodic boundary. Underlining indicates pronunciation appropriate for a late-closure sentence, and capitals indicate pronunciation appropriate for early closure. Since the syntactic clause boundaries and the prosodic boundaries coincide in each of the above sentences, these are examples in which the syntactic and prosodic cues cooperate.

(188) *Cooperating cues, early closure*
      BECAUSE HER GRANDMOTHER KNITTED% /PULLOVERS KEPT
      WARM IN THE WINTERTIME.

(189) *Cooperating cues, late closure*
      Because her grandmother knitted pullovers% /Kathy kept warm in the
      wintertime.

In the conflicting condition, cross splicing yielded prosody that conflicted with the syntactic structure:

(190) *Conflicting cues, early closure*
<u>Because her grandmother knitted /pullovers%</u> KEPT WARM IN THE WINTERTIME.

(191) *Conflicting cues, late closure*
BECAUSE HER GRANDMOTHER KNITTED% PULLOVERS /<u>Kathy kept warm in the wintertime.</u>

The underlined material in these examples came from sentences that were recorded with the late-closure prosody, while capitalized material came from sentences recorded with early-closure prosody. Since the syntactic (/) and prosodic (%) boundaries occur at different points in (190) and (191), they illustrate a conflict between syntactic and prosodic cues.

In the baseline condition, early-closure and late-closure sentences were recorded with the same prosodic contour. Pretesting showed that subjects judged the baseline and cooperating sentences to be equally acceptable.

In Kjelgaard and Speer (1999) subjects listened to the sentences and pressed a response key to indicate whether the sentence was uttered as the speaker had intended. The results appear in table 7.33. Kjelgaard and Speer (1999) found that response times were faster for cooperating sentences than for baseline sentences, which in turn produced faster response times than conflicting sentences. Response times were faster for late-closure sentences than for early-closure sentences in the baseline condition and in the conflicting condition. But in the cooperating condition, there was no difference in response times for early- versus late-closure sentences.

These results show that pseudosyntax relies greatly on prosodic patterns to develop an initial meaning-form hypothesis. The associative pattern is that a prosodic boundary corresponds to the completion of a semantic unit. In the absence of a clear prosodic boundary, the system relies on other nonprosodic patterns, such as NVN.

Table 7.33
Mean grammaticality judgment times (ms) depending on cues and sentence type

Sentence type	Nature of cues		
	Cooperating	Baseline	Conflicting
Early closure	1170	1490	1530
Late closure	1175	1270	1300

Source: Adapted from Kjelgaard and Speer 1999, fig. 3

Kjelgaard and Speer (1999, 1998) provide additional evidence that pseudosyntax uses prosodic patterns online. Subjects listened to sentence fragments in cooperating, baseline, and conflicting conditions, and then read aloud as quickly as possible a visually presented word. Examples of cooperating conditions are:

(192) *Cooperating cues, late closure*
    Whenever the guard checks the door%/' ... IT'S

(193) *Cooperating cues, early closure*
    Whenever the guard checks % /the door' ... IS

The word to be named was a plausible continuation according to the syntactic structure. For example, for late-closure fragments, *it's* could plausibly begin a new clause; for the early-closure condition, *is* could plausibly be a verb that has *the door* as subject. Again, % indicates a prosodic boundary and / a syntactic boundary; in the cooperating conditions, these boundaries coincide.

Examples of conflicting conditions are:

(194) *Conflicting cues, late closure*
    Whenever the guard checks % the door/' ... IT'S

(195) *Conflicting cues, early closure*
    Whenever the guard checks /the door%' ... IS

The results appear in table 7.34. Naming times were faster in the cooperating condition than in the baseline condition, and faster in the baseline condition than in conflicting condition. The late-closure sentences produced faster response times than early closure in the baseline and conflicting conditions but not in the cooperating condition.

This line of research indicates that speech provides additional patterns that pseudo-syntax uses to provide an initial meaning-form hypothesis. More recent research suggests that readers do not use corresponding patterns, even when they are available (Speer and Dobroth 1998).

Table 7.34
Mean naming times (ms) depending on cues and sentence type

Sentence type	Nature of cues		
	Cooperating	Baseline	Conflicting
Early closure	640	810	905
Late closure	670	675	740

Source: Adapted from Kjelgaard and Speer 1999, fig. 5

7.6.5 Subcategorization Preferences

The subcategorization requirements and preferences of verbs will influence the likelihood and strength of DO/S and other potential garden paths (see section 7.1.7). The
more frequently the verb is used as a transitive, the stronger the garden path when
it is discovered that the verb actually is used intransitively. The relevant factor,
however, may not be frequency of use of the verb as transitive, but instead, the
plausibility of the agent-action-patient sequence. Thus, the garden-path effect appears
stronger in (196) than in (197).

(196) *Plausible direct object*
       While Mary was mending the socks fell off her lap.

(197) *Implausible direct object*
       While Mary was mending the clouds grew in the sky.

A related case in which the system projects an argument structure is direct-object/
indirect-object ambiguities (DO/IO), as in (198) and the corresponding unambiguous
sentence (199).

(198) *Direct-object/indirect-object ambiguity*
       Fred pushed the dog the bone.

(199) *Unambiguous three-argument verb*
       Fred gave the dog the bone.

Sentence (198) is a mild garden path because the sequence *Fred pushed the dog* fits the
canonical NVN pattern. *Pushed* may take two arguments (agent and patient) or it
may take three (agent, patient, recipient). Only when *the bone* is received is it clear
that *the dog* should be assigned the role of recipient rather than the role of patient.
The garden-path effect does not occur with (199) because *gave* cannot occur with
only two arguments, except as an idiom such as *I gave blood*.

7.7 Conjoined Noun Phrase/Coordinate Clause

The conjoined noun phrase/coordinate clause type of ambiguity (NP/CC) is illustrated by

(200) *Conjoined noun phrase/coordinate clause ambiguity*
       Jacob kissed Miriam and her sister laughed.

Frazier and Clifton (1996) consider such sentences to be subject to a principle of "late
closure." The late-closure analysis converges with application of the NVN template.
Since the NVN pattern is present in *Jacob kissed Miriam*, the grammar uses the corresponding meaning-form hypothesis to generate a syntax, the system then checks the
derived syntax against the input, and accepts it. When *and her sister* is received, this

analysis is modified to a complex object noun phrase, and a new syntax is generated, checked and accepted. This new analysis is rejected when *laughed* is received. The second recovery is relatively easy because *her sister laughed* fits the NVN template as well, and it is plausible. These examples and the examples of DO/IO ambiguities (see section 7.6.5) suggest that the NVN template keeps applying as long as incoming material is consistent with a verb-appropriate common sentence pattern.

7.8   Interactions of Complex Subcategorizations

In this section, we discuss three different kinds of garden-path sentences that depend on subcategorization requirements that are more complex than two arguments. We discuss ambiguities that involve verbs that can take patient and recipient roles, verbs that require locative phrases, and verbs that can take complement clauses.

Frazier and Clifton (1996) explain direct-object/relative clause (DO/RC) ambiguities such as (201) in terms of minimal attachment of *the dog* as an argument of *gave*. This analysis must be revised when *bit* is received.

(201) *Direct-object/relative clause ambiguity*
       Fred gave the man [the dog bit] the package.

LAST explains the DO/RC ambiguity in terms of activation of sentence templates that verbs elicit. For example, *gave* is an "alternating dative" verb that optionally subcategorizes for two noun phrase and one prepositional phrase arguments (NVN + PP) as in (202), in which the second noun phrase (*a raise*) is patient and the object of the prepositional phrase (*Harry*) is recipient. The verb *gave* also optionally subcategorizes for three noun phrase arguments (NVNN) as in (203), in which the second noun phrase (*Harry*) is the recipient and the third (*a raise*) is patient (see section 6.4.4 for further discussion of alternating datives).

(202) *Two noun phrase and one prepositional phrase arguments*
       The boss gave a raise to Harry.

(203) *Three noun phrase arguments*
       The boss gave Harry a raise.

Thus, for (204) *dog* completes the NVNN template, thus assigning *Fred* as agent, *man* as recipient, and *dog* as patient.

(204) Fred gave the man [the dog bit] the package.

Template matching for DO/RC ambiguity

Fred	=	N	=	agent
gave	=	V	=	action
the man	=	N	=	recipient
the dog	=	N	=	patient

The comprehension system uses this meaning-form hypothesis to initiate a syntactic derivation, which is accepted. The garden path, however, is detected on receiving *bit*, which activates its own argument requirements. The NVNN template for *gave* must be partially deactivated, so that *dog* fulfills the agent role of *bit* and *man* the patient role of *bit*. *Package* is then assigned the role of patient of *gave*.

Reactivation of sentence templates in DO/RC ambiguity

Fred		=	N	=	agent
gave		=	V	=	action
the man		=	N	=	recipient
	the dog	=	N	=	agent
	bit	=	V	=	action
	[the man	=	N	=	patient]
the package		=	N	=	patient

The subcategorization information that *gave* requires both a recipient and a patient is an important factor in producing the DO/RC garden path. Notice, for example, that the garden path is weaker in (205).

(205) *DO/RC ambiguity with optionally three-argument verb*
   Fred pushed the man [the dog bit] the package.

In (205), the system presents the initial meaning-form hypothesis that *Fred* is agent and *man* is patient corresponding to NVN = agent, action, patient. Even though *pushed*, like *gave*, may take three noun phrase arguments, the tendency to assign *dog* to the role of patient is not as strong as with *gave*, since *pushed* also may take just two noun phrase arguments, and these complete the more common NVN pattern.

A similar garden path should occur when verbs require locative phrases. For example, *put* requires an agent, a patient, and a location, producing the template N + V + N + PP. In sentences (206) and (207) from Frazier and Clifton (1996), the system does not present a meaning to the system after *book* based strictly on the NVN template, since *put* also requires a locative phrase.

(206) *PP attachment to main verb*
   I put the book [that you were reading] in the library.

(207) *PP attachment to embedded verb*
   I put the book [that you were reading in the library] into my briefcase.

The phrase *in the library* completes this required N + V + N + PP template, presenting an initial meaning-form hypothesis for the grammar to generate a candidate syntactic structure, which the system checks and accepts. The processing of (207) is similar until *into my briefcase* is received, producing a garden path. The garden path in (207) depends on the fact that *reading* optionally takes a locative phrase, but *put* obligatorily takes a locative phrase. In the (208), *found* requires modification either with an agent or a location.

(208) I put the book [found in the library] in my briefcase.

For (208), *in the library* allows the system to present the meaning-form hypothesis about the reduced relative clause *found in the library* that *book* is patient of *found* and *in the library* is the location. Consequently, there is no garden path when *in my briefcase* is received.

Sentences like these, in which the main verb requires a locative argument, allow a comparison of the relative role of subcategorization information and minimal attachment. Frazier and Clifton (1996), for example, have proposed that the phrase *in the library* in (207) is initially attached to *reading*. There is evidence that comprehenders prefer to attach a locative phrase to *put* rather than to *apple* in *Put the apple on the towel in the box* (Tanenhaus et al. 1995; see also Britt 1994; Ferreira and Clifton 1986; Trueswell et al., forthcoming). But we know of no research on the processing of locative phrases that follow an embedded verb that optionally takes a locative phrase.

A related garden path occurs when the verb optionally takes a sentential complement. For example, *tell* may take two noun phrase arguments (agent and patient) in (209), three noun phrase arguments (agent, patient, and recipient) in (210), or two noun phrase arguments (agent and patient) and a sentential complement (theme), as in (211) and (212).

(209) *Two noun phrase arguments*
      Ian told a joke.

(210) *Three noun phrase arguments*
      Ian told the man a joke.

Two noun phrase arguments and a sentential complement
(211) Ian told the man [to leave].

(212) Ian told the man [that he hired a secretary].

A garden path arises in (212) because of the interaction of subcategorization requirements for *tell* and *hire*. *Hire* can take two noun phrase arguments, as in (212), where *he* is agent and *secretary* is patient, and in (213), where *he* is agent and *man* is patient. Alternatively, *hire* can take two noun phrase arguments and a sentential complement as in (214), where *he* is agent, *man* is patient, and *to plow the field* is theme.

(213) Hire *takes two noun phrase arguments*
      Ian told the man [that he hired] a story.

(214) Hire *takes two noun phrase arguments and a sentential complement*
      Ian told the man [that he hired to plow the field] a story.

A garden path occurs in (213) because the strength of the NVN template leads the
system to propose that *story* is patient of *hire*, just as *secretary* is patient of *hire* in
(212). Assigning *story* as patient of *hire* leaves unfilled a possible third argument
for *tell*.

   Sentence (214) above may or may not produce a garden path. It seems likely that
intonation in normal speech will prevent a garden path. However, the sentence does
raise the interesting question of the extent to which subcategorization information is
available to guide the system's development of an initial meaning-form hypothesis,
and the extent to which the system relies on an independent NVN template. If the
system relies strongly on the fact that *tell* requires either an additional noun phrase
argument or a sentential complement, we expect that *to plow the field* will complete a
semantic unit for *tell*. To present this initial meaning-form hypothesis, however, the
system would also have to override the NVN template in the relative clause, and
present the meaning that the patient of *hire* is *man*. Since this analysis requires
undoing the NVN template, such sentences provide an interesting test of the relative
importance of an independent NVN template and subcategorization information.

7.9   Conclusion

In chapter 5, we pointed out that the analysis-by-synthesis model explains why
sentence-level canonical templates will be the most reinforced of any associative
completion patterns in language. In this chapter, we have reviewed explorations
that reveal the explanatory power of the canonical NV(N(N)) = agent action
(patient(recipient)) template as a whole, and in its subparts. In general, structures
that violate the canonical sentence-mapping schema are relatively hard to understand. Correspondingly, sentences with apparent but incorrect NVN garden path
lures tend to be confusing. Most telling is the paradoxical but predicted fact that
 deleting the relative pronoun from an object relative clause actually makes it easier to
comprehend.

Note

1. Bever (1970a) reported that children actually understand transitive NVN sentences before
they understand intransitive NV sentences.

Chapter 8
Conceptual Knowledge, Modularity, and Discourse

Language exhibits simultaneous levels of structural representation. This raises an issue concerning the level at which the analysis-by-synthesis cycle occurs. The most salient levels are the word, phrase, clause, sentence, and discourse. We have focused on the clause and sentence levels for several reasons. Clauses and sentences are highly structured, which sets a crucial problem for models that assign structure directly. The clause and sentence levels are highly productive, which is a crucial problem for template and statistical models. The clause and sentence levels are the critical interface between form and compositional meaning, at which sufficient information is available to form complete propositions. As outlined in chapter 3, these levels are the minimal level for representation of fully productive recursion. By hypothesis, a specific sentence structure is not directly constrained by its meaning.

In this chapter, we first develop the idea that analysis by synthesis in fact may apply at each natural level of analysis. In each case, there is an initial pseudosyntactic component that assigns an approximate structure followed by a synthetic component that checks it for completeness. This provides a natural account for the strong intuition that comprehension builds up incrementally as we encounter sentences, rather than waiting until the end of each major unit. We then review recent evidence of the computational modularity of syntax processing independent of conceptual information. Finally, we review experimental evidence for how the sentence level of comprehension interacts with discourse-level structures and the relations between connected clauses.

8.1 Parallel Syntactic and Semantic Analyses

A strict interpretation of LAST for the sentence level would seem to require that the final analysis and interpretation occur only at the end of the sentence. This unlikely event is also a potential characteristic of many of the structural models that we reviewed in chapter 4, which assign structure independently of and prior to semantic analysis.

However, *all* models that give priority to the sentence level can accommodate the appearance of ongoing comprehension by postulating that meaning is computed "in parallel" with syntax. It is worth examining how this intuitively appealing notion cashes out in detail. It implies two parallel syntactic computations, the one that applies automatically to the incoming forms and one that provides the basis for semantic analysis of incomplete information. Thus, "parallel" assignment models have an inherent circularity at worst and a duplication of processes at best.

Consider our favorite example, as it appears word by word:

(1) The horse raced past the barn.

(2) a. The
    b. The horse
    c. The horse raced
    d. The horse raced past
    e. The horse raced past the
    f. The horse raced past the barn.

Let us assume a structural model in which syntactic and semantic analyses are pursued in parallel. A theoretically critical point is just after the first complete noun phrase *the horse*. In a structure-first model, this is assigned a phrase-level "noun phrase" as a function of fitting the pattern of "determiner noun." That phrase can then go to the parallel semantic analyzer, where several things happen. First, the conceptual analysis of *the horse* can be assigned. At the same time, a potential thematic role for the phrase is considered (but not assigned). In a structure-first model, assigning a potential thematic role can be done only if there is sufficient structure to determine what the range of possible thematic roles might be. What happens next depends on how much syntactic analysis the semantic processor performs.

An extreme view would be that the semantic processor directly triggers potential syntactic structure at each point. Thematic assignment in syntax-first models is dependent on prior and independent syntactic assignment. After the first noun phrase, there must be the postulation of a syntactic "dummy" analysis, with enough place-holders at least to arrive at a verb that can assign a thematic relation, as shown in figure 8.1.

With that information, *the horse* can be assigned the thematic role of "agent" of the (as yet unspecified) verb. However, this assignment and its associated structure cannot inform the ongoing syntactic analysis of the input form sequence, since in such models, the syntactic assignment is not informed by semantic analysis or plausibility. The dual assignment of syntactic structures allows such a model to meet the intuition that semantic and thematic information is assigned continuously and to maintain the claim that the "real" syntactic assignment occurs independently of semantic analysis.

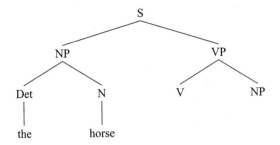

Figure 8.1
Dummy syntactic analysis for projected thematic assignment.

   This solution is forced and duplicative. The separation of the two ongoing syntactic assignments serves only the theoretical claim, and the duplication of syntactic
assignment is odd, at best. At worst, it implies circularity because the syntactic tree
with dummy elements certainly allows for semantic analysis of *them*. In the preceding
example, not only might *horse* be assigned the "agent" of V, there can also be a
projected semantic analysis of the V with the VP-internal argument as some kind of
thematic object. The result would be that the semantic analysis of basic thematic
relations can actually move ahead of the incoming syntactic analysis. This is not to
say that a structural model of this type could not be proposed; but in doing so, there
would be a theoretical corruption of syntactic autonomy in the "garden-path" model.
   Fortunately, structure-first models typically take a less extreme view, which, however, still implies some duplication of syntactic processing. For example, Frazier and
colleagues (Frazier 1987a; Rayner, Carlson, and Frazier 1983) propose that the
semantic analyzer develops various alternative sets of thematic relations as argument-
assigning words are received (e.g., *raced*). World knowledge points to the most
plausible thematic relations, given the arguments provided by the syntactic processor.
The semantic processor thus determines the phrases that carry arguments, and thematic roles. If the minimal syntactic structure provided by the syntactic processor
does not match the most plausible thematic roles, the semantic processor "guides"
the syntactic processor to reanalyze the input for an alternative structure that has the
arguments for the most plausible thematic roles. Clearly, this architecture implies
that the semantic processor is capable of some syntactic analysis. At the least, the
semantic processor is able to determine the correspondence between syntactic phrases
and thematic roles, to recognize when the proposed syntactic structure does not
match its favored semantic analysis. Even more problematically, the semantic processor may "suggest" an alternative syntactic analysis that supports its favored set of
thematic relations.
   LAST accounts for the intuition that meaning is computed immediately by way
of the pseudosyntactic assignment processes that map the surface sequence onto a

preliminary meaning. We have likened the mapping templates to automatic, statistically valid associative constructs, which are triggered differentially according to the strength of their input cues in the listener's experience. For example, the NVN template is triggered partially by the appearance of an initial noun phrase, *the horse*, on two grounds. First, it is a complete noun phrase at the beginning of the sequence. Second, the noun phrase is animate. Accordingly, to some extent, *the horse* will be assigned the thematic role of agent by the automatic initial activation of the NVN template.

Similar principles apply at lower and higher levels of representation to account for the intuition that processing is immediate, as opposed to delayed until the ends of the units. In chapter 5, we first outlined how LAST operates in isolating and recognizing words from a continuous speech stream. An initial phase involves mapping easily recognized features, morphemes, and words onto an hypothetical lexical sequence, which is then checked by internal regeneration of the sequence. The initial phase occurs immediately and explains the apparent immediacy of the recognition. The same sort of process can occur at the phrase level. Pseudosyntax consists of regularities such as

"det ... N" → [det N]$_{phrase}$

Because phrases with nouns are themselves potential arguments, they can be subject to a reconstitutive check of their structure. In this way, a cascade of analysis-by-synthesis modules can operate simultaneously to assign a lexical analysis, phrase structure hierarchy, and derivational sentence-level syntax.

The notion that lexical, phrasal, and sentential analyses proceed in parallel is relatively uncontroversial since all three have proper analysis as component parts of an autonomous "syntax." The next intuitive level of analysis is that above the single-clause sentence, namely, multiclause sentences and discourses. We consider the discourse level first, as the clearest case of a suprasentential level of representation. Then we return to the more complex case of multiclause sentences.

The most salient feature of discourses is that they have little language-specific structure, if any. In general, a multisentence narrative or essay in one language has an accurate, sentence-by-sentence translation in every other language (modulo sentence-internal constraints such as mechanisms for focus and topicalization). This inter-translatability suggests that the form of discourse representation is not syntactic but is more directly related to conceptual structures. In LAST, conceptual structures are themselves initially assigned by a set of low-level syntactic features and statistically valid templates. The initial conceptual analysis is then confirmed by its link to the syntactic reconstruction of the input. This means that the conceptual level associated with each sentence is never "generated" via some recursive processes, but is passively assembled and then checked via its implied syntactic infrastructure.

The distinction between conceptual and syntactic representations gives rise to a central concept in the cognitive sciences, the modularity of certain processes. Up to now, we have not mentioned this major issue, but consideration of the interface between conceptual and syntactic processes forces us to confront it directly. There are two main ideas associated with the notion of modularity:

1. Certain perceptual processes are modular. This means they characteristically are
a. Rapid and automatic.
b. Architecturally (e.g., "neurologically") segregated in such a way that they resist outside influence. In particular, their operations proceed independently of information from a "central processor."
2. Modular processes are computational, symbolic, and highly constrained. In contrast, the "central processor" operates associatively, can connect widely different kinds of information, and is largely unconstrained.

The first notion was discussed by Forster and associates (Forster 1970; Forster and Olbrei 1974), then elaborated by Marshall (1980) and, most articulately, by Fodor (1983). Fodor also clarified the second kind of distinction, between modular and central processes.

A great deal of recent psycholinguistic research has the credit or discredit of modularity as its underlying agenda. Indeed, much of the research on sentence comprehension we have reviewed in previous chapters was actually motivated by this controversy. In those chapters, we were concerned to show how the data support LAST, rather than whether they do or do not support the modularity hypotheses. In general, it is easy to see that evidence supporting the role of conceptually associative information in online comprehension is prima facie evidence against both premises of modularity. Evidence for the autonomy of syntactic parsing is evidence in favor of modularity. Put crudely for language comprehension, if meaning influences initial syntactic assignment processes, modularity is false; if it does not, modularity is true.

We are about to review research that bears more directly on the modularity hypothesis for language comprehension because it deals with the interaction of discourse and sentences, which necessarily forces a confrontation between the role of conceptual and syntactic processes. But our presentation will satisfy neither modular adherents nor opponents of modularity. The reason for this is that in fact, modularity of the sort described above is not an issue, for at least the following reasons:

1. *Scientific method.* The first premise of modularity is fundamental to accepted scientific method (see, e.g., Forster and Olbrei 1974). Therefore, modularity often appears to be substantively true when it is actually a methodological foundation of research (Marr 1976; Simon 1962; Spearman 1937). It is scientifically trite that we divide nature at her joints and study the properties of distinct "modular" processes free of outside influences.

2. *Unfalsifiability*. It is virtually impossible with today's methods to prove modularity, if it were true. We noted at the beginning of this chapter that it is intuitively obvious that comprehension appears to move word by word, or even in smaller increments. But the ability of the system to project ahead of the immediate input means that meaning can appear to be computed immediately. This point does not depend on whether the projections are via multiple incomplete analyses (which we do not advocate), or via overlapping pattern completion and synthesis mechanisms (which we do advocate). The "whole person" can understand a whole proposition in advance of the complete input regardless of the architectural independence of the component processes. This is not to say that it is impossible in principle to titrate out evidence for distinct internal processes when meaning is neutralized. But it is very hard to show that apparent evidence for the impact of meaning on syntax is *not* via direct interaction between conceptual and syntactic processes. Perhaps sufficiently sensitive measures will emerge in the future.

3. *The whole iguana*. Architectural modularity is the proposal that, for example, semantic information cannot inform ongoing syntactic processes because of architectural segregation of semantic and syntactic processes. But, even if this were false, it might appear to be true because of what we have called *informational independence* (Townsend and Bever 1991, 1982; see also Frazier 1985, 1990; Jackendoff 1990).

It is a point of logic underlying the necessity of modularity when different kinds of representational systems are concerned. If the computational language of two systems differ, one cannot affect the internal operation of the other. This does not necessarily demonstrate an architectural boundary between them, because their mutual computational opacity would lead to such discontinuities of influence anyway.

As an extreme, consider a cross-modal example such as the matching of pictures to words. At first, this appears to be an obvious example of two distinct modules at work, separated architecturally. Operationally speaking, to demonstrate their modular independence one would want to show that if a picture facilitates the perception of a corresponding word, it is only after the word is initially sensed. That is, a picture of an iguana cannot directly facilitate perception of the isolated letter sequences *i* or *ig*, or *igu*, or *igua*, but only of a representation of the word *iguana*. Such facts, if true, would support the assumption that picture processing and word finding are distinct modules. But in fact, the results show something weaker. It is empirically reasonable that the computational language of object recognition is not directly mapped onto phoneme sequences. It follows logically that object recognition cannot inform word recognition. That is, the picture of the iguana cannot constrain the word-finding process to search for words beginning with *i*, or *ig*, or *igu*, or even *iguana*. It can only constrain the word-finding process to find words with semantic structure related to that of iguanas. Of course, the word-finding process itself may quickly provide the information that the most important word that is semantically related to iguanas is *iguana* and thereby constrain its visual expectation for that word. But that constraint does not interact with letter recognition directly, only via conceptual and lexical levels of representation (see Schwartz and Schwartz 1984).

This logical point makes it necessary to be cautious about any evidence for architectural modularity between different sources of information relevant to language behavior. Because there are empirical reasons to believe that the internal computational languages of nonlinguistic knowledge, semantics, syntax, and phonology all differ, we must expect on those grounds alone to find discontinuities in the apparent influence of information from one system to another.

4. *Having it both ways.* Finally, LAST assumes an interaction between associative and syntactic information, of a specific kind, that resolves many apparent conflicts in research data that were initially touted by their discoverers as definitively proving or disproving modularity. LAST assumes the immediate projection of a conceptual representation, based in part on associatively accumulated information that can immediately interact with longer-term and current expectations. At the same time, the model assumes that, once launched from the initial analysis, the syntactic assignment operates autonomously from conceptual impact. Thus, LAST is both modular and nonmodular, depending on which aspect one emphasizes.

We can summarize four points as follows. We accept the idea that the modularity of different kinds of information involved in comprehension is a good working hypothesis, following the standard methodological stance (point 1). It is difficult to find unambiguous evidence for any kind of syntactic modularity (point 2), or crucial experimental evidence uniquely for architectural modularity (point 3). LAST offers a specific model to test against the kinds of experimental facts that the modularity hypothesis stimulated (point 4). We maintain that LAST fits the facts well, and thereby *replaces* the general claims about modularity with a specific and experimentally supported model.

Thus, we doubt that modularity is the constant primary question of cognitive science. But we also do not despair over the last decades of research on modularity in language comprehension. Just because it has focused on the relative roles of associative and computational language processes, it has turned up a great deal of data that we have organized and shown to favor LAST. We now turn to some of the classic investigations of modularity, having to do with discourse and multiclause relations.

LAST provides unique explanatory opportunities for considering the relation between context, meaning, and ongoing structural assignment. First, the most significant unit of the meaning-form relationship is at the clause/sentence level. This follows from the fact that the output of the pseudosyntax must be rich enough to trigger a syntactic sentence-level derivation, and that the output of the syntactic component will tend to be sentences (see the discussion of the grain problem in section 5.4.2). Thus, while there can be a modular cascade of analysis-by-synthesis loops, as suggested above, computational priority will naturally be given to the clause-level meaning-form relations. This leads to the natural prediction that the unit of interaction between context, meaning, and sentence-structure assignment will tend to be at the clause/sentence level.

A second feature of LAST is that its internal mechanisms require the formation of two sound-meaning pairs at each level during comprehension. First, pseudosyntax creates an initial meaning-form hypothesis related to the physical input. Then the syntactic component creates another meaning-form derivation, whose output is compared to the physical input. This computational architecture requires a memory store for the entire physical input of an utterance, at least a sentence in length. At the same time, the initial meaning-form hypothesis is also stored as part of the syntactic derivation. Thus, the analysis-by-synthesis model intrinsically requires a clause/sentence-level store for both an entire meaning and the entire physical sequence. This feature allows us to explain various phenomena in which one or the other kind of representation is accessed, depending on natural or experimental circumstances.

8.2   Intersentential Contexts

The influence of prior discourse information on sentence processing is a critical test for sentence-level syntactic modularity. On the strict interpretation of structure-first theories, structure is assigned independently of both generic and recent semantic in formation. This applies most strongly to information from prior sentences in a discourse. In LAST, the strategies of pseudosyntax apply directly and without inhibition from prior context. However, since the strategies arrive instantly at an initially hypothesized meaning, there is the possibility of certain kinds of behavioral interactions as a function of prior context.

8.2.1   Passive in Context
The assignment of pseudosyntax and an initial meaning relies predominantly on habits. The habit that NVN corresponds to agent-action-patient is so strong that the comprehension system follows it even when context suggests that it is not appropriate in a particular situation. Davison and Lutz (1985) demonstrated the resistance of the NVN template to context. They investigated whether a context sentence that focuses attention on a particular element could eliminate the processing complexity of a target sentence. They compared reading times for untransformed sentences that follow the NVN template versus transformed sentences that do not. The target sentences were preceded by context sentences that were neutral, supportive of the transformed version, or supportive of the untransformed version. Among the sentence types that Davison and Lutz investigated were passive, *there*-insertion, adverb preposing, raising to subject, and raising to object. We focus here on passive.

A specific example of the passive violation of the NVN template from Davison and Lutz (1985:35–41) is:

(3) *Passive target sentence*
    A six-year-old girl was abducted by a man in California.

(4) *Active target sentence*
    A man in California abducted a six-year-old girl.

The first sentence above does not conform to the NVN template, while the second does. Examples of context sentences for the active-passive pair are:

(5) *Neutral context*
    Police reported the details of a recent kidnapping.

(6) *Active-supporting context*
    Strange men have been on the prowl lately.

(7) *Passive-supporting context*
    Children should never be allowed to walk alone.

The passive-supporting context focuses on *children* by placing it in the initial position, while the active-supporting context focuses on *men*. If focus influences immediate reliance on the NVN pattern, a passive sentence will be easier to read in a passive-supporting context than in an active-supporting context. Average reading times for active versus passive target sentences appear in table 8.1.

Davison and Lutz found that overall reading times were 163 ms shorter for active sentences than for passive sentences. Compared to neutral contexts, the active-supporting contexts increased the advantage in reading time for active target sentences, but passive-supporting contexts had little effect on the reading time difference between active and passive target sentences. If passive-supporting contexts reduced the processing complexity of passive sentences, these contexts should at least have reduced the advantage in reading time for active sentences, compared to neutral contexts. Assuming that the notion of focus constitutes a reasonable model of dis-

Table 8.1
Mean reading times (ms) for active and passive target sentences

Context	Target sentence		Difference
	Active	Passive	
Neutral	2356	2455	99
Active-supporting	2264	2526	262
Passive-supporting	2319	2448	129

Source: Adapted from Davison and Lutz 1985, fig. 1.1

course, these results suggest that the pattern of NVN = agent-action-patient is so strong that the initial phase of comprehension reacts to this pattern even in passive-supporting contexts.

Liversedge et al. (1998) obtained similar results with more online measures. They used an eye-tracking methodology to examine how context influences the interpretation of a *by*-phrase in passive sentences. The *by*-phrase may be interpreted as identifying an optional agentive argument in passives, as in

(8) *Agentive interpretation*
    The shrubs were planted by the apprentice that morning.

or as a locative adjunct, as in

(9) *Locative interpretation*
    The shrubs were planted by the greenhouse that morning.

The optionality of the agent argument in a passive is shown by the fact that the following sentence is consistent with the meaning of the agentive interpretation:

(10) *Patient-only passive*
     The shrubs were planted.

Liversedge et al. (1998) found that an off-line measure showed a strong bias toward interpreting the *by*-phrase as agentive: 96 percent of sentence fragments like *the shrubs were planted by the* ... were completed as agentive, according to participants' judgments about their own completions. The materials included verbs that were predominantly transitive only.

In the online measure of eye tracking, Liversedge et al. found that fixation times on the second noun were longer for *greenhouse* than for *apprentice*, even though the target nouns were matched for frequency and plausibility. These results were interpreted to show that comprehenders prefer to interpret noun phrases as filling argument roles, consistent with their preferences in the off-line task.

Liversedge et al. then examined whether a discourse context could modify this preference. Participants first read either an agent-supporting context sentence or a location-supporting context:

(11) *Agent-supporting context*
     The gardener wondered who would plant the shrubs.

(12) *Location-supporting context*
     The gardener wondered where to plant the shrubs.

followed by either an agentive target sentence or a locative target sentence. The results appear in table 8.2.

Fixation times on the noun were longer for agentive context-locative target pairs than for the other three pairings of context and target. This result suggests that both

Table 8.2
Mean fixation times for the noun in the *By*-phrase (ms/character) depending on context and target

Context	Target sentence	
	Agentive	Locative
Agentive	31	36
Locative	32	31

Source: Adapted from Liversedge et al. 1998, fig. 3

context and the verb argument requirements can "prime" an agent role. Processing is disrupted when discourse context leads to the expectation of an agent that is not fulfilled by the noun in the *by*-phrase. In contrast, processing a passive with an agentive *by*-phrase is disrupted very little when discourse context leads to the expectation of a locative phrase.

The Liversedge et al. study shows that the initial assignment process is sensitive to verb-argument preferences. The initial processes assign noun phrases to the argument roles that a verb takes. The study also shows a strong tendency to assign to the noun in a *by*-phrase the role of agent. This fact helps explain why studies of relative clauses as discussed in chapter 7 sometimes have shown that good patients eliminate the reading-time effect on the Verb + *by* region. The word *by* together with a good patient and a transitive-only verb strongly suggests a relative clause structure.

The studies by Davison and Lutz (1985) and Liversedge et al. (1998) indicate that the basic mechanisms of comprehension are similar in and out of context. The pseudosyntax develops a quick rough approximation to meaning based on familiar sentence patterns and information that follows from the argument requirements of verbs.

8.2.2   The Grammar Generates a Syntax from Primed Concepts

In chapter 6 we saw that the initial assignment processes can project slots or dummy elements based on the thematic requirements of verbs. The comprehension system then looks for noun phrases that can fill these slots. For example, in

(13) Sam put ...

the initial projection is that there will be a patient and a location. All other factors being equal, a hypothesis about sentence meaning triggers the sentence synthetic component primarily when all required slots are filled.

The initial assignment processes may also project units that are of broader gauge than arguments. "Scripts" activate expectations of a particular proposition or event. A *script* is a stereotypical sequence of events such as eating in a restaurant or visiting a doctor (Bower, Black, and Turner 1979; Schank and Abelson 1977; Sharkey and Mitchell 1985). An activated event may function as an initial hypothesis about meaning, and allow the grammar to generate a candidate syntax. As before, the comprehension system then compares this candidate syntax with the input. If the candidate syntax matches the input, there is integration with the conceptual representation and loss of surface form. If the candidate syntax does not match, another hypothesis about meaning is formed and another candidate syntax generated.

We (Townsend and Bever 1988, 1989) obtained evidence for projection of a candidate sentence-level syntax from expected events. Subjects read stories based on scripts as in the following two examples:

(14) *Supportive story*
     Johnny woke up very hungry for breakfast.
     He found a bowl and a spoon in the kitchen.
     He got a pitcher of milk from the refrigerator.
     When he took down a box of cereal from the shelf . . .

(15) *Neutral story*
     Johnny was watching his favorite programs on TV.
     He started to get hungry for a snack.
     He waited for a commercial to go into the kitchen.
     When he took down a box of cereal from the shelf . . .

The first story was written from the events that college students listed when they were asked to describe what happens when one eats breakfast (see Bower, Black, and Turner 1979). One of the events that these students frequently listed for eating breakfast is that one takes out a box of cereal from the cupboard. Thus, the sentence

(16) He took down a box of cereal from the shelf.

expresses a typical event in eating breakfast. The first story strongly supports this sentence.

The second story was based on the events that college students listed for getting a TV snack, except that they never mentioned taking out a box of cereal as an event that occurs when one gets a TV snack. Thus, the target sentence is plausible in the neutral story, but it is not strongly supported by it.

In Townsend and Bever 1988, the target event appeared in either active or passive form. The stories were presented either one clause at a time or one word at a time in a self-paced reading task. We compared these reading paradigms because they appear to place different emphasis on conceptual and superficial representations.

We expected the whole-clause task to encourage the formation of conceptual representations so that the conceptually supportive contexts would decrease reading time, especially for the more complex passive construction. Since the initial analysis in the pseudosyntax may access semantic context, the conceptual representation of the underlying script of eating breakfast will prime the subject, verb, and object concepts of the target event, but in an unordered conceptual representation:

Johnny = agent
get   = action
cereal = patient

Thus, the conceptual representation of an anticipated event could neutralize the fact that the passive expression of the anticipated event is not in the canonical SVO order. Since both agent and patient concepts are primed, both noun phrases will be read more quickly, even though they are presented in the passive form.

But reading in the word-by-word paradigm should exert a different kind of pressure that encourages a more superficial representation of the anticipated event. Since the words disappear as subjects read through the sentence word by word, they must assign a structure to each word in sequence, and build up an ordered representation. Since the word-by-word reading format focuses attention on the superficial, ordered level, we expected less facilitation from conceptually supportive contexts. If the focus of attention is on the superficial level, subjects should represent predictions of upcoming events in a more superficial manner as well. That is, they should assign the anticipated event a syntactic form. Since the canonical form in English is agent-action-patient, we expected that that subjects would represent predicted events in a manner such as

(17) Johnny gets the cereal.

Thus, supportive contexts should facilitate word-by-word reading of active sentences. However, because the ordered prediction does not match the form of a passive sentence,

(18) The cereal was taken down from the shelf by Johnny.

we expected that supportive contexts would slow down word-by-word reading of passive sentences.

Overall, the subjects read active sentences more quickly than passives (375 ms/word vs. 432 ms/word; see table 8.3). Overall, they read target sentences faster in supportive contexts than in neutral contexts (382 ms/word vs. 425 ms/word). Reading times were faster in the clause format than in the word format (342 ms/word vs. 465 ms/word). Supportive contexts overall had larger effects for passives than for actives (a 50 ms/word facilitation vs. 27 ms/word facilitation).

The interactions between presentation format, context, and sentence structure were particularly revealing. In the clause format, supportive contexts reduced reading time more for the passive target sentence than for the active target sentence (by a factor of

Table 8.3
Mean reading times per word (ms) in target sentences depending on form, context, and presentation format

Context	Clause format		Word format	
	Active	Passive	Active	Passive
Neutral	322	436	465	477
Supportive	294	316	419	497
Facilitation	28	120	26	−20

Source: Adapted from Townsend and Bever 1988

4, 120 ms/word vs. 28 ms/word). In the word format, supportive contexts reduced reading time for active sentence (by 46 ms/word), but it significantly *increased* reading time for passive sentences (by 20 ms/word). Townsend and Bever (1988) found that this increase in reading time for the passive in supportive contexts occurred on both the initial noun phrase and the final noun phrase.

Knowledge of stereotyped scripts primes particular events, so that when these events actually appear, a projected initial meaning-form hypothesis may already be available. The grammar may use the initial hypothesis to generate and anticipate aspects of a particular surface syntactic form. All other things being equal, the form will be a canonical NVN. Thus, an actual sentence that does not match the canonical form may be harder to process, even though the context primes its meaning.

8.2.3 Contextual Integration at the Propositional Boundary
LAST proposes that semantic context can prime an initial hypothesis about meaning. Whichever meaning is most strongly primed from whatever source, that meaning is the basis for the grammar to generate a syntax, which is then checked against the input string stored in a temporary memory. If the generated syntax matches the input string, the corresponding meaning becomes integrated with conceptual information.

In this model, discourse context has two kinds of behavioral effects. As we just noted, it can prime an initial meaning-form hypothesis. It also can influence the integration of sentence meaning into a conceptual representation of discourse. The model predicts that a discourse context that supports sentence meaning will have larger behavioral effects when the grammar projects a relatively complete unit, and the corresponding meaning is integrated into a conceptual representation.

We (Townsend and Bever 1989) showed that story contexts have greater effects at the end of a sentence, which corresponds, by hypothesis, to the end of an analysis-by-synthesis cycle at the sentence level. As in Townsend and Bever (1988) we used script-based stories. We embedded a critical sentence in a passage that strongly or weakly supported the sentence. There was strong support for the critical sentence when it stated an event that was central to the underlying script for the story and weak support when it was peripheral.

In one study, subjects read texts line by line in a self-paced reading task. The lines randomly ended either at a clause boundary, or just before the final word of a clause. A major variable was whether the entire critical sentence,

(19) He took down some cereal.

appeared entirely on one line, as above, or with the last word of the sentence on the next line. The following two stories present the critical sentence entirely on one line, but differ in their support for the critical sentence:

(20) *Supportive, complete clause*
Johnny woke up very hungry for
breakfast. He found a bowl and a
spoon in the kitchen. He got a
pitcher of milk form the refrigerator.
He took down some cereal.
Then he filled the bowl
and ate until he wasn't hungry anymore.

(21) *Neutral, complete clause*
Johnny was watching his favorite
programs on TV. He started to get
hungry for a snack. He waited for
a commercial to go into the kitchen.
He took down some cereal.
Then he filled the bowl
and ate until he wasn't hungry anymore.

When the critical clause was presented on separate lines, it appeared as follows:

(22) He took down some
cereal. Then he filled the bowl

The critical data were times to read the line containing the complete target clause, *he took down some cereal*, compared to a line containing all but the last word of the target clause, *he took down some* ... To facilitate comparison, reading times were adjusted for number of words in the line. The results appear in table 8.4.

When the target clause appeared as a complete clause entirely on one line, target-line reading times were faster for passages that strongly supported the target than for passages that supported it only weakly (285 vs. 373 ms/word). When the target clause was not entirely on one line ("incomplete clause"), target-line reading times did not differ for passages with strong versus weak support for the target event (401 vs.

Table 8.4
Mean reading times (ms/word) depending on contextual support and clause completeness

Context	Clause completeness	
	Incomplete	Complete
Neutral	401	373
Supportive	404	285
Facilitation	−3	88

Source: Adapted from Townsend and Bever 1989, table 3

404 ms/word). Since discourse-level support had a positive effect on reading only complete clauses, much of its effect appears at the end of a clause. Discourse-level support does not eliminate structural processing prior to the end of a clause.

There is, of course, the alternative interpretation that a discourse effect does not occur with incomplete clauses because the context supports a key word such as *cereal* rather than an entire event, and this key word appears on the next line. Acknowledging this possibility, we tentatively take these results to demonstrate that integration of clause meaning into the representation of discourse is more likely to occur at the end of clause. It is at this point that the comprehension system checks the generated syntax against the input. In case of a match, the comprehension system integrates the corresponding meaning into the ongoing representation of discourse (see also Caplan 1972; Chang 1980; Jarvella 1971; Just and Carpenter 1980; Haberlandt and Graesser 1985; Sachs 1967).

8.2.4 Attention to Sentence Level vs. Discourse Level
Nevertheless, there is evidence that discourse context affects certain aspects of comprehension independently of the end of an analysis-by-synthesis unit. According to LAST, these effects will occur most naturally in the initial assignment of a meaning/form, or at conceptual integration of sentence meaning with local context and background knowledge.

• In the initial assignment of meaning, context effects will involve activating words and sentence frames.
• At conceptual integration, context effects will involve primarily propositions.

Thus, the mechanism by which meaning influences comprehension depends on the point at which meaning has its effect.

We (Townsend and Bever 1991) tested the hypothesis that context effects on word recognition and sentence integration can involve different mechanisms. We used a change-of-speaker detection task in which one word was uttered by a speaker other

Box 8.1
The change-of-speaker detection task

> The change-of-speaker detection task (Townsend and Bever 1991; O'Bryan et al. 2000) is a monitoring task in which subjects listen to a sentence or a discourse for a speech sound uttered by someone other than the primary speaker. Linguistic materials are recorded by a primary speaker and by a secondary speaker who usually is of a different gender than the primary speaker. Using the recording by the primary speaker, the target word is replaced by the secondary speaker's recording of the same word as it appears in the same context. For experiments that measure response time, a timing tone is placed on a second channel and is made inaudible to the subject. The timing tone initiates a timer that is stopped by the subject's detection response.
>
> Subjects are instructed to listen to the recorded linguistic materials for the purpose of making judgments about aspects of the story and the storyteller, such as the plausibility of the story or the mood of the storyteller. A secondary task is to determine whether there is a word spoken by someone other than the primary storyteller. Response-time measure can be taken online, or subjects can make their judgments about whether their was a change of speaker after the story has ended.
>
> The change-of-speaker detection task has the advantage that the material that subjects must detect is a part of the speech signal. In addition, it is not unnatural to listen to speech in which a word uttered by another speaker appears in the speech.

than the main storyteller (see box 8.1). Targets occurred at the end of a clause (high within-sentence constraint) or at the beginning of a clause (low within-sentence constraint), corresponding to the high- and low-constraint conditions in Marslen-Wilson and Welsh 1978. These within-clause constraint conditions differ based on the common notion that within-clause predictability tends to increase later in the clause. In the examples below, the target word is italicized.

(23) *High within-sentence constraint*
Because she is a sweet cute *girl* boys asked her out often.

(24) *Low within-sentence constraint*
- Because she is a sweet cute girl *boys* asked her out often.

The target-containing sentences were taken from Bever, Lackner, and Kirk 1969; see chapter 2. *Girl* is subject to a high within-sentence constraint because of syntactic and lexical-associative information, such as the fact that only an adjective or a noun can appear in the position that *girl* occupies. *Boys* is subject to a low within-sentence constraint because the position that *boys* occupies at the beginning of a clause may be filled with a pronoun, determiner, adjective, or noun. In addition to the within-sentence variation in constraints, the sentences that contained the target word itself were either highly or weakly constrained by the discourse context.

Table 8.5

Mean response times (ms) for detecting a change in speaker depending on discourse constraints and within-sentence constraints

Within-sentence constraints	Discourse constraints		Mean
	Low	High	
Low	510	544	527
High	470	490	480
Mean	490	517	

Source: Adapted from Townsend and Bever 1991, fig. 2

(25) *High discourse constraint*

Mary went to South Side High School. She was voted the most popular girl in the class. . . .

(26) *Low discourse constraint*

My friend has not lived at home for years. Through high school she constantly battled with her parents. . . .

The discourse materials were obtained from undergraduate students who wrote stories around the critical sentences. Discourses were selected for experimental materials if the critical sentence was either high or low in plausibility, as determined by graduate student ratings. Unlike the high-discourse-constraint condition shown here, the discourses did not contain another instance of the target word.

The results appear in table 8.5. Within-sentence constraints showed the expected result (see also Marslen-Wilson and Welsh 1978). Response times were faster in the within-sentence high-constraint condition than in the low-constraint condition (480 vs. 527 ms). Discourse-level constraints showed the opposite effect: response times to detect a change of speaker were significantly *slower* in the high-discourse-constraint condition (517 vs. 490 ms). A second experiment measured detection accuracy, and obtained corresponding results: increasing within-sentence constraints improved detection accuracy, but increasing discourse-level constraints reduced detection accuracy.

These results show that increasing discourse-level constraints interferes with reports of word-level processing. The slower response times in high-discourse-constraint contexts presents difficulties for a strictly constraint-based theory, which predicts that if there is any difference effect of discourse context at all, it is in the direction of more strongly constrained contexts facilitating recognition of a change of speaker.

LAST explains these results in terms of a series of overlapping processes:

1. *Extract words and major phrases.* The pseudosyntax deploys probabilistic information patterns to yield an initial meaning as soon as possible.

2. *Meaning proposed.* The words, phrase grouping, and most plausible sentence meaning are presented to the synthetic component.
3. *Syntax generated.* The grammar generates a candidate syntactic derivation for the proposed meaning.
4. *Surface attention for syntax checking.* Attention is focused briefly on surface form for the purpose of determining whether the generated syntax matches the input.
5. *Meaning integrated.* If the generated syntax matches the input, the corresponding meaning is integrated into a representation of discourse.

We assume that attention tends to focus on one process at a time (Kahneman 1973). In terms of LAST, the within-sentence effects may actually be end-of-clause effects. That is, the faster response times at the end of the clause (high within-sentence constraint) may involve checking of the candidate syntax to determine whether it accounts for all of the input. As a result, there is increased attention to the acoustic form. The discourse-level effects may be a result of a focus of attention on the initial meaning-form hypothesis. At the point of the target word, the system is determining a plausible initial guess about sentence meaning. When this initial guess is consistent with context, attention is drawn away from the acoustic details.

8.3   Sentence-Internal Contexts and Connectives

We turn now to the effect of the information in a clause on processing the immediately following clause within the same sentence. It is intrinsic to the architecture of LAST that surface and semantic representations can be developed simultaneously. The comprehension system stores the input surface representation for later syntax checking, while developing a semantic representation. This raises the obvious question of whether these representations from one clause influence the processing of the next clause. It also seems reasonable to ask whether higher-level processes use these representations. Discourse-processing models generally assume that the basic building blocks of discourse representations are propositions, produced by sentence-level processing mechanisms. Do these higher-level processes require only meaning representations, or do they take advantage of the availability of surface representations? LAST makes no particular prediction on this question, but it does raise the possibility. The studies we review in this section can inform us about how LAST is integrated into the processing of multiclause sentences, and discourses.

8.3.1   Resolving Ambiguities
Tyler and Marslen-Wilson (1977) reported a widely cited study that has been interpreted as showing that the semantic analysis of information in an initial subordinate clause can influence the immediate syntactic processing of the following main clause.

Table 8.6
Mean target naming times (ms) depending on ambiguity and probe type

Sentence type	Probe type	
	Appropriate	Inappropriate
Ambiguous	519	555
Unambiguous	554	581

Source: From Tyler and Marslen-Wilson 1977

In fact, the results of their study support LAST, since semantic context can influence the integration of the initial meaning into a full conceptual representation. Tyler and Marslen-Wilson presented spoken sentence fragments like the following:

(27) *Singular bias*

   If you want to take a cheap vacation, visiting relatives ...

(28) *Plural bias*

   If they arrive unexpectedly, visiting relatives ...

Subjects then had to name a visually presented word, such as *is* or *are* (see box 6.2). The word *is* signals that *visiting relatives* has a gerund structure, and, according to pretest ratings, this interpretation is more consistent with the first sentence fragment above (i.e., singular bias). The word *are* signals that the ambiguous phrase is an adjectival construction, which is more consistent with the second fragment. The results appear in table 8.6.

   Tyler and Marslen-Wilson (1977) found that target-word-naming times for *is* and *are* were faster when the context supported the interpretation of the ambiguous phrase that was determined by the target word (519 vs. 555 ms). Since the context effect was no smaller than the structural effect of unambiguous phrases (e.g., *mixing drinks, diving submarines*), this result has been interpreted as showing that the semantic context guides local syntactic decisions.

   There is another interpretation of the Tyler and Marslen-Wilson 1977 result that is uniquely consistent with LAST: semantic context is integrated with linguistic meaning once the comprehension system has checked the generated syntax against the input. This interpretation requires that much of the semantic-context effect occurs in sequences that have initiated synthesis and conceptual integration. To separate the locus of the semantic-context effect, Townsend and Bever (1982) introduced a number of controls into the materials of Tyler and Marslen-Wilson (1977; see also Cowart and Cairns 1987; Marslen-Wilson and Tyler 1987). These controls showed that the context effects on naming time are indeed due to a variety of sources of priming, including explicit morphological number information on the context verb, priming from specific lexical items, and conceptual integration at the completion of relatively complete semantic units. Following an explanation of how *landing planes* can lead to synthesis in some cases and not others, we review the evidence for priming from these sources.

The two interpretations of an ambiguous phrase like *landing planes* differ in functional completeness. That is, they differ in how explicitly they state the details of the canonical sentence (see Carroll 1978; Tanenhaus and Carroll, 1975). The transitive interpretation of *landing planes* corresponds to a gerund structure like *mixing drinks*, in which *drinks* is the object of the verb *mixing*. The intransitive interpretation of *landing planes* corresponds to an adjectival structure like *diving submarines*, in which *diving* is a modifier of the head noun *submarines*. The verb *is* in

(29) *Gerund structure*
Landing planes is easy.

signals that the ambiguous phrase has a gerund structure, while *are* in

(30) *Adjectival structure*
Landing planes are hazardous.

signals that it has an adjectival structure. The two structures differ in how closely they correspond to complete canonical NVN sentences. The gerund structure is closer than the adjectival because it presents the final phrase (verb-object) of the canonical common English sentence pattern, subject-verb-object. Since the gerund maintains a piece of the canonical order, it activates more strongly the NVN strategy:

polishing glasses = VN
glittering glasses = AN

Hence, we would expect that contextual information will interact with ongoing processing more for gerund structures than for adjectival structures (see the "whole iguana" point in section 8.1). This prediction follows from the assumption that the NVN template can match a sequence without a match of the initial noun—that is, that template matching is not strictly linear.

Morphological Number Context With respect to morphologically primed number, we (Townsend and Bever 1982) found that context effects occurred only when the context contained a singular verb and the target was singular as well (see also Cowart and Cairns 1987). We compared sentence fragments like the following:

(31) *Singular morphological bias, singular target*
If the pit crew works very efficiently, racing cars ... IS

(32) *Singular morphological bias, plural target*
If the pit crew works very efficiently, racing cars ... ARE

Table 8.7
Mean response times (ms) depending on morphological number bias

Bias	Target number		Bias effect
	Singular	Plural	
Singular	641	733	92
Plural	653	653	0

Source: Townsend and Bever 1982, table 5

(33) *Plural morphological bias, singular target*
    If the pit crews work very efficiently, racing cars ... IS

(34) *Plural morphological bias, plural target*
    If the pit crews work very efficiently, racing cars ... ARE

The materials above all have a singular nonmorphological (semantic) bias, as determined by pretest ratings. Additional materials context clauses with a plural nonmorphological bias were used as well (see below). The results for morphological number matching appear in table 8.7.

Table 8.7 shows that the morphological-bias effect occurs only for morphological contexts that match singular targets. In terms of LAST, there is priming of morphological number, but this priming exerts an effect only at the point of conceptual integration of the relatively complete gerund structure. Conceptual integration of the gerund phrase is most natural with singular targets.

Lexical Context   The morphological matching effect was largely due to lexical priming from an adversative context introduced by *though* (see section 8.3.3). Townsend and Bever (1982) included materials in which there was a specific present tense form of *be* in the context clause. Some examples are:

(35) *Singular lexical bias, singular target*
    If the pilot is required to attend flight school, landing planes ... IS

(36) *Singular lexical bias, plural target*
    If the pilot is required to attend flight school, landing planes ... ARE

(37) *Plural lexical bias, singular target*
    If the pilots are required to attend flight school, landing planes ... IS

(38) *Plural lexical bias, plural target*
    If the pilots are required to attend flight school, landing planes ... ARE

The context clauses were either an *if*-clause, a main clause, or a *though*-clause. The morphological-bias effects with and without a form of *be* in the context appear in table 8.8.

Table 8.8
Morphological bias effects (ms) for ambiguous fragments depending on presence or absence of IS/ARE in the context

| Connective | Context | | Bias effect |
	IS/ARE present	IS/ARE absent	
if	35	53	−18
main	5	28	−23
though	120	36	84

Source: From Townsend and Bever 1982, table 7

The results showed that the morphological-context bias effect was greatest when the context contained a form of *be* and was introduced by the connective *though*. We return to the implications of the connective effect later in the chapter. For now, it is sufficient to point out that specific lexical items may prime words in a following clause, at least under some conditions. This priming occurs in the earliest phase of LAST.

Conceptual Integration Townsend and Bever (1982) examined the independent effects of nonmorphological (semantic) bias as well. In addition to the singular non-morphological contexts for *racing cars* that were listed above, they used plural non-morphological contexts as well. Examples of plural nonmorphological bias for *racing cars* include the following:

(39) *Singular morphological bias, singular target*
If a young boy enjoys intense competition, racing cars ... IS

(40) *Singular morphological bias, plural target*
If a young boy enjoys intense competition, racing cars ... ARE

(41) *Plural morphological bias, singular target*
If young boys enjoy intense competition, racing cars ... IS

(42) *Plural morphological bias, plural target*
If young boys enjoy intense competition, racing cars ... ARE

The results for nonmorphological bias appear in table 8.9.

In general, the semantic-context effects were weaker than those in Tyler and Marslen-Wilson 1977, as expected when relevant controls are introduced into the materials, (as discussed earlier in this section and in section 8.3.4). In particular, the effects of context were limited to singular biases. These results follow from LAST. Since the sequence of words in the gerund interpretation (Verb + Noun → action +

Table 8.9
Mean response times (ms) depending on nonmorphological number bias and target number

Bias	Target number		Bias effect
	Singular	Plural	
Singular	623	710	87
Plural	658	666	−8

Source: Townsend and Bever 1982, table 5

patient) is a more reliable cue to meaning, this interpretation is strongest. The initial meaning hypothesis is the basis for generating a candidate syntax. The candidate syntax is checked against the input sequence and integrated with the meaning of the context. Hence, context effects are greater for *is* than for *are*.

Local Agreement   Farrar and Kawamoto (1993) replicated certain aspects of the results of Townsend and Bever (1982) and Tyler and Marslen-Wilson (1977). In two subject-paced word-by-word reading tasks (see box 6.3), Farrar and Kawamoto examined the effects of pragmatic bias and syntactic anomaly. In one experiment, the context was a separate sentence that preceded the target sentence that contained the ambiguous phrase. The context sentence contained a subject noun that was either singular or plural, and the entire context sentence was pragmatically biased toward either a singular or a plural form for the verb following the ambiguous phrase. Morphological bias and pragmatic bias were varied independently.

(43) *Singular morphological bias, singular pragmatic bias*
      The pilot must be observant. Flying planes does/do certainly ...

(44) *Singular morphological bias, plural pragmatic bias*
      An astronomer must be observant. Flying planes does/do certainly ...

(45) *Plural morphological bias, singular pragmatic bias*
      The pilots must be observant. Flying planes does/do certainly ...

(46) *Plural morphological bias, plural pragmatic bias*
      Astronomers must be observant. Flying planes does/do certainly ...

   The verb following the ambiguous verb was either *do*, signaling a gerund structure, or *does*, signaling an adjectival structure. The reading-time results for the verb following the ambiguous phrase and the next word appear in table 8.10.
   Farrar and Kawamoto (1993) found no effect of pragmatic context on reading times for the verb *does/do* following the ambiguous phrase. Pragmatic bias did have a significant effect on reading times for the adverb. For plural pragmatic context, subjects read the adverb 47 ms faster when it followed the plural verb *do* than when it

Table 8.10
Mean reading times (ms) on the verb and the next word depending on pragmatic bias and disambiguating verb

	Disambiguating verb	
Pragmatic bias	DOES	DO
DOES/DO reading times		
Singular bias	414	415
Plural bias	424	413
CERTAINLY reading times		
Singular bias	421	428
Plural bias	451	404

Source: From Farrar and Kawamoto 1993, table 1

followed the singular *does*. For singular pragmatic context, subjects read the adverb only 7 ms faster when it followed the singular verb than when it followed the plural verb. The interaction was significant by subjects but not by items.

It is not clear that there is any effect of pragmatic context, as Farrar and Kawamoto noted. First, the pragmatic effect does not appear on the disambiguating verb. Thus, it is difficult to make a claim that pragmatic information has an immediate effect on a syntactic decision about the phrase that preceded the verb. In addition, the pragmatic effect that does appear on the adverb is greater for the plural bias than for the singular. All other things being equal, we would expect plural bias effects to be greater than singular bias effects if subjects applied the NVN template locally (see also Nicol, Forster and Veres 1997, as discussed in chapter 6). That is, subjects may adopt a local agreement strategy and assume that a noun-verb pair (e.g., *planes do*) corresponds to agent-action. In this case, subjects would expect the verb to agree with the immediately preceding noun in number regardless of the structure of the phrase. Because of this, a plural noun produces more efficient processing when followed by a plural verb than by a singular verb. The fact that there is no apparent effect of the plural noun in cases of singular pragmatic bias may be interpreted as showing that singular pragmatic contexts cancel the effect of local structure. As we noted in section 8.2.2, it is reasonable to expect that subjects place greater reliance on superficial word order in self-paced word-by-word reading, and hence, we would expect them to be strongly influenced by local agreement (see also Bock and Miller 1991). In short, it is not clear that there is any effect of pragmatic context even on the adverb.

To determine whether the delayed effects of pragmatic bias might be attributed to peculiarities of the self-paced reading task, Farrar and Kawamoto (1993) introduced a word into the ambiguous phrase that made it either unambiguous or ungrammati-

Table 8.11
Mean reading times (ms) on the verb and the next word depending on structural bias and the disambiguating word

	Verb	
Structure	IS	ARE
IS/ARE reading times		
Singular structure	541	521*
Plural structure	552*	530
CERTAINLY reading times		
Singular structure	566	595*
Plural structure	616*	517

Note: * = ungrammatical sentence
Source: From Farrar and Kawamoto 1993, table 2

cal. Subjects read sentences like the following in a self-paced word-by-word reading task:

(47) *Gerund structure*
    Sinking those ship is/*are certainly not a pleasant job.

(48) *Adjectival structure*
    Those sinking ships *is/are certainly in need of help.

The initial noun phrase in the first sentence is unambiguously a gerund structure, so that the sentence is grammatical when *is* follows *ships* and it is ungrammatical when *are* follows *ships*. The initial noun phrase in the second sentence is unambiguously an adjectival structure, so that it is grammatical with *are* but not with *is*. The results appear in table 8.11.

  Once again, there were no significant effects on reading times for the verb. There was, however, an effect of structure on reading times for the following adverb. Reading times for adverbs were faster in grammatical sentences than in ungrammatical sentences (542 vs. 606 ms). The grammaticality effect was greater for the plural structure than for the singular (99 vs. 29 ms). Overall, the grammaticality effect on the adverb was more than double the pragmatic bias effect (59 vs. 27 ms). Thus, ungrammaticality has a larger effect than pragmatic unexpectedness.

  If we assume that the pragmatic bias effects on the adverb in the first experiment are reliable, the results of the two experiments support LAST. The pragmatic effects appear *earlier* than the syntactic effects. The mean reading times were more than 100 ms per word longer when there were syntactic violations, suggesting that the pragmatic information is available earlier than the syntactic information. In terms of LAST, pragmatic information may exert an effect on the initial meaning-form hypothesis, while syntactic information may exert its effect during the syntactic checking phase.

8.3.2 Multiclause Sentences vs. Discourse Structures

The preceding studies demonstrate that both conceptual and structural levels of representation can be maintained in parallel during comprehension. We now come to the question of whether multiclause sentences are treated as (complex) sentences or as the smallest instance of discourses. In terms of LAST, is there a sentence-level synthesis of the relations between clauses, or are the relations between clauses treated at the discourse level?

Interclause relations are governed by certain aspects of syntax, and accordingly must be subject to some degree of sentence-level synthesis. This is particularly clear in the processing of multiclause sentences that are formed by recursion of an element within one clause. In chapter 6, for example, we discussed the different kinds of processes that apply to *wh-* and NP-trace. Similar arguments apply to cases in which one clause fills an argument position of another. Indeed, clause recursion is one of the most important arguments that there are derivations (see chapter 3), and hence, a need for the synthetic process.

Adjunctive relations between clauses may call on a different kind of processing. By definition, adjuncts are added modifiers or extensions of existing phrases. There are various restrictions on the placement of adjuncts, but relatively weak syntactic constraints. Adjunct clauses characteristically are joined by connective conjunctions, such as *and*, *when*, and so on. Interclause connectives such as *because*, *if*, *although*, *after*, *before*, and so forth provide cues to the semantic relationship between the connected clauses (Caron 1997; Halliday and Hasan 1976; Noordman and Vonk 1997). These interclause semantic relations do not describe relations between elements within a clause, such as agent of action or patient of action, but rather are properties that apply to two clauses:

(49) Heidi felt very proud and happy
     because she won first prize at the art show.

In this sentence from Traxler, Bybee, and Pickering 1997, the event that appears in the *because*-clause is interpreted as the cause of the event that appears in the other clause. Sentences with *because* often can be integrated readily into a conceptual representation since they make explicit the causal relationships that underlie much of narrative discourse. The underlying causal nature of much of discourse has been established with studies on sentence reading time and sentence recall (Golding et al. 1995; Haberlandt 1982; Haberlandt and Bingham 1978; Keenan, Baillet, and Brown 1984; Murray 1995, 1997; Myers, Shinjo, and Duffy 1987; Noordman, Vonk, and Kempf 1992; Segal, Duchan, and Scott 1991; Townsend 1983).

Millis and Just (1994) proposed that in sentences with interclause connectives, comprehenders use working memory resources to integrate the two clauses during or at the end of the second clause. They had subjects read two-clause sentences one word a time in the moving-window paradigm (see box 6.3). The second clause contained either *because* or no connective; in the case of no connective, there was a period marking the end of the sentence. After reading the second clause, the subjects responded to a probe for a target word in either the first or second clause (see box 6.9), and then answered a comprehension question about each of the clauses. In the load condition, the two clauses were preceded by an unrelated clause. In this case, there was a cue between the probe and the comprehension questions for the subject to recall the last word of the unrelated clause.

Here is a sample trial (from Millis and Just 1994, table 1):

Load sentence
A series of waves approach parallel to the shore line.

Clause 1
The elderly parents toasted their only daughter at the party {because/.}

Clause 2
Jill had finally passed the exams at the prestigious university.

Probe
** toasted **

Cue
RECALL LAST WORD OF LOAD SENTENCE.

Question 1
Did the parents have several children?

Question 2
Did Jill succeed in her exams?

Millis and Just recorded word reading times as well as probe recognition times, accuracy in answering questions, and response time for answering questions. Response times on the probe recognition task appear in table 8.12.

Probe recognition response times were faster in the no-load condition than in the load condition (1229 vs. 1430 ms), but load condition did not interact with connective or clause. For target words in clause 1, Millis and Just found that connectives reduced response times for probes in both no load and load conditions. For target words in the final clause, connective did not reduce probe recognition times. The fact that connectives reduced response times for targets in the initial clause but not the final clause supports the view that connectives reactivate the surface properties of the initial clause for the purpose of integrating it with the final clause. Interestingly,

Table 8.12
Mean probe recognition times (ms) depending on target location, load condition, and connective

	Target location	
	Clause 1	Clause 2
No load		
No connective	1350	1130
Connective	1300	1135
Load		
No connective	1530	1330
Connective	1500	1360

Source: Adapted from Millis and Just 1994, fig. 1

Millis and Just found in a later experiment that *although* reduced probe recognition times for targets in both the first and second clause. As we will see in section 8.3.3, this result suggests that comprehenders process clauses in different ways when they are introduced by *because* versus *although*.

Comprehension questions were answered significantly more accurately in the connective condition than in the no-connective condition (88% vs. 86%), and response times to answer questions also were faster in the connective condition (2.1 vs. 2.2 sec).

Connectives increased reading times for the last word of the second clause, but they decreased reading times for the remaining words of the second clause. The finding that reading times increased on the last word of the second clause, especially for connective trials, may be interpreted to show that interclause integration occurs most naturally at the point of checking the syntax and integrating the meaning. This point occurs when the grammar has generated a possible syntax and successfully matched it against the input.

In a later experiment, Millis and Just tested for reactivation of the first clause at two points while reading the second clause. The probe (e.g., ** toasted **) was presented either after the first word of the second clause (e.g., after *Jill*), or after the last word of the second clause (e.g., after *university*). Whether the probe appeared early or late, the target word was the verb in the first clause (e.g., *toasted*):

The elderly parents toasted their only daughter at the party {because/.}

Jill {** toasted ** ϕ} had finally passed the exams at the prestigious university.

{ϕ ** toasted **}

The probe-recognition times appear in table 8.13. The results indicate that early in the processing of the second clause (at the "Early Probe" position), the connective

Table 8.13

Mean probe recognition times (ms) for initial-clause verb depending on probe position in second clause

Condition	Probe location	
	Early	Late
No connective	925	1160
Connective	1010	1100

Source: Adapted from Millis and Just 1994, fig. 3

because actually increases probe recognition times for the initial clause verb. At the end of the second clause, however, the connective reduces probe recognition times for the initial clause verb. Since the connective reduced probe recognition times only at the end of the second clause, Millis and Just conclude that information from the first clause is reactivated primarily at the end of the second clause. This result suggests that two clause sentences are processed differently than independent sentences. At the end of a two-clause sentence, the comprehension system regenerates the entire sentence for the purpose of checking the syntax and integrating sentence information into a conceptual representation. The presence of a connective facilitates this process. It is worth noting, however, that the connective *because* does have an immediate effect on processing, since it increased probe recognition times at the early probe position.

The integration of *because* sentences depends on clause order. Sentences with the clauses ordered as main-*because* are harder to integrate than sentences with the *because*-main order. This exception actually follows from a discourse-level statistical strategy: the canonical order of events in a story is cause-effect (e.g., van Dijk 1977; Townsend 1983; Trabasso and Sperry 1985; Trabasso, Secco, and van den Broek 1984; Trabasso and van den Broek 1985). If the discourse-processing system applies a cause-effect template as the default, the results of Millis and Just at both probe positions follow naturally. The connective *because* at the beginning of the second clause signals immediately that the default ordering of events is not fulfilled, and reorganization at the discourse level can proceed as the second clause is being read. We address clause-order effects in section 8.3.5. (A second exception to the generalization that *because* facilitates integration is that "diagnostic" statements with *because* are difficult; see Traxler, Bybee, and Pickering 1997.)

8.3.3 Adversative Connectives: The Discourse Level and Analysis by Synthesis

In Joseph Heller's novel *Catch-22* (1996:187), one of the characters yells out, "I see everything twice!" The comprehension system is similar: it accesses form twice, and it also accesses meaning twice. The surface form is stored in a memory buffer and the comprehension system accesses function morphemes (part of pseudosyntax) to organize words into major phrase groups. The surface form is also accessed at the point of checking the generated syntax against the memory-buffer representation of the surface form. Similarly, meaning is accessed when common sentence patterns activate an initial meaning-form hypothesis, and again when sentence meaning is integrated into a conceptual representation. Thus, in the normal course of comprehension, there will be alternations in accessibility to syntactic and semantic information. As Wundt put it (Blumenthal 1970; chapter 2), attention oscillates between the outside world (surface form) and the inside world (meaning).

In general, the structural models of comprehension describe the problem as mapping a surface representation onto a conceptual representation. In a left-right parsing model, the input is serially assigned a syntactic structure that either immediately, or with a delay, feeds semantic analysis. By the end of each unit, the comprehension system recodes the surface form into one or more potential syntactic structures and conceptual realizations (Caplan 1972; Chang 1980; Jarvella 1971; Just and Carpenter 1980; Haberlandt and Graesser 1985; Rodriguez, Ravelo, and Townsend 1980; Sachs 1967). Similarly, associative and spreading activation models seek to assign a complete structure at all levels at each point in the surface sequence. Thus, on all the models we reviewed in chapter 4, the default is that the surface-sequence representation is either erased or at least is no longer relevant as processing goes on.

Yet, buffers exist. For various reasons, particular models may assume that the input string is maintained for a fixed number of words. Usually, the goal of this is to allow for backtracking and reanalysis when parsing errors occur on the first pass through the string or to avoid parsing errors in the first place (see chapter 4). But no model except LAST is required by definition to maintain a complete representation of the surface string, at least for every major derivational unit—for example, the clause. LAST requires maintenance of the input surface string to verify that the candidate syntactic analysis produced by the synthetic component actually matches the surface string. This raises the following question: Is there evidence that comprehension activities take advantage of the availability of a complete surface representation of major syntactic units? If so, this tends to support LAST—other models could include such a complete buffer, but the only reason to do so would be to accommodate that evidence.

In some circumstances, it may be necessary to retain access to the surface form, and LAST affords a natural mechanism for doing this. A case in point is

(50) a. It's not that John doesn't like sandwiches ...

This is a complete sentence syntactically, but it is not complete pragmatically. Full conceptual interpretation requires completion of a contrast. The sentence may be continued as

(50) b. ... it's just that *Mary* doesn't like them.   *[handwritten: contrastive]*
     c. ... he just can't *eat* them on his diet.   *[handwritten: form — you have to pay]*
     d. ... he just doesn't like *white bread.*   *[handwritten: attend to intonation]*

These continuations demonstrate that almost any word in the sentence may serve as the basis for the contrast. Thus, the comprehension system needs some means of preventing information from being dumped out of short-term memory, even though the syntax is correct.

Another case in point is adversative conjunctions such as *although* (see Blakemore 1989; Dakin 1970; Halliday and Hasan 1976; Noordman and Vonk 1997; Quirk et al. 1972; Segal and Duchan 1997; Townsend 1983; Vonk and Noordman 1990). In

(51) a. Although Sally called up her aunt each night ...

the sentence can be continued to establish a contrast with the subject

(51) b. ... *Sam* never calls

with the verb

(51) c. ... she never *writes* to her aunt

or with the object

(51) d. ... she never calls her *grandmother.*

The use of *although* indicates that, while the information in the subordinate clause should be stored in memory as an event that did occur, the occurrence of this event did not cause the event that one would have expected. To integrate the meaning of an *although*-sentence into a coherent representation of text, the comprehender must determine what causal relation was expected but did not occur. The following sentences express the apparent causal relation (or diagnostic relation; see Traxler et al. 1997) that was expected for each of the three continuations above:

(52) Because Sally calls her aunt each night, Sam does the same.

(53) Because Sally calls her aunt each night, she writes to her as well.

(54) Because Sally calls her aunt each night, she calls her grandmother as well.

Thus, *although* is a cue that the pragmatic interpretation of a clause may depend on additional information. *Although* signals the comprehension system to use information from outside the clause to arrive at a pragmatic interpretation of the *although*-clause.

These facts show that the conceptual interpretation of an *although*-clause requires information from outside the clause. An *although*-clause generally cannot be conceptually integrated immediately. The conceptual interpretation of the information within the *although*-clause depends on which aspect of the clause is the source of the adversative relationship. Thus, the surface form must be maintained for the purpose of conceptual integration. Therefore, attention will be directed more to the lexical/syntactic level than to the semantic/conceptual level. On the other hand, since the conceptual integration of a *because* clause does not depend on information outside of it, it can be integrated as soon as there is an initial meaning hypothesis. Thus, we expect that conceptual integration will occur as rapidly as possible, and therefore attention will be focused on a more semantic/conceptual level while processing a *because*-clause.

Townsend and Bever (1978) obtained support for the view that adversative conjunctions shift attention toward a superficial level of linguistic representation. They presented two different probe tasks near the ends of spoken clauses that were introduced by one of several connectives. One probe task depended on structural information, while the other depended on semantic associations. The materials included the following examples using *if*, *though*, or main clauses without a connective and similar materials using the relatively neutral *when*:

(55) If, *early target, word probe*
     If Pete calls up his aunt each ... UP

(56) If, *late target, word probe*
     If Pete calls his aunt up each ... UP

(57) If, *associative-meaning probe*
     If Pete calls up his aunt each ... USING THE PHONE

(58) Though, *early target, word probe*
     Though Pete calls up his aunt each ... UP

(59) Though, *late target, word probe*
     Though Pete calls his aunt up each ... UP

(60) Though, *associative-meaning probe*
     Though Pete calls up his aunt each ... USING THE PHONE.

(61) *Main, early target, word probe*
     Pete calls up his aunt each ... UP

(62) *Main, late target, word probe*
     Pete calls his aunt up each ... UP

(63) *Main, associative-meaning probe*
     Pete calls up his aunt each ... USING THE PHONE

In all cases, the speech stopped immediately after *each* (i.e., before the end of the surface structure clause) and the probe item appeared visually. For the word-probe examples, subjects said whether *up* had appeared in the sentence fragment. This task

Table 8.14
Relative accessibility to surface form and meaning in the online processing of initial subordinate clauses

Connective	Task	
	Surface form[a]	Meaning[b]
if	−159	+136
when	−67	−19
though	+399	−340

a. Word probe response time for late targets—word probe response time for early targets in subordinate clause relative to main clause
b. Meaning probe response time for subordinate clause—meaning probe response time for main clause
Source: Adapted from Townsend 1983, fig. 1

requires attention to the words of the clause. Since the target *up* appears in different positions within the clause in the early and late target conditions, any difference in response times for the early versus late targets will indicate relative attention to the location of words within clauses. For the associative-meaning probe, subjects said whether *using the phone* is associated with any part of the sentence fragment. This task requires attention to information that is associated with words and phrases in the clause. In this case, *using the phone* and *calls up* are associated.

The results appear in table 8.14. The entries in the first column of table 8.14 are response times for late targets minus response times for early targets, relative to target position differences in main clauses. Response time differences between early and late targets were greater for *though*-clauses than for *if*-clauses. This result suggested that *though* directs attention to the surface order of words which results in a left-to-right serial search for the target word. However, on the associative-meaning probe, shown in the second column of table 8.14, response times were relatively faster for *if* than for *though*. These results show that *if* directs resources toward associative information. This pattern of results was replicated by Townsend (1983) using other tasks, by Townsend, Carrithers, and Bever (1987) using auditory probes, and by Lehman (1990; Townsend 1997) using visual materials.

Townsend, Hoover, and Bever (2000) confirmed that connectives influence how comprehenders allocate attention between levels of representation during sentence comprehension. Subjects first read a cue word or phrase, and then listened to sentences like those below.

(64) *Synonym target*, if
YOUNG PEOPLE: If Harry keeps snakes on the farm kids visit every day.

Table 8.15
Mean response times (ms) depending on conjunction and monitoring task

Conjunction	Monitoring task	
	Synonym	Nonsense
if	624	391
when	726	347
though	765	342

Source: Adapted from Townsend, Hoover, and Bever, forthcoming

(65) *Synonym target*, though
   YOUNG PEOPLE: Though Harry keeps snakes on the farm kids visit every day.

(66) *Nonsense syllable target*, if
   KIG: If Harry keeps snakes on the farm kig visit every day.

(67) *Nonsense syllable target*, though
   KIG: Though Harry keeps snakes on the farm kig visit every day.

The subjects' task was to monitor for either a synonym or a nonsense syllable. If the subjects received *young people* as a cue, they were to monitor for a word that was associated semantically with this phrase. If they received a nonsense syllable like *kig* as a cue, they were to monitor for a syllable that matched it. The results appear in table 8.15.

Response times for semantic associates were faster for *if* than for *though*. This result suggested that the availability of a causal chain, signaled by *if*, directs attention more to semantic associations. Response times for nonsense words, however, were faster for *though* than for *if*. This result suggested that the demand for determining the expected causal relation that is required by *though* directs attention to structural units (syllables). Since these differences between connectives occur in online monitoring tasks, they appear to depend on how comprehenders allocate attention resources during comprehension.

The series of studies on connectives fits naturally with LAST, which posits a late reaccess of both superficial form and conceptual information. Connectives that differ in their requirements for integration into a conceptual representation influence the focus of attention on form versus conceptual information. In this view, responses to *though*-clauses occur at the point of syntax checking, making superficial form including word order and syllables highly accessible. Responses to *if*-clauses occur at the point of conceptual integration. The studies reported in the next three sections elaborate on this conclusion.

8.3.4 Syntax Checking: Discourse-Level Effects

Townsend and Bever (1982; see section 8.3.1 of the present book) used the word-naming task from Tyler and Marslen-Wilson 1977 to examine how conjunctions affect accessibility to syntactic information. Subjects heard initial clause fragments that contained unambiguous phrases, such as

(68) *Initial* if
    a. If polishing glasses ... [gerund]
    b. If glittering glasses ... [adjectival]

(69) *Initial main*
    a. Polishing glasses ...
    b. Glittering glasses ...

(70) *Initial* though
    a. Though polishing glasses ...
    b. Though glittering glasses ...

Immediately after hearing *glasses*, subjects saw a single word such as *is* or *are*. Their task was to name the word as quickly as possible.

Polishing is transitive and *glittering* is intransitive. Hence, *polishing glasses* is a gerund structure with *glasses* as theme, and *glittering glasses* is an adjectival structure with *glasses* as the noun that it modifies. A gerund structure requires a main verb that is singular, as in

(71) Polishing glasses is tedious work.

If the main verb is plural, the sequence is ungrammatical. On the other hand, an adjectival structure requires a main verb that agrees with the head noun, in this case the plural *glasses*, as in

(72) Glittering glasses are sometimes found in chandeliers.

If the main verb for an adjectival phrase like *glittering glasses* is singular, the sequence is ungrammatical. Response times to name a singular versus plural verb indicate how closely comprehenders have processed the syntactic information at the time the target word appears.

Several factors in these materials operate to influence responses on the word-naming task. First, differences in processing of transitive and intransitive verbs involve filling the argument requirements of verbs, such as whether the verb requires a patient, as with transitive verbs such as *polishing*, or an agent experiencer, as with intransitive verbs such as *glittering*, as we noted in earlier chapters. If comprehenders utilize such information immediately to generate a syntactic structure, they should respond faster to congruent target words than to incongruent target words. Second, application of the NVN template locally will produce faster response times for plural target words,

Table 8.16
Effect of congruity of target word with structure bias: naming times for incongruent targets—naming times for congruent targets (in ms)

Connective	Structure	
	Singular	Plural
if	120	124
main	3	82
though	20	−18

Source: Adapted from Townsend and Bever 1982, fig. 1

which agree with the local noun (*glasses*). Third, connectives will influence attention to semantic information. Since initial *if* best fits the cause-effect template at the discourse level, a syntactic structure based on the argument requirements of verb will be generated quickly. Since *though* fits the cause-effect template worst and depends on extraclausal information, syntax generation will be delayed. Since a main clause provides no specific cues to discourse-level information, the more canonical sentence templates will apply, producing faster response times for plural bias.

The results appear in table 8.16. There was a large structural bias effect for both gerund and adjectival structures for *if*, no bias effect for either structure for *though*, and a large bias effect only for adjectival structures for main clauses. The results for *if* suggest that it shifts attention toward meaning. In LAST, activating the meaning of a verb such as *glittering* also activates the information that it is intransitive and requires an agent experiencer, and therefore must be a modifier of *glasses*. The results for *though* suggest that it shifts attention away from meaning, and hence, there is no effect of syntactic information.

The results for main clauses suggest that listeners apply the NVN template locally, to the noun and the verb. Subject nouns and verbs must agree in number (Bock and Miller 1991). Since the noun *glasses* is plural, it should take a plural verb. The NVN template appears to apply equally to adjectival and gerund structures. However, the fact that there was no target number effect for gerund structures suggests that the gerund requirement for a singular verb cancels the effect of the locally applied NVN template, which would require a plural verb for the plural noun. That is, the NVN template conflicts with the local-agreement strategy, producing no effect of gerund structures.

8.3.5 Syntax Checking: Clause-Order Effects
In general, memory is better when the clauses in a two-clause sentence are ordered as main-subordinate (Clark and Clark 1968; Flores d'Arcais 1978; Irwin and Pulver 1984; Jou and Harris 1990; Townsend 1983) and this order is preferred in production

as well (McCabe and Peterson 1988). In comprehension and memory, there are a number of reversals of results depending on the order of main and subordinate clauses (Clark and Clark 1968; Townsend and Bever 1978; Bever and Townsend 1979; Shedletsky 1975; Townsend 1983; Townsend, Ottaviano, and Bever 1979; Townsend and Ravelo 1980). The general finding is a variable that interacts with clause type in a particular way in the initial clause of a sentence but interacts in the *opposite* way in the final clause of the sentence. Reversals depending on clause order occur as a function of both the semantic role of the clause and the structural role. Reversals that depend on the structural role of a clause suggest that the entire two-clause sentence is a relevant unit in an analysis-by-synthesis cycle.

Consider, for example, the results we reviewed above (section 8.3.3) showing that information in *though*-clauses is accessed more readily in a surface form, while in *if*-clauses it is accessed more readily at a conceptual level. Those results were for initial clauses only. In the same study Townsend and Bever (1978) administered word-probe recognition and associative-meaning probe tasks for final clauses, as in:

(73) *Main first,* though *second, early target*
      There is little danger of a major depression though good jobs are now quite scarce in most large ... NOW

(74) *Main first,* though *second, late target*
      There is little danger of a major depression though good jobs are quite scarce now in most large ... NOW

(75) Though *first, main second, early target*
      Though there is little danger of a major depression good jobs are now quite scarce in most large ... NOW

(76) Though *first, main second, late target*
      Though there is little danger of a major depression good jobs are quite scarce now in most large ... NOW

The auditory presentation of the sentence was stopped just before the last word of the sentence, and the word probe *now* was presented. Similar materials were used for the associative-meaning probe task. The response-time results depending on the conjunction that introduces the final clause appear in table 8.17.

For both tasks, the pattern of results for final clauses was very nearly the opposite of the results for initial clauses (see table 8.15). Table 8.17 contrasts the relative accessibility to serial position of words in subordinate clauses, relative to main clauses, and the relative accessibility to associative meaning, relative to main clauses. The most notable exception to a mirror-image reversal between *if* and *though* for initial versus final clause probes is that the large surface form effect for initial *though* (399 ms; table 8.15) is much smaller for final *if* (86 ms; table 8.17). This result suggests that

Table 8.17
Relative accessibility to surface form and meaning in the online processing of final subordinate clauses

Connective	Task	
	Surface form[a]	Meaning[b]
if	+86	−295
when	−125	−117
though	−267	−21

a. Word probe response time for late targets—word probe response time for early targets in subordinate clause relative to main clause
b. Meaning probe response time for subordinate clause—meaning probe response time for main clause
Source: Adapted from Townsend and Bever 1978

increased access to surface form does not occur because the clauses are presented out of the normal cause-effect order in a main-*if* sentence, but rather, it occurs because an *if*-clause, unlike a *though*-clause, does not require information from outside the clause.

Following our earlier interpretation, the reversed results suggest that in final clause position, *though*-clauses actually are accessed at a conceptual level, while *if*-clauses are accessed more serially. We (Townsend and Bever 1978) interpreted the reversal for *though* as follows: In a final *though*-clause, a conceptual analysis provided by the initial assignment mechanisms can immediately identify the adversative component because the entire main event has been recoded into conceptual terms. A more literal analysis of *if*-clauses is required because a final *if*-clause is out of canonical cause-effect order, and the entire two-clause sentence has to be put back into a correct sequence, thereby emphasizing serial order in general.

We also (Townsend and Bever 1978) reported a reversal in the results for the word-probe task depending on the structural role (main versus subordinate) of the clause. In this case, we used the connective *when*, which is neutral as to causal and temporal order. The results appear in table 8.18.

The results showed that response times were significantly longer for late targets than for early targets in initial subordinate clauses, and also in final main clauses (see table 8.18). These results suggested a serial, left-to-right search in these types of clauses. In terms of LAST, these clauses are searched for the word target at the syntax-checking stage, when superficial form is reaccessed. According to the model, clauses that do not show evidence of serial left-to-right search are at the point of conceptual integration, when superficial form is no longer readily accessible. These results follow from the assumption that initial main clauses and final subordinate

Table 8.18
Response times (ms) on word probe task depending on clause type, clause position, and target position

Clause type	Initial clause			Final clause		
	Early	Late	L − E	Early	Late	L − E
Main	1098	1125	27	1117	1207	90
Subordinate	1085	1181	96	1157	1057	−100

Source: Adapted from Townsend and Bever 1978

clauses are readily integrated into a conceptual representation. Initial subordinate and final main clauses require further processing to integrate them with the other clause in the sentence.

Bever and Townsend (1979) reported a similar reversal in word-probe results depending on the number of syllables in the clause. Their experimental logic relied on the argument that an increasing relationship between set size and probe recognition time is evidence for a serial exhaustive scan of memory (e.g., Sternberg, 1966). Subjects heard two-clause sentences such as

(77) *Initial main, short*
The cat killed the parrot when Sam left the house for a week ... KILLED

(78) *Initial main, long*
The young sailor dropped the anchor when nobody had spotted any whales ... DROPPED

(79) *Initial subordinate, short*
When the cat killed the parrot Sam left the house for a week ... KILLED

(80) *Initial subordinate, long*
When the young sailor dropped the anchor nobody had spotted any whales ... DROPPED

Short clauses contained six or seven syllables, while long clauses contained eight or nine syllables. The results appear in table 8.19.

Response times were longer for long clauses than for short clauses. Length of clause had a larger effect in initial subordinate clauses and in final main clauses, compared to the other two conditions.

This series of studies on clause-order effects shows that the representation that is searched in a word-probe task is a more superficial representation when the target is located in a clause that does not appear in the canonical structural or semantic order. Since an initial subordinate clause, particularly one that denies the normal cause-effect organization of discourse, is dependent on the main clause, the syntax is checked

Table 8.19
Response times (ms) on word probe task depending on clause type, clause position, and clause length

Clause type	Initial clause			Final clause		
	Short	Long	L − S	Short	Long	L − S
Main	1342	1352	10	1243	1336	93
Subordinate	1374	1406	32	1274	1276	2

Source: Adapted from Bever and Townsend 1979, table 6.10

somewhat later than for sentences with an initial main clause. This late checking makes the superficial representation more accessible, producing target position effects and length effects.

8.3.6 Discourse, Connectives, and Conceptual Integration

After syntax checking for complete units, final conceptual integration with context is possible. Conceptual integration may clearly vary in complexity depending on the nature of the context (e.g., Haberlandt 1982). Townsend (1983) examined the interactions of connectives and a context sentence in conceptual integration. Subjects read a two-sentence story and created a sentence to continue the story. The first sentence had one clause and the second had two clauses, one of which was introduced by *although* or *because*. The sentences appeared in either main-first or subordinate-first order. The first sentence paraphrased either the main clause or the subordinate clause of the second sentence. Some sample materials for *although*-sentences are:

(81) *Paraphrase of* although-*clause*
   a. Harry takes care of reptiles in his house.
   b. Although he raises snakes, kids often visit Harry.

(82) *Paraphrase of main clause*
   a. Children are always hanging around Harry's place.
   b. Although he raises snakes, kids often visit Harry.

Some sample materials for *because*-clauses are:

(83) *Paraphrase of* because-*clause*
   a. Harry takes care of reptiles in his house.
   b. Because he raises snakes, kids often visit Harry.

(84) *Paraphrase of main clause*
   a. Children are always hanging around Harry's place.
   b. Because he raises snakes, kids often visit Harry.

Table 8.20
Mean continuation times (sec) depending on conjunction and paraphrased clause

Connective	Clause paraphrase	
	Subordinate	Main
because	9.1	9.7
although	9.3	6.3

Source: Adapted from Townsend 1983, fig. 7

As we have noted, sentences with *although* deny an expected causal relation. A pragmatic interpretation of an *although*-sentence requires determining what causal relation the speaker or writer had expected. This can be done by drawing an inference from the main clause of the sentence, or from context. Thus, discourses that paraphrase the main clause ought to make it easier to integrate an *although*-sentence conceptually. Townsend (1983) tested this hypothesis by measuring the time that subjects took to create a sentence that plausibly continued to discourse. The average continuation times appear in table 8.20.

Paraphrases of the main clause significantly reduced continuation times only for *although*-sentences (by 1.0 sec). The main clause of an *although*-sentence provides information that can be used to determine the expected causal relation that is being denied by *although*. The fact that paraphrases of the main clause reduced continuation times for *although*-sentences confirms that *although*-clauses are interpreted in terms of information outside of the clause, and, in this case, in terms of information outside of the sentence. When the information contained in the main clause is available at the time of reading an *although*-sentence, conceptual integration is facilitated.

We (Townsend and Bever 1989) found similar results with script-based contexts. Townsend and Bever used the materials described earlier (sections 8.22 and 8.23):

(85) *High support*
    Johnny woke up very hungry for breakfast. He found a bowl and a spoon in the kitchen. He got a pitcher of milk from the refrigerator. Although he took down some ... GETTING THE CEREAL

(86) *Low support*
    Johnny was watching his favorite programs on TV. He started to get hungry for a snack. He waited for a commercial to go into the kitchen. Although he took down some ... GETTING THE CEREAL

Subjects listened to the story until they heard a short tone after the word *some*. Three hundred ms later, a two- to four-word phrase (*getting the cereal*) appeared on a screen. The subject's task was to say whether or not the phrase was similar in mean-

Table 8.21
Mean probe recognition times (sec) depending on conjunction and contextual support

| | Connective | |
Context	because	although
Low support	2.31	2.39
High support	2.30	2.22
Facilitation	.01	.17

Source: Townsend and Bever 1989, table 2, Skilled Readers

ing to any part of the last sentence. Response times on this meaning-probe task appear in table 8.21. Supportive contexts significantly reduced response time only for *although* (by 170 ms) not for *because* (the facilitation effect for *because* was 10 ms).

These results show that a supportive context increases attention to meaning near the end of an *although*-clause. *Because*-sentences can be directly integrated conceptually as the phrases and corresponding meaning become available. But for their pragmatic interpretation, *although*-sentences require knowledge of what causal relation the speaker is denying. Since the stories in this study were based on a stereotypical sequence of events (i.e., script; see section 8.2.2), the subjects have this knowledge before hearing the story. Comprehenders can use this knowledge for conceptual integration of an *although*-clause as they hear it. Together with the results of Townsend 1983, these results suggest that discourse context influences the integration of sentence meaning into a coherent representation of discourse.

8.4   Conclusion: Representations, Discourses, and Modules

This chapter reviewed the role of different kinds of representations that flicker on and off during comprehension. One fundamental point is that LAST offers a way to explain both data that support apparent syntactic processing modularity, and data that support ongoing conceptual integration effects. The synthetic aspect of comprehension has some characteristics of modularity, but the initial meaning hypothesis is based on nonmodular processes.

We are now in a position to answer the question we posed earlier: Do higher-level discourse processes take advantage of the architecture of the sentence-comprehension system by utilizing the persistence of both meaning and surface representations? Many researchers have found evidence for the immediate postclause salience of meaning as we have with connectives like *because*. Studies of the processing of sentences with *although* suggest that the comprehension processes also maintain and use surface representations for developing discourse-level representations. These surface representations persist as a natural outcome of the requirement that syntax checking occurs after the synthesis of the surface form. The ease of access to phonological representations, the persistence of representations of superficial word order and lexical items, and clause-length effects on word-probe recognition that connectives such as *although* stimulate all demonstrate the availability of surface information. The availability of surface information has functions both in the normal course of sentence comprehension and in developing higher-level discourse representations. It is an intrinsic feature of LAST that two pairings of meaning and surface representations are retained and accessed during comprehension.

We must interpret the data we reviewed in this chapter cautiously. Both structure-first and constraint-based models can accommodate the facts regarding the maintenance of different types of representations. For example, we could add to these models a buffer that maintains superficial representations. While such a change could account for the data, it is an ad hoc change that does not follow from the basic assumptions of the model. The persistence of surface representations, however, is an intrinsic part of LAST.

Chapter 9 Next h̃c
Relation to Other Systems of
Language Use

Strictly speaking, this book is about a model of language comprehension, focusing on the integration of structural and statistical knowledge about language. But language is acquired and is processed in the brain. Thus, it is important to delineate at least a general perspective on acquisition and neurological representation that is consistent with our comprehension model. In doing this, we can also explore the extent to which our analysis of related language behaviors supports our comprehension model. Accordingly, what follows are sketches of possible models of acquisition and neurology. We do not intend them to be complete descriptions, but rather theoretically focused considerations that relate to LAST. In passing, we will mention some current tissues, but the fundamental goal is to show how the comprehension model could be integrated with other aspects of language, and to show that those other aspects of language exhibit properties consistent with the architecture of the comprehension model.

9.1 Acquisition and Comprehension

Comprehension theories that utilize statistical properties can tout themselves as simultaneous theories of acquisition: as the child builds up statistical pattern templates, she or he is thereby "learning" what there is to learn about the language. Comprehension theories that deal only with structural properties of language characteristically rationalize that approach within the framework of nativism. The child has access to a separately represented set of the essential structural aspects of language. In this view, learning a language is learning how those universals are expressed in the particular speech it experiences.

These two approaches to acquisition taken individually have virtues and failings corresponding to their implementations as comprehension models, reviewed in chapter 4. Statistical approaches to language acquisition in the end must partially presuppose certain kinds of structural dimensions along which linguistic abilities are defined and extended. The concepts in categorical knowledge cannot be causally created by frequency information, only confirmed or disconfirmed (Fodor and McLaughlin 1995). Inductive reinforcement of particular patterns requires a representational system that describes and isolates the patterns (Chomsky 1959). Conversely, it is theoretically perverse and probably impossible to assume that speech data confirm or disconfirm particular structural hypotheses without access to frequency information about particular kinds of structures. Just as the adult comprehender depends on both kinds of information, so should the language-learning child. The result of the learning process must also lay down a neurological organization that reflects the learning process and underlies the application of what is learned to adult behavior.

Many aspects of linguistic structure are not evident in actual utterances. This motivates the assumption that a great deal of language learning builds on innate substrates, with specific formal and substantive content. In one sense, every kind of cognitive theory must assume that the ability to master language is innate to humans, since we all do it. The critical questions have to do with the structure of what is innate and how much can be extracted from the linguistic environment without language-specific learning mechanisms. This dual question corresponds to the comprehension problem of how to integrate structural knowledge with probabilistic habits.

How might the child compute linguistically relevant structures from its linguistic environment? Recent research has been devoted to studying this in two ways. One approach is to examine the young child's ability to extract and generalize language-like patterns from regular input. A number of recent studies has shown that even an infant has prodigious pattern-extraction skills for learning structured sequences. The other approach is to examine the information in motherese, the kind of language caretakers address to children. It is becoming clear that a great deal of linguistic structure is regularly reflected in the distributional patterns of motherese.

The right kind of statistical analysis can isolate and differentiate a wide range of structural categories of information. This suggests that we might use the approach developed in our comprehension model to good effect in a model of acquisition. Our comprehension model suggests that sentence comprehension proceeds in several stages:

1. Build a likely semantic structure based on valid cues
2. Check the structure by recapitulating it syntactically, revising it as required by structural constraints

On the analogous acquisition model, at any given stage, the child builds linguistic representations with the kinds of structures it has mastered at that point; it then accumulates statistically valid canonical forms within that framework. Further analyses are coded as departures from that canonical form, mediated by structural linguistic analysis. That is,

1. Acquire a canonical pattern, based on general cognitive or perceptual principles (usually frequency, but not necessarily)
2. Acquire departures from the pattern, mediated by connections to increasingly complex grammatical levels of representation

This dialectical appeal to "theme and variation" as a mechanism of learning is not exactly a profound breakthrough. Rather, it offers a framework within which to segregate statistical compilations that children build up from representational constraints. In this way it serves as a demonstration that the architecture of the comprehension system itself may have its basis in more fundamental processes of language acquisition.

9.1.1 Statistical Learning at Different Levels of Structure
In this section, we summarize the implications of our approach for four kinds of linguistic representations that are shared across a wide range of grammatical theories: phonological constraints, lexical categories, phrase structure, and the mapping between conceptual and grammatical roles. In each case, we delineate the distinct role of statistical inference mechanisms and structural properties of language that they support and extend.

Phonological Constraints   The infant's first problem (logically) is to figure out where the words begin and end in fluent speech. A natural point of entry is the syllable, and Aslin, Saffran, and Newport (1998) demonstrated that infants pay attention to syllable sequences by measuring the time that infants spent looking at a speaker that emitted artificial words or nonwords. In one study, eight-month-old infants listened to a three-minute tape with a continuous sequence of artificially synthesized consonant-vowel syllables. The syllables were organized into four words of three syllables each: *pabiku*, *tibudo*, *golatu*, and *daropi*. Thus, a segment of the three-minute tape consisted of the sequence

pabikugolatudaropitibudodaropigolatu . . .

The only cue to the boundaries of words is the fact that any one of three other syllables may follow the last syllable of a word. For example, the last syllable of a word, such as /ku/ in *pabiku* may be followed by the initial syllables of the other three words /ti/, /go/, and /da/. On the other hand, a syllable within a word, such as /pa/ in *pabiku*, is always followed by the same syllable, /bi/. Thus, a syllable marks the end of a word if several other syllables may follow it.

Aslin et al. determined that infants are sensitive to transitional probability between syllables. After listening to the three-minute tape, infants heard a recording of one of

two artificial words, *pabiku* or *tibudo*, or one of two part-words consisting of the final
syllable of one word and the first two syllables of another, as in *todaro* or *pigola*. The
test tape began when the infant was gazing at the speaker, and it ended when the
infant's gaze left the speaker. Aslin et al. found that infants spent significantly more
time listening to the novel words than to the familiar words (7.36 vs. 6.78 sec). This
differential sensitivity at the least required that they compute the statistical likelihood
of syllable sequences, which is an initial step in recognizing repeated words.

Thus, the prelinguistic infant may be sensitive to transitional probabilities in
speech. But, of course, Aslin et al. did not demonstrate that the child discovered the
notion of syllable itself from the statistical patterns. Rather, they assume that the
child has the natural tendency to analyze the signal in terms of syllables. This kind of
assumption has been confirmed by other studies with newborns (Aslin, Saffran, and
Newport 1999; Aslin et al. 1996; Bertoncini et al. 1995; Bijeljack, Bertoncini, and
Mehler 1993; Moon, Bever, and Fifer 1992; Otake et al. 1993).

Lexical Categories   Suppose you knew where all the words begin and end in a language. The next (logical) step would be to discover their syntactic category. At first
this might seem an impossible task, since the number and variety of patterns of categories is quite large. However, it is possible to extract reasonably appropriate syntactic groupings of words, based strictly on similarities of local lexical environment.
Bever et al. (1995) developed a computational model that assigns words to lexical
categories. The model followed Mintz 1997 by analyzing the similarity of target
words depending on the immediately preceding and following words (see section
4.3.2). To apply the model to the child's linguistic environment, Bever and colleagues
used the preceding and following word only if they were among the 200 most frequent words in the CHILDES corpus of spontaneous adult speech to young children
(MacWhinney and Snow 1985). The analysis was restricted to speech directed to
infants under two years of age. For each word the program kept track of the frequencies with which all other words immediately preceded it and followed it. For
example, in *the truck is red* the precontext for *truck* is *the* and the postcontext is *is*.
For *the* the precontext is "beginning-of-utterance," and for *red* the postcontext is
"end-of-utterance."

The program mapped the word contexts onto multidimensional vectors that were
used to compute the similarity between words in terms of the degree of overlap in
their contexts. A hierarchical clustering analysis was applied to the similarity measures so that words that shared the same immediately preceding or following words
formed a category, while those that did not fell into different categories.

The program was reasonably good at assigning words to the linguistic categories
of noun and verb. Some sample groupings appear in table 9.1. The first two groups

Table 9.1
Groupings of words based on distributional evidence

N1:	ball barette boy button buttons cars cow dog finer hair horse house man mouse piece see-saw sheep train truck tunnel way wheel wheels home *finished *good *it *one *Patsy *right *too
N2:	airplane bag blocks box boys car donkey egg floor light slide top toys wagon *help *her *little *Mama *other *tape
V1:	close does fix get hit leave open pull push put putting take throw wind
V2:	are can could did do don't thank would *if
V3:	doing going know say see
V4:	gonna have like want
V5:	build make
V6:	I'll I'm give it's let that's there's they're we'll we're what's where's who's you're *I *and *how *who *why
M1:	awoh black come go he here hm huh is let's Lois look mmhm mmm more no now oh ok oops peekaboo Peter there they turn two uhhuh well what where white xxx yeah yes you
M2:	again around away back broken closed down goes off out up yet
M3:	in of on riding through
M4:	that this
M5:	all not
Singles:	a about another any at be big but can doesn't for got happened has just me my need one's over play recorder shall so some the them think those to very was we when with woof write your

Source: Adapted from Bever et al. 1995

(N1 and N2) clearly contain nouns, the next six (V1–V6) clearly contain verbs, and the next five (M1–M5) contain a miscellaneous set of words. The "Singles" were words assigned to different groups with only one member. These results show that there is important information to help language learners develop accurate groupings of words into lexical categories simply from distributional evidence.

In the case of major lexical categories, once a distributional analysis segregates words into groups, they can then be grounded by the priority of some aspects of their reference. Thus, nouns such as *pretense* and *silliness* can be given syntactic categorization as nouns by virtue of their codistributional properties with concrete nouns like *dog*. But even this apparently simple generalization requires several things:

1. Knowledge of the distinct syntactic categories—for example, verbs that take arguments, nouns that can be arguments

2. Knowledge that referentially concrete words are syntactically nouns

3. Knowledge that referentially concrete words should provide the base description for the category

4. A predilection to carry out "distributional analysis" on repeated sequential phenomena in its environment

Thus, the learner must not only know that there is a category, "noun," it must have some procedural information about what kinds of information to seek to determine what lexical category a given distributional group corresponds to.

It is tempting to conclude that Bever and colleagues (1995) refuted the nativistic claim that lexical categories are *innate*. However, they exemplified something importantly different: they have specified what particular kinds of knowledge and operations must be available to the language learner to account for the inductive extraction of a syntactically categorized lexicon. This is a useful step in making the nativistic claim more precise and testable. For example, various researchers (e.g., Aslin, Saffran, and Newport 1999; Saffran, Aslin, and Newport 1996; Saffran, Newport, and Aslin 1996; Gerken 1994, 1996) are developing evidence that infants have a predisposition to group speech stimuli according to their distribution. It remains to be seen how general this distributional sensitivity is. It may be initially focused on language input from adults, or it may be a general computational process. Furthermore, one cannot rule out in principle the possibility that the knowledge in points 1 to 4 above is acquired from other kinds of general operations on the input whose domain extends beyond language.

Phrase Structure   A similar division between structural expectation and learning procedure applies to higher-order grammatical structures. We noted in chapter 4 that phrase structure boundaries can be initially extrapolated from examination of lexical sequential regularities around utterance boundaries, themselves marked by falling intonation, breath intake, silence, and other extrinsic cues. Once the infant has built up lexical patterns that predict utterance boundaries, it can automatically generalize to phrase boundaries, because every utterance boundary is a phrase boundary (Juliano and Bever 1988). This results in a basic segmentation of lexical sequences into likely phrases. To embed such a scheme in a theory of phrase structure acquisition, at least the following would be required:

1. Knowledge of phrase structure as a hierarchy

2. Knowledge that each phrase has a head that defines its type

3. Knowledge of the categories of possible heads

4. A predisposition to isolate utterance boundaries

The knowledge of at least some of the categories might itself emerge from the scheme outlined above. Juliano and Bever (1988) suggested that young children might focus on discovering patterns that predict the ends of utterances because they mark turn-taking. That is, the child's goal might be to discover when it is its turn to make language-like behaviors. An offshoot of that social goal would be structural information of great use in acquiring sentence-internal syntax. Infants' sensitivity to function words and morphemes is the subject of intense research. The fact that young language-learning children characteristically omit function words has raised doubts about whether they are sensitive to them at all (Pinker 1984). However, various researchers have shown that infants are sensitive to function words in perception (Gerken 1996; Valian and Coulson 1988), and Gerken (1991) has suggested that they may omit them from early production because of the mechanisms of speech production. Syntactic structure includes more than categories and phrases. Many sentences have a characteristic pattern. For example, if we categorize the preceding sentence in terms of function (F) versus content (C) words along with simple phrase structure bracketing, it would be symbolized as:

((FC) (C (FCC)))

It is likely that English overall, and especially motherese, has a number of statistically characteristic subpatterns.

The acquisition of syntax would be assisted by sensitivity to such patterns, but we must first determine that infants are sensitive to such regularities. Gomez and Gerken (1999) used a head-turning methodology to show that infants are sensitive to patterns that are differentiated only by whether or not particular words are repeated. They trained infants on sequences made up of four nonsense syllables, in which the patterns were defined by a simple set of order restrictions on when particular syllables can be repeated. They then showed that the infants generalized to new sequences with new nonsense syllables if the new sequences followed the same kind of pattern restrictions as the training set. That is, the infants showed that they had learned the pattern of repeating syllables independent of the actual syllables in their experience. Like all the other statistical analyses we have discussed, this alone will not account for learning syntactic patterns. Here too the infant must have some kind of knowledge that such structures could be relevant to the discovery of both phrase structure and higher-order syntactic patterns. Most important, it is very impressive that infants can pick up patterns in the absence of any meaning. But it also highlights the importance of their knowing that in real language, isolating meanings is a critical goal, which, among other things, allows reinforcement of meaning-relevant patterns.

The Relation Between Conceptual and Syntactic Features Syntactic theorists of widely divergent views agree that the nature of the relation between form and meaning is an important aspect of linguistic theory. Within minimalist linguistics, language acquisition consists of learning which conceptual features have syntactic reflexes (Chomsky 1995; chapter 3).

Table 9.2
Percentages of occurrence of word-order types in Serbo-Croatian and Turkish speech

	Serbo-Croatian		Turkish	
	Children	Adults	Children	Adults
SVO	99	97	46	66
SOV	83	67	87	86
VSO	79	84	100	100

Source: Adapted from Slobin and Bever 1982, table 2

Languages appear to have canonical sentence forms for the expression of conceptual roles, and children learn them at an early age. Slobin and Bever (1982) examined children's interpretation of sentences between the ages of two and four. The children were learning one of four languages: English (strict word order, uninflected), Italian (weakly ordered, weakly inflected), Serbo-Croatian (weakly ordered, inflectional), and Turkish (minimally ordered, inflectional). Data from Bates 1976 showed that 82 percent of Italian-speaking parents' utterances were SVO, and 72 percent of children's utterances were SVO. Slobin and Bever's (1982) recordings of parent-child conversations in Serbo-Croatian and Turkish show that the most frequent word order in Serbo-Croatian is NVN (SVO) and in Turkish it is NNV (SOV), as shown in table 9.2.

Slobin and Bever (1982) then administered a task in which children had to act out with toy animals events such as *the squirrel scratches the dog*. All possible word orders were used: NVN, NNV, and VNN. Table 9.3 shows the percentage of choices of the first noun as agent in uninflected forms. The data are arranged according to eight groups of mean length of utterance.

The table shows a strong overall preference for interpreting the initial noun as agent. The tendency to interpret the initial noun in any order as agent is weaker in languages such as Turkish, which rely less on word order and more on morphological cues to agenthood. In general, the pattern of interpreting the initial noun as agent shows up most clearly in the canonical sentence form for the language. That is, the preference is strongest for the NVN order in English, Italian, and Serbo-Croatian, and it is strongest for the NNV order in Turkish. Thus, two-year-old English-learning children have a pattern of interpreting a noun that immediately precedes a verb as its agent and one that follows as its patient (Bever 1970a). Surely, by definition, the child's early acquisition of the canonical pattern of its language is a reflection of the statistically supported patterns it experiences. However, a strategy of this kind might seem to be dependent on general cognitive mechanisms (e.g., search first for an agent ...). So it is not until the child masters a set of systematic exceptions to

Table 9.3
Percentage of choices of first noun as agent

MLU	English			Italian			Serbo-Croatian			Turkish		
	NVN	NNV	VNN	NVN	NNV	VNN	NVN	NNV	VNN	NVN	NNV	VNN
1	50	58	46	64	61	43	53	50	68	54	17	35
2	60	56	33	61	49	50	80	57	68	64	74	65
3	81	32	40	95	56	53	75	67	63	58	62	51
4	90	40	43	90	47	70	73	67	57	53	42	52
5	80	44	40	81	43	71	80	55	72	67	73	53
6	92	46	61	93	43	56	77	47	57	65	70	50
7	80	51	42	90	29	20	58	67	58	53	82	60
8	92	56	56	79	52	58	72	67	72	52	67	44
Mean	78	48	45	82	48	53	71	60	64	58	61	51

Source: Adapted from Slobin and Bever 1982

such generalizations that we can be sure that it has mastered specific aspects of the mapping between conceptual features and the distributional patterns of its language. English passive construction is an exception to the canonical forms—it appears that the patient comes before the verb and the agent follows. However, there is a distributional distinction between "syntactic" and "lexical" passives. Lexical passives are past participle forms that distribute like adjectives, while syntactic passives do not (see chapters 3 and 5).

(1) *Lexical passives* (verbs can be adjectives)
   a. The ruined city . . .
   b. The abandoned city . . .

(2) *Syntactic passives* (verbs cannot be adjectives)
   a. *The attacked city . . .
   b. *The left city . . .

Most of the lexical passive verbs involve a state, as indicated by the fact that they can be used with the verb *remained*. Most of the syntactic passive verbs involve an act that has a point in time and involves the agent's activity only. Thus, in our program what we would look for first is evidence that motherese presents the child with agentless lexical passives—these maintain the generalization that the first noun is an agent or experiencer of the verb. Furthermore, it must be the case that such passive forms are the only ones that appear prenominally as adjectives. At the same time, we predict that full passives with agents in motherese will primarily be those with syntactic passive verbs.

Such predictions about the statistical properties of motherese remain to be examined. But, even if true, they could account for the acquisition of the distinction between different kinds of passives only if the child has available the following:

1. Knowledge of conceptual roles
2. Knowledge of verb-argument positions
3. Knowledge that conceptual features of verbs can determine the distribution of verb arguments
4. A predisposition to search for the distributional regularities of arguments

The isolation of arguments might emerge from some aspects of the phrase structure component (i.e., knowledge of the heads of phrases). Indeed, the other components might be accounted for by general cognitive properties interacting with cognitive and linguistic experience. We do not see how this would work, but that is the challenge for the distributional analysis—to show how general cognitive habits interact with distributional information to point the language-learning child in the right direction.

Is There a General Theory?   In each of the preceding cases, there is an interaction between the compilation of a frequent, canonical form, and the isolation of exceptions to it, expressed within the framework of another level of representation. Thus, the canonical syllable is divided into segmental units that express variation in a particular language; at the other extreme, the canonical sentence form provides the basis for acquisition of variations from it, expressed in terms of syntactic categories.

The preceding sketches outline how statistical information and structural categorizations of it may be built up during acquisition. We have suggested that an alternation between extending linguistic ability through reliance on statistically valid generalizations in motherese, and the compilation of new structural descriptions, provides a framework for a dynamic acquisition model for the integration of structural and statistically valid information. In this view, adult language skills are the residue of this acquisition sequence, which may explain how comprehension alternates between reliance on statistically valid patterns, and grammatical reconstruction of the surface forms.

9.1.2   The Acquisition of Sentence Templates
We now turn to the development of the primary syntactic-level sentence template in English, NV(N) = agent-action-(patient). As we noted, the child has access to a basic comprehension template at age two (Slobin and Bever 1982). This template allows for better-than-chance comprehension of nouns immediately preceding verbs as their agent. Thus, Bever (1970a) found that the two-year-old understands simple declara-

Table 9.4
Percentage of correct responses to active and passive sentences at different age levels

	Active	Passive	S-Cleft	O-Cleft
Girls				
2;0–2;7	64	60	94	63
2;8–3;3	66	23	71	71
3;4–3;7	66	32	89	43
3;8–3;11	80	56	95	44
4;0–4;3	90	42	90	74
4;4–4;7	96	60	90	73
4;8–5;7	97	93	82	78
Boys				
2;0–2;7	65	56	78	78
2;8–3;3	70	43	85	63
3;4–3;7	78	42	85	76
3;8–3;11	71	66	95	55
4;0–4;3	82	64	98	74
4;4–4;7	79	53	90	85
4;8–5;7	91	86	90	84

Source: Adapted from Bever 1970, figs. 6 and 7

tive sentences and subject-first cleft sentences better than chance, as measured by the task of acting out sentences with dolls (see table 9.4):

(3) a. The dog bit the cat.
    b. It was the dog that bit the cat.

At the same time, the child performs randomly on passives and on object-first cleft sentences:

(4) a. The cat was bitten by the dog.
    b. It was the cat that the dog bit.

Around age four, the child actually performs worse on the passive and object-first cleft sentences, while improving greatly on the subject-first clefts and simple declaratives. This is consistent with the view that the general NVN template itself develops as a function of experience with simple sentences. As the child accumulates experience with sentences, it can extract the more general fact that a noun at the beginning of an utterance is likely to be the agent, whether immediately preceding a verb or not. In critical cases, this can make it appear that the child is actually getting worse in comprehension, but those are the unusual cases to which the generalization does not apply (Maratsos 1974; de Villiers and de Villiers 1972). In general, the literature on the acquisition of comprehension of passives has focused on syntactic passives, which show the decrease in comprehension as predicted (Fox and Grodzinsky 1998; Maratsos 1974; Pinker, Lebeaux, and Frost 1987). But it remains to be shown that the comprehension of lexical passives actually *improves* at the same time.

Eventually, by age six, children understand all passive sentences fairly well. But exactly how they come to do that still remains to be understood.

The preceding approach to language acquisition requires that the child focuses at least in part on the level of the sentence, as opposed to acquiring information about individual words. This may seem counterintuitive, since knowledge of the words is critical to composing them into sentences. However, what is at issue is what the child attends to intuitively most strongly. To examine this, Bever (1975) asked subjects from age three to twenty to respond as quickly as possible to a particular three-word target sentence in a list of similar sentences. The subjects were either told the target was an entire sentence or was the first word of the sentence. Intuitively, one would think that being told the entire sentence target would always lead to faster recognition, but this was not so. Children between the ages of five and ten actually responded faster to targets given as the first word of the sentence, than to whole-sentence targets. This may correspond to the fact that during that age period, children are engaged in massive learning of new words, mostly content words. In contrast with this both young children and adults responded faster to whole-sentence targets. This suggests that young children who have mastered at least a working set of function words focus on sentence-level processes. Adults again return to this orientation, after having acquired a large vocabulary.

Our learning model predicts that the most common patterns are learned first, followed by learning of details and exceptions. Focusing on the NVN pattern should lead to rapid access to the semantic content of a sentence. Focusing on other components of the pseudosyntax should lead to rapid access to the words and their order within a sentence.

Townsend, Ottaviano, and Bever (1979) tested whether there are developmental differences in the level of representation on which listeners focus. They presented tape recordings of two-clause sentences with a main clause and a subordinate clause, as in:

(5) *Temporal, main verb first*
    The owl scratched the fox after he touched the monkey.

(6) *Temporal, main verb second*
    After the owl scratched the fox he touched the monkey.

(7) *Relative, main verb first*
    The owl scratched the fox that touched the monkey.

Table 9.5
Mean word probe recognition times (sec) to targets in main and subordinate clauses

	Main	Subordinate
3 years	2.40	2.78
4 years	2.08	1.78
5 years	1.69	1.31
Adult	1.20	1.12

Source: Adapted from Townsend, Ottaviano, and Bever 1979

(8) *Relative, main verb second*
   The owl that scratched the fox touched the monkey.

At the end of the sentence, the subjects heard a single word and had to say whether it had occurred in the sentence. In the critical positive trials, the target was either the main verb or the subordinate verb. The subjects were children aged three, four, and five years, and college students. If subjects adopt the strategy of focusing on the meaning of the main clause and the surface form of the subordinate clause, we would expect that response times would be faster for target words in subordinate clauses. The average response times to main versus subordinate verbs appear in table 9.5. Response times were faster for target words in subordinate clauses for all groups except for three-year-olds. This result suggests that older children and adults do focus on the pseudosyntactic level in subordinate clauses. By our assumption, the three-year-olds still focus on the pseudosyntactic details in main clauses.

There is, however, another interpretation: three-year-olds may restrict their processing to main clauses, on the grounds that the main clause conveys the more important information. If three-year-olds' processing resources are limited to the processing of one of the clauses, they may largely ignore the processing of subordinate clauses. Townsend and Ravelo (1980) tested this hypothesis with a picture-matching task (see box 9.1). Subjects heard a two-clause sentence, such as:

(9)   *Main first*
      a. The goat threw the ball after he pulled the wagon.
      b. The goat threw the ball before he pulled the wagon.

(10) *Subordinate first*
      a. After the goat threw the ball he pulled the wagon.
      b. Before the goat threw the ball he pulled the wagon.

The critical cases were those in which the event depicted in the picture matched the main-clause event or the subordinate-clause event. If listeners focus on meaning in main clauses, their response times will be faster for pictures about main clauses. The results appear in table 9.6.

Box 9.1
The sentence-picture matching task

In the sentence-picture matching task, subjects receive a sentence either visually or auditorilly. At the end of the sentence, a picture appears on a screen in front of the subject. The subject's task is to say or press a button to indicate whether the sentence is a true statement about the picture. The sentence-picture matching task has been used in a variety of studies that primarily have examined the processing of single-clause sentences (e.g., Chase and Clark 1972; Clark and Chase 1972; Slobin 1966).

In Townsend and Ravelo 1980, the subjects heard two-clause sentences, such as

The goat threw the ball after he pulled the wagon.

The sentences were presented through the right channel of headphones, and at the end of the last word, a 50-ms, 500-Hz tone was presented through the left channel. The tone started a millisecond time and triggered a shutter to present the picture on a screen. The picture was a cartoon drawing of animals engaging in various activities, such as a goat throwing a ball. The subject's instruction was to say whether the event shown in the picture was mentioned in the sentence. The subject's vocal response stopped the timer. Pictures for negative trials always showed one of the two actions mentioned in the sentence (e.g., either throwing or pulling), but either a different agent or a different patient. Townsend and Ravelo (1980) found that errors occurred on about one-third of the trials for three-year-old subjects. However, there was no significant correlation between errors and response times.

Table 9.6
Mean picture-matching times (sec) for events in main and subordinate clauses

	Main	Subordinate
3 years	4.11	4.25
4 years	3.41	3.41
5 years	3.46	3.54
Adult	1.19	1.24

Source: Adapted from Townsend and Ravelo 1980, table 2

Except for the four-year-old group, all age groups were numerically faster in responding to pictures about main clauses. While these differences were not statistically significant, the trends support the hypothesis that the older subjects focus on the semantic level in main clauses and on the pseudosyntactic level in subordinate clauses. They also suggest that the three-year-olds adopt the strategy of focusing on the meaning of the main clause, and, based on Townsend, Offaviano, and Bever 1979, on the pseudosyntactic details of the main clause as well. However, the youngest subject groups do not display the consistency of the older groups. The results suggest that the youngest children have learned the general principle that the main clause contains more important information, but that they are experimenting with alternative ways of processing sentences with two clauses. Other studies have demonstrated that preschool children process to some degree information in subordinate clauses (Mazuka 1998). For example, using children aged four to eight, Mazuka (1998) confirmed that children respond faster to the meaning of main clauses, but they tend to respond faster to lexical details of subordinate clauses.

At the same time children are learning the structural roles of clauses, they are also learning the semantic relationships between clauses. We can expect that children acquire common patterns at the discourse level as well, and these patterns may override structurally based strategies. A canonical discourse-level pattern is that events are described in the order in which they actually occurred—that is, first event followed by second event. To further examine the "theme-and-variation" principle in the allocation of attention to properties of the linguistic stimulus, Townsend and Ravelo (1980) systematically compared children's processing of sentences that express temporal relations between clauses.

(11) *Canonical discourse pattern*
    a. The goat threw the ball before he pulled the wagon.
    b. After the goat threw the ball he pulled the wagon.

(12) *Canonical discourse pattern*
    a. The goat threw the ball after he pulled the wagon.
    b. Before the goat threw the ball he pulled the wagon.

The average response times to first events versus second events appear in table 9.7.

For a picture that matched the initial-clause event, the three-year-olds and the adults responded significantly faster when it was the first event rather than the second event. But for a picture that matched the final-clause event, these groups responded faster when it was the second event rather than the first. Neither the four-year-olds nor the five-year-olds showed this pattern. At the least, this result shows that the three-year-old subjects represent at some level the order of events in sentences, and that this level influences their performance.

Table 9.7
Mean picture-matching times (sec) for first events and second events in initial and final clauses

	Initial clause		Final clause	
	First event	Second event	First event	Second event
3 years	3.72	4.65	4.43	3.96
4 years	3.52	3.49	3.45	3.18
5 years	3.31	3.52	3.53	3.64
Adult	1.17	1.25	1.30	1.15

Source: Adapted from Townsend and Ravelo 1980, table 3

Children adopt a mixture of strategies that vary in their influence at different ages. Townsend and Ravelo found that the four- and five-year-olds that did not respond faster to first events in initial clauses did respond significantly faster to main-clause events than to subordinate-clause events. Thus, children who are not organizing the events in a temporal order are attending more to structural properties of sentences.

The results of these studies therefore are consistent with the theme-and-variation model of learning: learn common patterns first, and learn details and exceptions later. Learning details and exceptions may persist for a period of time. Townsend, Carrithers, and Bever (1987) found that even children aged ten to thirteen years have not mastered the adult organization of structural and discourse-level processing strategies.

Online studies of comprehension in children provide supportive evidence that at first they do not integrate context and semantic information, but rely on local within-sentence structure. Trueswell et al. (1999) observed four- to five-year-old children's eye movements when following instructions like:

(13) *Ambiguous*
Put the frog on the napkin in the pot.

(14) *Unambiguous*
Put the frog that's on the napkin in the pot.

The paradigm is modeled on Tanenhaus et al. 1995, in which the dependent measure relies on the fact that the subject looks at the goal location that the object *frog* will be moved to. Adults show a clear effect of prior discourse, focusing more on the incorrect goal location (napkin) only when the discourse structure has one referent in it (i.e., one frog rather than two) and the sentence is ambiguous. But children look at the incorrect goal in ambiguous sentences regardless of the prior or referential context. In a later study, Trueswell and colleagues (Trueswell, Sekerina, and Logrip, forthcoming) show that children are sensitive to the local-verb constraints. For example, there are far fewer gazes at the incorrect goal when the verb does not require a goal:

Wiggle the frog on the napkin in the pot.

   To summarize this section, children acquire both structural and statistical pattern in their language. The emergence of evidence for templates such as NVN with age attests to their inductive nature. The emergence of evidence for structural features of language attests to some noninductive source. As the child becomes more facile with the language, she or he builds up both a structural and a strategic inventory.

   The child is parent to the adult: we have touched on recent approaches to language acquisition that reveal the emerging interaction between structural knowledge and statistical and referential properties of sentences. The data are broadly consistent with the following:

1. The child has an available set of structural representations at several levels, to apply to language. These can be termed *innate*, although that is not an explanation of their basis until it is cashed out in genetic or behavioral systems that underlie it.
2. The child uses initial representational systems to compute patterns of language that relate different levels of representation.
3. Frequency information is used on the patterns to isolate canonical sets that link different levels of representation. The canonical representations extend the scope of the initial systems.
4. The processes in 2 and 3 cycle to develop more elaborate and rich representational systems and statistically sensitive generalizations from them.

   It is a natural consequence of a model like this for the adult to have both a rich structural description of the language, and an accumulated set of statistically valid patterns. In this way, LAST can be built up gradually as the result of the process of acquisition.

9.2   Neurological Evidence for the Model

We cannot expect neurological investigations to provide direct evidence for (or against) functional architectures such as LAST. Neurological investigative tools today are largely limited to location of damage and timing of activities. While these tools are much too crude indicators to reveal particular computations, it is also true that our models often do not make clear predictions at finely grained levels of temporal analysis. However, certain kinds of facts can lend construct validity to the distinctions LAST makes, and in some cases at least bear on sequences of different kinds of computations. Indeed a number of emerging facts of the past few decades are consistent with LAST's architecture for comprehension. In particular, there is evidence that sentence templates are acquired as part of hemispheric lateralization. Furthermore, evidence for sentence templates as an early component of comprehension and for derivational syntactic structures can be seen in fast and slow event-related brain potentials, respectively. Finally, the loss of sentence templates may be the specific deficit in certain kinds of aphasia. We now turn to the evidence.

9.2.1   Hemisphere Asymmetries and Perceptual Strategies

One of the most stable claims about the neurological organization for language structure is that it is "in" the left hemisphere, generally in the temporal and parietal areas (see Kertesz 1999 for a review). This claim has been largely based on clinical data, showing that patients with lesions in those areas of the left hemisphere lose language ability more regularly and permanently than in other areas, or in the right hemisphere. More recently, brain-imaging techniques with normal populations have given general support for this picture, although they show more involvement in language behavior of the right hemisphere and of subneocortical structures than had been thought.

If sensitivity to sentence-level sequences is built up through experience, we might expect that the location of these sentence-level perceptual templates is also asymmetric, primarily in the left hemisphere, which more reliably represents linguistic structures. Bever (1970b) reported that the canonical pattern affects immediate memory for sentences more strongly in the right than the left ear. For example, if subjects must count backward by threes from a number presented right after the sentence, right-ear presentation elicits more sentence-recall errors and greater latency in noncanonical sentence forms:

(15) ~*Canonical, adverb*
      The boy quickly threw away the trash.

(16) *Canonical, adverb*
      Quickly the boy threw away the trash.

(17) ~*Canonical, passive*
      The boy was liked by the girl.

(18) *Canonical, active*
      The girl liked the boy.

This result suggests that the left hemisphere has more immediate access to the canonical NVN pattern. An alternative explanation is that backward counting interferes more with the left hemisphere than with the right, and that when the left hemisphere is occupied with backward counting, the right hemisphere can process either canonical or noncanonical patterns. Evidence from Faust and Chiarello (1998;

Chiarello, Liu, and Faust 1999), however, confirms that the right hemisphere attends much less to syntactic patterns than does the left.

Of course, traditionally, all linguistic functions are associated with the left hemisphere, so finding that the initial sentence templates are left-hemisphered may not implicate any special relationship between them and asymmetries. If we turn to the stages of acquisition, however, we see some evidence that asymmetries themselves emerge coincident with the emergence of the sentence templates. For example, Bever (1970b) used a measure of children's cerebral dominance for language. His measure was the extent to which they paid attention to animal names in one ear or the other (children had a number of small animals on inverted cups in front of them; the animals named on each trial had M&Ms under them). He found considerable variation in the extent to which two- to four-year-old children attended dominantly to the right ear. He then correlated individual children's use of the NVN template in comprehension with their ear preference. Two- to four-year-old children with a strong ear preference (usually for the right ear) showed a much greater reliance on the NVN template in their comprehension, than did children with a weak ear preference. This maturational (or individual) correlation suggested that there may be a unique relation between the early comprehension templates and cerebral asymmetry, in particular the dominance of the left hemisphere for language.

Friederici (1985) has recently developed this kind of theme. She noted that while adults can recognize function words faster than content words in sentences (see section 6.1.1), this pattern does not occur in children aged five to nine years. Only by age ten does the adult pattern appear. This is striking because children at age eight already have manifestly mastered the basic structure of their language. Friederici suggests that this may indicate that children at first use different kinds of strategies for comprehension; only after a great deal of experience do they have access to very rapid recognition of function words. We think her general interpretation is correct, but it is striking that the period when she finds that children recognize content words better than function words is also the period when Bever found that children access sentences best in terms of their initial (content) word. Friederici did not test children younger than five. We think it likely that such studies will show that those younger children are more like adults, in being able to access function words more quickly. Thus, we agree with Friederici that the initial syntactic pattern recognition strategies are learned with experience, but we think it likely that the essential ones are actually learned before age five.

9.2.2   Templates, Grammar, and Early vs. Late Components of ERPs
The adult and developmental correlation of templates with hemispheric specialization support the construct validity of strategies as functionally distinct components

of comprehension. The study of electrical activity of the brain has advanced steadily in the last decade. It is now possible to obtain reliable recordings relatively easily by attaching small sensors to various locations on the scalp. The location of the underlying source of the electrical activity, however, is still a subject of controversy. Nonetheless, evidence from event-related potentials (ERPs) can also support the construct validity of different components of a comprehension model. If different properties of the ERP are associated with particular components of processing, that lends support to the distinction between those components. More cautiously, we can interpret the temporal sequence of response within the ERP wave to reflect relative sequencing of the underlying processes. We must be tentative, however, because it is not clear that each component of ERP reflects a particular process occurring simultaneously with it, as opposed to following or preceding it. The appropriate analogy for understanding poststimulus ERPs may be like the ringing of a bell, which has different postring resonances as a function of where and how vigorously the clapper struck. Thus, it is entirely possible that late ERP components reflect early processes and conversely. With that caveat, however, the actual temporal sequence of certain ERP components appears to correlate with specific computational subprocesses of LAST, and with the order in which they occur in the model. (See table 9.8.)

To set the scene for this, we review the sequence of computational events in a typical comprehension sequence in LAST.

1. Assign initial segmentation into words of local phrases using function words
2. Perform obligatory movements of *wh*-phrases in situ
3. Assign initial hypothesized meaning, using sentence templates—for example, NVN
4. Access syntactically defined predicate subcategorization information
5. Regenerate syntactic derivation and check against input
6. Reanalyze if necessary

Table 9.8 summarizes the ERP evidence on these events that we will now review. The evidence in the table is consistent with the proposed sequence of events in comprehension.

Phrase Structure   The brain constantly yields electrical signals at the scalp. Thus, in principle, there could be a unique electrical pattern associated with every computational activity of the brain. However, it is difficult to associate particular patterns with particular computations at the least because the brain is doing so many different things at the same time. It is necessary to create a contrasting set of stimuli to reveal differences in ERPs associated with particular inputs. For example, Neville et al. (1991) contrasted the ERPs to *of* in the following sequences (in this section we italicize the word on which the ERP was observed):

Table 9.8
Summary of ERPs to various events in the LAST model

Event	ERP result	Study
Phrase structure	ELAN: N125	Neville et al. 1991
		Friederici, Pfiefer, and Hahne 1993
		Friederici, Hahne, and Mecklinger 1996
Wh-placement	LAN: 300–500 ms	Neville et al. 1991
		Kluender and Kutas 1993
NVN	LAN: 300–500 ms	King and Kutas 1995
	Positivity 300–500 ms	Mecklinger et al. 1995
Verb subcategories	LAN: 300–500 ms	Rösler et al. 1993
Grammar check	CEN 300–600 ms	Kutas and King 1996
		Friederici et al. 1996
		Osterhout and Mobley 1995
		Friedman et al. 1975
Reanalysis	P600: 500–1000 ms	Osterhout and Holcomb 1992
		Friederici 1997
		Friederici, Hahne, and von Cramon 1998
		Hagoort, Brown, and Groothusen 1993
		Neville et al. 1991
		McKinnon and Osterhout 1996

(19) a.   The man admired a sketch *of* the landscape.

   b.   *The man admired Don's *of* sketch the landscape.

They found a specific and rapid relative negativity in the front part of the left hemisphere at around 125 ms after presentation of the word *of* in the second sequence. (Perhaps a more appropriate comparison is between *The man admired Don's sketch of the landscape* and **The man admired Don's of sketch the landscape*.) They contrasted this effect with the effect of other kinds of sentence violations. For example, they contrasted normal and semantic violations by comparing the ERP to *sketch* and *headache* in

(20) a.   The man admired Don's *sketch* of the landscape.

   b.   *The man admired Don's *headache* of the landscape.

In the second sequence *headache* elicited a relative negativity at 400 ms, widespread throughout the brain. It has been demonstrated that this "N400 effect" is due to an unexpected or odd stimulus (Kutas and Hillyard 1983). Thus, it is reasonable to interpret the effect as due to the semantic oddness introduced by the word *headache*. While of interest in its own right, the presence of the N400 following semantic anomalies shows that the presence of the N125 following a phrase sequence violation may reflect a process particular to that kind of violation. This effect, dubbed *early left anterior negativity* (ELAN) by Friederici, was replicated in a number of studies by her (Friederici, Pfiefer, and Hahne 1993; Friederici, Hahne, and Mecklinger 1996). For example, in several studies, she contrasted ERPS to the final word in:

(21) *Acceptable*
Der Finder   wurde *belohnt.*
the discoverer was   rewarded

(22) *Semantic violation*
*Die Wolke wurde *begraben.*
*the cloud   was   buried

(23) *Phrase structure violation*
*Der Freund wurde im   *besucht.*
*the friend   was   in-the visited

The semantic violation elicited the standard N400 effect. But the phrase sequence violation (*in-the visited*) elicited the ELAN. Similarly, Friederici, Hahne, and Mecklinger (1996) found that the incorrect presentation of a noun or verb form elicited ELAN:

(24) Das Metall wurde zur *veredelung/*veredelt.*
the metal was for refining/*refined

This convergence of results in two languages establishes the ELAN as sensitive to the initial assignment of surface phrase structure. In the context of LAST, this establishes the concept that ELAN can be used in general to probe for early components of the comprehension process. That rationale reveals some results, surprising, but consistent with our theory.

Wh-Placement   We have noted that an early part of the process, prior to establishing a potential meaning, is to move *wh*-phrases back to their source position, so that canonical sentence templates can apply. Sequences that block the normal application of *wh*-repair elicit a somewhat later left anterior negativity (LAN, at 300–500 ms). For example, Neville et al. also found relative LAN in the ungrammatical sentence of the following triple:

(25) *Acceptable declarative*
The man admired Don's sketch *of* ...

(26) *Acceptable* wh-*question*
What did the man admire a sketch *of*

(27) *Specificity violation*
    *What did the man admire Don's sketch *of*?

Strictly speaking, the last sentence violates the specified subject constraint, which blocks *wh*-movement over filled noun phrases (*Don* versus *a*). If this is actually a constraint on processing (which many have suspected), then the *wh*-repair is blocked and a phrase structure violation results (*of* without an object). This is further evidence that *wh*-movement is a very early component of comprehension. Kluender and Kutas (1993) also found a greater LAN at 300–500 ms after *you* in *Who have you ...?* compared to *Have you ...?*

Agent Assignment Kutas (1997) reported greater left anterior negativity for object relatives than for subject relatives, as in:

(28) *Object relative*
    The fireman who *the* cop speedily rescued sued the city.

(29) *Subject relative*
    The fireman who *speedily* rescued the cop sued the city.

The difference appeared in the initial word of the relative clause—that is, in *the* in the object relative compared to *speedily* in the subject relative.

Mecklinger et al. (1995) recorded ERPs in German relative clauses. German has the property that whether a relative clause is a subject or object relative clause depends only on the verb, which is located at the end of the relative clause. Thus, the first sentence below is an object relative because the singular auxiliary verb *hat* requires a singular subject (*die Studentin*), whereas the second is a subject relative because the plural auxiliary verb *haben* requires a plural subject (*die Studentinnen*):

(30) *Object relative*
    Das sind die Professorinnen, die die Studentin gesucht hat.
    these are the professors   that the student   sought has

(31) *Subject relative*
    Das sind die Studentinnen, die die Professorin gesucht haben.
    these are the students   that the professor   sought have

Mecklinger et al. (1995) observed (for fast comprehenders) an increased positivity for object relatives than for subject relatives between 300 and 400 ms in the parietal region. The brain response appears to correspond to the assignment of words to the roles of agent and patient.

Auxiliary Selection A LAN may appear with violations of auxiliary-verb requirements. For example in German certain verbs require a form of *be* as the past auxiliary, and others a form of *have*. Knowledge of which verbs take which auxiliary is a function of the initial subcategorization information that goes with each verb. For example, *fall* and *laugh* take *have*, whereas *greet* and *go* take *be* (translations are from Rösler et al. 1993:360):

Acceptable

(32) Der Präsident wurde   *begrusst*.
     the president is-being greeted

(33) Der Clown hat *gelacht*.
     the clown has laughed

(34) Das Paket wurde   *geliefert*.
     the parcel is-being delivered

(35) Die Kerze hat *gebrannt*.
     the candle has burned

Syntactically unacceptable

(36) *Der Lehrer wurde   *gefallen*.
     *the teacher is-being fallen

(37) *Der Dichter hat *gegangen*.
      the poet   has gone

Semantically unacceptable

(38) *Der Honig wurde   *ermordet*.
     *the honey is-being murdered

(39) *Der Ball hat *geträaumt*.
     *the ball has dreamed

The syntactically unacceptable sequences violate auxiliary-verb requirements of the final word. Rösler et al. (1993) presented words of sentences like these through the auxiliary verb, *wurde* or *hat*, and then the last word of the sentence. The subject's task was to decide whether the last word in the sequence was a word. Sequences that violated auxiliary-verb requirements produced a negative effect, relative to acceptable controls, over the left frontal cortex within 400 to 700 ms of the final word. Sequences that violated semantic properties produced an N400 over both hemispheres in the parietal area and the posterior temporal area. These results confirm the generalization that it is primarily the left hemisphere that is sensitive to syntax, whereas both hemispheres are sensitive to semantic properties.

In sum, rapid ELAN appears when the local function-word context requires a particular syntactic lexical category and there is a mismatch. Somewhat slower LAN may occur when the mismatch is more driven by lexical auxiliary-verb requirements.

Finally, we can take the standard widespread N400 as a reflex of recognition that a semantic violation has occurred. Because of the complex nature of the source of different temporal components of the ERP, we cannot automatically take literally the order of these effects as indicating the actual order of processing. But it may be worth the exercise to consider that as one of the causal possibilities of that order, and see if it conforms to other aspects of a theory of comprehension. If we take ELAN as a reflex of recognition that an early stage of processing is a violation, and we take N400 to be a reflex of recognition of a meaning violation, then the results suggest that the first three stages of syntactic processing may be:

1. Local phrase building based on lexical categories and function-word templates (possibly also including higher-order template, such as NVN)
2. Recognition of basic meaning
3. Access of auxiliary-verb frames related to verb meaning

This sequence conforms quite well to the hypothesized initial pseudosyntax stage of LAST. Caution forbids celebrations, but the coincidence is intriguing.

Grammatical Checking   Friederici, Hahne, and Mecklinger (1996) noted a frontally distributed negativity over the left hemisphere 300 to 600 ms after the onset of a word that began a new phrase. This effect appeared during the word *von* in both grammatical and ungrammatical sentences, though it was somewhat more pronounced in ungrammatical sentences:

(40) *Grammatical*
     Das Metall wurde veredelt *von* dem Goldschmied den man auszeichnete.
     the metal was   refined by the goldsmith   who   was honored

(41) *Ungrammatical*
     *Das Metall wurde zur veredelt *von* dem Goldschmied den man auszeichnete.
      the metal was   for refined by the goldsmith   who   was honored

Friederici et al. attributed this effect to closure at the end of a major phrase (*the metal was refined*). Kutas (1997) reported similarly negative ERPs at the ends of English clauses.

Reanalysis   Osterhout and Holcomb (1992) described a late widespread positive shift at points where a preferred syntactic analysis must be abandoned. They examined ERPs in two types of reduced relative sentences. In one kind the first encountered verb would most likely be a reduced relative but could be a main verb with an appropriate continuation (e.g., *the broker persuaded the buyer*):

(42) *Reduced relative interpretation*
     The broker persuaded *to* sell the stock was sent to jail.

(43) *Main-verb interpretation*
    *The broker persuaded *to* sell the stock.

This contrasted with another type of verb that was more likely to be a main verb than a passive participle in a reduced relative clause:

(44) *Reduced relative interpretation*
    ? The broker hoped *to* sell the stock was sent to jail.

(45) *Main-verb interpretation*
    The broker hoped *to* sell the stock.

Osterhout and Holcomb (1992) found that the word *to* elicited a more positive wave in the sentence with *persuaded* than in the sentence with *hoped*. This increased positivity began at about 500 ms after the onset of *to* and continued until about 800 ms, with its midpoint at about 600 ms. Since the sentence with *persuaded* may continue as the less preferred reduced relative interpretation, Osterhout and Holcomb proposed that this P600 effect occurs because of the reanalysis of the preferred main-verb analysis to the less preferred reduced relative structure.

This finding has been widely replicated: all the studies reviewed above of syntactic malformed sentences show some kind of *syntactic positive shift* (Hagoort, Brown, and Groothusen 1993) relative to the control sentences, roughly between 500 and 1000 ms (Friederici 1997; Mecklinger et al. 1995; Osterhout and Holcomb 1993). A number of researchers associate this shift with a stage in which grammar is accessed after recognition of the error. That, too, is consistent with LAST, but of course it is consistent with any model on which repair attempts come after initial misassignments are recognized. In our view, the late positivity might reveal access to the grammar and recognition that there is no correct structure for the sequence (true of all the cases except the very complex reduced relatives).

There is one other piece of ERP evidence that the full grammar is accessed late in processing, which we have not mentioned until now. This evidence is that noun-verb inflection violations do *not* produce an ELAN but *do* produce LAN and widespread late positivity (Kutas and Hillyard 1983; Hagoort, Brown, and Groothusen 1993; Friederici, Pfiefer, and Hahne 1993). For example, in the sentence below, *bohnere* is a verb form but should be the past participle agreeing with the subject, rather than the first-person singular form. Friederici, Pfiefer, and Hahne (1993) found a LAN between 300 and 500 ms and a widespread late positivity to these cases.

(46) *Das Parkett wurde *bohnere.*
    the parquet is-being polish

Similarly, Kutas and Hillyard (1983) found a marginally significant LAN and a widespread late positive ERP to simple verb-number agreement violations:

(47) *As a turtle grows its shell grow too.

(48) *Some shells is even soft.

This consistent result is a puzzle for theories on which syntax is assigned first. Why should lexical category violations occasion ELAN, while agreement errors do not? It cannot be that the latter are not recognized, since we know that people are conscious of them, and the violations also elicit the slow positivity associated with all other syntactic violations. According to LAST, the fact that they are locally the correct category allows for an initial mapping onto meanings (i.e., they are at first treated as acceptable semisentences). Only after an initial meaning is arrived at and the system then checks the surface sequence by synthesizing a match for it, do the details such as morphological agreement actually come into play. This is not to say that there is no recognition of an oddity immediately when agreement is violated, but only that it does not impede the active processing in the initial stages of comprehension.

9.2.3 Templates, Aphasia, and Persistent Grammatical Knowledge

How can the comprehension system break down? If there is damage to the comprehension system, what patterns of comprehension follow from LAST? LAST is not sufficiently developed to make precise predictions on this question, but we can speculate about the possibilities.

The last fifteen years have provided a wealth of studies on aphasias, which are language disorders caused by brain damage. These studies have focused primarily on Broca's aphasia, which is characterized by nonfluent speech plus differences in understanding complex sentences, and Wernicke's aphasia, characterized by fluent but nonsensical speech, and also comprehension difficulties (Kertesz 1999). Broca's aphasia generally is associated with damage to areas of the left frontal lobe, while Wernicke's aphasia is associated with damage to areas of the left temporal lobe.

Unfortunately, much of the data on aphasia is difficult to interpret for a variety of reasons. One reason for this is that the sample sizes of studies often are low. Even when a reasonably sized group of patients is assembled for experimental testing, it is unlikely that all patients in the group have exactly the same pattern of brain damage. And even if all members of an experimental group had the same pattern of brain damage, there is no assurance that the members of the group are functionally similar, since there are individual differences in cerebral organization (see, for example, Bever et al. 1989; Bradshaw 1980; Hardyck 1977; Harsham, Hampson, and Berenbaum 1983; Hecaen, de Agostini, and Monzen-Montes 1981; Hecaen and Sauguet 1971; McKeever 1986; Townsend, Carrithers, and Bever, forthcoming; van Strien and Bouma 1995). Accordingly, any claims about the mechanisms underlying the language behavior of aphasic patients must be interpreted cautiously.

We find that some neuropsychological results can be explained more naturally by structural theories, and other results more naturally by constraint-based models. This pattern of results clearly implicates a hybrid model, such as LAST. Even though LAST does not uniquely explain any result, its architecture is such that both structural and constraint-based results follow from it. No other current approach can explain naturally this divergent pattern of results. Thus, for the moment, we offer LAST as a useful framework for organizing the clinical neuropsychological literature.

Two general kinds of deficits follow from loss of the two major components of LAST. If the architecture of comprehension is like LAST, we might expect that brain damage could cause a loss of pseudosyntax. Losing pseudosyntax could reveal itself as difficulty in obtaining an initial meaning-form hypothesis. If the pseudosyntax component were lost, we would find evidence of difficulty in accessing function words (at least early), segmenting low-level phrases, applying sentence-level templates such as NVN, assigning *wh*-trace, or accessing argument requirements of verbs. Alternatively, we might expect that brain damage could produce an inability to apply the grammar in synthesizing a complete surface structure. As it turns out, the evidence favors the loss of pseudosyntax rather than loss of the ability to deploy the full grammar.

The aphasia literature has revealed certain points that are consistent with LAST. The most important is that access to grammatical knowledge is spared typically in Broca's aphasics, while access to the comprehension system is not. For example, Broca's aphasics have difficulty matching pictures to passive sentences (Schwartz, Saffran, and Marin 1980; see box 9.1) and to sentences with object relative clauses (Caramazza and Zurif 1976):

(49) *Reversible passive*
      The boy is followed by the girl.

(50) *Reversible object-extracted relative clause*
      The cat that the dog is biting is black.

These patients perform much better when there are semantic cues to meaning, as in nonreversible passives. Because of these difficulties with reversible sentences, Broca's patients are often described as "agrammatic," even though careful testing has revealed that they are not completely without grammar.

Agrammatic aphasics perform at chance levels on sentence-picture matching of reversible passives, object-cleft sentences, and object-extracted relative clauses. For example, Linebarger, Schwartz, and Saffran (1983) found that sentence-picture matching, agrammatic aphasics scored an average of 76 percent on active sentences, and 52 percent on passives. Berndt, Mitchum, and Haendiges (1996) reviewed fifteen published studies on sentence-picture matching in agrammatic aphasics. In table 9.9, we list the number of subjects who scored above chance, at chance, and below

Table 9.9
Number of agrammatic patients who scored above, at, and below chance on active and passive picture matching

	Active	Passive
Above chance	42	23
At chance	22	37
Below chance	0	4

Source: Adapted from Berndt, Mitchum, and Haendiges 1996, appendix

chance on actives and on passives, as reported by Berndt and associates. While Berndt, Mitchum, and Haendiges suggest that there are several distinct patterns of agrammatic performance, we note that, overall, their summary appears to show that agrammatics perform better than chance on comprehending active sentences, but at chance on passives (see also Drai and Grodzinsky 1999; Grodzinsky et al. 1999).

Grammar   In a series of studies, Linebarger, Schwartz, and Saffran (1983) have shown that "agrammatic" aphasics can judge which sentences are grammatical and which are not. Among ten different sentence types, four aphasic patients generally obtained accuracy rates of at least 80 percent. For example, the average accuracy on gapless relatives was 91 percent:

(51)   *Mary ate the bread that I baked a cake.

(52)   *Mary ate the bread that I baked.

In an earlier study (Schwartz, Saffran, and Marin 1980), it was found that the same aphasic subjects that were 85 to 100 percent accurate in judging the grammaticality of passive sentences

(53)   John has finally kissed Louise.

(54)   *John was finally kissed Louise.

performed no better than chance in a comprehension task with the same sentences.

This result is astounding. How can it be that patients who cannot understand a sentence can nonetheless judge whether or not it is grammatical? In our view, these patients have lost the ability to use pseudosyntax to develop an initial meaning. But they have not lost the full grammar. These findings support the architectural separation of pseudosyntax and the full grammar in the analysis-by-synthesis model.

Default Strategies   Assuming that agrammatic patients do perform at chance on reversible passives, Grodzinsky (1986, 1995) explains this result in terms of their inability to assign traces, as is required when noun phrases move out of the canonical position. Consequently, according to Grodzinsky, the agrammatic patients try to make sense of such noncanonical sentences by deploying reasoning strategies outside the comprehension system. For example, they rely on the "default strategy" of interpreting the first noun in a passive sentence as the agent. And, since they assign the role of agent to the noun phrase in the *by*-phrase of a passive as well, they have two agents for a passive sentence, and simply guess. Thus, agrammatic aphasics perform at chance on passives, and on other noncanonical sentences such as object-cleft sentences and sentences with object-extracted relative clauses.

Chance performance on reversible passives and other noncanonical sentences may be interpreted in terms of a loss of pseudosyntax. If pseudosyntax were intact in agrammatic aphasics and they applied the NVN template, they would *consistently* misinterpret passives as though they were active, with the initial noun assigned the role of agent and the final noun the role of theme. Thus, their performance on reversible passives would be significantly poorer than chance. But the meta-analysis of Berndt, Mitchum, and Haendiges (1996), as summarized in table 9.9, shows little evidence that agrammatic aphasics perform below chance on reversible passives. Clearly, these patients are not applying the canonical NVN template to interpret reversible passives to obtain an initial-form hypothesis meaning. Thus, Grodzinsky's default strategy is an example of a nonlinguistic reasoning strategy. Other studies may be interpreted to show that agrammatic aphasics have lost other aspects of pseudosyntax and rely on nonlinguistic default strategies.

Function Words   There is evidence that aphasics have difficulty in accessing function words. In section 6.1.1, we discussed evidence from Friederici (1985) that normal subjects detect function words faster than content words in a word-monitoring task. Freiderici (1985) also found that Broca's aphasics have a very long recognition time for function words in sentences, much slower than recognition of content words (see table 9.10). Pulvermuller (1995) presented evidence that when normal subjects interpret "pruned" sentences, in which some portion of function words is deleted, their responses duplicate the aphasic comprehension pattern.

Table 9.10
Mean word-monitoring times (ms) for agrammatic subjects and normal controls

Word class	Type of subject	
	Agrammatic	Normal
Content	630	350
Function	782	298

Source: Adapted from Friederici 1985, table 3

These peculiar facts are consistent with LAST. The initial comprehension strategies depend greatly on frameworks set up by function words and morphemes. If the damaged brain area is responsible for Broca's aphasics' selective loss of access to the initial surface syntactic patterns that are input to recognition strategies, then they will not be able to access an initial hypothesis about meaning, and will not be able to understand the sentences. But if the knowledge of the grammar lies in another brain region (either bilaterally represented, or represented in another area of the left hemisphere than the typically damaged one), they will still have a synthetic grammar and be able to match surface strings with correct grammatical sequences. These data follow naturally from LAST.

Wh-Trace   There is evidence that certain patients have difficulty in filling gaps (Swinney et al. 1996; Zurif et al. 1993; Swinney and Zurif 1995). Zurif et al. (1993) examined online processing of subject-extracted relative clauses in four Wernicke's aphasics and four Broca's aphasics. They used a cross-modal lexical decision task with sentences like:

(55) *Subject-extracted relative clause*
The gymnast loved the professor$_1$ from the northwestern city * who * t$_1$ complained about the bad coffee.

The asterisks indicate possible test locations in which the lexical decision materials were presented. The probes were either related to the antecedent (*teacher*) or unrelated to the antecedent (*address*).

The results appear in table 9.11. There was priming only for Wernicke's aphasics at the gap location, that is, after *who* in the above example. Broca's aphasics did not show significant priming in either the pregap or gap location.

Table 9.11
Mean response times (ms) to related vs. unrelated probes at the pregap vs. gap location in Wernicke's vs. Broca's aphasics

	Pregap	Gap
Wernicke's		
Related	1017	982
Unrelated	1061	1107
Broca's		
Related	1145	1126
Unrelated	1125	1058

Source: Adapted from Zurif et al. 1993, table 2

Table 9.12
Mean response times to related vs. unrelated probes at the pregap vs. gap position for Broca's vs. Wernicke's aphasics

	Pregap	Gap
Broca's		
Related	1257	1183
Unrelated	1379	1174
Wernicke's		
Related	1511	1378
Unrelated	1514	1486

Source: Adapted from Swinney et al. 1996, table 1

Swinney et al. (1996) extended these results to agrammatic aphasics' processing of object-extracted relative clauses. They again used the cross-modal lexical decision task. Their subjects consisted of four Broca's aphasics and four Wernicke's aphasics. Sample materials were:

(56) *Object-extracted relative clause*
The priest enjoyed the drink₁ that the caterer was * serving * t₁ to the guests.

Subjects heard the sentences and received a visual probe probe at one of two locations, marked by asterisks above. The probes were either related to the antecedent (*drink*) or unrelated. For example, a related probe is *wine* and an unrelated probe is *boat*. On seeing the probe word, the subject's task was to say whether or not the letter sequence was a word. The results appear in table 9.12. The results showed a significant effect of probe relatedness only for Wernicke's patients in the gap position. Broca's aphasics did not show a significant relatedness effect at either the pregap or gap position. The 122-ms pregap effect for Broca's patients was not significant. Swinney et al. attributed this nonsignificant difference to residual activation of the antecedent.

The studies by Zurif, Swinney, and colleagues indicate that agrammatic aphasics have difficulty filling gaps created by the movement of *wh*-words. In LAST, *wh*-gap filling is in the domain of pseudosyntax (see chapter 5). Blumstein et al. (1998) obtained evidence that agrammatic aphasics do access antecedents at the point of a gap. However, because of the design of their materials, these results may also be interpreted as demonstrating end-of-sentence processes (see also Balogh et al. 1998).

Syntax Checking   We find evidence that agrammatic aphasics engage in end-of-sentence processes that normally are attributed to checking the syntax and integrating sentence meaning. These end-of-sentence processes occur despite the apparent loss of a pseudosyntactic representation of meaning.

Friederici, Hahne, and von Cramon (1998) demonstrated selective loss of semantic systems and pseudosyntax with the preservation of end-of-sentence processing. Friederici and colleagues measured evoked potentials in one Broca's aphasic, one Wernicke's aphasic, and eight normals. Example sentences are:

(57) *Correct*
   Der Finder wurde belohnt.
   the finder was   rewarded

(58) *Semantic violation*
   Die Wolke wurde begraben.
   the cloud was   buried

(59) *Phrase stucture violation*
   Der Freund wurde im   besucht.
   the friend was   in-the visited

(60) *Morphosyntactic violation*
   Der Schatz wurde bewache.
   the treasure was   guard

The sentences were presented auditorily and subjects had to press a button to indicate whether the sentence was grammatical or ungrammatical. Evoked potentials were measured from the onset of the critical word, which was always in the sentence final position.

The results for normal subjects were consistent with earlier studies (see section 9.2.2). Compared to the control sentences:

1. Phrase structure violations produced an ELAN, a left anterior negativity between 100 and 300 ms after the onset of the critical word. These violations also produced a positive wave 300–700 ms after the critical word.
2. Semantic violations produced an N400, a negative wave over the left and right centroparietal areas 400 ms after the critical word.
3. Morphosyntactic violations produced a P600, a positive wave in the centroparietal region 600 ms after the critical word. Friederici et al. attribute this brain response to reanalysis or repair, which, in terms of LAST, is a by-product of syntax checking.

The results for the Broca's aphasic showed the following:

1. Phrase structure violations produce no ELAN. These violations did produce a positive wave 400–1100 ms after the critical word.
2. Semantic violations produced an N400-like wave that was delayed, appearing 500–950 ms after the critical word.
3. Morphosyntactic violations produced a P600 lasting from about 600 to 1200 ms after the critical word.

The results for the Wernicke's aphasic showed a different pattern of brain response:

1. Phrase structure violations produced an ELAN between 200 and 350 ms after the critical word.
2. Semantic violations produced no N400.
3. All three violations produced a late positive component around 1200 ms after the critical word.

In sum, the Broca's patient did not show the early left anterior negativity that normally occurs in phrase structure violations but did show a late positive component to syntactic violations, and did show the N400 to semantic violations. On the other hand, the Wernicke's patient did show the early negativity to phrase structure violations but did not show the N400 to semantic violations. Once again, we must interpret these data cautiously. Nevertheless, the correspondence between the hypothesized specific deficit in pseudosyntax for Broca's aphasia is striking.

Postcomprehension Processes   After a sentence is understood, its syntax is checked and its meaning integrated. An example of a task that occurs after comprehension is a conscious, explicit judgment of the plausibility of a sentence (see chapter 5).

Saffran, Schwartz, and Linebarger (1998) have demonstrated several factors that influence aphasics' judgment of plausibility. They presented auditory versions of sentences and asked seven aphasic patients (five of whom were classified as Broca's aphasics) to indicate whether or not the sentence was "silly" versus "OK." Saffran and colleagues measured errors in their aphasic subjects, and they used the same materials to measure reaction times in normal subjects. The relatively long reaction times for normal subjects (about 600–1300 ms) supports the view that plausibility judgments occur after they have understood the sentence.

Saffran and associates varied how strongly the noun phrases were semantically constrained to take on a particular thematic role. For example, both *man* and *child* plausibly can take on the agent role for *pick up* (they both can pick up something), and both plausibly can take on the patient role for *pick up* (they both can be picked up), though it is implausible that a child could pick up a man. Similarly, both *mouse* and *cat* can both carry or be carried, though it is implausible that a mouse could carry a cat. These sorts of constraints are called *proposition-based constraints*. In the examples below, a # indicates an implausible sentence.

Proposition-based constraints
(61)   The man picked up the child.

(62)   #The mouse is carrying the cat.

On the other hand, in (63)–(66) *performance* cannot take on the agent role for *watch*, *crash* cannot take on the experiencer role for *frighten*, *music* cannot take on the agent role *listen*, and *idea* cannot take on the experiencer role for *surprised*. These constraints are called *verb-based constraints*.

Verb-based constraints

(63)   The audience was watching the performance.

(64)   The crash frightened the children.

(65)   #The music was listening to the woman.

(66)   #The professor surprised the idea.

Thus, one cue to the thematic role of each noun was the meaning of the noun.

A second cue to thematic role was whether the noun appeared first in the sentence. Nouns appeared either as the first noun in the sentence or as a later noun. For example,

(67)   The child was picked up by the man.

provides a strong cue (but invalid in this case) that *the child* takes on the agent role of the verb. The sentences appeared as active or as passive.

A third cue to thematic role was whether the noun was topicalized by occupying its own clause. Nouns that occupy their own clause are more likely to be agent. For example,

(68)   It was the child that the man picked up.

provides a strong cue (again invalid) that *the child* takes on the agent role. Saffran et al. included subject-cleft and object-cleft sentences. Table 9.13 shows the mean percentage of errors.

Errors were more frequent overall on implausible sentences than on plausible sentences (35% vs. 14%). Errors also were more frequent overall on verb-based con-

Table 9.13
Mean percentage of errors for aphasic patients

	Active	Passive	SC	OC	Mean
Plausible					
Proposition	13	13	16	27	17
Verb	7	14	7	16	11
Mean	10	14	11	21	14
Implausible					
Verb	43	56	34	50	46
Mean	27	39	24	48	35

Source: Adapted from Saffran, Schwartz, and Linebarger 1998, table 7

straints than on proposition-based constraints (28% vs. 20%); the advantage for verb-based constraints in plausible sentences was not significant. Syntactic structure also influenced errors overall, with the fewest errors on subject-cleft sentences (18%) and the most errors on object-cleft sentences (35%).

Inspection of table 9.13 reveals that all three cues to thematic roles had an effect. Errors were less frequent in verb-constrained sentences than in proposition-constrained sentences (20% vs. 28% overall), less frequent for active sentences than for passives (19% vs. 27% overall), and less frequent when the topicalized noun phrase was the agent (17% vs. 35%). Thus, aphasic patients appear to use all three cues to make judgments about sentence plausibility.

Saffran and colleagues suggest that aphasic patients use the various constraints during online interpretation of the sentences. They see the aphasic difficulty as an inability to relate syntactic arguments with thematic roles online due to loss of verb-specific mapping information. If the sentence-plausibility judgments were in fact made online, response times should be relatively fast.

Unfortunately, Saffran and associates did not record reaction times for the aphasic subjects. Their basis for believing that this task taps online decisions is the fact that in normal subjects, response times, measured from the onset of the last syllable of the sentence, were faster when the NP whose role is more constrained appears earlier in the sentence, at least among noncleted sentences. But it is risky to assume that aphasics make online decisions in the same way as normals, particularly in view of evidence that aphasic patients have reduced working-memory capacity (Miyake, Carpenter and Just, 1994; see Schwartz et al. 1987). Table 9.14 shows mean response times for normal subjects and mean error rates for aphasic subjects on the verb-constrained sentences. An italicized phrase indicates the noun phrase whose role is constrained by the thematic requirements of the verb. The data in table 9.14 show that the case for online assignment of thematic roles is more compelling for normal subjects than for aphasic subjects. For normals, the interaction between semantic

Table 9.14
Performance of normals (RT in ms) and aphasics (percent error) on plausible active and passive sentences

	Normal	Aphasic
Patient constrained		
The artist disliked *the painting*.	764	6
The painting was disliked by the artist.	640	17
Agent constrained		
The crash frightened the children.	578	9
The children were frightened by *the crash*.	823	11

Source: Adapted from Saffran, Schwartz, and Linebarger 1998, tables 4 and 8

constraint and syntactic structure was significant: response times were faster when the more constrained noun phrase occurred earlier. To interpret the aphasic data in terms of online decisions in the absence of corresponding reaction-time data, we would at least like to see that aphasics show a pattern of error rates similar to the normal pattern of response time. This was not the case. As table 9.14 shows, errors were more frequent for passives than for actives regardless of the semantic constraint.

We view these data in terms of the application of the various constraints in a nonlinguistic reasoning process that occurs after linguistic processing. In this view, aphasics have an impoverished representation of sentence meaning, due to their difficulties with pseudosyntax. Nevertheless, the comprehension system runs through its analysis-by-synthesis cycle, and subjects must decide whether the sentence is plausible or not. The comprehension system may have revealed bits and pieces of evidence, including thematic requirements of verbs, initial noun phrases, and topicalization, which the subject now uses as the basis for making a judgment about plausibility.

9.3 Conclusion

Several lines of research suggest that the sentence templates are distinct from grammatical knowledge, both in acquisition and in the neurological organization of adults. In particular, the superiority of the left hemisphere for language may have a privileged relation to the initial sentence templates, which, according to LAST, elicit the initial meaning-form hypothesis. The ability of left-hemisphere damaged aphasics to recognize ungrammatical sentences, while not understanding them or their grammatical counterparts, may implicate a selective impairment of the initial comprehension templates, which leaves intact access to grammatical knowledge. Cerebral lateralization for language emerges in concert with the appearance of these templates; left-hemisphere effects of constructions that violate the strategies appear early in the ERP, and prior to semantic violations. ERP effects of syntax errors that do not violate the strategies (e.g., morphological agreement) appear only late in the overall ERP, and are of the same quality as the late ERP to other syntactic errors. The data thus far are consistent with the view that syntactic errors that violate strategies are detected early by virtue of the early application of strategies, and detected late by virtue of being syntactic errors. Errors that do not violate the strategies are detected only late.

Is this really the true story? Of course, we do not know, and the data vastly underdetermine what we can be sure of. But whether true or not, it demonstrates a general consistency of the processes hypothesized in LAST, with salient and enduring facts about acquisition, and an otherwise heterogeneous set of facts about ERPs. At the very least, the behavioral separation of pseudosyntax and statistical patterns from structural knowledge in acquisition and neurological responses gives credence to their separation in the comprehension model.

Chapter 10

Implications

We have presented a model of language comprehension that incorporates and integrates both habit-based and rule-governed aspects of language. This model has implications for the broader field of cognitive science. In this final chapter, we first summarize the main points of our model, the historical background for it, and the evidence for it, roughly in the order of the preceding chapters. Then we review some topics on the implications of our model for cognitive science as a whole.

10.1 Summary

There are two foundational approaches to the study of sentence comprehension, the habit-based approach of behaviorists such as Skinner and Osgood and the rule-governed approach that emerged from the work of Miller and Chomsky (chapter 2). The greatest advantage of the habit-based approach was its characterization of the associative nature of many aspects of language behavior, and its goal of explaining the acquisition of language behavior through inductive mechanisms. In the end, however, the habit-based approach of the 1950s and 1960s failed largely because it did not have sufficiently sophisticated algorithms for modifying associative strength, it was limited by behaviorist restrictions, and it had no means of identifying the appropriate unit of reinforcement.

During the same period, experimental research on language perception gave special prominence to the sentence level of representation and the view that the natural unit of comprehension is larger than the word but smaller than the discourse. The natural unit of comprehension was thought to be the sentence, which was defined by a set of generative rules. We observed that a critical and enduring fact is that words seem to be physically clearer when they are arranged in sentences. This basic psychophysical phenomenon heightened the importance of understanding the psychological mechanisms for understanding and manipulating sentences.

The then-nascent transformational grammar offered a generative model for sentences, which sparked two decades of research on the "psychological reality" of grammar. The outcome of this research was that the relation between grammar and comprehension was seen as indirect. Consequently, psycholinguistic models became more detached from linguistic theory.

Psycholinguistic research has been further complicated by rapid changes in grammatical theory. However, most syntactic theories since the 1950s share some central ideas about language (chapter 3). First, sentences have a hierarchical structure, in which larger units consist of two or more smaller units. Second, sentences have derivations, in which rules are applied to abstract structures that modify the linguistic representation. Third, derivations are cyclic, operating over sentence-like units. These theories converge on the view that a representation of meaning is based on the content of a sentence. The evolution of syntactic theory reflects greater insight into how best to describe the relation between the meaning of a sentence and its form. In the generative framework, meaning was based on an initial inner form, the "deep structure" of sentences, which was deformed by transformations under a surface representation. This was then supplemented by sensitivity to aspects of surface form, with concomitant constraints on the derivational relation between the deep and surface structures. More recently, it has become clear that there are many formal and empirical advantages to building up a sentence syntactic derivation, phrase by phrase, with concomitant intermediate stages in access to the meaning representation.

Current approaches to sentence comprehension come in two basic flavors, rule-based and habit-based (chapter 4). Modern variants of Marcus's rule-based model adopted the view that syntactic structure is essential and logically prior to the construction of sentence meaning. Accordingly, these models assume that the apprehension of syntactic structure comes first in the understanding of sentences. There are also modern variants of habit-based models, which adopt the view that sentence comprehension is primarily a process of applying associative knowledge that is represented as connections between simple processing units. Connectionist models have made tremendous progress in solving the methodological half of Osgood's dilemma: the development of sophisticated mathematical procedures for distributing feedback to associative connections, so that the model converges on language-like behavior. However, connectionist models have not been able to solve the other half of the dilemma that faces all inductive associative models: What is the appropriate linguistic unit that determines how feedback is distributed?

This set the stage for the development of a model of sentence comprehension that integrates the two types of linguistic behavior, an analysis-by-synthesis model that we call *Late Assignment of Syntax Theory* (LAST, chapter 5). LAST uses associative, habit-based knowledge, or pseudosyntax, to form an initial hypothesis about the relation between meaning and form. This initial representation of meaning and form is the input to a synthetic component. The synthetic component consists of abstract grammatical knowledge that generates a full syntactic representation and its corresponding meaning. The comprehension system compares the output of this full syntactic derivation to a stored representation of the input sequence. If the two representations match, the corresponding meaning is stored and the syntactic details become less available.

LAST has two critical implications. First, it is completely compatible with current syntactic theory. The output of pseudosyntax consists of overt lexical items, basic phrase grouping, and an associated meaning that specifies basic grammatical values and semantic functions. This pseudosyntactic representation corresponds well to the input to a derivation in current syntactic theory, the "numeration."

A second critical feature of LAST is that we understand sentences twice. The first time, an initial meaning-form pair is based on associative connections and templates in the pseudosyntax. The second time we understand a sentence it is based on the meaning-form pair derived by the grammar. Successful comparison of the derived form and the stored input confirms the final interpretation. This process explains a number of phenomena including the most important classical finding that words are clearer when they appear in sentences. In the dual-representation model, two surface forms are created and compared with the input, thus focusing extra processing and attention to the physical input.

There is considerable classical evidence for LAST (chapter 6). Current theories can explain different parts of this evidence, but LAST explains all of it without adding ad hoc assumptions. The initial representation of the relation between form and meaning approximates the final representation. It can be syntactically incorrect, as in the initial representation of passive sentences as adjectival, but "good enough" to arrive at a likely meaning-form, which then sparks a complete derivation (cf. Ferreira and Stacey 2000). The evidence shows that there is rapid access to low-level phrases, which are established in part by using function words and morphemes to identify the boundaries of phrases. In addition to function words and morphemes, pseudosyntax consists of sentence-level templates like NVN = agent-action-patient and its fuller form based on learned argument requirements for verbs, NV (N) (N) = agent-action-patient-recipient. The presence of explicit markers for wh-movement enables the pseudosyntax to identify the location of wh-traces. The evidence also shows that subcategorization frames and knowledge about word meanings quickly influence sentence processing. The synthetic component uses the initial representation of meaning and pseudosyntax to generate a detailed syntactic representation. The synthetic process is similar in certain ways to the processes of recalling or producing sentences. Some aspects of the syntactic representation, such as detailed phrase structure and the source location of moved noun phrases, become available only late in the process of sentence comprehension, after the grammar has generated a complete syntactic representation and the corresponding meaning. The results of studies that examined introspection about sentences were found to depend on whether the task uses prospective introspection, which precedes full comprehension, or retrospective introspection, which follows full comprehension.

Sentence-level templates in pseudosyntax have tremendous explanatory power (chapter 7). The sentence template NVN = agent-action-agent and its variants NV (N) (N) = agent-action-(patient)-(recipient) can explain virtually all the experimental evidence on sentences with a reduced relative clause as in *the horse raced past the barn fell*, much of which has appeared contradictory. The reliance of pseudosyntax on sentence-level templates also explains a vast amount of the literature on full subject and object relative clauses and garden-path sentences other than reduced relatives. In each case, the comprehension difficulty occurs because of the initial application of the NVN sentence template and its variants.

The architecture of LAST entails that representations of the relation between meaning and form appear twice during comprehension, once in the initial representation of meaning based on pseudosyntax, and once in the complete representation of meaning based on grammar. This architecture has implications for the issues of syntactic modularity and discourse processing (chapter 8). We noted that LAST can be seen as both nonmodular, in the formation of the initial hypothesis about meaning and form, and modular, in the generation of a complete syntactic representation, which uses grammatical knowledge exclusively. The formation of two representations of meaning and form also has implications for the processing of multiclause sentences and discourses, since, in principle, representations of both meaning and form may be available for integration during ongoing sentence processing. There is corresponding evidence that ongoing comprehension involves fluctuations of attention to different kinds of representations depending on the requirements of the comprehension system as described by LAST. As far as we know, much of this evidence remains unexplained by other theories, except by ad hoc assumptions.

LAST also has implications for the acquisition and neurological representation of language (chapter 9). Much evidence from acquisition indicates that children develop early sensitivity to pseudosyntax, including sentence templates and grammatical morphemes. A review of studies of neurological processing during sentence comprehension reveals a surprising amount of evidence for LAST. In general, pseudosyntax and aspects of associative meaning produce very rapid brain responses, while more detailed syntactic representations produce relatively slow brain responses. Evidence from studies of agrammatic aphasia also can be interpreted naturally in terms of LAST.

Our discussion has focused on the need for a model of comprehension that integrates habit-based and rule-based knowledge, the organization of such a model, and the evidence for it. Along the way, we have referred to critical and complementary failures of habit-based and rule-based approaches, such as the grain problem for habit-based approaches and the learning problem for rule-based approaches. We turn now to a summary of these issues and some broader implications of LAST for an integrated theory of language behavior and consciousness.

10.2   Cognitive Architecture, the Grain Problem, and Consciousness

Sentence comprehension may be one of the more complex cognitive capacities of humans. But its principles may have analogues in other cognitive behaviors. We now explore three implications of the analysis-by-synthesis model for cognitive science in general.

10.2.1   Habits and Rules Are Segregated in Modules

A constant theme of this book has been the construct validity of both habit-based and structural explanations of language behavior. In general, most of ongoing language behavior has a clear habitual component, while it also affords the possibility of constructing and understanding quite novel utterances. It has long been a puzzle how to integrate the two kinds of information in a single approach. Indeed, much of the antecedent history of cognitive science has involved radical swings back and forth between statistical and structural treatments of all behaviors, roughly three decades at a time for each approach since the turn of the twentieth century.

For example, the cognitive revolution of the 1960s was a triumph of rationalist structuralism over behaviorist associationism that had dominate the field since the 1920s. Abstract structures, such as the level of representation of sentences, were recognized by all as a dangerous challenge to the "terminal meta-postulate." The *terminal meta-postulate* refers to the behaviorist claim that all theoretical terms and all corresponding inner psychological entities are grounded in more superficial entities, and ultimately in explicit behaviors and stimuli (see Bever, Fodor, and Garrett 1968). There is no obvious way in which inner syntactic forms are extracted from outer ones. Indeed, syntactic theory suggests that the relation is in the opposite direction. Rational structuralism sharpened the focus of research on the behavioral role of such inner forms, and gradually behaviorist strictures lapsed into the obscurity of irrelevance.

But arguments against behaviorism are not direct arguments against associationism. Associationism is merely the doctrine that all mental relations are associative rather than categorical, usually built up out of repeated experiences or co-occurrences. The compelling argument against the idea that absolutely everything is based on associative habits is the complexity and underdetermined nature of normal behaviors, such as the comprehension of language. The traditional answer by associationists has been that we underestimate the subtlety of behavior that a large complex associative network can compute. Even inner, abstract representations might be connected by a myriad of associations that is so complex as to mimic the appearance of hierarchies, part-whole relations, relations at a distance, and other kinds of categorical facts. The thrust of connectionism, the major school of modern associationism, is to apply relatively complex networks of associatively connected simple processing units, and thereby explain apparent categorical and rule-like structures as the result of pattern completion and the exigencies of associative information compression. The idea is that with enough experience, associative networks produce behavior that looks structural in nature, but we allegedly know it really is not because we can manufacture a machine of associative networks in computer model of selected language behaviors.

That, of course, is just one of many human conceits. We manufacture electric generators, but we do not make the laws or the electrons that the laws govern. Rather, we construct machines that manipulate those phenomena to our own ends. Similarly, suppose that we wired up an associative network as complex as a human brain and placed it in a completely human environment and that it started to learn language. The process by which the associative network learns language would be as much a mystery as how a child learns language. We would be back to the 1960s' cognitive psychology joke. Someday the researchers in artificial intelligence will create a very human-like robot, and then we will have to practice psychophysics, theoretical psychology, and experimental "neuro"science on it to figure out how it works. We will have new sections of international psychological associations in "robopsychology" and the closely related field, "virtual cognitive neuroscience." In short, our creation of a language-learning machine would not mean that we have created language or the laws of language learning.

Similar modesty is indicated about mimicking the achievements of specific connectionist models. The ability of a model to converge on 90 percent accuracy in computing a specific syntactic structure after thousands of training trials or to differentiate lexical classes based on repeated exposure to local contexts is an important achievement. Such an achievement stands as an existence proof that statistically reliable information is available in the language stimulus world and can support the induction of recognition patterns. But to claim that such achievements show we can account for actual categorical syntactic structure is not warranted. It would be like claiming that the amazing height of a medieval church spire shows that humans can reach the heavens. The church steeple is a prototype of humanity's ambition, but the ambition itself refers to categorical concepts.

So, after the cognitive shouting and bombast of the 1960s and the more recent connectionist enthusiasms are absorbed, we are left with the same truth as before: Behavior is affected both by categorical and statistical processes. Some current models in cognitive science respond to this by proposing "hybrid models" that commingle elements of symbolic and associative processes. This can create conceptual puzzles if the two kinds of information are truly blended. What does it mean to state that a "rule" applies a particular percentage of time, especially if the rule is a stage in a complex derivation? What does it mean to state that an "associative regularity" defines a structural category? In both cases, the attempt by one kind of information to modify the other can lead to theoretical incoherence.

The analysis-by-synthesis model we have sketched allows both kinds of information to play explanatory roles in behavior, and much of this book has been devoted to showing the empirical power of this model. But while it can be counted as a "hybrid" model, it clearly segregates the two kinds of information into separate computational domains. This maintains theoretical consistency and clarity, while allowing each kind of information to explain what it can explain in actual data.

10.2.2 The Grain Problem and Its Solution

The basic proposal of induction is that experience reinforces certain internal states, which then modify future behavior. This principle runs through the work of Skinner, Osgood, and current connectionist models. The problem has been repeatedly noted, starting with Chomsky's review of Skinner's book on language, that associative models generally do not have independent definitions of what counts as a stimulus in the world and a response pattern to it. That is, these models do not define what should be connected by each reinforcing experience independently of the intuition of an observer who already possesses the knowledge to be learned. In research on language behavior, this has become known as the "grain problem," the question of what level of linguistic analysis is confirmed by each environmentally successful use of an utterance.

We noted in chapter 5 that the analysis-by-synthesis model offers a very specific solution to the grain problem. There are two sets of constraints that must be met for the model to work. First, the output of the associative pseudosyntax must provide what is needed for the input to the syntactic derivation. In current grammatical terms, this includes a list of the (inflected) lexical items, phrase information, and information about functional relations, the latter most relevant to sentence/clause-level thematic roles. Accordingly, the levels for learning include mapping low-level information relevant for isolating words, higher-level information for grouping phrases, and semantic-pattern information relevant to sentence-level thematic roles. The last kind of information naturally emphasizes sentence/clause-level structures. This emphasis on sentence/clause-level structures is further confirmed by the fact that the sentence/clause is the natural unit of a complete grammatical derivation, produced by the syntactic component. The result is that the dominant focus of behavior is on sentence/clause-level information. Interpreted as a learning device, the analysis-by-synthesis model will reinforce connections between input information and the assignment of sentence-level structure.

This solves the grain problem for language comprehension. What we show here is that it is possible to extract an answer to the grain problem from the intrinsic structure of a behavioral model. But is this idea generalizable to other kinds of cognitive behaviors? It would be in the spirit of learning theorists to expect that there will be universal features, following on the general idea that there are common laws of learning. That is for others to argue in relation to specific models of other behaviors. Perhaps the solution will be different in every modality; perhaps it will have fundamental universal features that are similar to those we have developed.

10.2.3 Consciousness: The Universality of Analysis by Synthesis and Multiple Drafts

We close this book with a discussion of one of the broadest problems in cognitive science: consciousness. In its preoccupation with issues of structuralism and associationism since the 1960s, psycholinguistics has tended to be quite dry. Big psychological issues such as "beauty" or "happiness" are usually untouched by linguists and psycholinguists alike. A sensible interpretation of this situation is that the disciplines of linguistics and psycholinguistics are highly rarefied and technical. These disciplines illustrate an aspect of the structure of knowledge and a sketch of how that structure is deployed in certain behaviors. But even the most technical matter, such as the architecture of a model of sentence comprehension, may have extensions to broader questions.

Some of today's thinkers on consciousness divide it into technical (also known as "easy") problems of cognitive science, and traditional (also known as "hard") philosophical problems of epistemology. A leading example of the former is Dennett (1991), and a leading example of the latter is Chalmers (1996). We leave the philosophical problems (whatever they may be) to the philosophers. But we find the cognitive science approach to be compatible with our model, and we think that our model may have something to contribute to the problem of consciousness. In Dennett's model, what we think of as conscious representations of the world are actually a set of partially independently formed representations, some of which supplant the others in time, some of which merge. Each representation is a "draft" of reality, which blends in a stream of awareness and occasionally crystallizes into a relatively permanent form. Thus, "consciousness" does not occur in a set mental place, where we project reality to ourselves. Rather, what we mean and experience as consciousness is itself dynamic and self-reforming. Dennett draws on many different kinds of facts from cognitive science to support his view. We think our model has a small additional contribution to make to this enterprise.

We have sketched a comprehension model that chases its tail at least once. It starts with an associatively primed meaning, and then uses that to begin a syntactic derivation that rearrives at a detailed surface form and syntactically enriched meaning. This presents the comprehension process as a set of emerging representations of meaning and structure that converge. We have sketched the representations as occurring in a series, but of course, they could be computed partially in parallel in many actual cases.

Thus, in our model we understand everything twice. This claim flies in the face of our phenomenological experience that we understand sentences once. Intuitively, we think we understand a sentence and are conscious of it and its meaning as a unified experience. Yet, the analyses and experiments we review in this book suggest that this apparently unified process is actually composed of converging operations of quite different kinds. The lack of consistency between our analytic and experimental results on the one hand and our phenomenological experience on the other is a problem that we eventually will have to face.

We can infer that our model of comprehension is an instance of Dennett's "multiple-drafts" model of consciousness. As in the multiple-drafts model, one representational draft has prominence over others, but all drafts are there as a part of the process. The compatibility of our model with the multiple-drafts view of consciousness allows us to enrich methods of studying how the drafts can work together and apart. It is a natural extension of our comprehension model to interpret the initial associative meaning-form hypothesis as one draft of a sentence and its meaning, and the syntactically derived representation of meaning-form as another draft. Thus, our model allows us to specify the nature and structure of each kind of draft, and to study how the formal attributes of each interact with conscious intuitions about them. A particular puzzle about the multiple-drafts theory of consciousness is the frequent intuition that one draft seems to have priority over the others—that is, one draft seems to be the "real" representation. In the case of sentences, the final computed sentence may appear to be the "real" one. What might this tell us about which kinds of drafts dominate others as part of reportable consciousness? There are various options:

· The "latest" draft seems to be the most real by co-opting those that precede it.
· The most "complete" draft seems to be the most real.
· The draft that depends most on internal computations seems to be the most real.

In a real machine, these explanations tend to co-occur. The latest draft is often the most "complete" by virtue of having had more internal computations involved in its production. But it is possible to test at least some of these alternatives by varying the computational complexity of the linguistic stimulus in specific ways, and studying the effects on its perceptual clarity. For example, we can make sentences that are relatively complex in terms of the associative pseudosyntax by violating canonical forms. Or we can make sentences more complex in terms of the formal grammar by requiring longer derivations. We can then examine the behavioral effects of different kinds of complexity. This may lead to some surprising predictions, in particular, that sentences that are more complex actually result in greater acoustic enhancement so long as they are still comprehensible. A similar prediction may follow from certain ungrammatical sentences, namely, those that seem plausible at first.

Such predictions are highly unintuitive, which is why we like them. We have emphasized throughout this book the importance of being able to predict and explain phenomena that are prima facie unlikely or very puzzling. Any old theory can explain the obvious. We look ahead to predicting and explaining the nonobvious. This is the real meaning of the much-misunderstood saying: the exception proves the rule.

References

Aaronson, D., and Scarborough, H. S. (1976). Performance theories for sentence coding: Some quantitative evidence. *Journal of Experimental Psychology: Human Perception and Performance, 2*, 56–70.

Abrams, K., and Bever, T. G. (1969). Syntactic structure modifies attention during speech perception and recognition. *Quarterly Journal of Experimental Psychology, 21*, 280–290.

Altmann, G. T., Garnham, A., and Dennis, Y. (1992). Avoiding the garden path: Eye movements in context. *Journal of Memory and Language, 31*, 685–712.

Altmann, G. T. M., Garnham, A., and Henstra, J. A. (1994). Effects of syntax in human sentence parsing: Evidence against a structure-based proposal mechanism. *Journal of Experimental Psychology: Learning, Memory, & Language, 20*, 209–216.

Altmann, G. T. M., and Steedman, M. (1988). Interaction with context during human sentence processing. *Cognition, 30*, 191–238.

Aslin, R. N., Saffran, J. R., and Newport, E. L. (1998). Computation of conditional probability statistics by 8-month-old infants. *Psychological Science, 9*, 321–324.

Aslin, R. N., Saffran, J. R., and Newport, E. L. (1999). Statistical learning in linguistic and nonlinguistic domains. In B. MacWhinney (Ed.), *The emergence of language* (pp. 359–380). Mahwah, NJ: Erlbaum.

Aslin, R. N., Woodward, J. Z., LaMendola, N. P., and Bever, T. G. (1996). Models of word segmentation in fluent maternal speech to infants. In J. L. Morgan and K. Demuth (Eds.), *Signal to syntax: Bootstrapping from speech to grammar in early acquisition* (pp. 117–134). Mahwah, NJ: Erlbaum.

Baird, R., and Koslick, J. D. (1974). Recall of relations within clause-containing sentences. *Journal of Psycholinguistic Research, 3*, 165–171.

Balogh, J., Zurif, E., Prather, P., Swinney, D., and Finkel L. (1998). Gap-filling and end-of-sentence effects in real-time language processing: Implications for modeling sentence comprehension in aphasia. *Brain and Language, 61*, 169–182.

Bartlett, F. C. (1932). *Remembering.* New York: Cambridge University Press.

Bates, E. (1976). *Language and context: The acquisition of pragmatics.* New York: Academic Press.

Bates, E., and MacWhinney, B. (1982). Functionalist approaches to grammar. In E. Wanner and L. Gleitman (Eds.), *Language acquisition: The state of the art* (pp. 173–218). New York: Cambridge University Press.

Bates, E., and MacWhinney, B. (1987). Competition, variation, and language learning. In B. MacWhinney (Ed.), *Mechanisms of language acquisition* (pp. 157–193). Hillsdale, NJ: Erlbaum.

Bechtel, W., and Abrahamsen, A. (1991). *Connectionism and the mind: An introduction to parallel processing in networks*. Cambridge, MA: Blackwell.

Bennett, P. (1995). *A course in generalized phrase structure grammar*. London: University College London Press.

Berndt, R. S., Mitchum, C. C., and Haendiges, A. N. (1996). Comprehension of reversible sentences in "agrammatism": A meta-analysis. *Cognition, 58*, 289–308.

Bertoncini, J., Floccia, C., Nazzi, T., and Mehler, J. (1995). Morae and syllables: Rhythmical basis of speech representations in neonates. *Language and Speech, 38*, 311–329.

Berwick, R. C., and Weinberg, A. S. (1986). *The grammatical basis of linguistic performance: Language use and acquisition*. Cambridge, MA: MIT Press.

Bever, T. G. (1968a). Associations to stimulus-response theories of language. In T. R. Dixon and D. L. Horton (Eds.), *Verbal behavior and general behavior theory* (pp. 478–494). Englewood Cliffs, N.J.: Prentice-Hall.

Bever, T. G. (1968b). A survey of some recent work in psycholinguistics. In W. J. Plath (Ed.), *Specification and Utilization of Transformational Grammar: Scientific Report Number Three*. Yorktown Heights, NY: Thomas J. Watson Research Center, International Business Machines Corporation.

Bever, T. G. (1970a). The cognitive basis for linguistic structures. In J. R. Hayes (Ed.), *Cognition and the development of language* (pp. 279–362). New York: Wiley.

Bever, T. G. (1970b). The integrated study of language behavior. In J. Morton (Ed.), *Biological and social perspectives in psycholinguistics* (pp. 158–209). Urbana: University of Illinois Press.

Bever, T. G. (1972). The limits of intuition. *Foundations of Language, 8*, 411–412.

Bever, T. G. (1973). Serial position and response biases do not account for the effect of syntactic structure on the location of brief noises during sentences. *Journal of Psycholinguistic Research, 2*, 287–288.

Bever, T. G. (1975). Psychologically real grammar emerges because of its role in language acquisition. *Georgetown University Roundtable on Languages and Linguistics, 1*, 63–75.

Bever, T. G., Carrithers, C., Cowart, W., and Townsend, D. J. (1989). Language processing and familial handedness. In A. Galaburda (Ed.), *From reading to neurons* (pp. 331–357). Cambridge, MA: MIT Press.

Bever, T. G., Fodor, J. A., Garrett, M. F., and Mehler, J. (1966). *Transformational operations and stimulus complexity*. Unpublished manuscript, MIT.

Bever, T. G., Fodor, J. A., and Garrett, M. F. (1968). A formal limitation of associationism. In T. R. Dixon and D. L. Horton (Eds.), *Verbal behavior and general behavior theory* (pp. 582–585). Englewood Cliffs, N.J.: Prentice-Hall.

Bever, T. G., Garrett, M. F., and Hurtig, R. (1973). The interaction of perceptual processes and ambiguous sentences. *Memory and Cognition, 1*, 277–286.

Bever, T. G., and Hurtig, R. (1975). Detection of a nonlinguistic stimulus is poorest at the end of a clause. *Journal of Psycholinguistic Research, 4*, 1–7.

Bever, T. G., Hurtig, R., and Handel, A. (1975). *Response biases do not account for the pattern of click location errors.* Unpublished manuscript, Columbia University.

Bever, T. G., Kirk, R., and Lackner, J. (1969). An autonomic reflection of syntactic structure. *Neuropsychologia, 7,* 23–28.

Bever, T. G., Lackner, J. R., and Kirk, R. (1969). The underlying structures of sentences are the primary units of immediate speech processing. *Perception and Psychophysics, 5,* 225–231.

Bever, T. G., Lackner, J. R., and Stolz, W. (1969). Transitional probability is not a general mechanism for the segmentation of speech. *Journal of Experimental Psychology, 79,* 387–394.

Bever, T. G., and Mehler, J. (1967). The coding hypothesis and short-term memory. *AF Technical Report.* Cambridge, MA: Harvard Center for Cognitive Studies.

Bever, T. G., Mehler, J., Valian, V., Epstein, J., and Morrissey, H. (1969). Linguistic capacity of young children. (Unpublished.) Referred to in J. Fodor, T. G. Bever, and M. F. Garrett (1974), *The psychology of language* (p. 502). New York: McGraw-Hill.

Bever, T. G., Newport, E. L., Aslin, R. N., Mintz, T. H., Juliano, C., and LaMendola, N. P. (1995). *Computational studies of motherese.* Unpublished manuscript, University of Rochester.

Bever, T. G., and Sanz, M. (1997). Empty categories access their antecedents during comprehension: Unaccusatives in Spanish. *Linguistic Inquiry, 28,* 68–91.

Bever, T. G., and Townsend, D. J. (1979). Perceptual mechanisms and formal properties of main and subordinate clauses. In W. C. Cooper and E. C. T. Walker (Eds.), *Sentence processing: Psycholinguistic studies presented to Merrill Garrett* (pp. 159–226). Hillsdale, NJ: Erlbaum.

Bijeljack, B. R., Bertoncini, J., and Mehler, J. (1993). How do 4 day old infants categorize multisyllable utterances? *Developmental Psychology, 29,* 711–721.

Blakemore, D. (1989). Denial and contrast: A relevance theoretic analysis of "but." *Linguistics and Philosophy, 12*(1), 15–37.

Bloomfield, L. (1914). *The study of language.* New York: Holt.

Bloomfield, L. (1933). *Language.* New York: Holt.

Blumenthal, A. L. (1967). Prompted recall of sentences. *Journal of Verbal Learning and Verbal Behavior, 6,* 203–206.

Blumenthal, A. L. (1970). *Language and psychology: Historical aspects of psycholinguistics.* New York: Wiley.

Blumenthal, A. L. (1975). A reappraisal of Wilhelm Wundt. *American Psychologist, 30,* 1081–1088.

Blumenthal, A. L., and Boakes, R. (1967). Prompted recall of sentences: A further study. *Journal of Verbal Learning and Verbal Behavior, 6,* 674–676.

Blumstein, S. E., Byma, G., Kurowski, K., Hourihan, J., Brown, T., and Hutchinson, A. (1998). On-line processing of filler-gap construction in aphasia. *Brain and Language, 61,* 149–168.

Bock, K., and Miller, C. A. (1991). Broken agreement. *Cognitive Psychology, 23,* 45–93.

Boland, J. E. (1993). The role of verb argument structure in sentence processing: Distinguishing between syntactic and semantic effects. *Journal of Psycholinguistic Research, 22,* 133–152.

Boland, J. E. (1997a). The relationship between syntactic and semantic processes in sentence comprehension. *Language and Cognitive Processes, 12*, 423–484.

Boland, J. E. (1997b). Resolving syntactic category ambiguities in discourse context: Probabilistic and discourse constraints. *Journal of Memory and Language, 36*, 588–615.

Boland, J. E., Tanenhaus, M. K., Carlson, G. N., and Garnsey, S. M. (1989). Lexical projection and the interaction of syntax and semantics in parsing. *Journal of Psycholinguistic Research, 18*, 563–576.

Boland, J. E., Tanenhaus, M. K., and Garnsey, S. M. (1990). Evidence for the immediate use of verb control information in sentence processing. *Journal of Memory and Language, 29*, 413–432.

Boland, J. E., Tanenhaus, M. K., Garnsey, S. M., and Carlson, G. N. (1995). Verb argument structure in parsing and interpretation: Evidence from *wh*-questions. *Journal of Memory and Language, 34*, 774–806.

Bower, G. H., Black, J. B., and Turner, T. J. (1979). Scripts in memory for text. *Cognitive Psychology, 11*, 177–220.

Bradshaw, J. L. (1980). Right hemisphere language: Familial and nonfamilial sinistrals, cognitive deficits and writing hand position in sinistrals, and the concrete-abstract, imageable-nonimageable dimensions in word recognition. A review of interrelated issues. *Brain and Language, 10*, 172–188.

Branigan, H. P., Pickering, M. J., Liversedge, S. P., Stewart, A. J., and Urbach, T. P. (1995). Syntactic priming: Investigating the mental representation of language. *Journal of Psycholinguistic Research, 24*, 489–506.

Bransford, J. D., and Franks, J. J. (1971). The abstraction of linguistic ideas. *Cognitive Psychology, 2*, 331–350.

Bransford, J. D., and Franks, J. J. (1972). The abstraction of linguistic ideas: A review. *Cognition, 1*, 211–249.

Bresnan, J., and Kaplan, R. M. (1983). Grammars as the mental representation of language. In J. Bresnan (Ed.), *The mental representation of language*. Cambridge, MA: MIT Press.

Britt, M. A. (1994). The interaction of referential ambiguity and argument structure. *Journal of Memory and Language, 33*, 251–283.

Britt, M. A., Perfetti, C. A., Garrod, S., and Rayner, K. (1992). Parsing in discourse: Context effects and their limits. *Journal of Memory and Language, 31*, 293–314.

Caplan, D. (1972). Clause boundaries and recognition latencies for words in sentences. *Perception & Psychophysics, 12*, 73–76.

Caramazza, A., and Zurif, E. B. (1976). Dissociation of algorithmic and heuristic processes in language comprehension: Evidence from aphasia. *Brain and Language, 3*, 572–582.

Carlson, G. N. (1977). *References to kinds in English*. Unpublished doctoral dissertation, University of Massachusetts, Amherst.

Caron, J. (1997). Toward a procedural approach of the meaning of connectives. In J. Costermans and M. Fayol (Eds.), *Processing interclausal relationships* (pp. 53–73). Hillsdale, NJ: Erlbaum.

Carpenter, P. A., and Daneman, M. (1981). Lexical retrieval and error recovery in reading: A model based on eye fixations. *Journal of Verbal Learning and Verbal Behavior, 20*, 137–160.

Carpenter, P. A., and Just, M. A. (1975). Sentence comprehension: A psycholinguistic processing model of verification. *Psychological Review, 82,* 45–73.

Carroll, J. M. (1978). Sentence perception units and levels of syntactic structure. *Perception & Psychophysics, 23,* 506–514.

Carroll, J. M., and Tanenhaus, M. K. (1975). Functional clauses and sentence segmentation. *Journal of Speech and Hearing Research, 21,* 793–808.

Carroll, P. J., and Slowiaczek, M. L. (1987). Modes and modules: Multiple pathways to the language processor. In J. L. Garfield (Ed.), *Modularity in knowledge representation and natural language understanding* (pp. 221–247). Cambridge, MA: MIT Press.

Chalmers, D. J. (1996). *The conscious mind: In search of a fundamental theory.* New York: Oxford University Press.

Chang, F. R. (1980). Active memory processes in visual sentence comprehension: Clause effects and pronominal reference. *Memory and Cognition, 8,* 58–64.

Chase, W. G., and Clark, H. H. (1972). Mental operations in the comparison of sentences and pictures. In L. W. Gregg (Ed.), *Cognition in learning and memory* (pp. 205–232). New York: Wiley.

Chiarello, C., Liu, S., and Faust, M. (1999). Cerebral asymmetries in sentence priming and the influence of semantic anomaly. *Brain and Cognition, 40,* 75–79.

Chomsky, N. (1957). *Syntactic structures.* The Hague: Mouton.

Chomsky, N. (1959). Review of Skinner's "Verbal Behavior." *Language, 35,* 26–58.

Chomsky, N. (1965). *Aspects of the theory of syntax.* Cambridge, MA: MIT Press.

Chomsky, N. (1966). *Cartesian linguistics.* New York: Harper and Row.

Chomsky, N. (1981). *Lectures on government and binding.* Dordrecht, The Netherlands: Foris.

Chomsky, N. (1985). *Knowledge of language.* New York: Praeger.

Chomsky, N. (1995). *The Minimalist Program.* Cambridge, MA: MIT Press.

Chomsky, N., and Miller, G. A. (1958). Finite state languages. *Information and Control, 1,* 91–112.

Chomsky, N., and Miller, G. A. (1963). Introduction to the formal analysis of natural languages. In D. Luce, R. Bush, and E. Galanter (Eds.), *Handbook of mathematical psychology* (pp. 269–321). New York: Wiley.

Christianson, K., Hollingworth, A., Halliwell, J., and Ferreira, F. (Forthcoming). Thematic roles assigned along the garden path linger. *Cognitive Psychology.*

Clark, H. H., and Chase, W. G. (1972). On the process of comparing sentences against pictures. *Cognitive Psychology, 3,* 472–517.

Clark, H. H., and Clark, E. V. (1968). Semantic distinctions and memory for complex sentences. *Quarterly Journal of Experimental Psychology, 20,* 129–138.

Clarke, C. M., Bever, T. G., and Townsend, D. J. (2000). The role of verb and preposition variables in reduced relative complexity. Poster presented at the annual CUNY Conference on Human Sentence Processing.

Clifton, C., Kurcz, I., and Jenkins, J. J. (1965). Grammatical relations as determinants of sentence similarity. *Journal of Verbal Learning and Verbal Behavior, 4,* 112–117.

Clifton, C., and Odom, P. (1966). Similarity relations among certain English sentence constructions [Special issue]. *Psychological Monographs, 80* (613).

Cofer, C. N. (Ed.). (1961). *Verbal learning and verbal behavior.* New York: McGraw-Hill.

Cofer, C. N., and Musgrave, B. S. (Eds.). (1963). *Verbal behavior and learning: Problems and processes.* New York: McGraw-Hill.

Cohen, L., and Mehler, J. (1996). Click monitoring revisited: An on-line study of sentence comprehension. *Memory & Cognition, 24,* 94–102.

Compton, A. J. (1967). Aural perception of different syntactic structures and length. *Language and Speech, 10,* 81–87.

Cook, V. J., and Newson, M. (1996). *Chomsky's universal grammar.* Cambridge, MA: Blackwell.

Cowart, W., and Cairns, H. S. (1987). Evidence for an anaphoric mechanism within syntactic processing: Some reference relations defy semantic and pragmatic constraints. *Memory and Cognition, 15,* 318–331.

Crain, S., and Fodor, J. D. (1985). How can grammars help the parser? In D. Dowty, L. Kartunnen, and A. M. Zwicky (Eds.), *Natural language parsing: Psychological, computational, and theoretical perspectives* (pp. 94–128). New York: Cambridge University Press.

Crain, S., and Steedman, M. (1985). On not being led up the garden path: The use of context by the psychological parser. In D. R. Dowty, L. Karttunen, and A. M. Zwicky (Eds.), *Natural language parsing: Psychological, computational, and theoretical perspectives* (pp. 320–358). New York: Cambridge University Press.

Crocker, M. W. (1996). *Computational psycholinguistics: An interdisciplinary approach to the study of language.* Boston: Kluwer.

Dakin, J. (1970). Explanations. *Journal of Linguistics, 10,* 199–214.

Davidson, D. (1967). The logical form of action sentences. In N. Rescher (Ed.), *The logic of decision and action* (pp. 81–95). Pittsburgh: University of Pittsburgh Press.

Davidson, R. E. (1969). Transitional errors and deep structure differences. *Psychonomic Science, 14,* 293.

Davison, A., and Lutz, R. (1985). Measuring syntactic complexity relative to discourse context. In D. R. Dowty, L. Karttunen, and A. M. Zwicky (Eds.), *Natural language parsing: Psychological, computational, and theoretical perspectives* (pp. 26–66). New York: Cambridge University Press.

Dennett, D. C. (1991). *Consciousness explained.* Boston: Little, Brown.

deVilliers, P. A., and deVilliers, J. G. (1972). Early judgments of semantic and syntactic acceptability by children. *Journal of Psycholinguistic Research, 1,* 299–310.

van Dijk, T. A. (1977). *Text and context.* London: Longman.

Dowty, D. R. (1979). *Word meaning and Montague grammar.* Dordrecht, The Netherlands: Reidel.

Dowty, D. R. (1991). Thematic proto-roles and argument selection. *Language, 67,* 547–619.

Drai, D., and Grodzinsky, Y. (1999). Comprehension regularities in Broca's aphasia? There's more of it than you ever imagined. *Brain and Language, 70,* 139–143.

Elman, J. L. (1990). Finding structures in time. *Cognitive Science, 14,* 179–211.

Farrar, W. T. IV, and Kawamoto, A. H. (1993). The return of "visiting relatives": Pragmatic effects in sentence processing. *Quarterly Journal of Experimental Psychology*, *46A*, 463–487.

Faust, M., and Chiarello, C. (1998). Constraints on sentence priming in the cerebral hemispheres: Effects of intervening words in sentences and lists. *Brain and Language*, *63*, 219–236.

Feldman, J. A. (1986). *Neural representation of conceptual knowledge*. Cognitive Science Technical Report. Rochester, NY: University of Rochester.

Ferreira, F., and Clifton, C. (1986). The independence of syntactic processing. *Journal of Memory and Language*, *25*, 348–368.

Ferreira, F., and Henderson, J. M. (1991). Recovery from misanalyses of garden-path sentences. *Journal of Memory & Language*, *30*, 725–745.

Ferreira, F., and Henderson, J. M. (1995). Reading processes during syntactic analysis and reanalysis. In J. M. Henderson, M. Singer, and F. Ferreira (Eds.), *Reading and language processing* (pp. 119–147). Mahwah, NJ: Erlbaum.

Ferreira, F., Henderson, J. M., Anes, M. D., Weeks, Jr., P. A., and McFarlane, D. K. (1996). Effects of lexical frequency and syntactic complexity in spoken-language comprehension: Evidence from the auditory moving-window technique. *Journal of Experimental Psychology: Learning, Memory, and Cognition*, *22*, 324–335.

Ferreira, F., and Stacey, J. (2000). *The misinterpretation of passive sentences*. Unpublished manuscript, Michigan State University.

Filip, H., Tanenhaus, M. K., Carlson, G. N., Allopenna, P. D., and Blatt, J. (1997). Reduced relatives judged hard require constraint-based analyses. In P. Merlo and S. Stevenson (Eds.), *Lexical representation and sentence processing* (pp. 349–399). Cambridge, England: Cambridge University Press.

Flores d'Arcais, G. B. (1978). The perception of complex sentences. In W.J.M. Levelt and G. B. Flores d'Arcais (Eds.), *Studies in the perception of language* (pp. 155–185). London: Wiley.

Fodor, J. A. (1965). Could meaning be an r_m? *Journal of Verbal Learning and Verbal Behavior*, *4*, 73–81.

Fodor, J. A. (1966). More about mediators: A reply to Berlyne and Osgood. *Journal of Verbal Learning and Verbal Behavior*, *5*, 412–415.

Fodor, J. A. (1983). *The modularity of mind*. Cambridge, MA: MIT Press.

Fodor, J. A., and Bever, T. G. (1965). The psychological reality of linguistic segments. *Journal of Verbal Learning and Verbal Behavior*, *4*, 414–420.

Fodor, J. A., Bever, T. G., and Garrett, M. F. (1974). *The psychology of language: An introduction to psycholinguistics and generative grammar*. New York: McGraw-Hill.

Fodor, J. A., and Garrett, M. F. (1967). Some syntactic determinants of sentential complexity. *Perception and Psychophysics*, *2*, 289–296.

Fodor, J. A., and McLaughlin, B. P. (1995). Connectionism and the problem of systematicity: Why Smolensky's solution doesn't work. In C. MacDonald and G. MacDonald (Eds.), *Connectionism: Debates on psychological explanation* (Vol. 2, pp. 199–222). Cambridge, MA: Blackwell.

Fodor, J. D. (1978). Parsing strategies and constraints on transformations. *Linguistic Inquiry*, *9*, 427–473.

Fodor, J. D., and Inoue, A. (1998). Attach anyway. In J. D. Fodor and F. Ferreira (Eds.), *Reanalysis in sentence processing* (pp. 101–141). Dordrecht, The Netherlands: Kluwer.

Fodor, J. D., Ni, W., Crain, S., and Shankweiler, D. (1996). Tasks and timing in the perception of linguistic anomaly. *Journal of Psycholinguistic Research, 25,* 25–57.

Ford, M., Bresnan, J., and Kaplan, R. M. (1982). A competence-based theory of syntactic closure. In J. Bresnan (Ed.), *The mental representation of grammatical relations,* 727–796. Cambridge, Mass.: MIT Press.

Forster, K. I. (1970). Visual perception of rapidly presented word sequences of varying complexity. *Perception and Psychophysics, 8,* 215–221.

Forster, K. I. (1979). Levels of processing and the structure of the language processor. In W. E. Cooper and E.C.T. Walker (Eds.), *Sentence processing: Psycholinguistic studies presented to Merrill Garrett* (pp. 27–85). Hillsdale, N.J.: Erlbaum.

Forster, K. I. (1981). Priming and the effects of sentence and lexical contexts on naming time: Evidence for autonomous lexical processing. *Quarterly Journal of Experimental Psychology, 33A,* 465–495.

Forster, K. I., and Olbrei, I. (1973). Semantic heuristics and syntactic analysis. *Cognition, 2,* 319–347.

Forster, K. I., and Ryder, L. A. (1971). Perceiving the structure and meaning of sentences. *Journal of Verbal Learning and Verbal Behavior, 10,* 285–296.

Foss, D. J. (1969). Decision processes during sentence comprehension: Effects of lexical item difficulty and position upon decision times. *Journal of Verbal Learning and Verbal Behavior, 8,* 457–462.

Fox, D., and Grodzinsky, Y. (1998). Children's passive: A view from the *by*-phrase. *Linguistic Inquiry, 29,* 311–332.

Frauenfelder, U., Segui, J., and Mehler, J. (1980). Monitoring around relative clauses. *Journal of Verbal Learning and Verbal Behavior, 19,* 328–337.

Frazier, L. (1978). *On comprehending sentences: Syntactic parsing strategies.* Unpublished doctoral dissertation, University of Connecticut.

Frazier, L. (1985). Modularity and the representational hypothesis. In *NELS 12.* GLSA, University of Massachusetts, Amherst.

Frazier, L. (1987a). Sentence processing: A tutorial review. In M. Coltheart (Ed.), *Attention and performance: Vol. 12. The psychology of reading* (pp. 559–586). Hove, England: Erlbaum.

Frazier, L. (1987b). Theories of sentence processing. In J. L. Garfield (Ed.), *Modularity in knowledge representation and natural-language understanding* (pp. 291–307). Cambridge, MA: MIT Press.

Frazier, L. (1990). Exploring the architecture of the language-processing system. In G.T.M. Altmann (Ed.), *Cognitive models of speech processing: Psycholinguistic and computational perspectives* (pp. 409–433). Cambridge, MA: MIT Press.

Frazier, L., and Clifton, Jr., C. (1996). *Construal.* Cambridge, MA: MIT Press.

Frazier, L., and Clifton, Jr., C. (1998). Comprehension of sluiced sentences. *Language and Cognitive Processes, 13,* 499–520.

Frazier, L., Clifton, C., and Randall, J. (1983). Filling gaps: Decision principles and structure in sentence comprehension. *Cognition, 13,* 187–222.

Frazier, L., and Rayner, K. (1982). Making and correcting errors during sentence comprehension: Eye movements in the analysis of structurally ambiguous sentences. *Cognitive Psychology, 14*, 178–210.

Frazier, L., and Rayner, K. (1987). Resolution of syntactic category ambiguities: Eye movements in parsing lexically ambiguous sentences. *Journal of Memory and Language, 26*, 505–526.

Freedman, S. E., and Forster, K. L. (1985). The psychological status of overgenerated sentences. *Cognition, 19*, 101–132.

Friederici, A. D. (1985). Levels of processing and vocabulary types: Evidence from online comprehension in normals and agrammatics. *Cognition, 19*, 133–166.

Friederici, A. D. (1997). Diagnosis and reanalysis: Two processing aspects the brain may differentiate. In J. D. Fodor and F. Ferreira (Eds.), *Reanalysis in sentence processing* (pp. 177–200). Dordrecht, The Netherlands: Kluwer.

Friederici, A. D., Hahne, A., and Cramon, D. Y. von. (1998). First-pass versus second-pass parsing processes in a Wernicke's area and Broca's area aphasic: Electrophysiological evidence for a double dissociation. *Brain and Language, 62*, 311–341.

Friederici, A. D., Hahne, A., and Mecklinger, A. (1996). Temporal structure of syntactic parsing: Early and late event-related brain potential effects. *Journal of Experimental Psychology: Learning, Memory, and Cognition, 22*, 1219–1248.

Friederici, A. D., Pfiefer, E., and Hahne, A. (1993). Event-related brain potentials during natural speech processing: Effects of semantic, morphological, and syntactic violations. *Cognitive Brain Research, 1*, 183–192.

Friedman, D., Simson, R., Ritter, W., and Rapin, I. (1975). The late positive component (P300) and information processing in sentences. *Electroencephalography and Clinical Neurophysiology, 38*, 255–262.

Garnsey, S. M., Pearlmutter, N. J., Myers, M., and Lotocky, M. A. (1997). The contributions of verb bias and plausibility to the comprehension of temporarily ambiguous sentences. *Journal of Memory & Language, 37*, 58–93.

Garrett, M. F. (1965). *Syntactic structures and judgments of auditory events*. Unpublished doctoral dissertation, University of Illinois.

Garrett, M. F. (1999). Remarks on the architecture of language processing systems. In Y. Grodzinsky, L. Shapiro, and D. Swinney (Eds.), *Language and the brain: Representation and processing* (pp. 31–69). San Diego, CA: Academic Press.

Garrett, M. F., Bever, T. G., and Fodor, J. A. (1966). The active use of grammar in speech perception. *Perception and Psychophysics, 1*, 30–32.

Gazdar, G., Klein, E., Pullum, G., and Sag, I. (1985). *Generalized phrase structure grammar*. Cambridge, MA: Harvard University Press.

Gerken, L. (1991). The metrical basis for children's subjectless sentences. *Journal of Memory and Language, 30*, 431–451.

Gerken, L. (1994). Sentential processes in early child language: Evidence from the perception and production of function morphemes. In J. C. Goodman and H. C. Nusbaum (Eds.), *The development of speech perception: The transition from speech sounds to spoken words* (pp. 271–298). Cambridge, MA: MIT Press.

Gerken, L. (1996). Phonological and distributional information in syntax acquisition. In J. L. Morgan and K. Demuth (Eds.), *Signal to syntax: Bootstrapping from speech to grammar in early acquisition* (pp. 411–426). Mahwah, NJ: Erlbaum.

Gibson, E. (1998). Linguistic complexity: Locality of syntactic dependencies. *Cognition, 68,* 1–76.

Golding, J. M., Millis, K. M., Hauselt, J., and Sego, S. A. (1995). The effect of connectives and causal relatedness on text comprehension. In R. F. Lorch and E. J. O'Brien (Eds.), *Sources of coherence in reading* (pp. 127–143). Hillsdale, NJ: Erlbaum.

Gomez, R. L., and Gerken, L. (1999). Artificial grammar learning by 1-year-olds leads to specific and abstract knowledge. *Cognition, 70,* 109–135.

Gorrell, P. (1995). *Syntax and parsing.* New York: Cambridge University Press.

Gorrell, P. (1998). Syntactic analysis and reanalysis in sentence processing. In J. D. Fodor and F. Ferreira (Eds.), *Reanalysis in sentence processing* (pp. 201–245). Dordrecht, The Netherlands: Kluwer.

Gough, P. B. (1965). Grammatical transformations and speed of understanding. *Journal of Verbal Learning and Verbal Behavior, 4,* 107–111.

Gough, P. B. (1966). The verification of sentences: The effects of delay of evidence and sentence length. *Journal of Verbal Learning and Verbal Behavior, 5,* 492–496.

Grodzinksy, Y. (1986). Language deficits and the theory of syntax. *Brain and Language, 27,* 135–159.

Grodzinksy, Y. (1995). A restrictive theory of agrammatic comprehension. *Brain and Language, 50,* 27–51.

Grodzinsky, Y., Pinango, M. M., Zurif, E., and Drai, D. (1999). The critical role of group studies in neuropsychology: Comprehension regularities in Broca's aphasia. *Brain and Language, 67,* 134–147.

Haberlandt, K. F. (1982). Reader expectations in text comprehension. In J. F. Ny and W. Kintsch (Eds.), *Language and comprehension* (pp. 239–250). Amsterdam: North Holland.

Haberlandt, K. F., and Bingham, G. (1978). Verbs contribute to the coherence of brief narratives: Reading related and unrelated sentence triples. *Journal of Verbal Learning and Verbal Behavior, 17,* 419–425.

Haberlandt, K. F., and Graesser, A. C. (1985). Component processes in text comprehension and some of their interactions. *Journal of Experimental Psychology: General, 114,* 357–374.

Hagoort, P., Brown, C., and Groothusen, J. (1993). The syntactic positive shift (SPS) as an ERP measure of syntactic processing. *Language & Cognitive Processes, 8,* 439–483.

Hakes, D. T., Evans, J. S., and Brannon, L. L. (1976). Understanding sentences with relative clauses. *Memory & Cognition, 4,* 283–290.

Halle, M., and Stevens, K. N. (1964). Speech recognition: A model and a program for research. In J. A. Fodor and J. J. Katz (Eds.), *The structure of language: Readings in the philosophy of language.* Englewood Cliffs, NJ: Prentice-Hall.

Halliday, M.A.K., and Hasan, R. (1976). *Cohesion in English.* London: Longman Press.

Hanna, J. E., Barker, C., and Tanenhaus, M. (1995). Integrating local and discourse constraints in resolving lexical thematic ambiguities. Poster presented at the Eighth Annual CUNY Conference on Human Sentence Processing, Tucson, AZ.

Hardyck, C. (1977). A model of individual differences in hemispheric functioning. In H. Whitaker and H. A. Whitaker (Eds.), *Studies in neurolinguistics*, vol. 3 (pp. 223–256). New York: Academic Press.

Harley, H. (1998). *Papers from the UPenn/MIT Roundtable on argument structure and aspect*. Cambridge, MA: Department of Linguistics and Philosophy, MIT.

Harris, Z. (1957). Co-occurrence and transformation in linguistic structure. *Language, 33*, 283–340.

Harris, Z. (1958). Linguistic transformations for information retrieval. *Proceedings of the International Conference on Scientific Information* (Vol. 2). Washington, DC: NAS-WRC.

Harsham, R. A., Hampson, R., and Berenbaum, S. A. (1983). Individual differences in cognitive abilities and brain organization: Part I: Sex and handedness differences in ability. *Canadian Journal of Psychology, 37*, 144–192.

Haviland, S. E., and Clark, H. H. (1974). What's new? Acquiring new information as a process in comprehension. *Journal of Verbal Learning and Verbal Behavior, 13*, 512–521.

Hecaen, H., de Agostini, M., and Monzon-Montes, A. (1981). Cerebral organization in left-handers. *Brain and Language, 12*, 261–284.

Hecaen, H., and Sauguet, J. (1971). Cerebral dominance in left-handed subjects. *Cortex, 7*, 19–48.

Heller, J. (1961). *Catch-22, a novel*. New York: Simon and Schuster.

Hickok, G., Zurif, E., and Canseco-Gonzales, E. (1993). Structural description of agrammatic comprehension. *Brain and Language, 45*, 371–395.

Higginbotham, J. (1996). *On events in linguistic semantics*. Unpublished manuscript.

Hirst, W. (1988). *The making of cognitive science: Essays in honor of George A. Miller*. New York: Cambridge University Press.

Holmes, V. M. (1973). Order of main and subordinate clauses in sentence perception. *Journal of Verbal Learning and Verbal Behavior, 12*, 285–293.

Holmes, V. M. (1979). Some hypotheses about syntactic processing in sentence comprehension. In W. E. Cooper and E.C.T. Walker (Eds.), *Sentence processing: Psycholinguistic studies presented to Merrill Garrett* (pp. 227–247). Hillsdale, NJ: Erlbaum.

Holmes, V. M., and Forster, K. I. (1970). Detection of extraneous signals during sentence recognition. *Perception and Psychophysics, 7*, 297–301.

Holmes, V. M., and Forster, K. I. (1972). Click location and syntactic structure. *Perception and Psychophysics, 12*, 9–15.

Holmes, V. M., and O'Reagan, J. K. (1981). Eye fixation patterns during the reading of relative-clause sentences. *Journal of Verbal Learning and Verbal Behavior, 20*, 417–430.

Holmes, V. M., Stowe, L. A., and Cupples, L. (1989). Lexical expectations in parsing complement-verb sentences. *Journal of Memory and Language, 28*, 668–689.

Hull, C. L. (1943). *Principles of behavior*. New York: Appleton-Century-Crofts.

Humboldt, W. V. (1835/1903). *Über Verschiedenheit des menschlichen Sprachbaues und ihren Einfluss auf die geistige Entwicklung des Menschengeschlechts*. In *Gesammelte Schriften* (Vol. 7). Berlin: Königlich Preussiche Akademie der Wissenschaften.

Irwin, J. W., and Pulver, C. J. (1984). Effects of explicitness, clause order, and reversibility on children's comprehension of causal relationships. *Journal of Educational Psychology, 76,* 399–407.

Jackendoff, R. (1969). An interpretative theory of negation. *Foundations of Language, V,* 218–241.

Jackendoff, R. (1990). *Semantic structures.* Cambridge, MA: MIT Press.

James, W. (1890). *Principles of psychology.* New York: Holt.

Jarvella, R. J. (1971). Syntactic processing of connected speech. *Journal of Verbal Learning and Verbal Behavior, 10,* 409–416.

Jenkins, J. J., Fodor, J. A., and Saporta, S. (1965). *An introduction to psycholinguistic theory.* Unpublished manuscript, University of Minnesota.

Jennings, F., Randall, B., and Tyler, L. K. (1997). Graded effects of verb subcategory preferences on parsing: Support for constraint-satisfaction models. *Language and Cognitive Processes, 12,* 485–504.

Johnson, N. F. (1965). The psychological reality of phrase structure rules. *Journal of Verbal Learning and Verbal Behavior, 4,* 469–475.

Jou, J., and Harris, R. J. (1990). Event order versus syntactic structure in recall of adverbial complex sentences. *Journal of Psycholinguistic Research, 19,* 21–42.

Juliano, C., and Bever, T. G. (1988). *Clever moms.* Unpublished manuscript, University of Rochester.

Juliano, C., and Tanenhaus, M. K. (1994). A constraint based lexicalist account of the subject/object attachment preference. *Journal of Psycholinguistic Research, 23,* 459–471.

Jurafsky, D. (1996). Probabilistic model of lexical and syntactic access and disambiguation. *Cognitive Science, 20,* 137–194.

Just, M. A., and Carpenter, P. A. (1980). A spreading activation theory of reading: From eye fixations to comprehension. *Psychological Review, 87,* 329–354.

Just, M. A., Carpenter, P. A., and Woolley, J. D. (1982). Paradigms and processes in reading comprehension. *Journal of Experimental Psychology: General, 111,* 228–238.

Kahneman, D. (1973). *Attention and effort.* Englewood Cliffs, NJ: Prentice-Hall.

Kaplan, R. M., and Bresnan, J. (1982). Lexical Functional grammar: A formal system for grammatical representation. In J. Bresnan (Ed.), *The mental representation of grammatical relations* (pp. 173–281). Cambridge, MA: MIT Press.

Katz, J. J., and Bever, T. G. (1975). The fall and rise of empiricism. In T. G. Bever, J. J. Katz, and D. T. Langendoen (Eds.), *An integrated theory of linguistic ability* (pp. 11–64). New York: Crowell.

Katz, J. J., and Postal, P. M. (1964). *An integrated theory of linguistic descriptions.* Cambridge, MA: MIT Press.

Keenan, J. M., Baillet, S. D., and Brown, P. (1984). The effects of causal cohesion on comprehension and memory. *Journal of Verbal Learning & Verbal Behavior, 23,* 115–126.

Kendler, H. H., and Kendler, T. S. (1962). Vertical and horizontal processes in problem-solving. *Psychological Review, 69,* 1–16.

Kertesz, A. (1999). Language and the frontal lobes. In B. L. Miller and J. L. Cummings (Eds.), *The Human Frontal Lobes: Functions and Disorders* (pp. 261–276). New York: Guilford Press.

King, J., and Just, M. A. (1991). Individual differences in syntactic processing: The role of working memory. *Journal of Memory and Language, 30*, 580–602.

King, J. W., and Kutas, M. (1995). Who did what and when? Using word- and clause-related ERPs to monitor working memory usage in reading. *Journal of Cognitive Neuroscience, 7*, 378–397.

Kjelgaard, M. M., and Speer, S. R. (1998). *Levels of prosodic phrasing and the on-line resolution of temporary syntactic closure ambiguity.* Unpublished manuscript, University of Kansas.

Kjelgaard, M. M., and Speer, S. R. (1999). Prosodic facilitation and interference in the resolution of temporary syntactic closure ambiguity. *Journal of Memory and Language, 40*, 153–194.

Kluender, R., and Kutas, M. (1993). Bridging the gap: Evidence from ERPs on the processing of unbounded dependencies. *Journal of Cognitive Neuroscience, 5*, 196–214.

Koffka, K. (1935). *Principle of Gestalt psychology.* New York: Harcourt, Brace & World.

Kratzer, A. (1995). *The event argument and the semantics of voice.* Unpublished manuscript, University of Massachusetts, Amherst.

Kutas, M. (1997). Views on how the electrical activity that the brain generates reflects the functions of different language structures. *Psychophysiology, 34*, 383–398. (Presidential address to the Society for Psychophysiological Research)

Kutas, M., and Hillyard, S. A. (1983). Event-related brain potentials to grammatical errors and semantic anomalies. *Memory & Cognition, 11*, 539–550.

Kutas, M., and King, J. W. (1996). The potentials for basic sentence processing: Differentiating integrative processes. In I. Ikeda and J. L. McClelland (Eds.), *Attention and performance* (Vol. 16, pp. 501–546). Cambridge, MA: MIT Press.

Ladefoged, P., and Broadbent, D. F. (1957). Information conveyed by vowels. *Journal of the Acoustical Society of America, 29*, 98–104.

Lakoff, G. (1971). On generative semantics. In D. Steinberg and L. Jakobovits (Eds.), *Semantics* (pp. 232–296). New York: Cambridge University Press.

Lakoff, G. (1972). The arbitrary basis of transformational grammar. *Language, 48*, 76–85.

Lakoff, G. (1973). Fuzzy grammar and the performance/competence terminology game. *Papers from the Ninth Regional Meeting of the Chicago Linguistic Society* (pp. 271–291). Chicago: Chicago Linguistic Society.

Lakoff, G., and Ross, J. R. (1976). Is deep structure necessary? In J. McCawley (Ed.), *Syntax and semantics* (Vol. 7, pp. 159–164). New York: Academic Press.

Lashley, K. (1951). The problem of serial order in behavior. In L. A. Jeffress (Ed.), *Cerebral mechanisms in behavior* (pp. 112–136). New York: Wiley.

Lehman, M. (1990). *The effect of format, context, and connective on reading and understanding of medical terms by skilled and average readers.* Unpublished master's thesis, Montclair State University.

Levelt, W.J.M. (1970). A scaling approach to the study of syntactic relations. In G. B. Flores d'Arcais and W.J.M. Levelt (Eds.), *Advances in psycholinguistics* (pp. 109–121). New York: American Elsevier.

Lewis, R. (1998). Reanalysis and limited repair parsing: Leaping off the garden path. In J. D. Fodor and F. Ferreira (Eds.), *Reanalysis in sentence processing* (pp. 247–285). Dordrecht, The Netherlands: Kluwer.

Liberman, A. M., Cooper, F. S., Shankweiler, D. P., and Studdert-Kennedy, M. (1967). Perception of the speech code. *Psychological Review, 74,* 431–461.

Linebarger, M. C., Schwartz, M. F., and Saffran, E. M. (1983). Sensitivity to grammatical structure in so-called agrammatic aphasics. *Cognition, 13,* 361–392.

Liversedge, S. P., Pickering, M. J., and Branigan, H. P. (1995). The comprehension of sentences that are ambiguous between agentive and locative interpretations. Poster presented at the Eighth Annual CUNY Sentence Processing Conference, Tucson, AZ.

Liversedge, S. P., Pickering, M. J., Branigan, H. P., and van Gompel, R.G.P. (1998). Processing arguments and adjuncts in isolation and context: The case of by-phrase ambiguities in passives. *Journal of Experimental Psychology: Learning, Memory, & Cognition, 24,* 461–475.

Lombardi, L., and Potter, M. C. (1992). The regeneration of syntax in short term memory. *Journal of Memory and Language, 31,* 713–733.

MacDonald, M. C. (1993). The interaction of lexical and syntactic ambiguity. *Journal of Memory and Language, 32,* 692–715.

MacDonald, M. C. (1994). Probabilistic constraints and syntactic ambiguity resolution. *Language and Cognitive Processes, 9,* 157–201.

MacDonald, M. C., Pearlmutter, N. J., and Seidenberg, M. S. (1994). The lexical nature of syntactic ambiguity resolution. *Psychological Review, 101,* 676–703.

MacWhinney, B. (1987). The competition model. In B. MacWhinney (Ed.), *Mechanisms of language acquisition* (pp. 249–308). Hillsdale, NJ: Erlbaum.

MacWhinney, B., and Snow, C. (1985). The child language data exchange system. *Journal of Child Language, 12,* 271–295.

Mandler, G., and Mandler, J. (1964). Serial position effects in sentences. *Journal of Verbal Learning and Verbal Behavior, 3,* 195–202.

Maratsos, M. (1974). Children who get worse at understanding the passive: A replication of Bever. *Journal of Psycholinguistic Research, 3,* 65–74.

Marcus, M. P. (1980). *A theory of syntactic recognition for natural language.* Cambridge, MA: MIT Press.

Marr, D. (1976). Early processing of visual information. *Philosophical Transactions of the Royal Society of London, B, 275,* 483–524.

Marshall, J. C. (1980). The new organology. *Behavioral and Brain Sciences, 2,* 472–473.

Marslen-Wilson, W. D., and Tyler, L. K. (1980). The temporal structure of spoken language understanding. *Cognition, 8,* 1–71.

Marslen-Wilson, W. D., and Tyler, L. K. (1987). Against modularity. In J. L. Garfield (Ed.), *Modularity in knowledge representation and natural-language understanding* (pp. 37–62). Cambridge, MA: MIT Press.

Marslen-Wilson, W. D., Tyler, L. K., and Seidenberg, M. S. (1978). Sentence processing and the clause boundary. In W.J.M. Levelt and G. Flores d'Arcais (Eds.), *Studies in the perception of language* (pp. 219–246). London: Wiley.

Marslen-Wilson, W. D., and Welsh, A. (1978). Processing interactions and lexical access during word recognition and continuous speech. *Cognitive Psychology*, *10*, 29–63.

Mauner, G., and Koenig, J. (1999). Lexical encoding of event participant information. *Brain and Language*, *68*, 178–184.

Mauner, G., Tanenhaus, M. K., and Carlson, G. N. (1995). Implicit arguments in sentence processing. *Journal of Memory and Language*, *34*, 357–382.

Mazuka, R. (1998). *The development of language processing strategies: A cross-linguistic study between Japanese and English*. Hillsdale, NJ: Erlbaum.

McCabe, A., and Peterson, C. (1988). A comparison of adult's versus children's spontaneous use of because and so. *Journal of Genetic Psychology*, *149*, 257–268.

McCawley, J. (1968a). Lexical insertion in a transformational grammar without deep structure. *Papers from the Fourth Regional Meeting of the Chicago Linguistic Society* (pp. 71–80). Chicago; Chicago Linguistic Society. (Reprinted in J. McCawley, *Grammar and meaning*, 1976, New York: Academic Press)

McCawley, J. (1968b). The role of semantics in grammar. In E. Bach and R. Harms (Eds.), *Universals in linguistic theory* (pp. 127–170). New York: Holt, Rinehart and Winston.

McClelland, J. L., and Rumelhart, D. E. (1986). Distributed memory and the representation of general and specific information. *Journal of Experimental Psychology: General*, *114*, 159–188.

McElree, B., and Bever, T. G. (1989). The psychological reality of linguistically defined gaps. *Journal of Psycholinguistics Research*, *18*, 21–35.

McElree, B., and Griffith, T. (1995). Syntactic and thematic processing in sentence comprehension: Evidence for a temporal dissociation. *Journal of Experimental Psychology: Learning, Memory, and Cognition*, *21*, 134–157.

McElree, B., and Griffith, T. (1998). Structural and lexical constraints on gap-filling: A time course analysis. *Journal of Experimental Psychology: Learning, Memory, and Cognition*, *24*, 432–460.

McKeever, W. F. (1986). The influences of sex, familial sinistrality, and androgyny on language laterality, verbal ability, and spatial ability. *Cortex*, *22*, 521–537.

McKinnon, R., and Osterhout, L. (1996). Constraints on movement phenomena in sentence processing: Evidence from event-related brain potentials. *Language and Cognitive Processes*, *11*, 495–523.

McKoon, G., Allbritton, D., and Ratcliff, R. C. (1996). Sentential context effects on lexical decisions with a cross modal instead of all visual procedure. *Journal of Experimental Psychology*, *22*, 1494–1497.

McKoon, G., and Ratcliff, R. C. (1994). Sentential context and on-line lexical decision. *Journal of Experimental Psychology: Learning, Memory, and Cognition*, *20*, 1239–1243.

McMahon, L. (1963). *Grammatical analysis as part of understanding a sentence*. Unpublished doctoral dissertation, Harvard University.

McRae, K., Ferretti, T. R., and Amyote, L. (1997). Thematic roles as verb-specific concepts. *Language and Cognitive Processes*, *12*, 137–176.

McRae, K., Spivey-Knowlton, M. J., and Tanenhaus, M. K. (1998). Modeling the influence of thematic fit (and other constraints) in on-line sentence comprehension. *Journal of Memory and Language*, *38*, 283–312.

Mecklinger, A., Schriefers, H., Steinhauer, K., and Friederici, A. D. (1995). Processing relative clauses varying on syntactic and semantic dimensions: An analysis with event-related potentials. *Memory & Cognition, 23*, 477–494.

Mehler, J. (1963). Some effects of grammatical transformations on the recall of English sentences. *Journal of Verbal Learning and Verbal Behavior, 2*, 346–351.

Mehler, J., Bever, T. G., and Carey, P. (1967). What we look at when we read. *Perception and Psychophysics, 2*, 213–218.

Mehler, J., and Carey, P. (1967). Role of surface and base structure in the perception of sentences. *Journal of Verbal Learning and Verbal Behavior, 6*, 335–338.

Melinger, A., and Mauner, G. (1999). When are implicit agents encoded? Evidence from cross-modal naming. *Brain and Language, 68*, 185–191.

Miller, G. A. (1951a). *Language and communication.* New York: McGraw-Hill.

Miller, G. A. (1951b). Speech and language. In S. S. Stevens (Ed.), *Handbook of experimental psychology* (pp. 769–810). New York: Wiley.

Miller, G. A. (1957). Some effects of intermittent silence. *American Journal of Psychology, 70*, 311–314.

Miller, G. A. (1962a). Decision units in the perception of speech. *IRE Transactions on Information Theory, 2*, IT-8.

Miller, G. A. (1962b). Some psychological studies of grammar. *American Psychologist, 17*, 748–762. (Presidential address to the Eastern Psychological Association, April 1962)

Miller, G. A., and Chomsky, N. (1963). Finitary models of language users. In D. Luce, R. Bush, and E. Galanter (Eds.), *Handbook of mathematical psychology* (Vol. 2, pp. 419–491). New York: Wiley.

Miller, G. A., Galanter, E., and Pribram, K. (1960). *Plans and the structure of behavior.* New York: Holt.

Miller, G. A., Heise, G. A., and Lichten, W. (1951). The intelligibility of speech as a function of the context of the test materials. *Journal of Experimental Psychology, 41*, 329–335.

Miller, G. A., and Isard, S. (1963). Some perceptual consequences of linguistic rules. *Journal of Verbal Learning and Verbal Behavior, 2*, 217–228.

Miller, G. A., and McKean, K. O. (1964). Chronometric study of some relations between sentences. *Quarterly Journal of Experimental Psychology, 16*, 297–308.

Miller, G. A., and Selfridge, J. A. (1950). Verbal context and the recall of meaningful material. *American Journal of Psychology, 63*, 176–185.

Millis, K. K., and Just, M. A. (1994). The influence of connectives on sentence comprehension. *Journal of Memory and Language, 33*, 128–147.

Mintz, T. H. (1997). *The roles of linguistic input and innate mechanisms in children's acquisition of grammatical categories.* Unpublished doctoral dissertation, University of Rochester.

Mitchell, D. C. (1989). Verb guidance and other lexical effects in parsing. *Language and Cognitive Processes, 4*, SI123–SI154.

Mitchell, D. C., Corley, M. M., and Garnham, A. (1992). Effects of context in human sentence parsing: Evidence against a discourse-based proposal mechanism. *Journal of Experimental Psychology: Learning, Memory, & Cognition, 18*, 69–88.

Mitchell, D. C., Cuetos, F., Corley, M.M.B., and Brysbaert, M. (1995). Exposure based models of human parsing: Evidence for the use of coarse-grained (nonlexical) statistical records. *Journal of Psycholinguistic Research, 24,* 469–488.

Miyake, A., Carpenter, P. A., and Just, M. A. (1994). A capacity approach to syntactic comprehension disorders: Making normal adults perform like aphasic patients. *Cognitive Neuropsychology, 11,* 671–717.

Moon, C., Bever, T. G., and Fifer, W. P. (1992). Canonical and non-canonical syllable discrimination by two day old infants. *Journal of Child Language, 19,* 1–17.

Murray, J. D. (1995). Logical connectives and local coherence. In R. F. Lorch and E. J. O'Brien (Eds.), *Sources of coherence in reading* (pp. 107–125). Hillsdale, NJ: Erlbaum.

Murray, J. D. (1997). Connectives and narrative text: The role of continuity. *Memory and Cognition, 25,* 227–236.

Murray, W. S., and Liversedge, S. P. (1994). Referential context effects on syntactic processing. In C. Clifton, L. Frazier, and K. Rayner (Eds.), *Perspectives on sentence processing* (pp. 359–388). Hillsdale, NJ: Erlbaum.

Murray, W. S., and Rowan, M. (1998). Early, mandatory, pragmatic processing. *Journal of Psycholinguistic Research, 27,* 1–22.

Myers, J. L., Shinjo, M., and Duffy, S. A. (1987). Degree of causal relatedness and memory. *Journal of Memory and Language, 26,* 453–465.

Neisser, U. (1967). *Cognitive psychology.* New York: Appleton-Century-Crofts.

Neville, H. J., Nicol, J. L., Barss, A., Forster, K. I., and Garrett, M. F. (1991). Syntactically based sentence processing classes: Evidence from event-related brain potentials. *Journal of Cognitive Neuroscience, 3,* 151–165.

Newmeyer, F. (1980). *Linguistic theory in America.* New York: Academic Press.

Nicol, J. L., Fodor, J. D., and Swinney, D. (1994). Using cross-modal lexical decision tasks to investigate sentence processing. *Journal of Experimental Psychology: Learning, Memory, and Cognition, 20,* 1229–1238.

Nicol, J. L., Forster, K. I., and Veres, C. (1997). Subject-verb agreement processes in comprehension. *Journal of Memory & Language, 36,* 569–587.

Nicol, J. L., and Swinney, D. (1989). The role of structure in coreference assignment during sentence comprehension. *Journal of Psycholinguistic Research, 18,* 5–19.

Noordman, L. G., and Vonk, W. (1997). The different functions of a conjunction in constructing a representation of the discourse. In J. Costermans and M. Fayol (Eds.), *Processing interclausal relationships* (pp. 75–93). Hillsdale, NJ: Erlbaum.

Noordman, L. G., Vonk, W., and Kempf, H. J. (1992). Causal inferences during the reading of expository texts. *Journal of Memory and Language, 31,* 573–590.

O'Bryan, E., Bever, T. G., Townsend, D. J., and Nicol, J. (2000). Reduced relatives and *wh*-gaps in spoken sentence comprehension. Poster presented at the annual CUNY Conference on Human Sentence Processing.

O'Seaghdha, P. G. (1997). Conjoint and dissociable effects of syntactic and semantic context. *Journal of Experimental Psychology: Learning, Memory, and Cognition, 23,* 807–828.

Osgood, C. E. (1963). On understanding and creating sentences. *American Psychologist, 18,* 735–751.

Osgood, C. E., and Maclay, H. (1967). Hesitation phenomena in spontaneous English speech. In L. A. Jakobovits and M. S. Miron (Eds.), *Readings in the psychology of language* (pp. 305–324). Englewood Cliffs, NJ: Prentice-Hall.

Osgood, C. E., and Sebeok, T. A. (Eds.). (1954). *Psycholinguistics: A survey of theory and research problems.* Supplement to the *International Journal of American Linguistics, 20*(4). (Reprinted by Indiana University Press, 1969)

Osgood, C. Suci, G., and Tannenbaum, P. (1957). *The measurement of meaning.* Urbana: University of Illinois Press.

Osterhout, L., and Holcomb, P. J. (1992). Event-related brain potentials elicited by syntactic anomaly. *Journal of Memory and Language, 31,* 785–806.

Osterhout, L., and Holcomb, P. J. (1993). Event-related potentials and syntactic anomaly: Evidence of anomaly detection during the perception of continuous speech. *Language & Cognitive Processes, 8,* 413–437.

Osterhout, L., and Mobley, L. A. (1995). Event-related brain potentials elicited by failure to agree. *Journal of Memory and Language, 34,* 739–773.

Osterhout, L., and Swinney, D. A. (1993). On the temporal course of gap-filling during comprehension of verbal passives. *Journal of Psycholinguistic Research, 22,* 273–286.

Otake, T., Hatano, G., Cutler, A., and Mehler, J. (1993). Mora or syllable? Speech segmentation in Japanese. *Journal of Memory and Language, 32,* 258–278.

Parson, T. (1990). *Events in the semantics of English.* Cambridge, MA: MIT Press.

Pearlmutter, N. J., and MacDonald, M. C. (1992). Plausibility and syntactic resolution. In *Proceedings of the annual meetings of the Cognitive Science Society* (pp. 498–503). Hillsdale, NJ: Erlbaum.

Peterson, M. A. (1994). Object recognition processes can and do operate before figure-ground organization. *Current Directions in Psychological Science, 3,* 105–111.

Pickering, M. J., and Traxler, M. J. (1998). Plausibility and recovery from garden paths: An eye-tracking study. *Journal of Experimental Psychology, 24,* 940–961.

Pinker, S. (1984). *Language learnability and language development.* Cambridge, MA: Harvard University Press.

Pinker, S., Lebeaux, D. S., and Frost, L. A. (1987). Productivity and constraints in the acquisition of the passive. *Cognition, 26,* 195–267.

Postal, P. M. (1967). Linguistic anarchy notes. In J. McCawley (Ed.), *Syntax and semantics* (Vol. 7, pp. 201–226). New York: Academic Press.

Potter, M. C., and Lombardi, L. (1990). Regeneration in the short-term recall of sentences. *Journal of Memory and Language, 29,* 633–654.

Potter, M. C., and Lombardi, L. (1998). Syntactic priming in immediate recall of sentences. *Journal of Memory and Language, 38,* 265–282.

Pritchett, B. L. (1992). *Grammatical competence and parsing performance.* Chicago: University of Chicago Press.

Pulvermuller, F. (1995). Agrammatism: Behavioral description and neurobiological explanation. *Journal of Cognitive Neuroscience, 7,* 165–181.

Pylyshyn, A. (1984). *Computation and cognition.* Boston: MIT Press.

Quirk, R., Greenbaum, S., Leech, G., and Svartvik, J. (1972). *A grammar of contemporary English*. New York: Seminar Press.

Radford, A. (1997). *Syntax: A minimalist introduction*. Cambridge, England: Cambridge University Press.

Rayner, K., Carlson, M., and Frazier, L. (1983). The interaction of syntax and semantics during sentence processing: Eye movements in the analysis of semantically biased sentences. *Journal of Verbal Learning and Verbal Behavior, 22*, 358–374.

Rayner, K., Garrod, S., and Perfetti, C. A. (1992). Discourse influences during parsing are delayed. *Cognition, 45*, 109–139.

Rodriguez, C., Ravelo, N., and Townsend, D. J. (1980). Bilinguals' memory for the language of sentences in discourse. *The Bilingual Review, 7*, 8–14.

Rösler, F., Puetz, P., Friederici, A. N., and Hahne, A. (1993). Event-related brain potentials while encountering semantic and syntactic constraint violations. *Journal of Cognitive Neuroscience, 5*, 345–362.

Ross, J. R. (1974). Three batons for cognitive psychology. In W. B. Weimer and D. S. Palermo (Eds.), *Cognition and the symbolic processes* (pp. 63–124). Hillsdale, NJ: Erlbaum.

Rumelhart, D. E. (1989). The architecture of mind: A connectionist approach. In M. I. Posner (Ed.), *Foundation of cognitive science* (pp. 133–159). Cambridge, MA: MIT Press.

Rumelhart, D. E., Hinton, G. E., and Williams, R. J. (1986). Learning internal representations by error propagation. In D. E. Rumelhart, J. L. McClelland, and the PDP Research Group (Eds.), *Parallel distributed processing: Explorations in the microstructure of cognition* (pp. 318–362). Cambridge, MA: MIT Press.

Rumelhart, D. E., and McClelland, J. L. (1986). On learning the past tenses of English verbs. In J. L. McClelland, D. E. Rumelhart, and the PDP Research Group (Eds.), *Parallel distributed processing: Explorations of the microstructure of cognition* (Vol. 2, pp. 216–271). Cambridge, MA: MIT Press.

Sachs, J. S. (1967). Recognition memory for syntactic and semantic aspects of connected discourse. *Perception and Psychophysics, 2*, 437–442.

Saffran, E. M., Schwartz, M., and Linebarger, M. C. (1998). Semantic influences on thematic role assignment: Evidence from normals and aphasics. *Brain and Language, 62*, 255–297.

Saffran, J. R., Aslin, R. N., and Newport, E. L. (1996). Statistical learning by 8 month old infants. *Science, 274*, 1926–1928.

Saffran, J. R., Newport, E. L., and Aslin, R. N. (1996). Word segmentation: The role of distributional cues. *Journal of Memory and Language, 35*, 606–621.

Saltz, E. (1971). *The cognitive bases of human learning*. Homewood, IL: Dorsey Press.

Sanz, M. (1996). *Telicity, objects, and the mapping onto predicate types: A cross-linguistic analysis of the role of syntax in processing*. Unpublished doctoral dissertation, University of Rochester.

Sanz, M., and Bever, T. G. (forthcoming). A theory of syntactic interference in the bilingual. In J. Nicol (Ed.), *One mind, two languages: Bilingual language processing*. Cambridge, England: Blackwell.

Savin, H., and Perchonock, E. (1965). Grammatical structure and the immediate recall of English sentences. *Journal of Verbal Learning and Verbal Behavior, 4*, 348–359.

Schank, R. C. (1973). Identification of conceptualizations underlying natural language. In R. C. Schank and K. M. Colby (Eds.), *Computer models of thought and language* (pp. 187–247). San Francisco: Freeman.

Schank, R. C. (1976). The role of memory in language processing. In C. N. Cofer (Ed.), *The structure of human memory* (pp. 162–189). San Francisco: Freeman.

Schank, R. C., and Abelson, R. P. (1977). *Scripts, plans, goals, and understanding: An inquiry into human knowledge structures.* Hillsdale, NJ: Erlbaum.

Schlesinger, I. M. (1981). Semantic assimilation in the development of relational categories. In W. Deutsch (Ed.), *The child's construction of language* (pp. 223–243). London: Academic Press.

Schwartz, M. F., Linebarger, M. C., Saffran, E. M., and Pate, D. S. (1987). Syntactic transparency and sentence interpretation in aphasia. *Language and Cognitive Processes*, *2*, 85–113.

Schwartz, M. F., Saffran, E. M., and Marin, O. S. (1980). The word order problem in agrammatism: I. Comprehension. *Brain and Language*, *10*, 249–262.

Schwartz, M. F., and Schwartz, B. (1984). In defence of organology. *Cognitive Neuropsychology*, *1*, 25–42.

Segal, E. M., and Duchan, J. F. (1997). Interclausal connectives as indicators of structuring in narrative. In J. Costermans and M. Fayol (Eds.), *Processing interclausal relationships* (pp. 95–119). Hillsdale, NJ: Erlbaum.

Segal, E. M., Duchan, J. F., and Scott, P. (1991). The role of interclausal connectives in narrative processing: Evidence from adults' interpretation of simple stories. *Discourse Processes*, *14*, 27–54.

Seidenberg, M. S. (1997). Language acquisition and use: Learning and applying probabalistic constraints. *Science*, *275*, 1599–1603.

Seidenberg, M. S., and Tanenhaus, M. K. (1986). Modularity and lexical access. In I. Gopnick and M. Gopnick (Eds.), *From models to modules: Studies in cognitive science from the McGill Workshops* (pp. 135–157). Norwood, NJ: Ablex.

Seidenberg, M. S., Tanenhaus, M. K., Leiman, J. L., and Bienkowski, M. (1982). Automatic access of the meanings of ambiguous words in context: Some limitations of knowledge-based processing. *Cognitive Psychology*, *14*, 489–537.

Seitz, M. (1972). *AER and the perception of speech.* Unpublished doctoral dissertation, University of Washington.

Sells, P. (1985). *Lectures on contemporary syntactic theories.* Palo Alto, CA: CSLI Publications.

Sharkey, N. E., and Mitchell, D. C. (1985). Word recognition in a functional context: The use of scripts in reading. *Journal of Memory and Language*, *24*, 253–270.

Simon, H. A. (1962). The architecture of complexity. *Proceedings of the American Philosophical Society*, *106*, 467–482.

Simpson, G. B. (1981). Meaning, dominance, and semantic context in the processing of lexical ambiguity. *Journal of Verbal Learning and Verbal Behavior*, *20*, 120–136.

Skinner, B. F. (1957). *Verbal behavior.* New York: Appleton-Century-Crofts.

Slobin, D. I. (1966). Grammatical transformations and sentence comprehension in childhood and adulthood. *Journal of Verbal Learning and Verbal Behavior*, *5*, 219–227.

Slobin, D. I., and Bever, T. G. (1982). Children use canonical sentences schemas: A cross-linguistic study of word order and inflections. *Cognition*, *12*, 229–265.

Slowiaczek, M. L. (1981). *Prosodic units as language processing units.* Unpublished doctoral dissertation, University of Massachusetts, Amherst.

Spearman, C. (1937). *Psychology down the ages.* London: Macmillan.

Speer, S. R., and Dobroth, K. M. (1998). *Effects of prosodic constituency on ambiguity resolution in auditory and visual sentence processing.* Unpublished manuscript, Northeastern University.

Speer, S. R., Kjelgaard, M. M., and Dobroth, K. M. (1996). The influence of prosodic structure on the resolution of temporary syntactic closure ambiguities. *Journal of Psycholinguistic Research, 25,* 249–271.

Spivey, M. J., and Tanenhaus, M. K. (1998). Syntactic ambiguity resolution in discourse: Modeling the effects of referential context and lexical frequency. *Journal of Experimental Psychology: Learning, Memory, and Cognition, 24,* 1521–1543.

Spivey-Knowlton, M. J., and Tanenhaus, M. K. (1994). Referential context and syntactic ambiguity resolution. In C. Clifton, L. Frazier, and K. Rayner (Eds.), Perspectives on Syntactic Processing (pp. 415–439). Hillsdale, NJ: Erlbaum.

Spivey-Knowlton, M. J., Trueswell, J. C., and Tanenhaus, M. K. (1993). Context effects in syntactic ambiguity resolution: Discourse and semantic influences in parsing reduced relative clauses. *Canadian Journal of Experimental Psychology, 47,* 276–309.

Staats, A. W. (1961). Verbal habit families, concepts, and the operant combination of word classes. *Psychological Review, 68,* 190–204.

Steedman, M. (1996). *Surface structure and interpretation.* Cambridge, MA: MIT Press.

Sternberg, S. (1966). High speed scanning in human memory. *Science, 153,* 652–654.

Stevenson, S. (1994). Competition and recency in a hybrid network model of syntactic disambiguation. *Journal of Psycholinguistic Research, 23,* 295–322.

Stevenson, S., and Merlo, P. (1997). Lexical structure and parsing complexity. *Language and Cognitive Processes, 12,* 349–399.

Stewart, C., and Gough, P. B. (1967). Constituent search in immediate memory for sentences. Presentation at the annual meetings of the Midwestern Psychological Association.

Stowe, L. A. (1986). Parsing WH-constructions: Evidence from on-line gap location. *Language and Cognitive Processes, 1,* 227–245.

Sturt, P., and Crocker, M. W. (1998). Generalized monotonicity for reanalysis models. In J. D. Fodor and F. Ferreira (Eds.), *Reanalysis in sentence processing* (pp. 365–400). Dordrecht, The Netherlands: Kluwer.

Suci, G., Ammon, P., and Gamlin, P. (1967). The validity of the probe-latency technique for assessing structure in language. *Language and Speech, 10,* 69–80.

Swinney, D. A. (1979). Lexical access during sentence comprehension: (Re)consideration of context effects. *Journal of Verbal Learning and Verbal Behavior, 18,* 645–659.

Swinney, D., and Zurif, E. (1995). Syntactic processing in aphasia. *Brain and Language, 50,* 225–239.

Swinney, D., Zurif, E., Prather, P., and Love, T. (1996). Neurological distribution of processing resources underlying language comprehension. *Journal of Cognitive Neuroscience, 8,* 174–184.

Tabor, W., Juliano, C., and Tanenhaus, M. K. (1997). Parsing in a dynamical system: An attractor-based account of the interaction of lexical and structural constraints in sentence processing. *Language and Cognitive Processes, 12,* 211–271.

Tabor, W., and Tanenhaus, M. K. (1999). Dynamical models of sentence processing. *Cognitive Science, 23,* 491–515.

Tabossi, P., Spivey-Knowlton, M. J., McRae, K., and Tanenhaus, M. K. (1994). Lexical effects on syntactic ambiguity resolution: Evidence for a constraint-based resolution process. In C. Umilta and M. Moscovitch (Eds.), *Attention and performance 15: Conscious and nonconscious information processing* (pp. 589–615). Cambridge, MA: MIT Press.

Tanenhaus, M. K. (1988). Psycholinguistics: An overview. In F. Newmeyer (Eds.), *Linguistics: The Cambridge survey: Vol. 3. Biological and psychological perspectives* (pp. 1–37). New York: Cambridge University Press.

Tanenhaus, M. K., and Carlson, G. N. (1989). Lexical structure and language comprehension. In W. D. Marslen-Wilson (Ed.), *Lexical representation and process* (pp. 529–561). Cambridge, MA: MIT Press.

Tanenhaus, M. K., Carlson, G. N., and Seidenberg, M. S. (1985). Do listeners compute linguistic representations? In D. R. Dowty, L. Kartunnen., and A. M. Zwicky (Eds.), *Natural language parsing* (pp. 359–408). New York: Cambridge University Press.

Tanenhaus, M. K., and Carroll, J. M. (1975). Functional clause hierarchy . . . and nouniness. In R. Grossman, J. San, and T. Vance (Eds.), *Papers from the parasession on functionalism* (pp. 499–511). Chicago: Chicago Linguistics Society.

Tanenhaus, M. K., Spivey-Knowlton, M. J., Eberhard, K. M., and Sedivy, J. C. (1995). Integration of visual and linguistic information in spoken language comprehension. *Science, 268,* 1632–1634.

Tanenhaus, M. K., Spivey-Knowlton, M. J., and Hanna, J. E. (2000). Modeling thematic and discourse context effects within a multiple constraints framework: Implications for the architecture of the language processing system. In M. Pickering, C. Clifton, and M. Crocker (Eds.), *Architecture and mechanisms of the language processing system* (pp. 90–118). Cambridge, England: Cambridge University Press.

Tenny, C. (1987). *Grammaticalizing aspect and affectedness.* Unpublished doctoral dissertation, MIT.

Tenny, C. (1994). *Aspectual roles and the syntax-semantic interface.* Dordrecht, The Netherlands: Kluwer.

Townsend, D. J. (1983). Thematic processing in sentences and texts. *Cognition, 13,* 223–261.

Townsend, D. J. (1997). Processing clauses and their relationships during comprehension. In J. Costermans and M. Fayol (Eds.), *Processing interclausal relations in the production and comprehension of text* (pp. 265–282). Hillsdale, NJ: Erlbaum.

Townsend, D. J., and Bever, T. G. (1978). Interclause relations and clausal processing. *Journal of Verbal Learning and Verbal Behavior, 17,* 509–521.

Townsend, D. J., and Bever, T. G. (1982). Natural units of representation interact during sentence comprehension. *Journal of Verbal Learning and Verbal Behavior, 21,* 688–703.

Townsend, D. J., and Bever, T. G. (1988). Knowledge representations during reading depend on reading skill and reading strategy. In M. Gruneberg, D. Sykes, and P. Morris (Eds.),

Practical aspects of memory: Current research and issues: Vol. 2. Clinical and educational implications (pp. 309–314). New York: Wiley.

Townsend, D. J., and Bever, T. G. (1989). Expertise and constraints in interactive sentence processing. In *Proceedings of the Eleventh Annual Conference of the Cognitive Science Society* (pp. 582–589). Hillsdale, NJ: Erlbaum.

Townsend, D. J., and Bever, T. G. (1991). The use of higher-level constraints in monitoring for a change in speaker demonstrates functionally distinct levels of representation in discourse comprehension. *Language and Cognitive Processes, 6,* 49–77.

Townsend, D. J., Carrithers, C., and Bever, T. G. (1987). Listening and reading processes in college- and middle school-age readers. In R. Horowitz and J. L. Samuels (Eds.), *Comprehending oral and written language* (pp. 217–242). New York: Academic Press.

Townsend, D. J., Carrithers, C., and Bever, T. G. (Forthcoming). Lexical processing and familial handedness. *Brain and Language.*

Townsend, D. J., Hoover, M., and Bever, T. G. (2000). Word-monitoring tasks interact with levels of representation during speech comprehension. *Journal of Psycholinguistic Research, 29,* 265–274.

Townsend, D. J., Ottaviano, D., and Bever, T. G. (1979). Immediate memory for words from main and subordinate clauses at different age levels. *Journal of Psycholinguistic Research, 8,* 83–101.

Townsend, D. J., and Ravelo, N. (1980). The development of complex sentence processing strategies. *Journal of Experimental Child Psychology, 29,* 60–73.

Townsend, D. J., and Saltz, E. (1972). Phrases vs. meaning in the immediate recall of sentences. *Psychonomic Science, 29,* 381–384.

Trabasso, T. Secco, T., and van den Broek, P. (1984). Causal cohesion and story coherence. In H. Mandl, N. L. Stein, and T. Trabasso (Eds.), *Learning and Comprehension of Text.* Hillsdale, NJ: Erlbaum.

Trabasso, T., and Sperry, L. L. (1985). Causal relatedness and importance of story events. *Journal of Memory and Language, 24,* 595–611.

Trabasso, T., and van den Broek, P. (1985). Causal thinking and the representation of narrative events. *Journal of Memory and Language, 24,* 612–630.

Traxler, M. J., Bybee, M. D., and Pickering, M. J. (1997). Influence of connectives on language comprehension: Eye-tracking evidence for incremental interpretation. *Quarterly Journal of Experimental Psychology: Human Experimental Psychology, 50A,* 481–497.

Traxler, M. J., Sanford, A. J., Aked, J. P., and Moxey, L. M. (1997). Processing causal and diagnostic statements in discourse. *Journal of Experimental Psychology: Learning, Memory, & Cognition, 23,* 88–101.

Trueswell, J. C. (1996). The role of lexical frequency in syntactic ambiguity resolution. *Journal of Memory and Language, 35,* 566–585.

Trueswell, J. C., and Kim, A. E. (1998). How to prune a garden path by nipping it in the bud: Fast priming of verb argument structure. *Journal of Memory and Language, 39,* 102–123.

Trueswell, J. C., Sekerina, I., Hill, N. M., and Logrip, M. L. (1999). The kindergarten-path effect: Studying on-line sentence processing in young children. *Cognition, 73,* 89–134.

Trueswell, J. C., Sekerina, I., and Logrip, M. L. (1999). *Children's on-line use of verb information: Evidence from eye movements during listening.* Unpublished manuscript, University of Pennsylvania.

Trueswell, J. C., and Tanenhaus, M. K. (1991). Tense, temporal context, and syntactic ambiguity resolution. *Language and Cognitive Processes, 6*, 303–338.

Trueswell, J. C., Tanenhaus, M. K., and Garnsey, S. M. (1994). Semantic influences on parsing: Use of thematic role information in syntactic ambiguity resolution. *Journal of Memory and Language, 33*, 285–318.

Trueswell, J. C., Tanenhaus, M. K., and Kello, C. (1993). Verb-specific constraints in sentence processing: Separating effects of lexical preference from garden-paths. *Journal of Experimental Psychology: Learning, Memory, & Cognition, 19*, 528–553.

Tyler, L. K., and Marslen-Wilson, W. D. (1977). The on-line effects of semantic context on syntactic processing. *Journal of Verbal Learning and Verbal Behavior, 16*, 683–692.

Underwood, B., and Schultz, R. (1960). *Meaningfulness and verbal learning.* Philadelphia: Lippincott.

Valian, V., and Coulson, S. (1988). Anchor points in language learning: The role of marker frequency. *Journal of Memory and Language, 27*, 71–86.

van Strien, J. W., and Bouma, A. (1995). Sex and familial sinistrality differences in cognitive abilities. *Brain and Cognition, 27*, 137–146.

Vendler, Z. (1967). *Linguistics and philosophy.* Ithaca, NY: Cornell University Press.

Vonk, W., and Noordman, L.G.M. (1990). On the control of inferences in text understanding. In D. A. Balota, G. B. Flores d'Arcais, and K. Rayner (Eds.), *Comprehension processes in reading* (pp. 447–464). Hillsdale, NJ: Erlbaum.

Walker, E., Gough, P. B., and Wall, R. (1968). Grammatical relations and the search of sentences in immediate memory. Presentation at the annual meeting of the Midwestern Psychological Association.

Wanner, E. (1968). *On remembering, forgetting, and understanding sentences: A study of the deep structure hypothesis.* Unpublished doctoral dissertation, Harvard University.

Wanner, E., and Maratsos, M. (1978). An ATN approach to comprehension. In M. Halle, J. Bresnan, and G. A. Miller (Eds.), *Linguistic theory and psychological reality* (pp. 119–161). Cambridge, MA: MIT Press.

Warren, R. M., and Warren, R. P. (1970). Auditory illusions and confusions. *Scientific American, 223*, 30–36.

Watson, J. B. (1919). *Psychology, from the standpoint of a behaviorist.* Philadelphia: Lippincott.

Wundt, W. (1874). *Grundzüge der physiologischen Psychologie.* Leipzig: Engelmann.

Wundt, W. (1911). *Völkerpsychologie: Erster Band. Die Sprache.* Leipzig: Engelmann.

Zurif, E., Swinney, D., Prather, P., Solomon, J., and Bushell, C. (1993). An on-line analysis of syntactic processing in Broca's and Wernicke's aphasia. *Brain and Language, 45*, 448–464.

Author Index

Subject Index

A-attachment, 109
Achievement, 79–81
Accomplishment, 79–81
Activity
  as event, 79–81, 179, 369
  in brain, 380
  in units, 3, 123, 134, 136–138
Acquisition, 2, 8, 20, 43, 123, 127–128, 130, 174, 176, 193, 361–377, 379, 397, 399, 402. *See also* Grain problem; Learning; Theme-and-variation principle
Action type, 77–81, 179
Active node stack, 88, 90, 91
Active trace strategy, 109
Adjuncts. *See* Sentence structures, adjunct
Adversative conjunctions, 338, 346, 348, 349, 355. *See also* Connectives; Discourse
Agent-requiring verbs, 266–268
Ambiguity. *See also* Garden-path sentences
  and animacy, 255–258
  and competitive attachment, 143
  and conceptual fit, 258–271
  and dynamic systems, 140
  and ergativity, 271–272
  and syntactic (lexical) category, 254–255
  and NVN template, 249–251
  and plausibility, 258–271, 291–296, 308–309
  and prosody, 309–312
  and reanalysis, 117
  and referential context, 273–283
  and subcategorization, 154, 195, 251–253, 266–271, 274–285, 313–316
  and temporal context, 283–285
  conjoined noun phrase/coordinate clause (CNP/CC), 312–313
  direct object/indirect object (DO/IO), 312–313
  direct object/sentential complement (DO/SC), 293–300
  direct object/subject (DO/S), 305–312
  DO/SC vs. MC/RC, 298–300
  lexical vs. syntactic, 129

lexical, 46–47
main clause/reduced relative (MC/RC), 7, 248–285, 293–300
nonstructural resolution of, 149 (*see also* Ambiguity, and plausibility; Ambiguity, and animacy; Ambiguity, and conceptual fit; Ambiguity, and referential context; Ambiguity, and temporal context)
reference, 64
sentential complement/relative clause (SC/RC), 300–305
Ambiguity effect, 253, 254, 256, 257, 259, 261–266, 268–270, 281, 285, 295, 296. *See also* Garden-path effect.
Analysis-by-synthesis. *See also* Late Assignment of Syntax Theory (LAST)
  and aphasia, 397
  and cognitive science, 403
  and context, 332
  and grain problem, 173–175, 405
  and grammar, 172–173, 176–177, 187, 389
  and habits vs. rules, 400, 405
  and LAST, 6–9, 162–167, 175–176
  and main clause/relative clause ambiguity, 247
  and minimalist program, 178–179
  and sentence templates, 316
  and speech perception, 160–161
  and two surface representations, 185, 324
  and word recognition, 162
  cyclic nature of, 252–253, 262–263, 273, 290, 308, 317, 330, 354
  modularity of, 320, 323
Anaphor, 51, 63, 64
Animacy, 8, 122, 129, 149, 237, 240, 255–260, 286, 293. *See also* Plausibility; Features, semantic
Aphasia, 378, 387, 388, 394, 402
  agrammatic aphasia, 402
  Broca's aphasia, 387, 394
Architectural modularity, 322, 323
Arguments, 48, 52, 246. *See also* Thematic roles
  and aphasia, 388–392, 396

Language, Speech, and Communication

The Syntax of American Sign Language: Functional Categories and Hierarchical Structure, Carol Neidle, Judy Kegl, Dawn MacLaughlin, Benjamin Haban, and Robert G. Lee, 1999

Presumptive Meanings: The Theory of Generalized Conversational Implicature, Stephen C. Levinson, 1999

Converging Methods for Understanding Reading and Dyslexia, edited by Raymond M. Klein and Patricia A. McMullen, 1999

Optimality-Theoretic Syntax, edited by Géraldine Legendre, Jane Grimshaw, and Sten Vikner, 2000

Sentence Comprehension: The Integration of Habits and Rules, David J. Townsend and Thomas G. Bever, 2001